COMPARATIVE LEGAL DOCTRINE

STUDIES IN RUSSIAN, EAST EUROPEAN, AND EURASIAN LAW

WILLIAM E. BUTLER (SERIES EDITOR)

1. Butler, W. E., Russian Law and Legal Institutions. 3d ed.; 2021. ISBN 978-854901449

2. Il'in, I. A., On the Essence of Legal Consciousness, ed., introduced, & transl. W. E. Butler, P. T. Grier, and Paul Robinson. 2d rev. ed.; 2023. ISBN-13 978-1-61619-679-03.

3. Butler, W. E., Russian-English Legal Dictionary. 2d rev. ed.; Clark, New Jersey, Talbot Publishing, 2023. ISBN 978-1-61619-682-0

4. Butler, W. E., Russian Inheritance Law. 2d rev. ed.; Clark, New Jersey, Talbot Publishing, 2025. ISBN 978-1-61619-692-9

5. Butler, W. E. (ed. and transl.), G. I. Tunkin Selected Works. Clark, New Jersey, Talbot Publishing, 2025. ISBN 978-1-61619-695-0

6. Boshno, Svetlana V., Comparative Legal Doctrine. Clark, New Jersey, Talbot Publishing, 2025. ISBN 978-1-61619-697-4

Studies in Russian, East European, and Eurasian Law

COMPARATIVE LEGAL DOCTRINE

Svetlana V. Boshno
Доктор юридических наук; профессор
SJD (Pennsylvania State University)

TALBOT
PUBLISHING
Clark, New Jersey
2025

ISBN: 978-1-61619-697-4

TALBOT PUBLISHING AN IMPRINT OF
The Lawbook Exchange, Ltd.
33 Terminal Avenue
Clark, New Jersey 07066-1321

Please see our website for a selection of our other publications and fine facsimile reprints of classic works of legal history www.lawbookexchange.com

Library of Congress Cataloging-in-Publication Data

Names: Boshno, S. V. (Svetlana Vladimirovna) author
Title: Comparative legal doctrine / Svetlana V. Boshno, Доктор юридических наук; профессор,
SJD (Pennsylvania State University).
Description: First edition. | Clark, New Jersey : Talbot Publishing, an Imprint of The Lawbook Exchange, Ltd, 2025. | Series: Studies in Russian, East European, and Eurasian law ; 6 | Includes bibliographical references and index. | Summary: "An interdisciplinary study of global legal doctrine aiming to clarify the concept of doctrine and develop recommendations for its detection and application using methods from sociology, statistics, and data analysis"-- Provided by publisher.
Identifiers: LCCN 2025030703 | ISBN 9781616196974 hardcover
Subjects: LCSH: Comparative law | Law--Documentation
Classification: LCC K559 .B67 2025 | DDC 340/.2--dc23/eng/20250703
LC record available at https://lccn.loc.gov/2025030703

First published in 2025 by
Talbot Publishing Ltd

Printed in the United States of America on acid-free paper

GRAPHS & TABLES

Tables

Figures

Diagrams

RUSSIAN LEGAL DOCTRINE IN COMPARATIVE LEGAL STUDIES:

AN INTRODUCTION

William E. Butler

John Edward Fowler Distinguished Professor of Law,
Penn State Dickinson Law
Emeritus Professor of Comparative Law,
University College London

Back in earlier times I was asked with some frequency, when people learned that I was a specialist in Soviet law, whether the Soviet legal system was closer to the Romanist continental civil law systems than to the Anglo-American common law systems – does Soviet law have judicial precedent, they asked. Upon being told that the Soviet legal system was code-based and rejected the notion of binding judicial precedent, that response seemed to help orient the interlocutors, laymen always, in the spectrum of legal traditions.

In fact, the existence and possible role of judicial precedent as a defining feature of legal systems or traditions has been under severe questioning for some time in Russian, Soviet, and post-Soviet legal studies, and deservedly so. Soviet jurists themselves explored the possibility of introducing American-style casebooks into Soviet legal education,[1] which would have meant greater attention to reported cases. American specialists who taught Soviet law in the law-school curriculum prepared case materials based on interviews with Soviet jurisconsults and advokats[2] or collected case reports and contextual materials for instructional purposes.[3] In the post-Soviet period, excellent

[1] W. E. Butler, "The American Case Method and Soviet Legal Education", *The International Lawyer*, XIV (1977), pp. 206-209.

[2] Harold J. Berman (ed.), *Soviet Law in Action: :The Recollected Cases of a Soviet Lawyer* (1953) (with Boris A. Konstantinovsky).

[3] John N. Hazard, *Materials on Soviet Law* (1947);Hazard and Isaac Shapiro, *The Soviet Legal System: Post-Stalin Documentation and Historical Commentary* (1962);(2d

studies by Russian jurists[4] and foreign comparatists[5] have identified an important and subtle role for judicial practice, sometimes in forms unknown to foreign legal structures, in all periods of Russian legal history. The ultimate result is that judicial precedent no longer serves as a "black and white" distinction between types or families of legal systems, but requires a highly nuanced analysis of the role of judges and courts in the process of law-making and law-application.

The present study is strongly indicative that the role of legal doctrine deserves consideration of a similar nature. The author has devoted more than three decades to empirical studies, some comparative, of the role of actors or "players" in the highly formalist Russian legal context in applying or using doctrinal principles implicitly or – rarely – explicitly in their professional activities.

In Russia that means, in particular, recourse to ideological sources during the Soviet era – citations to the works of Karl Marx, Friedrich Engels, V. I. Lenin, J. V. Stalin, or others in support of legal positions taken in administrative or judicial proceedings, or to legal doctrinal sources – the treatises, textbooks, articles, or analogous materials which are used in teaching law at university law faculties or other legal educational institutions or which form part of the larger sources of legal ideas and principles that influence legal professionals in the course of their duties.

ed., 1969 (with P. B. Maggs and I. Shapiro); (3d ed.; 1977) (with P. B. Maggs and W. E. Butler); (4th ed.; 1984) (with P. B. Maggs and W. E. Butler); also see: Butler (transl.), "Cases on Soviet Criminal Law and Procedure", *Soviet Statutes and Decisions*, I, no. 4 (1964), pp. 1-110 (with H. J. Berman).

[4] The best study in English is A. Vereshchagin, *Judicial Law-Making in Soviet Russia* (2007); Vereshchagin, Кассационный сенат: Очерки устройства и деятельности [Cassational Senate: Survey of Structure and Activity of the Supreme Court of the Russian Empire] (2023); also see Butler, "Judicial Precedent as a Source of Russian Law", in James A. R. Nafziger and S. C. Symeonides (eds.), *Law and Justice in a Multistate World: Essays in Honor of Arthur von Mehren* (2002), pp. 583-594.

[5] For my own part, W. E. Butler, "The Duty to Rescue in Soviet Civil Law", in *Hommage ä René Dekkers* (1982), pp. 443-458; Butler, "Necessary Defense, Judge-Made Law, and Soviet Man", W. E. Butler. P. B. Maggs, and J. B. Quigley, Jr. (eds.), *Law After Revolution* (1988), pp. 99-130. Also see K. Hendley and P. Solomon, Jr., *The Russian Judicial System* (2023).

The author of this study has undertaken pioneering studies, taking advantage of the access to judicial materials that modern technologies permit, to identify instances where reliance on doctrinal sources is explicitly in evidence and then, with exceptional access to actors in the Russian legal system, considered these issues on the basis of extensive detailed questionnaires, reinforced by lengthy personal conversations with legal personnel willing and interested to reflect on these matters.

As for the ideological dimension, Soviet courts were instructed to apply "revolutionary legal consciousness",[6] when appropriate, and in the early days following the 1917 October Revolution, to fill gaps in the law by reference to the works of Karl Marx and V. I. Lenin as "undoubted sources of law and justice".[7] The citation to specific references of ideological classics seems to have been uncommon and certainly without specific references to secondary Soviet doctrinal writings, which were few and far between. On the other hand, English courts on at least one occasion accepted expert evidence that the works of V. I. Lenin are in effect a source of law in the Soviet Union and to be taken into account when interpreting and applying the law.[8] This evidence was uncontested and decisive in the case.

Russian jurists, for their part, during the Soviet period vehemently and without exception adhered to the view that the Soviet socialist legal model was distinct from the continental civil law systems and the Anglo-American systems on ideological grounds alone. In their view at the time, the Soviet Union was at the center of a socialist family of legal systems. As the author of this study demonstrates, her studies indicate that about two-thirds of Russian jurists sampled consider Russia now to be

[6] On the acceptance of this term, see Ivan A. Il'in, *On the Essence of Legal Consciousness*, ed. intro. and transl. W. E. Butler, P. T. Grier, and Paul Robinson (2d rev. ed.; 2023), pp. 116-119.

[7] I. V. Sternik, «В. И. Ленин и первые судебные декреты» [V. I. Lenin and the First Soviet Dekrets], Советское государство и право [Soviet State and Law], №4 (1976), p.. 112, fn. 4 cited in Butler, *Soviet Law* (2d ed.; 1988), p. 54.

[8] See *Re Banque des Marchands de Moscou (Koupetschesky)* (1957] 3 All ER 182.

part of the Romano-Germanic family of legal systems. This is a remarkable finding for several reasons. First, most Russian jurists consider affiliation with a family of legal systems to be a legal fact rather than an analytical template to be used to identify certain characteristics associated with models of legal systems. Second, this conclusion underestimates the extent to which the Soviet legal model truly departed from other legal models and embedded approaches, principles, traditions, and ideas that are not easily dispensed with during a transition away from that legal model. Third, the remarkable formalism of the contemporary Russian legal model, in practice, suggests that the formalistic requirements of the past Planned Economy sit uneasily with the freedoms of discretion inherent in a market economy, that these survive in the Russian legal mentality with deep roots in the Russian psyche, and that these persist in Russian legal education. Fourth, perhaps there are indicia of legal formalism in prerevolutionary Russian law and practice that encouraged the Planned Economy in the first place and continue to operate – a matter deserving of further investigation.

Comparisons with American practices are necessarily not so extensive in this study, but the United States judicial practices with respect to the explicit citation of doctrinal sources differ considerably from those in Russia. American judges make virtually routine reference to doctrinal writings as part of the judicial process and are under no formal restrictions in this respect.

On a more personal note, I have been privileged to supervise the dissertations of two established Russian scholars (Vereshchagin and Boshno), each obtaining an advanced foreign research degree after having done the same in Russia, both deeply involved in the analysis of Russian judicial processes, neither of whom knew one another, both of whom have produced seminal contributions to legal scholarship, and both of whom have, as they should have done, raised fascinating and important questions for the next stage of academic inquiry.

Given that Dr. Boshno has sustained the burden of persuasion that the use or nonuse of doctrine in judicial decision-making is a key distinction between the Russian and American legal systems with a strong indication that this may be generally true of post-Soviet and Anglo-American legal systems generally, a next step might be to determine whether the Russian approach to the judicial use of doctrine is true of the other fourteen post-Soviet legal systems, including the three Baltic States. If the Russian approach is perceived as a manifestation of "formalism", then the roots of that phenomenon deserve further investigation, including the historical origins of legal forms in Russia (petitions, contracts, supplications, powers of attorney, and so on) and the role of the development of printing and the reforms of the Cyrillic alphabet in these processes. The role of the Planned Economy in shaping these phenomena likewise deserves detailed consideration as part of the transition to an economy more market-oriented than previously. All these dimensions need to be assessed against the background, role, and orientations in Russian legal theory, which has doubtless played its own part in shaping and justifying these phenomena.

The major achievement of Dr. Boshno is that she has now identified the use of legal doctrine in judicial processes to be a major distinguishing mark of difference between the Anglo-American and the socialist/transitional/Romano-Germanic legal models. This volume is a significant benchmark in comparative legal studies, an empirically documented original and pathbreaking socio-legal study of a legal system in which studies on this scale are virtually unprecedented.

INTRODUCTION

The introduction to a book enables the author to connect with the reader, captivate, and guide him through the entire text, from the first page to the last. The purpose of the introduction is to keep readers interested and motivated and help them understand the substance of the material presented. In this introduction, I draw attention to the most valuable and exciting things to ensure that the relationship with the reader continues throughout the book.

This book, a revision and expansion of my second doctoral dissertation, was undertaken at Penn State Dickinson Law. Although my first doctoral dissertation (habilitation) was defended at the age of 36, this early success did not allow me to fully grasp the significance of this achievement. Now, two decades later, I present a new dissertation as the mature culmination of my contributions to legal scholarship. I am grateful to my mentors and colleagues for their support and faith in me, which allowed me to continue working and reach my scientific peak.

This book was not written alone and not only for me. Petty domestic worries distracted me. However, a person at my side – Arthur Tsatyan – supported me in my writing and protected me from the daily routine. The book would not have been written without him.

I likewise felt the support of my parents and son Romik, even though physically they could not be with me. I dedicate this book to them, as well as to those who have passed away and to those who will read it in the future. I am grateful to everyone who supported me and gave me new strength.

My teachers and mentors, especially Academician William E. Butler, greatly influenced me. The value of a book lies in its creation with love and passion. This book was written by a worker for workers, for those who do not separate weekdays from weekends, who consider their vocation to be essential, and who serve their calling faithfully and unrequitedly. I admire the legal scholars who inspire me. In the book, they are called Doctrine Personas.

The book is devoted to the phenomenon of global legal doctrine, distinguished by its polysemy and extensiveness. Introducing novelty and originality, this study discovers a new dimension of the legal system and doctrine, making the book valuable and relevant for legal researchers and practitioners. Its practical significance lies in its universal applicability for various categories of users: researchers, general public, and those employed in State legislative and law enforcement structures. The book has developed and tested a model for collecting, storing, and processing textual information of a legal nature, which can be helpful in legal research and lawmaking.

The study analyzes various software tools for content analysis, including artificial intelligence. This model is universal and can be used to analyze a wide range of legal data, which makes it valuable for those engaged in legal science.

The representativeness and universality of the study are provided by well-thought-out criteria for selecting objects of analysis. They include a theoretical and legal orientation, various subject areas, and the coverage of various legal systems, making it possible to superimpose the analytical templates of Anglo-American, Romano-Germanic, and ideologized legal systems. The book also considers different types of legal understanding, including positivist, libertarian, and sociological, as reflected in the analysis of the influence of the type of legal understanding or legal comprehension of doctrines.

The chronological approach, covering the period from 1865 to the present, makes it possible to study the evolution of legal doctrine over time and identify trends evident in large informational spectrums. The analysis of personal data allows for a deeper understanding of the influence of legal understanding or comprehension on the formation of legal doctrines.

Thus, the developed model can be successfully used in the academic sphere, in public discussion, and in the development of legislative initiatives.

The term "doctrine" has a wide range of applications and can denote scientific theories, opinions of lawyers, law enforcement practice, and doctrinal documents. An essential feature of doctrine is its ability to influence the formation and development of law, sometimes acting as an independent form of law and directly regulating social relations.

Despite the attempts of legal scholars to develop a single definition of legal doctrine, a generally recognized and practical concept does not exist. Criteria must be developed for recognizing a legal object as a doctrine to ensure its unambiguous application. Identifying the unique features of a doctrine is essential for its correlation with other forms of law.

Legal doctrine is closely related to concepts of law, legislation, and law enforcement authorities, as well as to the elements of legal regulation, such as legal consciousness, principles, and analogies. It helps to interpret laws and fill legal gaps.

This study aims to clarify the concept of doctrine and develop recommendations for its detection and application. Doctrine has a complex vocabulary and requires special training. That is why teaching how to use it to protect rights and freedoms is necessary.

This book does not confine itself to retelling or commenting on legal texts. Rather, it offers a new approach based on original empirical data collected since 2003. The book uses a unique empirical base, including data collected using the author's programs and methods. The novelty lies in applying extensive data analysis, content analysis, and modern information processing technologies using artificial intelligence.

This study develops a model for processing legal texts applicable not only to the analysis of legal doctrine but also to other objects of research. In an interdisciplinary approach, the author integrates legal knowledge with elements of sociology, statistics, and data analysis, which meets the needs of the modern scientific community in applying quantitative methods in jurisprudence.

In addition, the book offers a structured bibliographical database that includes information about the authors and their works, such as ORCID ID, DOI, and ISBN, as well as their professional characteristics. This facilitates access to scientific materials.

The study also highlights the importance of modern technologies for the analysis of legal objects. This makes it possible to draw verifiable conclusions and overcome the limitations of traditional legal research methods. The study analyzes various textual objects using mathematical and statistical approaches because most publications are descriptive and do not meet the requirements for standards of scholarly innovation. The main challenge is to move from repeating published theories to creating original approaches through an in-depth analysis of accumulated knowledge.

One task of the book is to adapt modern technologies for the collection, storage, and analysis of bibliographic data. ZOTERO and similar tools allow you to efficiently structure scientific materials and display data for subsequent analysis. Using computer programs to analyze the content of the texts, the author was able to identify hidden patterns in legal doctrines.

The contribution of the book lies in the application of the method of content analysis to legal doctrines. A significant result is the creation of a dictionary of terms that define the essence of doctrine, dividing them into satellite words and marker words. Satellite words such as "ideas" and "views" describe the general essence of doctrine. In contrast, marker words such as "State" or "official" define a specific type of doctrine.

A significant result was identifying changes in using the term "doctrine" in time and space. This made it possible to discover the dominant meanings of the term and their changes depending on the temporal and geographical context, as well as on the personal characteristics of the researchers.

I used three groups of methods to achieve my goals. The first group includes general scientific methods, such as abstraction and historical and legal analysis. The second group consists of methods of the legal sciences, including comparative law and the system-functional method. The third group covers interdisciplinary methods, such as programming, content analysis, and sociological approaches.

Especially significant are the original sets of empirical data collected by the author based on a survey of judges, civil servants, and legal scholars. The data obtained through the expert survey were used to develop the concept of "Persona-Doctrine".

The author has unique access to observations of Persona-Doctrine status holders due to personal experience of cooperation with them within the framework of councils of experts, working groups, and attendance at or participation in scientific events. These observations played a vital role in forming the socio-professional portrait of the "Persona-Doctrine". A tool was created for comparing educational levels and degrees of the United States and Russia, which may be helpful for people seeking a transnational career in law.

In addition, the book contains recommendations concerning the use of content analysis to determine the frequency of word use in texts and help identify hidden meanings.

The book highlights the possibility of using legal doctrine in judicial practice. The author proposes an algorithm for the selection of sources for legal documents. This algorithm includes a check of citation, authorship, place of publication, and the attitude of the courts to the sources used, which makes the doctrine suitable for practical application in court proceedings.

The book considers the influence of ideology on legal doctrine at the State and society levels, showing how it can be transformed from State doctrine to ideological. One finding is that researchers who adhere to a State or political ideology have a higher chance of career success.

The empirical foundation of the book is law enforcement practice data, including that drawn from Lexis+, Westlaw, Consultant+, and Garant, as well as data on the volume of dissertation repositories and citations of scientific sources. The author collected data from national libraries: Russian State Library in Moscow and the Library of Congress in Washington D.C.

Thus, the book offers original methodological approaches to studying legal doctrine and creates a valuable database for researchers and practitioners.

I processed empirical data using the PROVALIS and AntCon programs, this emphasizing new interdisciplinary and bilingual methods. The study also includes a combination of sociological methods, such as questionnaires, interviews, and expert surveys.

One major innovation is the concept of "Persona-Doctrine" – a legal scholar with high citation rates and significance in the professional community that forms legal directions and approaches. The term "Doctrine-Form" has been introduced as a form of external expression of doctrine, ranging from scholarly publications to State and judicial acts.

The study pays special attention to legal doctrines in various branches of law (civil, criminal, constitutional, and others), emphasizing the importance of universal theoretical legal doctrines that impact the legal system.

The comparative analysis of the legal systems of the United States and the Russian Federation helps to better understand the differences in approaches to legal doctrine and its application in these countries. The study examines the importance of content analysis, which in the author's opinion should be introduced into training programs for lawyers at all levels.

As a result, the book highlights the critical points of legal doctrine, its classification, indicia, and features. The use of the latest technologies and methods of analysis of legal texts makes the book relevant to contemporary legal research.

SECTION I

THEORETICAL AND METHODOLOGICAL FOUNDATIONS OF THE DOCTRINE OF LEGAL DOCTRINE

Chapter 1
Theoretical Foundations of the Doctrine of Doctrine

Doctrine is an ever-evolving phenomenon. This study explores doctrinal writings by legal scholars from different countries and legal systems, written at different times. This approach is called the space-time continuum of the critical concept "doctrine". We consider the proposition advanced by Roscoe Pound (1870-1964) to be very important: one obstacle to the development of any research is the dominance of the ghosts of ancient masters. Their sensible methods are forgotten, and their unfounded conclusions are taken as gospel. Legal doctrinal scholarship has not escaped this tendency. We will not worship authorities and their achievements. However, we must analyze their writings and formulate our opinions. This is how the methodological foundation is laid.

Within the framework of the sociological school,[1] Pound devoted much attention to studying the forms of law within the framework of different legal systems.[2] Legal doctrine has traditionally been considered to concern forms of law and the interpretation of the law for several objective and subjective reasons. Interpretation clarifies existing law. The need for interpretation arises from the incomprehensibility and the need to clarify the meaning of the law.[3] Interpretation can be academic (research), judicial, and doctrinal.

[1] R. Pound, "Fundamental Law in the Society of Today", *Tennessee Law Review*, XIII, no. 1 (1934), pp. 1-13.

[2] Pound, "Hierarchy of Sources and Forms in Different Systems of Law", *Tulane Law Review*, VII (1933), pp. 475-487.

[3] J. D. Ohlin, *International Law: Evolving Doctrine and Practice* (2018).

Regarding legal force, current law is divided into normative and individual, official (or legal), and unofficial.[4] For the purposes of the present study, the most valuable are doctrinal interpretations which acquire official status and are applied as forms of law – imperatively. We relied on research addressing the relationship between economic and legal relations, legislation, and economics.[5]

A person on the doctrinal level is Academician William Elliott Butler. He has contributed significantly to the general theory of forms and sources rights,[6] comparative studies,[7] and international law.[8] An exceptional connoisseur of Soviet academic bibliography[9] and Russian legislation,[10] Butler's publications, life, and service to jurisprudence have become doctrine.[11] His astonishing academic research has become a source of inspiration for the author of these lines, an example of academic historiography.[12]

[4] W. Baude and S. E. Sachs, "The Law of Interpretation", *Harvard Law Review*, CXXX (2017), pp. 1079-1147.

[5] R. Pound, "The Economic Interpretation and the Law of Torts", *Harvard Law Review*, LIII (1940), pp. 365-385.

[6] W. E Butler (ed.), *Russian Legal Theory* (1996), p. 11.

[7] W. E. Butler (ed.), *International Law in Comparative Perspective* (1980); Butler (ed.), *Justice and Comparative Law: Anglo-Soviet Perspectives on Criminal Law, Evidence, Procedure, and Sentencing Policy* (1987), followed by a half dozen or so works based on Anglo-Soviet symposia.

[8] W. E Butler (ed.), *International Law and the International System* (1987).

[9] Butler, *Soviet Law* (1982; rev. ed.; 1988); Butler. *Russian Law* (1999); 2d ed.; (2003); 3d ed.; (2009); Butler, *Russian Law and Legal Institutions* 3d ed.; (2021).

[10] Butler, *Russian Public Law* (3d ed.; 2013).

[11] Butler, *Russia and the Law of Nations* (2009). Butler has translated numerous works by Russian, Soviet, and post-Soviet jurists, including F. F. Martens, I. A. Il'in, V. É. Grabar, G. I. Tunkin, Á. L. Kolodkin, B. Tuzmukhamedov, A. Kapustin, V. I. Lafitsky, M. I. Braginskii, A. A. Rubanov, V. P. Mozolin, V. A. Tomsinov, and many others. His translations are based on Butler, *Russian-English Legal Dictionary* (rev. ed.; 2023).

[12] V. Mostecky and W. E Butler (eds.), *Soviet Legal Bibliography: A Classified and Annotated Listing of Books and Serials Published in the Soviet Union since 1917 as Represented in the Collection of the Harvard Law School Library as of January 1, 1965* (1965); Butler, *Russia and the International Legal System: A Bibliography of Writings by Russian Jurists on Public and Private International Law to 1917 with Reference to*

Many publications are devoted to legal doctrine and policy. Indeed, the ruling class and political parties influence ideological, State, and judicial doctrines.[13] An influential doctrine is an instrument quite comparable to the law. It is not uncommon for a legal doctrine to be more potent than the law. The strength of the doctrine lies in its vagueness and, as a result, the possibility of ambiguous interpretation and application.

Iuri Aleksandrovich Tikhomirov inspires researchers with his creativity, achievements, and academic authority.[14] I am personally acquainted with this "classic" of Russian jurisprudence. I had the opportunity to see and hear a genius. His modesty and academic steadfastness are astonishing. Russia and the USSR are States with entirely different ideologies. It was not easy to maintain one's views consistently when changing the country in which the researcher lives. Tikhomirov was able to maintain his moral position and is deservedly considered a "classic" of Soviet and Russian law. His works on "Comparative Law" and "Legal Models and Reality"[15] formed the methodological basis of the present work.

Butler and Tikhomirov studied the doctrine and became the doctrine themselves. We call this phenomenon "Persona-Doctrine".

Works on the theory of law, which have paid great attention to sources and forms, are of methodological importance for

Publications in Emigration (2006). For a bibliography of Butler's own publications, see Butler, *International and Comparative Law: A Personal Bibliography* (2015).

[13] N. R. A. Matasar, "Treatise Writing and Federal Jurisdiction Scholarship: Does Doctrine Matter When Law Is Politics?", *Michigan Law Review*, LXXXIX (1991), pp. 1499-1519.

[14] Iu. A. Tikhomirov, *Теория закона* [Theory of Law] (1982).

[15] Tikhomirov (ed.), Правовые модели и реальность [Legal Models and Reality] (2014).

this study. These are textbooks,[16] monographs,[17] a thesis, and articles[18] about sources of law and forms of law.[19]

American scholars have traditionally shown considerable interest in the forms of law.[20] Thus, Ronald Dworkin (1931-2013) significantly contributed to studying the position of legal doctrine and legal theory in the system of forms of law.[21] There is a process of studying the interaction and mutual influence of doctrine, precedents, and judicial customs.[22]

Legal scholars understand doctrine as the highest form of judicial practice, legal interpretation, and precedents. Judicial practice and doctrine interact and assimilate each other. These methodological foundations are essential for studying judicial doctrine.[23] Russian legal scholars have suggested that legal provisions be relegated to being considered as doctrinal forms of law. They use the term "judicial doctrine" when considering the peculiarities of Russian legislation and understanding of law.[24]

Many scholars understand doctrine as a legal theory, an authoritative study.[25] We call this type of doctrine a research doctrine.

[16] John W. Salmond, *Jurisprudence* (4th ed.; 1913); Pound, *Jurisprudence* (1959); C. S. M. Phillipps, *Jurisprudence* (1909).

[17] A. N. Chashin, Правовая доктрина как источник (форма) российского права [Legal Doctrine as a Source (Form) of Russian Law] (2022).

[18] J. Bell, "Sources of Law", *Cambridge Law Journal*, LXXVII, no. 1 (2018), pp. 40-71.

[19] Boshno, "*Form of Law*"; Pound, note 2 above.

[20] H. Silving, *Sources of Law* (1968).

[21] R. A. Dworkin, *Matter of Principle* (1985).

[22] R. Piszko, "Role of Custom in the Formation of the Directives of Law Interpretation". *Juridical Science*, no. 6 (2013), pp. 12-20.

[23] V. V. Chibizov, Правоприменительное усмотрение и его роль в преодолении юридических коллизий [Law Enforcement Discretion and Its Role in Overcoming Legal Conflicts] (2020) (dissertation candidate of legal sciences).

[24] Chashin, note 17 above.

[25] H. Cairns, *The Theory of Legal Science* (1941).

Some legal scholars believe that doctrine emanates from the development of law through its interpretation.[26] Perhaps this approach diminishes the status of doctrine because it becomes a phenomenon derived from legislation. However, research doctrine does more than explain the meaning and substance of legislation. It creates law directly and indirectly.[27] Law can be formed by interpreting custom or morality.[28] A law can maintain a connection with its prior sources by sanctioning customs. The law may enshrine a rule contrary to custom, such as the legal prohibition of blood feuds. We include conventional doctrine in the general typology of doctrine but do not discuss it in detail in this study.

Legal theorists pay great attention to the relationship between legal principles and doctrine.[29] Many principles are well-known and universally recognized legal frameworks. Such principles are a construct as close to a doctrine as possible.[30] Some scholars refer to legal principles as doctrine.[31]

Doctrine in international law is a source and form of law. This thesis is not in doubt.[32] However, this does not preclude discussing the substance of international law doctrine.[33] The

[26] A. Coan, "Amending the Law of Constitutional Interpretation", *Duke Journal of Constitutional Law and Public Policy*, XIII (2018), pp. 83-102.

[27] M. Greenberg, *What Makes a Method of Legal Interpretation Correct? Legal Standards vs. Fundamental Determinants*, SSRN Scholarly Paper (2017).

[28] S. E. Sachs, "The Law and Morals of Interpretation", *Duke Journal of Constitutional Law and Public Policy*, XIII, no. 2 (2018), pp. 103-114.

[29] "A Discussion of Legal Principles Suggested by Recent Decisions", *Law Review Board of Albany Law School*, I, no. 4 (1933); Dworkin, note 21 above; A. V. Iliukhina, "Доктринальные принципы права: понятие и специфика [Doctrinal Principles of Law: Concept and Specifics]", Актуальные проблемы государства и права [Current Problems of State and Law], V, no. 17 (2021), pp. 9-21.

[30] T. J. Halstead and Library of Congress (eds.), *The Separation of Powers Doctrine: Rationale, Applications and Bibliography* (2002).

[31] A. Devlin, *Fundamental Principles of Law and Economics* (2015).

[32] A. I. Dmitriev and W. E. Butler, История международного права [History of International Law] (2d ed.; 2013).

[33] H. W. A. Thirlway, *The Sources of International Law* (2014).

diversity of approaches to understanding and applying doctrine as a source and form of law is significant[34] in the interaction of municipal and international law.[35]

To comprehend the diversity of approaches to understanding doctrine, different types of understanding of law and different concepts of law are of great importance. One objective of this study is to trace the relationship between the type of an author's legal understanding and his or her approaches to doctrinal forms of law.

We have paid great attention to the pure theory of law of Hans Kelsen.[36] Positivism formed the basis of the legal theory of the former USSR. Jurists of the late Soviet era conceived of the legal profession in the context of the dominance of positivism in legal culture and the model of legal regulation in the USSR and later in Russia. The study has established that many modern Persona-Doctrines follow this theory.

Law, morality, and customs closely interact. In fact, they are the sources and forms of one another. We have studied publications on customary law, morality, and justice.[37] The positivist basis for the separation of social regulation and the separation of law and morality was investigated by H. L. A. Hart (1907-1992).[38]

We have formulated an alternative to primary or secondary, the derivative nature of social relations in the origin and recognition of doctrine. Our hypothesis is that social relations,

34 A. Carty, *Philosophy of International Law* (2d ed.; 2017).

35 M. M. Abgomenou, Концепция права развития в доктрине международного права [The Concept of Development Law in the Doctrine of International Law] (1990) (dissertation candidate of legal sciences).

36 L. Duarte d'Almeida, J. Gardner, and L. Green (eds.), *Kelsen Revisited: New Essays on the Pure Theory of Law* (2013).

37 L. Green, "Positivism and the Inseparability of Law and Morals Symposium: The Hart-Fuller Debate at Fifty", *New York University Law Review*, LXXXIII (2008), pp. 1035-1058; L. L. Fuller, *The Morality of Law* (1977).

38 H. L. A. Hart, "Positivism and the Separation of Law and Morals". *Harvard Law Review*, LXXI (1957), pp. 593-629.

preceding law in the form of legislation, can acquire the status of a source and even a form of law, such as custom or doctrine.[39] However, legal theory is dominated by the opposite thesis about the importance of law and the derivative nature of legal relations. In Russian educational and academic literature, legislation always precedes legal relations. Legal relations arise based on law. Accordingly, the law always precedes legal relations.

According to Marxist theory, law is a superstructure above the base, that is, the economy. The positivist legal conception asserts the rule of law as the only form of law. A law is a document that reflects the will of the economically dominant class. Soviet ideology, legislation, and legal theory adopted Marxist and positivist concepts. Foreign researchers have made exciting observations and conclusions[40] about Soviet doctrine, evaluating the doctrine of Marxism on entirely different ideological, political, and legal attitudes. Such cross-ideological observations formulate alternative conclusions. Unexpected theses significantly expand the horizons of the academic picture.

A complex set of reasons led to Soviet legal theory rejecting Marxism in the mid-1980s. Later, Russian jurisprudence became embarrassed by its former association with Marxism. V. I. Lenin (1870-1924) lost the status of the central classic; Marxism ceased to be the only ideological true theory. Universal boundless devotion was abruptly replaced by harsh criticism and a complete rejection of this methodology. However, as time has shown, the categorical rejection of this teaching has been groundless. It was just as thoughtlessly and uncritically that more than 100 years ago (in 1917), Marxist-Leninist theory was proclaimed the sole State ideology. Extremes are not conducive to the dialectical development of knowledge. Ill-considered political decisions interrupt academic schools. The mistakes of politicians cast doubt on research based on an obsolete ideology and break

[39] S. E. Stumpf, "Austin's Theory of the Separation of Law and Morals Studies in Legal Philosophy," *Vanderbilt Law Review* XIV, no. 1 (1960), pp. 117-150.

[40] L. Althusser, *Lenin and Philosophy, and Other Essays* (1972).

the connection between generations of researchers. History is aware of proposals to rewrite history, burn inconvenient books, or at least ban the free circulation of illegal works. A doctrine is, among other things, a research school as a set of researchers working on an everyday methodological basis. The change of ideology to the diametrically opposite leads to the interruption of academic schools and the disunity of the generations of researchers.

Researchers understand doctrine the same way as ideology, including State ideology.[41] In this connection, we have included in the methodology of our study views that refer to ideological doctrinal phenomena.[42] American scholars note the strong influence of politics on judicial doctrine and often mention the influence of ideology on the recognition of precedents as doctrine.[43] Daliell Pinello has studied the influence of political parties on legal ideology in the American judicial system in many academic and judicial sources.[44]

Judicial lawmaking creates doctrinal forms of law as legal provisions, generalizations of judicial practice, legal positions, precedents,[45] and other comparable phenomena. A doctrine can be created by collective bodies of the judiciary, judges considering specific cases, and interpretations of court decisions by judges.[46]

41 N. V. Butusova, "Государственная идеология России: понятие, содержание, проблемы формирования и правового закрепления [State Ideology of Russia: Concept, Content, Problems of Formation and Legal Consolidation]", Вестник Воронежского государственного университета. Серия: Право [Herald of Voronezh State University. Series: Law], no. 1 (2006), pp. 4-19.

42 S. V. Matsko, Государственная идеология и право современной России: теоретико-правовое исследование [State Ideology and Law of Modern Russia: Theoretical and Legal Research] (2003) (dissertation candidate of legal sciences).

43 C. Porter, Automated Content Analysis and the Development and Utilization of Legal Doctrine in the Federal Courts (2018) (dissertation candidate of political science).

44 D. R. Pinello, "Linking Party to Judicial Ideology in American Courts: A Meta-Analysis", *XX*, no. 3 (1999), pp. 219-254.

45 C. J. Peters (ed.), *Precedent in the United States Supreme Court* (2013).

46 M. Simic, "The Role of Judges in the Interpretation of Law: (Some Issues in the

In their monograph *How to Do Things with Legal Doctrine*, Pierre Schlag and Amy J. Griffin examined the characteristics of doctrine.[47] They investigated types of doctrinal sources. Researchers have generalized (periodized) the historical stages of the formation of the concept of doctrine, tracing the relationship between the concept of doctrine and interpretation, doctrinal interpretation. Schlag and Griffin caution all readers – law students, researchers, lawyers, and judges – against simplifying the issue. Researchers criticized the article "What is a Legal Doctrine?"[48] They found the following thesis erroneous: "In many respects, a doctrine or precedent is law, at least as it emanates from the courts. Judicial opinions create the rules or standards that make up legal doctrine".[49] Schlag and Griffin pointed out that the article failed to understand the true meaning of legal doctrine.[50] They regretted that there is no uniform understanding of doctrine, which is understood differently in different social relations and research areas. Doctrine is not taught in law schools.

Schlag and Griffin said that users do not refer to doctrine as general ideas that reflect patterns. They immediately rush to specific examples from judicial practice, calling them doctrines. However, it is highly probable that these accidental examples are not doctrines and do not deserve such a high status. A specific example may contain an illegal, erroneous, excessively novel solution when examined closely. For various reasons, an accidental example may fall outside the relevant doctrine.

The practical value of doctrinal works varies from one era to another and from country to country. For example, the English scholar R. Walker pointed to a classical doctrinal work for each

Theory of Interpretation of Law)", *Collection of Papers, Faculty of Law, Nis* (1975), no. 15, pp. 139-144.

[47] P. Schlag and A. J. Griffin, *How to Do Things with Legal Doctrine* (2020).

[48] E. H. Tiller and F. B. Cross, "What Is Legal Doctrine?", *Northwestern University Law Review*, C, no. 1 (2006), pp. 517-534.

[49] Ibid, p. 517.

[50] Schlag and Griffin, note 47 above.

branch of law. The judge is likely to follow this doctrine. He proposed to distinguish two types of legal literature, dividing them according to publication dates. Walker referred to ancient manuals as obligatory primary sources of common law. This is the first group. The second group consisted of up-to-date manuals written by respected authoritative authors. They are not a collection of binding norms or a source of law. They serve as a pointer for finding primary sources.[51] Walker admitted that educational literature might be recognized as a source for the text of a precedent. In fact, this is a precious function of literature and especially significant for the time when the sources have not been preserved or are not available. The wide dissemination of such historical sources was achieved through legal literature.

Finding the texts of precedents from the fifteenth to seventeenth century in England was difficult. Books with significant quotations from primary sources played a unique role as a secondary (derivative) source. In the absence of a first (original) source, they are the only source of English case law. Such sources include: 1) Ranulf de Glanvill (*alias* Glanvil, Glanville, Granville, 1130-1190). *On the Laws and Customs of England* (1187),[52] known from the author's name as "Glenville"; 2) Henry de Bracton, (1210-1268), *On the Laws and Customs of England* (ca. 1250);[53] 3) Thomas Littleton (1407-1481) *On Holdings* (late fifteenth century),[54] 4) Edward Cocke (Edward Coke, 1552-1634), *The Institutions of English Law* (1628),[55] 5) William Blackstone (1723-1780) *Commentaries on the*

51 R. Walker, *The English Legal System* (4th ed.; 1976), p. 191.

52 R. de Glanville, *The Treatise on the Laws and Customs of the Realm of England Commonly Called Glanvill*, ed. G. D. G. Hall (1983).

53 H. de Bracton, *On the Laws and Customs of England.*, ed. G. E. Woodbine and S. E. Thorne (1968).

54 T. Littleton, *Treatise of Tenures* (1841).

55 E. Coke, *The First Part of the Institutes of the Laws of England* (1823; reprinted 1999).

Laws of England (1765-1769).[56] The recognition of the latter as a source of law is questioned by Walker by reason of its general nature. Blackstone preferred earlier works in the event of a conflict between the works of Glanville, Bracton, Littleton, and Coke.[57]

Similar examples exist in Spain, Portugal, and Germany. Petrażycki determined that a decree deriving from ancient law cited by Roman jurists was adopted in modern history. He found Caccialupus (de modo studenti, V1. inf.) to the effect that, in case of disagreement of the doctors' opinions, the opinion of Bartolus should be preferred.[58] For international law, the dictates of Hugo Grotius (1583-1645) played the role of normative fact. The doctrinal level was occupied by the opinions of Emer de Vattel (1714-1767).[59]

It is uncommon to equate research between specific people and the law. Undoubtedly, the pinnacle of doctrinal law was the law of 426 by Emperor Valentinian III (425-456) which established the great influence of the writings of the five jurists of earlier times: Papinianus (c. 150-212), Paul (late 150-212), Ulpian (170-228), Modestinus (3rd century), and Gaius (130-180).[60] The status of law was also accorded to the writings of those of their predecessors to which they refer. If their opinions differed, Papinian's opinion was decisive. This right of academic origin was equated with law by an act of the emperor.

Russian jurists before 1917 studied the status of doctrine in the context of the doctrine of forms of law. This period is represented in the publications of M. V. Khvostov (1868-1920),[61]

[56] W. Blackstone, *Commentaries on the Law of England: In Four Books*, ed. R. Burn and J. Williams (11th ed.; 1794).

[57] Walker, note 51 above, p. 196.

[58] L. I. Petrazhitsky, Теория права и государства в связи с теорией нравственности [Theory of Law and the State in Connection with the Theory of Morality] (1907), II, p. 585.

[59] Ibid. p. 591.

[60] Ibid. p. 589.

[61] V. M. Khvostov, Общая теория права: элементарный очерк [General Theory

G. F. Puchta (1798-1846) in translation,[62] S. A. Muromtsev (1850-1910),[63] Iu. S. Gambarov (1850-1926),[64] D. Grimm (1864-1941),[65] and L. I. Petrazhitskiy[66] (1867-1931).

F. Regelsberger (1831-1911) wrote at the end of the nineteenth century:

> A feature of jurisprudence's creations is the absence of external binding force. On one hand, this appears quite clearly in the legal interpretation of the academic interpretation of law provisions. Meanwhile, a well-known external authority is not completely alien to the positions of lawyers.[67]

Doctrine is among the legal phenomena that have constantly changed and are changing their status but are elusive. Doctrine tends to dissolve into legal scholarship, jurisprudence, religion, general principles, and other forms and sources of law. In 1911 Gambarov noted the controversial question: "Whether such a right is an independent source of law, or it forms an integral part of customary and legislative law".[68] Perhaps this inconstancy and uncertainty explain the absence of specialized doctrinal works in connection with the doctrine of the form and source of law. It is identified with one of these phenomena, as well as with religion for Muslim States and with ideology for authoritarian States. The term is referred to in the context of

of Law: An Elementary Essay] (6th ed.; 1914), p. 147.

62 G. F. Puchta, Энциклопедия права Г.Ф. Пухты [Encyclopedia of Law], transl. P. Karasevich (6th ed.; 1872), p. 99.

63 S. A. Muromtsev, Статьи и речи: вып. 1-5 [Articles and Speeches: Vols. 1-5] (1910). 2 vols.

64 Iu. S. Gambarov, Курс гражданского права [Course of Civil Law] (1911), I.

65 D. D. Grimm, К вопросу о понятии и источнике обязательности юридических норм [On the Question of the Concept and Source of Binding Legal Norms] (1896).

66 Petrazhitsky, note 58 above.

67 F. Regelsberger, Общее учение о праве [General Doctrine on Law], ed. Iu. S. Gambarov, A. S. Belkin, and P. G. Vinogradov; transl. I. A. Bazanova (1897), p. 85.

68 Gambarov, note 64 above, p. 334.

interpretation and legal awareness issues. Pre-revolutionary academic research has specific achievements in reconstructing the system of doctrinal legal forms. The broadest range of doctrinal forms of law is proposed by Petrazhitskiy. Doctrine itself is rarely mentioned as an independent source of law.

In most scholarly studies, the authors understand doctrine as a multifaceted phenomenon that can exist and operate differently. This means that researchers simultaneously recognize as doctrine acts of the judiciary, acts of legislation, and acts of academic creativity.[69]

The doctrine is addressed in the works of F. Parsons,[70] A. I. Ovchinnikov, A. O. Dalgatova, V. I. Fathi,[71] E. O. Madaev,[72] A. N. Chashin,[73] A. A. Zozulya,[74] and other researchers. There are studies on the action and application of the doctrine by which we understand its place in the mechanism of legal regulation[75] in the sphere of legal regulation.[76]

[69] T. E. Shubert, Доктрина, законотворчество, судебная практика: вопросы взаимовлияния [Doctrine, Law-making, Judicial Practice: Issues of Mutual Influence] (2019).

[70] F. Parsons, *Legal Doctrine and Social Progress* (1982).

[71] A. I. Ovchinnikov, A. O. Dalgatova, and V. I. Fathi, "Правовая доктрина как источник права в Российской Федерации [Legal doctrine as a source of law in the Russian Federation]", Философия права [Philosophy of Law], no. 2 (2016), pp. 59-64.

[72] E. O. Madaev, "Место и роль правовой доктрины в правовой системе Российской Федерации [Place and Role of Legal Doctrine in the Legal System of the Russian Federation]", Вестник Бурятского Государственного Университета. Педагогика. Филология. Философия. [Herald of Buriat State University. Pedagogy. Philology. Philosophy], no. 2 (2015), pp. 193-197.

[73] A. N. Chashin, "Судебная доктрина как источник (форма) права [Judicial Doctrine as a Source (Form) of Law]", Европейская адвокатура [Eurasian Advokatura], no. 5 (2016), pp. 70-75.

[74] A. A. Zozulya, Доктрина в современном праве [Doctrine in Modern Law] (2006) (abstract of dissertation candidate of legal sciences).

[75] A. R. Gilmullin, Правовая доктрина в механизме Российского государства (теория и практика) [Legal Doctrine in the Mechanism of the Russian State (Theory and Practice)] (2019).

[76] R. V. Puzikov, Юридическая доктрина в сфере правового регулирования: проблемы теории и практики [Legal Doctrine in the Sphere of Legal Regulation: Problems of Theory and Practice] (2003) (abstract of dissertation candidate of legal

According to A. A. Vasiliev, legal doctrine is a system of ideas and representations of law that reflect social interests. Legal doctrine determines the content and functioning of the legal system. It influences the consciousness and will of the subjects of law. The State officially recognizes legal doctrine by authorization in normative acts or use in legal practice under authority and general recognition.[77] This way of understanding doctrine, positivist in essence, is identical to the popular understanding of custom as a form of law. According to positivist theory, State sanctions make customs and doctrines become law. This position seems simplistic. Such an approach makes it possible to have a simplified interpretation of legal phenomena. Nonetheless, it is impossible to simplify this complex problem of transitioning a research doctrine into a judicial one through sanctioning.

Academician T. Ia. Khabrieva defines doctrine as "an authoritative opinion of researchers expressed in the form of legal ideas, hypotheses, theories, and concepts".[78] It is not easy to agree with this approach, although its origin is evident, and its application is known. This approach applies only to doctrine in the form of legal scholarship. It cannot be applied to doctrine in all its diversity, to all species.

A. N. Chashin emphasizes that the doctrine is a prevalent authoritative source of law and law enforcement with an academic origin. Legal doctrine includes "a system of legal principles, definitions, ideas, concepts and theories aimed at streamlining social relations, systematizing the institutions of the legal system, and forming legal consciousness".[79]

sciences).

[77] A. A. Vasiliev, Правовая доктрина как источник права: историко-теоретические вопросы [Legal Doctrine as a Source of Law: Historical and Theoretical Issues] (2007) (abstract of dissertation candidate of legal sciences).

[78] T. Ia. Khabrieva, "Доктринальное значение российской Конституции [Doctrinal Significance of the Russian Constitution]", Журнал российского права [Journal of Russian Law], no. 2 (2009), pp. 34-38.

[79] Chashin, note 73 above, p. 16.

According to N. Ia. Embulaeva and A. A. Mikhailik,

> Legal doctrine is a scientifically grounded, formed by the scientific community, authoritative, widespread source of law and law enforcement activities, including a system of legal principles, definitions, ideas, concepts, and theories aimed at streamlining social relations, systematizing the institutions of the legal system, and forming legal consciousness.[80]

This is a typical variant of the proclamation of doctrine produced by legal scholars, which is synonymous with the broader concept of legal doctrine. We will not reject this understanding of doctrine, but we will not confine ourselves to it either. The concept of doctrine seems broader than legal theory of academic origin, both in content and form.

R. V. Puzikov and D. A. Polianskii follow legal theory – doctrine, which is a well-known method. In their view, doctrine is:

> A system of views on the problem of legal regulation of social relations, expressed in the form of principles, presumptions, axioms, and other fundamentals, developed by legal science, a model of positive law, serves as a regulator of social relations and determines priority directions, patterns, and trends in the development of legislation, regardless of whether its provisions are recorded in any document.[81]

This approach is much broader. It covers the model and regulatory properties of legal doctrine, which is convincing.

Professor N. L. Granat, sharing this position, emphasizes the effectiveness of doctrinal provisions:

80 N. Iu. Embulaeva and A. A. Mikhailik, "Правовая доктрина как источник права и правоприменения [Legal Doctrine as a Source of Law and Law Enforcement]", Власть закона [Rule of Law], no. 2 (2017), p. 117.

81 D. A. Polianskii and R. V. Puzikov, "Правовая доктрина как особое правовое явление [Legal Doctrine as a Special Legal Phenomenon]", Вестник Тамбовского университета. Серия: Гуманитарные науки [Herald of Tambov University. Series: Humanities], no. 11 (2013), p. 8.

> Doctrine as a source of law is understood as legal science (theory, concept, or idea), which in all cases, without exception, is used in the lawmaking and law-enforcement process ... Doctrine is essentially the result of research.[82]

In general, while we agree with the effective approach to doctrine, we consider it to be one-sided. A concept of doctrine associated only with legal research unjustifiably simplifies this phenomenon. It is a reduction of the part to the whole, which violates the laws of logic. A doctrine can be exploratory, State, judicial, ideological, or conventional. The statement "doctrine = research = research doctrine" is partially true, only for one type of doctrine.

Such a narrow approach is incomplete. The idealistic picture of the legislator's unambiguous perception of the results of academic research, outlined by Professor Granat, is far from reality. Instead, it is possible to speak of a specific influence of legal theory on lawmaking and law enforcement. The research results embodied in doctrinal works do not constitute a doctrine. Some individual studies have such great authority that they are always used, necessarily, without alternatives, and imperatively, as a normative legal act. However, this can happen without attribution or by anonymous publication. Doctrine is applied as a part of legal consciousness, an omnipresent law.

Thus, most Russian legal scholars understand doctrine as an authoritative part of legal theory embodied in ideas, theories, and concepts. Earlier, we said that doctrine is a set of theoretical provisions that are confirmed by established research, which, due to its depth and authority, is in demand by social practice and acts as a regulator of social relations.[83] However, after almost two decades of research analyzing more sources and using different research methods, we have concluded that it is unacceptable to identify all types of legal doctrine with doctrine

[82] N. L. Granat, "Источники права [Sources of Law]", Юрист [Jurist], no. 9 (1998), p. 12.

[83] S. V. Boshno, Форма права: теоретико-правовое исследование [Form of Law: Theoretical-Legal Research] (2005), p. 18 (dissertation doctor of legal sciences).

of legal scholarship. This essentially and unjustifiably narrows the concept of legal doctrine.

Studies have been devoted to doctrine as an active legal phenomenon, its role, purpose, and operation. There is a discussion of the methodological problems of the development of legal theory, the continuity of legal research, the impact of judicial practice on legislation (M. A. Udodova),[84] and the role of legal research in the development of law (M. Ia. Osipov).[85]

Osipov wonders why legal theory and researchers do not play a leading role in the development of Russian law. The reason is that legal scholars in Russia are not highly respected by the authorities because State authorities consider their laws to embody their will. And this will of the State is not bound by laws or common sense. Osipov pointed to the complex relationship between opposition legal scholars and the State. We are not talking about an active confrontation between these two systems, which are representatives of the academic community. Suppose a Russian scholar constructively criticizes the State and legal order. In that case, the Criminal Code may be relevant. At present, scholars should follow the general context of the political order. Otherwise, their original proposals may be assessed as anti-State, possibly constituting a crime. Professor Osipov wrote: "Scholars must understand that the final decision and the last word in the development of Russian law still remains not with them but with the authorities".[86] However, the State is indifferent to the opinions of legal scholars if they differ from its visions. Legal practitioners and scholars,

[84] M. A. Udodova, Преемственность научных исследований роли воздействия судебной практики на законодательство [Legal Succession of Scientific Research on the Role of the Impact of Judicial Practice on Legislation] (2016), pp. 52-53.

[85] M. Iu. Osipov, О роли юридической науки в развитии российского права [On the Role of Legal Science in the Development of Russian Law] (2016), p. 90.

[86] Ibid., p. 91.

and deputies or senators (A. A. Klishis,[87] P. A. Krashennikov)[88] are at the service of the State in the person of the President. Nobody can be free of the system once he (or she) is within the system. Accordingly, a deputy and a senator, each in their own way, are bound hand and foot by elections and appointments, obligations, and agreements. In this regard, publications on the freedom of a legal scholar's creativity,[89] a dissertation on this topic,[90] and ideology are a doctrine.

Nevertheless, Osipov, turning to the future, hopes to organize "a normal dialogue between legal scholars and the authorities, in which both sides feel that they are needed by each other".[91] We do not see this dialogue to be probable. On the contrary, we observe a deepening alienation.[92]

The study of the phenomenon of doctrine should be pursued in at least two directions. The first is examining the regulatory role of doctrine as an independent form of law. Such independence, however, does not preclude that doctrinal provisions acquire an external form, a written shell at the expense of other legal phenomena (above all, judicial practice). The second direction is to explore the influence of doctrine on the development of law in all its forms. This is especially evident in cases where

[87] A. A. Klishas, Конституционный контроль и конституционное правосудие в зарубежных странах [Constitutional Control and Constitutional Justice in Foreign Countries] (2007) (abstract of dissertation doctor of legal sciences).

[88] P. B. Krasheninnikov et al. (eds.), Законотворческая история современного Гражданского кодекса [Legislative History of the Contemporary Civil Code] (2019).

[89] L. G. Berliavskii, Свобода научного творчества в международном и национальном праве [Freedom of Scientific Creativity in International and National Law] (2006), pp. 93-97.

[90] M. V. Rostova, Конституционно-правовое регулирование свободы преподавания и научного творчества [Constitutional-Legal Regulation of the Freedom of Teaching and Scientific Creativity] (2018) (abstract of dissertation candidate of legal sciences).

[91] Osipov, note 85 above, p. 93.

[92] S. V. Boshno, "Доктринальные формы и источники права" [Doctrinal Forms and Sources of Law], Государство и право [State and Law], no. 9 (2018), pp. 5-15.

doctrinal concepts or tenets accepted in mass consciousness lead to a change in legislation.

Doctrine is not entirely an independent form of law, but is the basis of all legal phenomena. Other forms of law act as a shell in which doctrine is clothed: a principle of law, a doctrinal writing, judicial practice, a generally-recognized, omnipresent law, and a normative legal act. Other forms of perceiving doctrine detail its provisions, giving them the character of concrete rules of conduct.

The development of the term "doctrine" generates several problems. On one hand, this concept has no legal meaning. A doctrine can be philosophical, sociological, or political. On the other hand, some terms overlap with doctrine, such as ideology or academic research.

The study of the phenomenon of doctrine as a form of law is related to the following questions:

- the occurrence of this phenomenon,
- the form (shell) of its existence,
- combination with other forms of law in terms of legal force and content, the degree to which it is binding,
- the possibility of protection by State coercion.

In recent years, another aspect of the problem has emerged. Modern lawmaking has used this term for bureaucratic legal acts of State power. These are military, environmental, climate, and other doctrines.

The opinions of authoritative jurists which have become on par with the law are of great importance in the study of doctrine. There are many historical examples. Such a role was played by the works of glossators-commentators (Italian legal scholars of the twelfth and thirteenth centuries). Interpretations of value are known as *Glossa Ordinaria*. Their authority was exceptional. Petrazhitsky, however, pointed out that the legislative consolidation of academic research as a form of law was derivative. Accordingly, disparate historical examples are not a reason to identify academic research and law.

Petrazhitsky developed the author's classification of legal studies that can be recognized as doctrine: 1) the law of lawyers, the direct consolidation of such a fact in legislation; 2) the opinions of legal scholars (commune doctoral opinion); 3) the law developed in groups (schools); 4) the teachings of great jurists.

A compromise seems to be appropriate. In today's conditions of the rule of law, it is not easy to imagine any State recognizing some books as equal to law. But that is only one side of the problem. On the other hand, denying the possibility of some legal studies enjoying exceptional legal authority is not helpful. Although their authority is not established by law, that authority has the right to exist. In the absence of a resolution of the problem, the publications of legal scholars may be equated to law. It was about this effect of the doctrine that Petrazhitsky wrote:

> Just as customary law does not cease to be customary law because its application is regulated by law, the law of scholars' opinions does not lose its (psychological) nature because its application is regulated by law.[93]

The Russian jurist N. M. Korkunov (1853-1904) proposed to see the differences between academic research and doctrine in the degree to which they are binding:

> A sign of the obligatory nature of the principles developed by academic research can only be their assimilation by judicial practice, in other words: not theory, but only practice is an independent source of law.[94]

We consider this opinion to be constructive. Legal scholars must distinguish between the source of the origin of the norm, on one hand, and its application in legal relations as a form of

[93] Petrazhitsky, note 58 above, p. 590.

[94] N. M. Korkunov, *Лекции по общей теории права* [Lectures on the General Theory of Law] (3d ed.; 1894), p. 289.

law, on the other. This division is seen as follows. Academic research or its ideas can be used in courts or law-making bodies. They can often be used in a personified and impersonal form (without indicating the author and a specific publication). Frequent use of the idea strengthens its authority and can be enshrined in judicial practice or given the form of law. Thus, an idea is born in legal research and becomes a doctrine in legal practice.

Academic freedom is an important concept. Legal scholars offer new, original solutions to social problems. In conditions of freedom and diversity of opinions, research conclusions are not identical. As a result, not just one solution is offered to the same challenge of social relations, but several. In publications and theses, researchers can express and substantiate diametrically opposed opinions. Due to objective and subjective circumstances, some ideas, theories, and concepts dominate. In this ideal example, there is rivalry, organic and age dominance, and the acceptance of some decisions of academic origin.

The path from an idea to a uniform application may be extended or lightning-fast. Ideas can become dominant in one day: the day of elections, a coup, or a revolution. This phenomenon was identified by Ia. M. Magaziner (1882-1961). He gave it an unusual name: non-law, "which became the starting point of a new legal order".[95] He found that the negation of legislation could be the source of a new right.

In addition to the revolutionary, there may be an evolutionary path of doctrinal development. A long journey can have different durations. The legislator may not decide on a topical issue of public life for a long time. The need to resolve disputes leads to using ideas from secondary sources. This is a standard situation of a legislative gap. It can take decades to legislate, and all the while, a doctrine that fills the gap is applied. However, it is not the measurement of this period that is important. This must not

[95] Ia. M. Magaziner, *Лекции по государственному праву: (Общее государственное право)* [Lectures on State Law: (General State Law)] (1919), p. 50.

be a one-time action. This lengthy process leads to the elevation of doctrine to the status of a regulator of social relations.

In legal theory, there are developments in expert law or the law of experts. The right of legal expertise can have the status of both a source and a form of law. As a rule, expert opinions have a force proportional to the authority of the author and the success of the content thereof. Expert law acquires the status of a form of law only when there is an "attribution of legal obligations and rights concerning a normative fact, to someone's expertise on a matter relating to the case".[96]

For a more precise understanding of the role and significance of expertise, it is necessary to determine the variants of its correlation with academic research and doctrine. An expert is a specialist in a particular field with exceptionally high qualifications. Experts can be specialists in different professions. They may have academic degrees. As a rule, law professors are experts in legal matters. Experts should have methodological tools, a database, and a system of methods based on which they draw conclusions. The results of an expert examination must be substantiated and verifiable.

The historical roots of expert law lie in Roman practice, more precisely in the decision of Emperor Augustus (63 BC-AD 14) to give the expertise of eminent jurists imperial sanction and authority. In addition, the authority of experts and the trust of the addressees of opinions played a significant role in the emergence of expert law. Petrazhitsky distinguished stages in the formation of expert law. The first stage consisted of recognizing the expertise given in a specific case for its resolution. The second stage is the validity of the expert opinion to resolve other similar cases.[97]

The expert makes significant written or even oral findings. These opinions can be used by the legislator or the court. Researchers call the results of such activities expert law. For

[96] Petrazhitsky, note 58 above, p. 591.

[97] Ibid., pp. 467-468.

example, the Constitutional Court of the Russian Federation summons a qualified professor to hear a case under discussion. Considering the expert's opinion, the court decides. It reproduces (without quotation, in an impersonal form) the expert's opinion in a court document. This is expert law.

An urgent problem is assessing the role, significance, and effectiveness of legal expertise in the modern mechanism of legal regulation. Despite the controversial status of expert law, legislation contains references to this source of law (for example, anti-corruption expertise in Russian legislation).

Doctrinal sources and forms of law include *Principles of Law,* which are the main areas of legal action. Attribution of principles of law to the sources of law is not accepted in domestic jurisprudence. Nevertheless, such a possibility is suggested in textbooks by V. V. Lazarev and S. V. Lipen, A. S. Pigolkin, G. Alpo,[98] and W. Henszey.[99] As a rule, the principle of law may be applicable in international legal relations.[100]

Because one method of this study is content analysis, we have made considerable effort to collect studies on doctrine – more than 1,000 works in two languages. The bibliography is a significant achievement of this study. Sources were collected from various databases, libraries, and legal reference systems. Each source is assigned a unique ID, which makes it easy to find these sources.

A review of scholarly literature on research is an essential preparatory stage of creative research work. There is a considerable body of academic research on doctrine, which is diverse and heterogeneous. All genres of publications are represented. Knowledge in this matter has been accumulated for centuries in different countries. The abundant publications are an argument against a new study on this topic. With each

98 G. Alpa, "General Principles of Law", *Comparative Law,* no. 1 (1994), pp. 1-39.

99 B. N. Henszey and Benjamin N. Henszey (eds.), *Introduction to Basic Legal Principles* (5th ed.; 1991).

100 Butler, note 8 above.

successive study, the chance of novelty decreases. The novelty of this study lies in collecting a database of publications on doctrine and analyzing them using advanced software. Thus, the multitude of sources on the topic of this study is a guarantee of the representativeness of the materials on which this study is based. The bibliography of publications is analyzed by using content analysis.

Chapter 2

Computer Tools and Databases on Doctrinal Studies

BIBLIOGRAPHIC, INFORMATIONAL, AND LEGAL DATABASES FOR USE IN DOCTRINAL RESEARCH

The primary information resources used in this study are the Russian Science Citation Index, HeinOnline, Lexis+, Consultant+, Library of Congress, Russian State Library, ProQuest, and certain others. Some of these resources have built-in analytics tools. We refer to the bibliography and related databases by the term "object".

DATABASES OF RESEARCH OBJECTS

Many objects have been compiled and published in different languages. The comparative-legal task predetermined the territories of the objects collected. Considering the space-time continuum, we chose the United States (a representative of the Anglo-American legal systems) and Russia (a representative of a transitional legal system with some Romano-Germanic characteristics). The collection of objects was undertaken in the databases of these two countries. Each database was analyzed, the possibility of comparing them was evaluated, and a comparative assessment was made. For this purpose, we selected the databases in Table 1.

Table 1. Databases for the Storage of Study Objects

Object view	United States	Russia
Books	Books Ngram Viewer	
court documents*	Lexis+ (unofficial)	Consultant+ (unofficial)

academic articles	HeinOnline (unofficial)	e-library (RSCI), CyberLeninka (unofficial/official**)
all publications (comprehensive collections)	Library of Congress (unofficial)	Russian State Library (partially official)
	Web of Science (not official for the United States and official for the Russian Federation)	
thesis	ProQuest (unofficial)	aleph.rsl.ru RSL (official)
official documents (current version of legislation)	US CODE (official)	pravo.gov.ru (unofficial 1)**
	Lexis+ (unofficial)	Consultant+ (unofficial)

*It is noteworthy that neither in the United States nor in the Russian Federation is judicial practice collected as an official resource.

**Sources are not collected officially, but the result is officially recorded.

In the Russian Federation, the pravo.gov.ru website is an official publication portal.

ProQuest has been collecting dissertations worldwide since 1939 and claims to be the world's most comprehensive collection. The database includes more than five million works and has functional search and reference references. Works are deposited by authors or universities.

Figure 1. ProQuest database

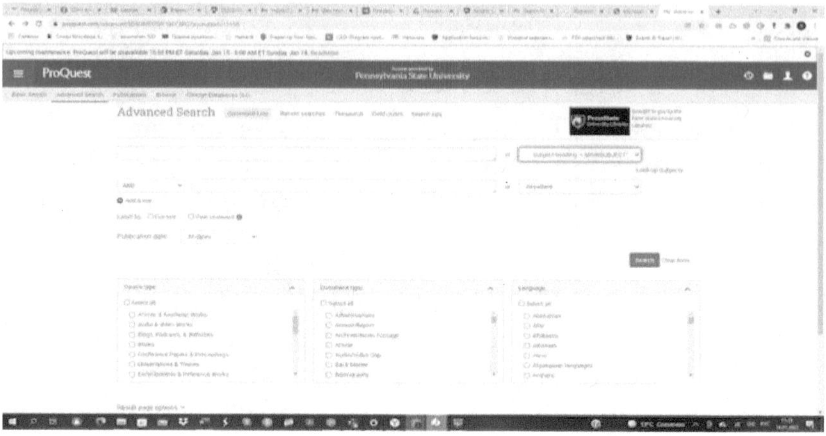

The **HeinOnline** database, established in 2000, contains an extensive collection of 6journals in different languages. 175 countries have access to the database. The database is designed to provide legal information to libraries. It is the world's largest distributor of legal information from periodicals. The database has its own full-text materials in pdf. (txt.) Format. HeinOnline has innovative search features. The database is integrated with the Library of Congress; it correctly transmits bibliographic information to Zotero. HeinOnline keeps track of citations of academic publications in court documents. The system maintains a rating of authors by the number of citations, including academic and forensic citations.

Figure 2. HeinOnline Database

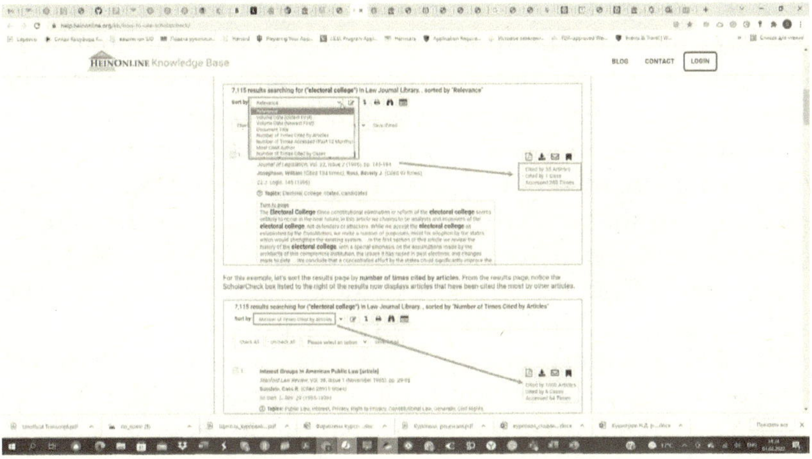

Figure 3. HeinOnline Database. Academic and Judicial Citation System

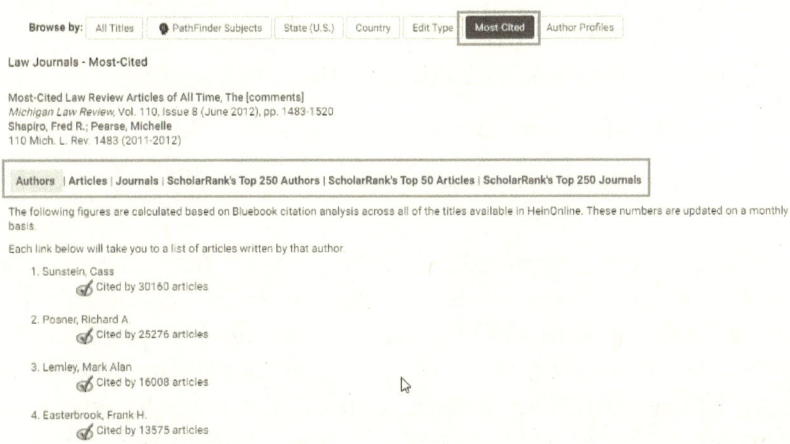

The Russian State Library (RSL, "Leninka") is the largest repository of all types of materials, including academic publications. In Russia, all publishers of printed products with ISBN and ISSN, following the requirement for the legal deposit of a copy, send printed copies of their publications to authorized libraries, including the RSL. Abstracts and dissertations are objects of storage for the RSL.

Abstracts of dissertations are available free of charge in electronic form at any point of access. Dissertations in electronic form are only available in authorized libraries. Paper texts are stored in the library's collections. The Ministry of Science / academic organization / educational organization obliges authors to submit the dissertation and abstract to the RSL in electronic and paper forms. This is a condition for awarding a candidate or doctor of legal sciences academic degree. The existing system is being reformed to expand the rights of academic and educational organizations. Over time, we expect changes in how dissertations and abstracts are submitted. As of 2025, the RSL is the central repository of dissertations and abstracts defended in Russia.

The degree of completeness of the Unified Electronic Catalogue on the official website of the RSL is as follows:

- receipt of books in the Russian language since 2003 and mainly receipt from 1831 to 2002 (omissions are due to technical problems of digitization of catalogs),
- receipt of dissertations since 1944,
- receipt of dissertation abstracts since 1986 (partly for previous years).

At the beginning of 2024, more than 317,000 abstracts on jurisprudence were included in the electronic catalog of the Russian State Library. The first abstract on jurisprudence is dated 1976. However, the process of creating these documents began long before the specific date of the start of retention. Information about previously defended dissertations (before 1976) is available in the paper catalog of the Russian State Library. Undigitized abstracts in paper form are also stored there, but are not available in the electronic catalog. Newly defended dissertations and any dissertations for the previous period have been entered (appeared) in the database. The library provides access to scanned copies of some sources for which copyright protection has elapsed. Other sources in electronic form can only be accessed in virtual rooms.

The Russian Science Citation Index (RSCI) is a Russian bibliographic database of more than 45 million publications. RSCI collects citation information from more than 6,000 journals. Most authors and publications are Russian and in the Russian language. Foreign authors and publications are collected by citing Russian sources.

The database has been in existence since 2005. Over the past years, data on publications have been entered by the author's representatives of the organization where the researcher works. This resource requires the placement of research publications from journals. Publishers extract data metadata from logs. Publishers of books, brochures, and other printed formats voluntarily (not necessarily) submit bibliographic data of printed publications (with or without texts of publications). In this way, the data entry system is derived from several sources. There is no transparent model for supplying the RSCI with publications and data on publications. There is no reason to assert that the RSCI contains academic publications. Establishing the period for which all publications are entered is also challenging.

RSCI cooperates with Zotero with some data transmission failures. Transitions are saved for registered users when working on the same computer. From Zotero to RSCI, unregistered users do not have access to texts.

The RSCI provides different forms of familiarization with full texts depending on the contractual relationship between the RSCI and the publishers. Use of part of the collection is free of charge. Metadata extraction for publishers and authors is subject to a fee. Not all publications are available for download. Use is mainly free, but there are exceptions. The copyright holder may charge a fee for downloading sources.

The Russian Science Citation Index maintains its own citation record and calculates the Hirsch index on its basis. The database does not have citation evaluation functions ("positive" or "negative" or other ratings). It provides access to the place of citation in the original source (if the text is available), allowing scholars to independently see how the author evaluates the sources (approves, criticizes, and so on). Thus, from the reference, it is possible to establish the author's attitude of the citing publication to the quotation. This is a two-step process of psycho-emotional assessment manually, without an automatic tool.

Google Books Database Ngram Viewer is a valuable service with unique content and a user-friendly interface. It is derivative, taking sources from the library systems Google Scholar, Google Book Search, Amazon, and WorldCat. The Google Books database provides access to selected data following the user's request. In fact, Google Books Ngram Viewer redirects to the copyright holder website. The advantages of the resource are the tools search and lightning-fast query execution. This is an entirely free resource; no registration is required. Google Books Ngram Viewer analyzes bibliographic information by time and language. The disadvantage of Google Books Ngram Viewer is that it requires some pre-training for the user to generate executable search queries and interpret them. Using Google Books Ngram Viewer helps compile bibliography lists and select text fragments for content analysis. This resource allows scholars to use the most straightforward abstract notation using the "*" symbol – wildcart. This sign replaces the L-gram within the N-gram.

Figure 4. Books Ngram Viewer – Legal Doctrine

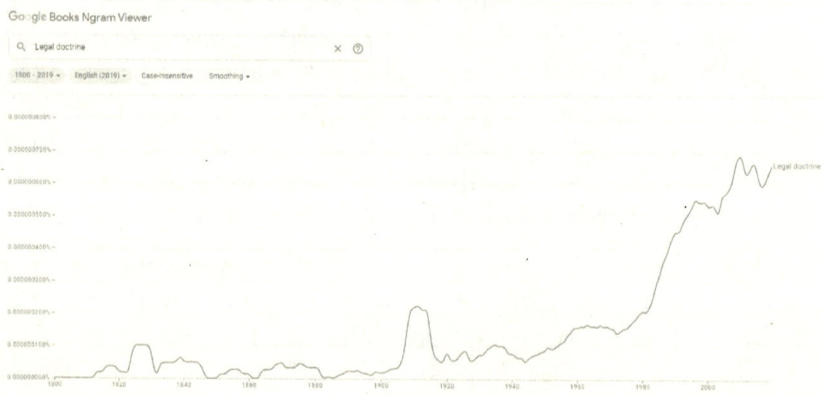

We can enter a specific year on the Google Books Ngram Viewer timeline. After that, we can open posts with a keyword phrase (word). Opening the text on the page with the key phrase (word) is possible. From Google Books, Ngram Viewer in Zotero correctly downloads the bibliographic data of the publication.

The array of objects that Books Ngram Viewer selects is large and diverse. We select only legal publications. The difficulty lies in the work being carried out online, and the search result is not saved. A new login to the program begins with the creation of a request. Thus, it is desirable to complete the selection without leaving the program. However, this is not easy due to the large amount of material.

Court decisions and related legal information in the United States and Russia are downloaded into legal databases. There are formal legal frameworks and many informal ones. For our study, we selected the term doctrine in the Russian legal framework Consultant+ and in the American legal framework in Lexis+. Both databases are unofficial.

For this study, the results of judicial activity are essential. Doctrine is the factual source and form of law used as the basis for adjudication in both States. However, it is a form of law (secondary source) only in the United States. We selected documents that defined the word doctrine as part of the request. The application of content analysis to court documents of the two countries differs significantly because the application of doctrine in the United States is open. In the Russian Federation it is latent.

Zotero inserts citations into the text and form a bibliographic list. However, the actual potential of this program is much greater. Zotero is an assistant in collecting, processing, and storing bibliographic data. Zotero assigns tags that automatically store a complete description of all data about the author and publication. It allows the researcher to take notes and save the URLs of the texts.

For sources and databases not protected by passwords, redirects from Zotero via UTL work confidently. Suppose the information system is entered by password from the same computer where Zotero is running. In that case, we can enter the text of the original source (seamless integration). Zotero extracts metadata from some .pdf files. This feature does not apply to all files now. However, it is generally available and beneficial for the researcher.

However, citations and compilations of bibliographic lists should be carried out under personal supervision and require constant attention from the user. The final word rests with the user.

Zotero assigns a unique ID to selected objects for legal doctrinal research (for example, the rights line). Zotero is a wrapper for selecting objects, organizing them (for example, adding them to folders), and maintaining an association with an object as a file or URL.

Zotero is a shell for collecting objects, organizing them (by adding them to folders), and maintaining a link to an object as a PDF file or URL. Zotero performs various search queries and creates a bibliographic record of the object on request. This tool is synchronized with Word and allows scholars to add footnotes and bibliographic lists to Word from Zotero.

The assortment of fields to be filled in Zotero makes it possible to use them for different purposes, including coding, depending on the needs of a particular researcher. The system has a dictionary memory, which frees scholars from the need to enter repetitive texts. It provides high-quality search. It is an open-source program that allows scholars to adapt to specific needs. An additional collection of footnote styles and bibliographies is available. However, not all program functions are Russified in terms of the rules of bibliographic work. The user must control the automatic data entry and output results. There are also questions about American citation styles and bibliography.

Figure 5. Entering an ID into the Zotero Program

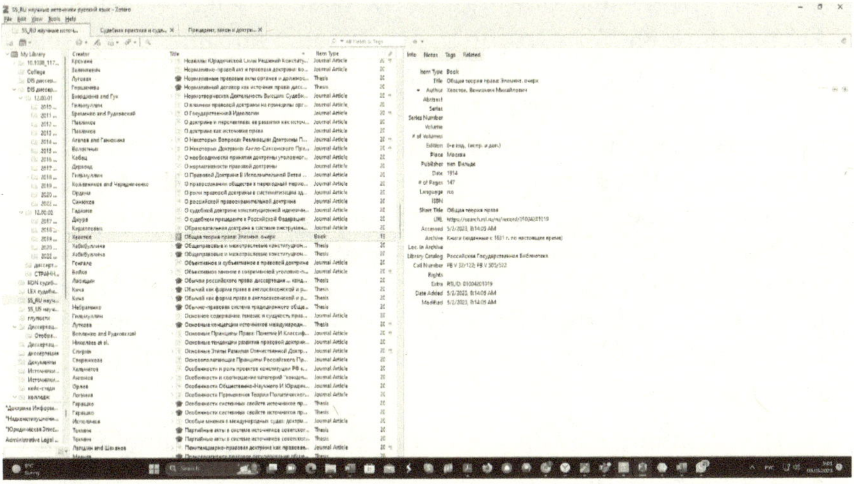

This way, all collected objects are consolidated in Zotero for further processing.

Consultant+ (C+). Legal Framework Consultant+ was established in 1992. As of 2023, it stores more than 200 million objects. C+ has the "Judicial Practice" database, which includes more than 11 million documents. The "Documents of the USSR" database contains documents dating back to October 1917. The database includes "Comments on legislation" and "Comments and books." They perform only an informational function and are not connected to the "Judicial Practice" database. Consultant+ contains some documents of judicial practice since 1917. The database is neither complete nor official. In fact, it is a random collection of different documents. However, it is a popular resource.

Consultant+ performs a contextual search for a word, several words in a title, in a paragraph, or as a phrase. When searching, scholars can set the maximum number of words between a keyword and other words, for example, in a phrase or paragraph within a set number of words. However, to form such a search query, a scholar must already have a dictionary of words that can be entered. Thus, the frequency of using a keyword, a known combination of words, is easily calculated by the Consultant+ system. The system does not know how to select words in the keyword range. Accordingly, we cannot automatically select words according to the formula "5 – key – 5" or key + words in a sentence. It searches for words as a phrase, a word in a paragraph, within a document. Scholars can set the number of words included in the search. Accordingly, at the first stage of forming the data business dictionary, Consultant+ cannot be used with its own tools. However, the program allows us to manually select 5 words around or insert specially selected groups of words into CheinWord-SB or AntCon. Consultant+ has context-selection models that cannot be automatically used in this study.

The Consultant+ database does not have a timeline, and accordingly, it does not have a temporal visualization. To construct a timeline manually, the researcher must transfer quantitative data from C+ to Excel. In this program, data can be processed and visualized into charts. Consultant+ provides statistics for each type of document. It is possible to process a request for the number of documents of a particular type with the word «doctrine» adopted in a certain period. C+ has a database of legal publications, which the company selects independently according to criteria that are not publicly announced. According to the oral comment of the C+ manager, the basis for the selection is the practical value of the publications. C+ contains comments on legislation, some textbooks, and articles.

The fundamental problem with data processing from Consultant+ is that in Russian legislation, the word "doctrine" refers to documents of different legal force issued by different State authorities. These documents are issued as laws, edicts, decrees, regulations, orders, and other forms. However, there is a type of document – a doctrine approved by an official. Thus, it is necessary to distinguish between the document "doctrine" as a type of document and "doctrine" as a word in the title, for example, Edict confirming a "Doctrine for the Development of the South Pole".[1] The word "doctrine" in the title emphasizes the document's general, strategic nature. It is a declaration of principles and basic ideas on some subject of legal regulation (subject area). Such documents do not have a direct regulatory effect. These are documents – declarations. The title of such documents may indicate the areas where they will be used (education, military, information security, foreign policy, and others).

Court documents for this study were selected from the "Judicial Practice" database of the Consultant+ system. In that system, *object analysis* can be (1) personalized, individual (database), e.g., ProQest; (2) within objects of the same type (for example, the type of object is academic research); (3) a comparison of objects of different types (e.g., academic research and court documents); (4) comparison of an object of the same type in different databases (for example, court documents in C+ and L+).

References and quotations in United States court decisions provide rich material for doctrinal research: it is a kind of "forensic scintigraphy". From these references, it is possible to compile a convincing rating of all sources and authors that the court uses. The source's creation date is significant; the "age" gives the source more authority.

For the Russian Federation, the assessment is absolutely the opposite. More relevant are academic sources that are as close as possible to the date of adoption of a regulatory act or court decision. The main reason for the rapid obsolescence of research sources is the variability of Russian legislation. For the United States, the older the judicial source, the more authoritative it is unless overridden or replaced.

Lexis+. The American legal framework **Lexis+** was created in 1966. It contains documents dating back to 1850. Secondary sources, including doctrine, are sometimes synchronized with

[1] The name is fictitious.

judicial practice, as facts are collected by citing a secondary source in court documents.

In Lexis+, the psycho-linguistic data of the text are combined with the timeline and a variety of visualizations justified by the United States judicial system. Lexis+ has a unique color chart tool for the intensity of word usage in text. Navigating this intensity scale allows scholars to select keyword document entry points. There is a convenient tool for combining words and expressions in a selected array of "and," "or" dependencies.

In American legal space, an advanced tool is Shepardizing.[2] This service is built into United States legal databases (Lexis+, WestLaw). Shepardizing collects and analyzes bibliographic legal information, citation data, and related sources.

Figure 6. Shepardizing

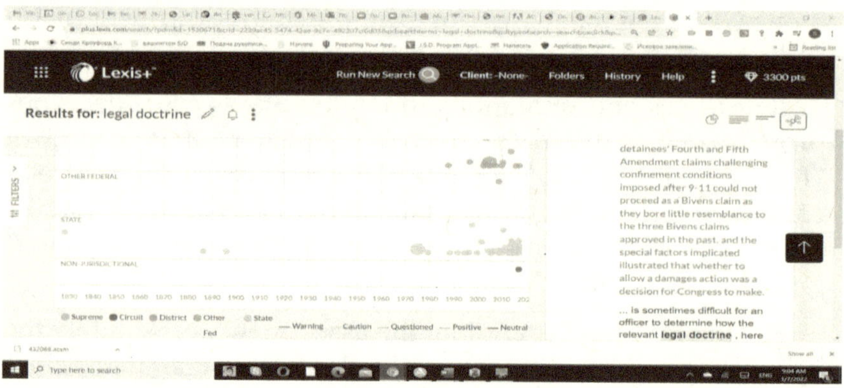

The service also evaluates the texts used in court documents positively and neutrally, requires attention, and is dangerous (rather negatively) to some ideas, cases, and publications (Figure 6). This tool has both advantages and disadvantages. Shepardizing's problematic tools are explored in detail in a PhD thesis, *Automated Content Analysis and the Development and*

[2] Library Guides: CRIMJ 420: Criminal Law and Procedure: Shepardizing E. Reed (available online).

Utilization of Legal Doctrine in the Federal Courts (2018), by Chase Porter.[3]

This analytical tool runs the Lexis+ legal database (See Figure 7).

Figure 7. Describes Meanings of Shepardizing Symbols

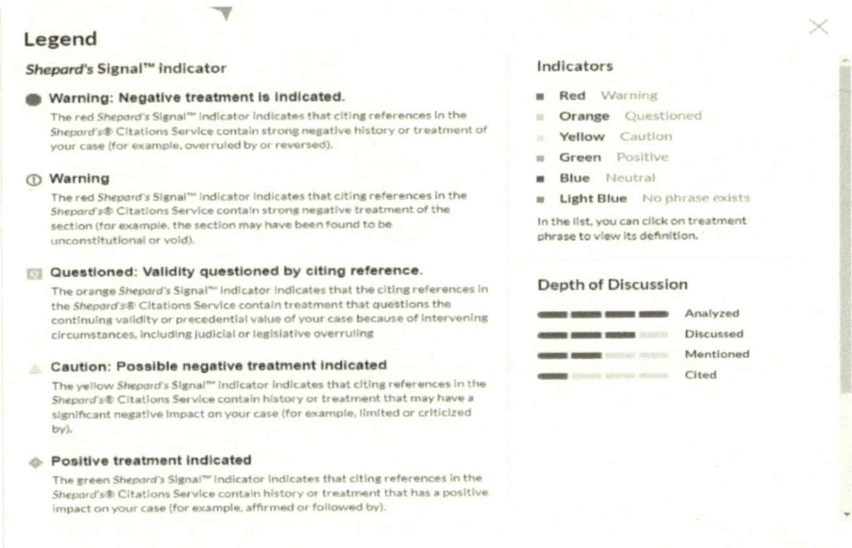

The program must not evaluate primary sources that are cited (mentioned). The program collects data on the tone (assessment) of the evaluation of the original source in other documents, for example, in court case articles. For example, the article's author writes that one should agree with some court decisions and use them in future decisions. This is a secondary assessment. This is used in Lexis+ as a tonality, for example, "positively." Technically, this is implemented as a content analysis in the form of finding words like "agrees". "corresponds to", "true", and other words-markers of some emotional evaluations.

[3] C. Porter, Automated Content Analysis and the Development and Utilization of Legal Doctrine in the Federal Courts (2018) (dissertation candidate of political science).

Figure 8. Display Source Citations in Lexis+

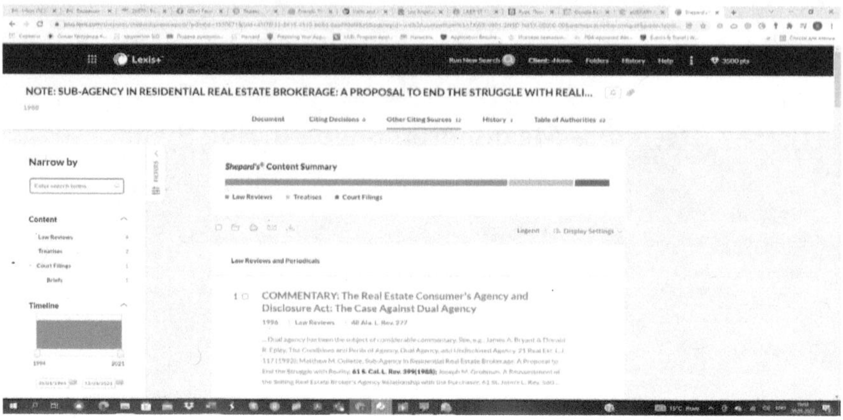

For example, the Court decision uses Boshno's book. The Court evaluates Boshno's book. In a simplified form, this mechanism looks like this: "Agreeing with Boshno book". This is an example of a positive assessment. However, neither judicial nor bibliographic databases retain estimates of secondary sources.

The Russian Consultant+ does not give a psycho-emotional assessment in court documents since, in most cases, references are given only to normative legal acts. Assessments of "positive" or "negative" with regard to a normative legal act are inadmissible in Russian legal culture. The Lexis+ system evaluates their suitability for a specific application. For example, the information "document canceled", "outdated", and "declared unconstitutional" in the Consultant+ system is synonymous with "attention" in Lexis+ but is applied to the law. In Russian documents, the courts assess the law as applicable or inapplicable in a particular case. Other forms of law in Consultant+ are not evaluated from the point of view of the possibility of their application since their application as a form of law is generally unacceptable.

It should be borne in mind that the Russian legal system openly classifies only normative legal acts as forms of law. Russian court documents, with rare exceptions, do not cite other court decisions. The exceptions are the documents of the Constitutional Court of the Russian Federation, which are used as normative legal acts, and others.

STATISTICS ON CONCEPT OF DOCTRINE IN EDUCATIONAL LITERATURE. QUANTITATIVE AND QUALITATIVE ANALYSIS OF EDUCATIONAL LITERATURE ON LEGAL DOCTRINE OF SOURCES OF LAW

To identify patterns in recognizing the doctrine in the system of sources and forms of law, we analyzed textbooks on the Theory of State and Law from 1868 to 2022 for the presence of information about legal doctrine in a chapter (or paragraph) of the textbook. Using electronic catalogs. 684 textbooks were reviewed, and 72 objects were selected for analysis by random sampling. All years have a selected specimen. In the 17 selected textbooks, doctrine is mentioned in the context of forms and sources of law, which is 23 % of the total.

Diagram 1. Analysis of the Recognition of Doctrine as Form of Law in Textbooks on Theory of Law

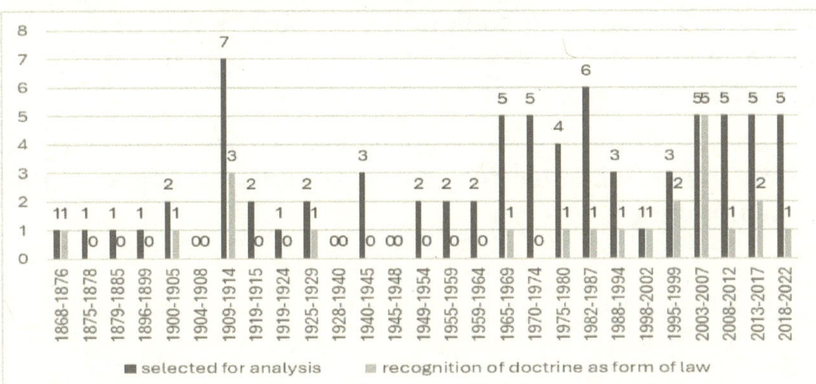

Two periods of elevating the status of doctrine to the level of a source or form of law in educational literature have been revealed. The first period was 1909 to 1914, and the second was 2003 to 2007. It is noteworthy that from 2003 to 2007, each selected textbook included the concept of doctrine, which indicates a strengthened recognition of the status of doctrinal law as a form and source of law.

The application of the content analysis method requires sources of funding. Logins to many databases are subject to a fee, especially for individual access. Corporate access can partially help solve the financial problem if the researcher can use corporate access. Suppose there are no free or corporate logins to the databases. In that case, the researcher can use (if possible) public access points, such as libraries. Legal reference programs (Consultant+, Lexis+) and library systems (HeinOnline, Znanium, Urait) are fee-based. Some software tools are free (Books Ngram Viewer, VAAL-mini), while other computer programs require payment (ABBYY, SimStat). User options can be unrestricted, storage can be paid (Zotero), essential functions are accessible, and advanced functions are fee-based (Questionnaire).

Coding of research objects for processing purposes in databases. Any file machined for content analysis must have a coded name. It is stored in a search folder with a coded name (ID). This encoding provides access to the bibliographic description. Thanks to coding, the researcher can analyze all data about the author, work, and other information from Zotero and other resources, if necessary.

For this study, we have developed a *method for encoding sources*: ID with a letter designation of the source type and its serial number.

Table 2. Object IDs for Content Analysis

Name of the object	Object ID (# number in the general list)	Explanation of the object	In the storage worksheet, the ID is entered into an Excel spreadsheet	ID in Zotero
Dissertations, abstracts	DIS_RU_# Full name	dissertations of the Russian Federation	2	rights
	DIS_a_RU_# Last Name	Dissertation abstracts in Russian Federation		
	DIS_EN_# Full name	United States Dissertations	3	
Court Documents	P D_RU_#	Consultant+ Garant	4	
	P D_EN_#	Lexis+	5	
Academic Research Publications	SS_RU_# Full name and 2 – 3 words of the title	Russian Academic Research sources in the Russian language	6	
	SS_EN_# Full name and 2 – 3 words of the title	American Academic Research Sources in English	7	
Official documents	ODOC_RU_#	normative legal acts of the Russian Federation – doctrines	8	
	ODOC_US__#	normative U.S. Legal Acts – doctrines	9	
Researchers' Personal Data	RS_RU_#_ Full name	method of identification of the author (researcher/scholars) Russian space	10	
	RS_EN_# Full name	method of identification of the author, American space	11	
Miscellaneous Sources	GB_RU_#	sources that are not included in the other types are in Russian language	12	
	GB_EN_#	sources not included in other species in English	13	
Persona-Doctrine	PD_RU_# Full name	identification of the Persona-Doctrine Russian space, Persona-Doctrine	14	
	PD_EN_# Full name	Identification of the Person-Doctrine of the American Space, Persona-Doctrine	15	
Form-Doctrine	FD_RU_# 2–3 words of the title	Identification of the Form-Doctrine (Russian space)	16	
	FD_EN_# 2–3 words of the title	Form-Doctrine Identification (American Space)	17	

We have introduced a division for each type of object based on the language used. Texts in different languages can hypothetically be entered into one database, but this has no effect. In any case, text search is performed in a specific language. For this reason, we have created an ID system indicating the language – RU for Russian and EN for English. Difficulties arise with authors who are researchers in the United States; their language is English, but they have publications in Russian. We will consider such a researcher and such a work according to the language of the work. For example, Professor William Butler may have an ID: SS_EN for publications in English and SS_RU for publications in English. Butler himself, as an author, is identified as an American researcher by his affiliation, although for much of his career he would identify as a British author.

This coding method has made it possible to create a data storage system and a form for analyzing the factors influencing the relevant research criteria. For example, the ID system makes it possible to know in what years sources containing a particular understanding of doctrine were written. Scholars can build a timeline for saved sources. Zotero will allow scholars to download data from it for further processing directly into Excel from Zotero.

To encode and record the information, including Zotero, we have developed a criteria system that may be relevant to understanding doctrine. We use two main criteria: **"object (text)" and "subject (author)"**. Accordingly, if a Russian researcher writes in Russian, his ID is his work SS_RU_# Full Name 2–3 words of the title; if in English – SS_EN_# Full Name 2–3 words of the title. If he is known as a Russian scholar but is affiliated with the United States, he is marked as RS_EN_# Last Name First Name. Russian researchers have the code RS_RU_#_Full Name

Name **Criterion "object (text)"**:

- year of publication of the object,
- country of publication of the object (language),

- country that is the object of the study,
- type of object (article, dissertation, abstract, book, court document, state regulatory document, etc.),
- understanding doctrine (judicial, state, scholarship, ideological, and other types).

Criterion "subject (author)":

- age is typed as modern (living now), deceased (with dates), and ancient. Typifying the spelling: one date "1936- the author is alive", two dates "1936-2023" – the author is deceased. For researchers of Russia, the following typifications are used: ancient, pre-revolutionary, Soviet, Russian, historical,
- legal views, type of legal understanding (positivism, sociological approach to law, natural law theory, and other types),
- the type of legal system (Romano-Germanic, Anglo-American, and so on),
- academic degree (lawyer without academic degree, master, PhD, associate professor, doctor of legal sciences or doctor of laws, professor, academician),
- dominant, including the self-identified type of activity (teacher, judge, civil servant, and so on),
- research specialty of the author (theory of law, history of law, family law, labor law, or others).

All these criteria are desirable and useful. Accordingly, they are given if the relevant information is available. Suppose a criterion is recognized as critical, especially important for research. In that case, it is necessary to concentrate maximum efforts on it. The information is collected during the study without extraordinary effort unless it is critical.

Chapter 3 Content Analysis Doctrinal Studies

EMERGENCE AND DEVELOPMENT OF CONTENT ANALYSIS AS METHOD OF LEGAL RESEARCH

Content analysis is a tool for transforming the qualitative-descriptive form of expression into a quantitative-digital one. Text objects can be lengthy or eloquent. The exact meanings can be expressed in different verbal forms. The exact words can have different meanings. Descriptive text objects are difficult to compare, and the results of such comparisons are easy to dispute. The results of such descriptions are difficult or impossible to verify. In fact, it is not a result but an opinion about the result.

In contrast to texts, digital data is convincing, calculable, and verifiable. With numerical units, scholars can perform mathematical operations and conduct quantitative analysis. Thus, there is an objective need to translate qualitative, textual data into quantitative, digital data. This will allow the content analysis of legal texts.

The method of content analysis has a long history. The foundation of the content analysis method was laid down by Harold Lasswell (1902-1978).[1] The Festschrift dedicated to this outstanding specialist[2] outlined the general concept of the method and its application to social research. Geller, Kaplan, and Lasswell had published on flexible and rigid content analysis procedures during the Second World War.[3] In 1955,

[1] H. D. Lasswell and N. Leites, *Language of Politics: Studies in Quantitative Semantics* (1949)

[2] H. D. Lasswell and A. A. Rogow (eds.), *Politics, Personality, and Social Science in the Twentieth Century: Essays in Honor of Harold D. Lasswell* (1969).

[3] A. Geller, D. Kaplan, and H. D. Lasswell, *The Differential Use of Flexible and Rigid Procedures of Content Analysis* (1943), p. 16.

sufficient research material was accumulated for a Working Conference on Content Analysis, later published in book form.[4] In 1963, one of the earliest practical recommendations for using content analysis in political studies was published by North (1914-2002).[5] In the early 1960s, research on content analysis was sufficiently extensive and diverse to be summarized in a special bibliographical publication.[6] Significant works on content analysis methodology in the twenty-first century have been published in England.[7]

The United States has taken a leading position in advancing computer technologies in content analysis,[8] developed by GOOGLE[9] and other companies. Before the advent of the computer, word processing, coding, and analysis was done manually. With the advent of computers and special software, content analysis became a tool for researchers, including those working individually. Artificial intelligence capabilities have brought research using content analysis to a new qualitative level.

The researchers left the library reading rooms and sat in front of computers in their offices. Instead of a pen, they picked up a mouse and used a computer display rather than hand-coded paper cards. AI and computer technology make analyzing an immense amount of information possible.

Russian legal scholars have made significant contributions to content analysis theory. Content analysis is actively used in

[4] I. de S. Pool (ed.), *Trends in Content Analysis* (1959).

[5] R. C. North, *Content Analysis: A Handbook with Applications for the Study of International Crisis* (1963)

[6] Richard W. Budd and Robert K. Thorp, *An Introduction to Content Analysis: Including Annotated Bibliography* (1963).

[7] R. Franzosi (ed.), *Content Analysis* (2008).

[8] M. D. West (ed.), *Applications of Computer Content Analysis* (2001); M. D. Hardee (ed.), *Content Analysis as a Research Tool for Higher Education* (1972).

[9] Google Cloud, "Cloud Natural Language" (available online).

linguistics, sociology, and political research.[10] At the junction of specialties, a new profession has developed – ontoengineering – a symbiosis of a linguist and a programmer.[11] Lawyers have proposed to use this profession to optimize the drafting of legal acts. Legal ontoengineering, in their opinion, will be undertaken by the profession of "normowriter".[12]

Programmers use a professional tool for the content analysis of such objects as historical documents.[13] Scholars from the Faculty of Mathematics, Moscow State University, undertook a content analysis of prisoner publications from 1925 to 1930.[14] Unexpected and important information opened up new horizons in legal materials and research content analysis.

The method of content analysis is not yet widely used in legal research. There are examples of content analysis of normative legal acts in the field of medicine[15] and publications on the use of the method for analyzing political and legal documents[16] and

10 N. N. Samorodova, "Контент-анализ посланий В. В. Путина Федеральному Собранию РФ (2000-2014 гг.)" [Content-Analysis of V. V. Putin's Addresses to the Federal Assembly of the Russian Federation (2000–2014)], Современные политические процессы [Contemporary Political Processes], no. 2 (15) (2015), pp. 7-13.

11 "ScienceHub #06: Компьютерная лингвистика [Computer Linguistics]," Хабр [Hubr] (available online).

12 I. V. Ponkin and A. I. Lapteva, Методология научных исследований и прикладной аналитики [Methodology of Scientific Research and Applied Analytics] (2d ed.; 2021).

13 M. E. Gusarova and K. V. Makarov, "Система компьютерного контент-анализа исторических документов [The System of Computer Content Analysis of Historical Documents]", Алгоритмы, методы и системы обработки данных [Algorithms, Methods and Data Processing Systems], no. 1 (2012), pp. 23-32.

14 K. A. Zingis, "Публикации заключённых: контент-анализ газеты 'новые соловки' (1925-1930 гг.) [Prisoner Publications: Content Analysis of the Newspaper Novye Solovki (1925-1930)]", Историческая информатика. информационные технологии и математические методы в исторических исследованиях и образовании [Historical Computer Science. Information Technologies and Mathematical Methods in Historical Research and Education], no. 3-4 (2015), pp. 45-55.

15 M. B. Erugina, I. L. Krom, and A. B. Shmerkevich, "Контент-анализ правовых актов и определение направлений оптимизации паллиативной помощи в современной России [Content Analysis of Legal Acts and Identification of Ways to Optimize Palliative Care in Modern Russia]", Саратовский научно-медицинский журнал [Saratov Scientific and Medical Journal] 11, no. 4 (2015), pp. 506-510.

16 A. I. Golovnia, "Военная доктрина и стратегия национальной безопасности

regulations of public authorities.[17] These studies are not in the field of law; they address some object (health, culture, and the like) regulated by law. Nonetheless, these examples prove that it is possible to use content analysis for normative legal acts and other legal documents. The application of the method extends to other forms of law, such as court documents, legal doctrine, legal customs, and other sources of law. Content analysis has been used to analyze unique literature and academic research in economics, sociology, and political research, which is close to this study from the object's point of view.[18] These examples allow us to conclude that content analysis can analyze any text. This method is universal for text objects. In 2005, Borishpolets adapted the content analysis method to study political processes.[19] Her innovative ideas were transformed into everyday tools.

Luzan's dissertation substantiated using content analysis in the field of philosophy. The object of his analysis was normative legal acts. Luzan's research focused exclusively on the frequency aspect of content analysis. However, frequency analysis without variables, determination of justifications, and reasons for the frequency of use of phrases does not correspond to content analysis as a research method. Without considering

России: контент-анализ с политико-правовых позиций [Military Doctrine and National Security Strategy of Russia: Content Analysis from Political and Legal Positions]", Право и политика [Law and Politics], no. 6 (2011), pp. 944-953.

[17] Iu. V. Goriushina and V. V. Trofimov, "Регламенты законодательных собраний как документально-фиксированное выражение функциональных направлений современной законотворческой деятельности: начальный исследовательский опыт контент-анализа (на примере Регламента Тамбовской областной Думы) [Regulations of Legislative Assemblies as a Documented Expression of the Functional Directions of Modern Legislative Activity: the Initial Research Experience of Content Analysis (on the Example of the Regulations of the Tambov Regional Duma)]", Правовая культура [Legal Culture], no. 1 (2021), pp. 37-45.

[18] S. V. Rastorguev, "Применение метода контент-анализа к экономическим, социологическим и политологическим исследованиям [Application of the Method odf Content Analysis to Economic, Sociological and Political Research]", Вестник Финансового университета [Herald of the Financial University], no. 6 (2011), pp. 76-80.

[19] K. P. Borishpolets, Методы политических исследований [Methods of Political Research] (2005).

significant variables, the frequency of word use does not give a significant academic result. Nevertheless, the merit of Luzan is that he explored the possibility of applying quantitative analytical methods to legislation. According to Luzan, the law has unique characteristics that make it a permissible object of content analysis. He specifically noted that the text of normative legal acts is a formalized, professionally processed text. A normative legal document is a structured system with several semantic series. These semantic sequences can only be recognized by content analysis methods.[20] We support this thesis, especially regarding the multi-layered structure of legislative texts, in which the real meaning is hidden. On the surface, only the text is in the zone of visual familiarization and intuitive understanding. The motivational and psychological meanings of the legislative text are encoded. However, these psychological meanings operate regardless of whether they are visible to the subject of law.

The legislator may embed hidden meanings and implicit objectives in legislation. The meaning, which is assumed, conceived, or hidden from society, may not correspond to the officially formulated and publicly proclaimed meaning. The goals, objectives, and principles of legislation are the most susceptible to mutations. These declarative fragments of documents give society socially approved signs of wishful thinking. They are talking about what is not yet there in the present tense. They provide ideological or programmatic guidelines, such as "to increase", "to ensure, develop", and so on. This strengthens the importance of methods for revealing the hidden meanings of legislation.

Despite the prohibition of connotation in normative texts, it is used, *inter alia,* to lull vigilance, conceal the fundamental

[20] V. S. Luzan, "Контент-анализ основных нормативных правовых документов, обеспечивающих реализацию государственной культурной политики (федеральный и региональный аспекты) [Content-Analysis of the Basic Normative Legal Documents Providing Realization of the State Cultural Policy (Federal and Regional Aspects)]", Журнал Сибирского федерального университета [Journal of Siberian Federal University. Humanities & Social Sciences], III, no. 4 (2011), pp. 342-362.

goals of public authorities and officials, and create a positive emotional background for harmful and dangerous decisions. Let us recall a well-known example. The public authority defines its prescription as a recommendatory or informative text for voluntary implementation. It looks as if the authorities are asking citizens to do something. At the same time, the authority assumes that citizens are obliged to do this. Such legislative norms are recommendatory (dispositive) in the form of presentation; in actual regulation, they are imperative.

There are two methods of content analysis: analytical and statistical. We believe it is possible to apply statistical analysis to the results of analytical analysis. Textual analytical forms such as dissertations and articles can be the object of statistical analysis. The results of the quantitative analysis should be analyzed by a specialist. Accordingly, analytical and statistical methods can be applied sequentially several times.

An important question arises with respect to the variables that affect the semantic content of the key concept. These variables are set by the author in the study program. For doctrinal learning, variables include time, place, concepts, and others.

Experts in *qualitative content analysis* point out that most challenging is the establishment of the concept or semantic content of the keyword – the concept. In our study, the keyword concept is "doctrine". Our task is to describe the open explicit and reveal the hidden meanings of this term in various textual objects created over a long period in different countries. We have created pairs of doctrinal properties, which may be opposite but coexistent; that is, the plural and the singular in doctrine. We have identified and investigated more than two dozen pairs of alternative properties of doctrine.

Quantitative content analysis "can be presented as a systematic study of the content of a written or spoken text, fixing the most frequently repeated phrases or plots".[21] This type of content

[21] Borishpolets, note 19 above, p. 58.

analysis is called *non-directional* analysis. This type of text analysis is implemented by selecting words that express the meaning of the text and calculating the frequency of word use based on the idea that a string of words is representative. This group of words can represent a piece of text or an entire object. Representative words "meet two requirements: 1) not be of a functional nature; 2) have a greater frequency of occurrence in the text".[22]

We selected nouns (law, doctrine, act, and others) and adjectives (ideological, among others) for the content analysis. However, sometimes verbs are needed to investigate an action (preserves, authorizes, and so on). Cognate verbs and nouns are sometimes not equivalent to the keyword context. For example, sanction (noun) and sanction (verb) differ significantly. The word "sanction" has no value in the analysis of doctrine. It is an element of the rule of law. The word "authorization" can describe the process by which a State recognizes different forms of law, such as custom or doctrine. Scholars do not need to use low-occurrence words to form an artificial text.

An example *of a non-directed word* selection is a word search. There can be several words. Their relative position does not matter. The possibility of directional selection analysis can be implemented by querying for words as phrases. When performing a query, the database will select phrases with different keyword endings.

Directed qualitative analysis is based on the exact sequence of words in a phrase, which are vectors and, in this sense, have a direction.[23] Programs that select an invariable sequence of words as phrases are tools for directed content analysis.

Analysis can be statistical and, in this sense, quantitative. "Statistical analysis implies only the quantitative expression of a feature in its physical expression. Counting, adding, multiplying, and so on, that is, performing some quantitative

22 Ibid.

23. Ibid., p. 64.

operations, can only be performed with physical objects as units of a statistical distribution".[24] Physically, the object of analysis is a word (phrase). Quantitative indicators are comparable. "A word, a sentence, a theme, an idea, a character, a social situation can be taken as a unit of text analysis".[25]

Quantitative information gathering is the calculation of the frequency of occurrence of any unit of analysis. The researcher records the frequency and analyzes this quantitative indicator. Quantitative content analysis is not a semantic study. It deals *exclusively with the frequency distribution of semantic units in a text*, or in other words, with the analysis of static patterns of the frequency distribution of semantic units in a text.[26] Identification of patterns is the main task of theoretical and legal research. Identifying patterns is the goal of legal theory and content analysis so they collaborate effectively.

QUANTITATIVE AND QUALITATIVE CONTENT ANALYSIS OF RESEARCH ON LEGAL DOCTRINE

The term "*qualitative content analysis*" means "content". "Qualitative content analysis is aimed at an in-depth, meaningful study of textual material. The final conclusions are formulated here, considering the interrelations of the content elements and their relative importance (rank) in the structure of the text".[27] In passing, Borishpolets touched upon the assessment of the emotional coloring of the texts. We consider this direction valuable and promising.

In this study, we use content analysis to identify correlations between the frequency of word use and to determine significant characteristics and variables. Factors that affect the frequency of

[24] L. Ia. Averianov, Контент-анализ [Content Analysis] (2007).

[25] I. A. Pashinian, "Контент-анализ как метод исследования: достоинства и ограничения [Content-Analysis as a Research Method: Advantages and Limitations]", Научная периодика: проблемы и решения [Scientific Periodicals: Problems and Solutions], no. 3 (2012), p. 15.

[26] Averianov, note 24 above, p. 16.

[27] Borishpolets, note 19 above, p. 55.

word use may not be related to the keyword. These factors may be outside the text. Factors for document creation can be found in social, political, historical, and other contexts. A tautology of the words "content" and "context" emerges. In the textual object research method, *content* refers to the words around a critical concept. *Contextual analysis* means that the meaning of a keyword is revealed by analyzing satellite words (surrounding words). "*Context*" is widely used in various fields outside of philology and texts. *Context (continuum)* is the environment, environment, and significant facts that influence and determine a fundamental phenomenon, event, and other meanings.

Stages of Content Analysis

Content analysis, according to the Borishpolets method, includes several stages in the research process:

1. definition of a set of objects,
2. text decomposition,
3. counting or quantifying multiple elements of a text array,
4. meaningful interpretation of the results of the decomposition of the text array and the quantification of the selected elements,
5. verify the results obtained and record them in the final document.[28]

Experienced researchers suggest the following stages of content analysis:

1. data preparation,
2. data collection and systematization,
3. data counting and analysis,
4. reflection of the results of the analysis[29].

[28] Ibid., p. 57.

[29] Методика проведения контент-анализа [Methods of Conducting Content Analysis] (available online).

Averianov pays attention to preliminary work, which includes the following activities:

1. determine a list of leading, authoritative, knowledgeable political scholars, for example, of, say, 100 people,
2. make a list of significant research and randomly select the direct object of content analysis,
3. choose the dominants, which are the words-concepts that have received the most votes,
4. create artificial conceptual spaces with a given word concept. In turn, from this artificial conceptual text, dominant words are selected, that is, concepts that have received the most significant number of votes,
5. establish the degree of connection (strong, weak) between the dominants, making it possible to obtain the full content of the concept studied in the text.[30]

At the preparatory stage, the researcher selects sentences with a keyword (dominant). Then, these sentences need to be cleaned. That is, the natural text must be reworked into an artificial one. *Cleanup* means removing unnecessary characters, footnotes, hyphenations, and other defects from the text that would interfere with computer processing. The text is clear of word forms, derivatives, and other words with the same meaning.[31]

Averianov describes the difference between a narrative (organic, natural) and artificial text. The original source text is organic. The essence of creating an artificial text is "to extract from the source text that part that will contain the feature of interest to the researcher ... Only those sentences containing a given word are selected from the source text (e.g., automatically by an electronic program)".[32]

30 Averianov, note 24 above, p. 284.

31 Ibid., p. 190.

32 Ibid., p. 194.

The task of preliminary preparation is to make the text suitable for processing by machine learning algorithms. To do this, the following operations are performed on the text:

Tokenization is the division of long sections of text into smaller ones (paragraphs, sentences, words). Some programs do this automatically. Such AI tools distinguish sentences by identifying dots. They can also identify paragraphs by automatically marking hyphenation. They will combine the words into groups. Phrase search is the most challenging tool.

Normalization is reducing the text to a uniform form (without format, style) (a single case of words, absence of punctuation marks, deciphered abbreviations, the verbal spelling of numbers, if it is essential for research, etc.).

Stemization is bringing a word to its root by eliminating appendages (suffixes, prefixes, endings). Special programs do this by searching for the root of a word.

Lemmatization means reducing a word to its semantic canonical form. For example, for nouns and adjectives, this form is the nominative singular and the infinitive for the verb.

Vectorization is the transformation of text into vectors.

A "bag of words" is an array of words without regard to grammar or word order.

In the initial stages of an investigation, scholars identify words as units to attach meanings to certain selected words. For example, in the study of legal doctrine, words important for defining doctrine as a whole or its individual types are selected in the bag of words. In the Provalis program, this selection is done by creating a dictionary.

An important concept is *N-grams,* combinations of N consecutive terms to simplify textual content recognition.[33]

[33] M. Vichugova, "Оцифровываем текст: как превратить слова в числа для Data Mining – 5 NLP-операций Feature Extraction [Digitizing Text: How to Turn Words into Numbers for Data Mining – 5 NLP-operations Feature Extraction. Digitizing the Text]" (available online).

Thus, an artificial or purified text consists only of meaningful words; there are no words in it – conjunctions, prepositions, abbreviations, redundant spaces, or numbers. It is imperative to control the presence of periods at the end of sentences. When transitioning texts from PDF format, they may disappear. If we omit (fail) these pre-processing steps, then the extra units of text will be selected and processed. Ultimately, we will still have to remove them from the processing program. Using Word's "find and replace" tools to eliminate common prepositions, adverbs, and other unnecessary elements is better when working with a text file.

Microsoft Word has a built-in tool to help researchers normalize text. For example, this tool makes non-printable characters visible and can automatically remove them. It is also necessary to eliminate numbers, hyphenations, extra spaces, and other text defects for subsequent machine processing.

Some programs can work without human intervention, but the tools we know are adapted only to English. Researchers cannot avoid text cleanup. In any case, it will have to be done before or after the selection of words around the key concept. The researcher chooses time and instrument.

The RSL displays only a paragraph when contextually searching the electronic catalog. The selection of pages with the selected value (keyword or phrase) is made exceptionally well by the Books Ngram Viewer program. In addition, any library database, such as the Russian State Library, selects lines (paragraphs) with a given word (combination of words). When comparing these two tools, we prefer Books Ngram Viewer as it curates pages. Such selection makes it possible to inspect the text before and after and analyze keywords in context. More generous amounts of information are provided by expensive paid resources such as Lexis+ and HeinOnline. They provide input to the text during contextual search and do not restrict access to the entire document. Under no circumstances does the RSL provide remote access to an e-book (or even a fragment thereof). The exceptions known to us are abstracts of dissertations and works of the "historical heritage" category, for which the term of copyright protection has passed (75+ years).

Specialists in content analysis attach great importance to *the pre-processing of texts.* Agreeing with this thesis in general, we note that in 2024 there are programs that, based on AI technologies, work with the raw language of any computer format. For example, AntCons similarly extracts data from text files (.txt).

At the same time, the pre-preparation of texts remains relevant for some programs used for certain types of content analysis. This study uses programs that work only with prepared text (.txt). This significantly lengthens the preparatory stage of the study. However, such high-quality training reduces labor costs at subsequent stages of the study.

A system of indicators should be used for a qualitative content analysis of data on satellite words of a critical concept of doctrine (or phrase). Beyond that, the absolute number of words does not matter.

In our study, the type of legal doctrine is a significant indicator. In this regard, we have placed marker words according to the types of doctrines, giving them the meaning of a marker. Words that can be used equally in different doctrines are not markers. They can acquire the value of a marker if they have an original and meaningful combination with a keyword. It is necessary to check the objective and subjective factors to interpret the features and possibilities of each type of legal doctrine. Suppose there is a significant correlation between the type of doctrine and the factor. In that case, it is possible to conclude about the conditions and prerequisites of a specific type of doctrine and the prospects and possibilities of managing the state of a particular type of legal doctrine.

For example, the relationship with time is essential for an ideological doctrine. It is most developed during revolutionary events, a period of the weakening or excessively strengthening of State power. It should be borne in mind that an ideological doctrine can be a State doctrine; such a State will be ideologized.

The uncontested dominance of the State ideology may be associated with the prohibition of other views. Other views are challenging to capture in the context of rampant censorship. The level of criticality in the decisions of State authorities is decreasing. Consent and then praise are the dominant styles of interaction between society and the authorities of a non-democratic political regime. State ideology is associated with the strengthening of the State. An ideology not associated with the State may oppose the State, which is another doctrine. In terms of content, it is an alternative. This non-right weakens the State or arises during periods of weakening of the State. Marker words of the State ideology – president, national, State, official, organ, political, ideology, and others.

We draw attention to the relationship between the ideological unofficial and the ideological State official doctrine, loyalty to the State, and State ideology. The main difference is in the form in which the doctrine is anchored. There is only one form of expression for the official doctrine of the State: official documents. Unofficial ideology can take many forms, including literature, party programs, and so on.

Qualitative analysis allows for using subjective factors from the author's curriculum vitae. Subjective factors are not usually expressed in marker words. Subjective, personal factors can be applied after establishing the type of legal doctrine to which we attribute this author or he identifies himself. Otherwise, it is just an analysis of one person's statement based on his words and biographical data. This is not content analysis, as no typed body of knowledge exists. However, we can type biographical data. This makes it worthwhile to check the text using content analysis. For example, a set of texts created for a certain period is selected. For example, 2015, 2016, 2021, and 2025 are the dates of writing (publishing) the object. Typing can be based on the years of the author's life. For example, it is possible to distinguish typified groups as Soviet, Russian, and pre-revolutionary researchers. With this sampling, it is possible to select doctrinal understanding in groups based on the typed biographical data of the authors. Then, continuing the research, it is possible to identify the type of selected group using content analysis of satellite words in the text (for example, the understanding of doctrine by Soviet scholars).

Cross-sectional qualitative content analysis can be carried out. It is possible to select from the general array of objects the objects identified as ideological doctrines.

The method of content analysis has *the following advantages*: (1) validity, (2) reliability, (3) objectivity, (4) consistency, (4) representativeness, (5) verifiability,[34] (6) formality, and (7) rigor.[35]

The *reliability of* content analysis is ensured by computer tools. Technical text processing distinguishes content analysis from other methods of legal research. Technology makes it possible to move from a descriptive genre to a fundamental research one.

The *systematic nature* of content analysis lies in the fact that this method reveals the regularities and patterns of an object in the system of objective and subjective context.

The *representativeness* of the content analysis method is ensured by well-grounded criteria for sampling material from the general information array. Rejected elements can be replaced with others relatively easily since there are many objects, and they are replaceable. For example, suppose we reject the abstract of the dissertation. In that case, we can replace it since the sample is 1 out of 10. We have 9 abstracts in reserve. One of the goals of content analysis is to type an array. Accordingly, its selected objects are replaceable since they are typically selected. This does not preclude the application of content analysis to unique texts, to the object as the only one. Each piece is unique. However, this is a different methodology compared to this study. Our goal is to establish the typical type of unique objects in the future.

[34] Borishpolets, note 19 above, p. 55.

[35] Pashinian, note 25 above, p. 16.

The *verifiability* of content analysis results is ensured by preserving the empirical base of the study. This creates prerequisites for the researcher or an external expert's subsequent verification of the initial data. It is easy to check the sampling method and its result, representativeness, and other study parameters. The information is stored conveniently and can be accessed on the researcher's workstation and anywhere using cloud technologies.

Quantitative indicators guarantee reasonable and verifiable results. Researchers divide large amounts of data into groups chronologically on various grounds, for example, by the type of legal understanding. Quantitative, numerical data can be visualized in charts and tables. Visualizations allow researchers to make the study results visible, visual, understandable, and editable.

Content analysis is applied to large amounts of information. The study's most relevant results can be obtained from the information array collected from various sources. The material may be publicly available or available to the author due to some of his or her characteristics (for example, official position, unique relationships, status, corporate access, or others). Closed access to databases increases the value of the study because non-public data is analyzed; however, closed access prevents verification of the source data. The discreteness of the database can skew the results of the study. For example, some dissertations and abstracts in the Russian State Library are stored only in paper form, and some in both paper and electronic form. The degree of availability of paper and electronic copies naturally differs. Only electronic objects are available remotely. The level of accessibility of different types of objects in digital form also differs. For 2023, abstracts in electronic form are available to all users free of charge from any access point. Dissertations in electronic form are available only in libraries that agree with the RSL. As a result of such objective circumstances, the basis of research on some objects may be gaps.

Content analysis is *a non-contact method.* The researcher contacts only the texts, mainly in electronic form. The author does not interview the respondents, observe the objects, or contact the media. However, content analysis can be carried out on the data collected from the respondents of sociological surveys, which combines contact and non-contact methods of collecting information.

Based on the analysis of academic literature and our own experience, we propose the following stages of content analysis:

1. Development of the research concept: goal, objectives, and hypothesis.
2. Selection of objects for analysis.
3. Selection of programs for object processing.
4. Keeping track of objects and assigning IDs.
5. Preparation of pre-processing of objects (if necessary).
6. Computer processing of objects by special programs.
7. Interpretation of results.
8. Conclusion on the results of the content of the critical concept.

The *disadvantages of the content analysis method* include the following:

- a technically complex method requires additional training from the researcher, which is broader than his research field and qualifications,
- use of special tools and software, which can have a high cost,
- content analysis is the collection of information for the final analysis of which other additional human analytical skills or tools are used,
- to use traditional Microsoft programs such as Word, Excel, and Access in content analysis, a higher level of user training is required than that of a humanitarian,
- a team style of work is desirable. A team may include a research supervisor (a carrier and generator of the

research goal), a philologist, a programmer, and a mathematician. Expanding the number of team members at the expense of other necessary specialists is possible depending on research and incomplete analysis. This may incur costs.

It is inexpedient to use the content analysis method to process objects (such as a dissertation, a monograph, or even an article) in their entirety. From these objects, the researcher selects fragments that should be representative of the object as a whole. Selecting research objects from the total number should also be based on sampling. We strive for 10 % representativeness for any object of research. If there is a need and opportunity, then at the stage of qualitative analysis, it is possible to additionally ensure the representativeness of the influencing factors. Legal scholars must set the number to increase the sample for a particular factor. For example, there are no or few features in the sample for the period from 2010 to 2020. This time factor is essential for the study. It is necessary to check this period in depth in such a situation. Based on the results of the in-depth inspection, the following reasoned conclusions can be made: 1) there were not enough objects during this period, 2) all objects were selected, or 3) another conclusion. The absence of an object in a period is as important as its presence.

Content analysis software can automatically select objects from text. The automatic selection of objects has advantages and disadvantages that can negatively affect conclusions and results. Here is an example of the distortion of the meaning in the automatic selection of objects: the author in the text states his critical and other attitude to some other publications and cites them for these purposes. There is a risk that the quotation in the main text may be mechanically attributed to the object's author. In this case, two distortions arise: (1) the object's author is not ascribed to his opinion, and (2) this other person's opinion differs from or is opposite to the author's position. Other errors are also possible.

Errors can be avoided by manually selecting and processing each fragment from the object. In addition to citations, which are relatively easy to detect in the text and eliminate using the "find" function, the object's author can provide an analysis or description of another researcher. Such a somersault can only be detected manually. But we must remove it in the process of preliminary preparation, as it distorts the author's opinion of the object.

What has been said is of no significance if the researcher observes an array without personification of objects (without authorship). In this case, the authorship does not matter. For example, suppose we analyze a collection of views on the definition of doctrine. In that case, all the quotations collected in one place do not bother us. This is used at the stage of dictionary formation. What matters to us is the presence of words, not authorship.

Another distortion that cannot be eliminated is the chronology of views. Suppose the text uses quotations from works published in different years. In that case, this will significantly distort the time continuum considered by the date of the leading publication. Any citation or analysis of other sources should be eliminated in the analysis that considers the author and publication date. Insignificant errors in applying the content analysis method are covered by the large volume of objects under study.

A significant disadvantage of the content analysis method is that it requires much preliminary preparation on the researcher's part at the program development stage. The researcher should have a clear idea of the concept of the study. At the program development stage, the researcher must have in-depth knowledge of the research object to formulate a hypothesis. At the project design stage, the researcher develops attributes and factors that may affect the research object. The influence of factors will be checked in the process of qualitative analysis. At the outset of the study, it was unknown what factors affected the object. However, the author must anticipate and assume them.

There are obvious influences. For example, place and time usually matter. If we analyze academic publications, then the academic degree of the author can probably be relevant. However, the data needs to be collected sooner. When selecting objects, all possible factors should be considered, and the author should develop a hypothetical idea of them before the study. This means that the researcher anticipates the factors that are likely to have an impact on the object of study.

A content analysis program will be more successful for a researcher with experience in the research topic. The researcher should know the sources on the topic. We call these steps the preliminary stages of the author's preparation. These actions are not counted as a content analysis step. This is the researcher's personal preparatory work for applying content analysis.

At the stage of collecting empirical data for the study, definitions of doctrine from various sources were collected and systematized. They were selected based on the keyword "doctrine" in publications. After selecting many objects (text fragments), we worked them out using AntCons and Wordstat9 Provalis. This is part of the research using the content analysis method.

A sociological survey is considered in conjunction with content analysis. It serves as a form of verification of specialist respondent use of marker words. In general, it can be stated that there is a positive attitude towards the approbation of the content analysis method, legal doctrine in general, and the typology of the doctrine in particular. Moreover, respondents with publications with the studied definitions willingly provided them for content analysis. It can be said that a synergy has emerged, a connection of the professional community in support of collective research. In fact, the Legal Doctrine Club was formed with its own discussion platform. Respondents provided their own or supported definitions of doctrine in response to open-ended questions. Respondents sent lists of publications, the texts of publications, collections of articles on doctrine, and even monographs. The creative association of the respondents was also manifested in the fact that they are recommended by name or even with the titles of significant works of scholarship for the status of a Persona-Doctrine or an authoritative person in their lives.

These were not only personally known colleagues, but also researchers whom respondents know from publications. It can be assumed that the personal passion of the author of the questionnaire was transferred to the respondents. The questionnaire turned from a tedious formal questionnaire into a platform for a club of research interests because of the combination of the author's and respondents' energy and interest.

Content analysis of the text is used to select the words surrounding the keyword "doctrine". The selected words are summarized and further used to analyze the objects of study (texts). At the beginning of the study, we formulated the hypothesis that doctrine is described in a certain number of words. In the future, after the word selection is complete, we will use the dictionary to find pairs of words "doctrine" + "..."; for example, "doctrine" + "idea". Perhaps one or more words from the dictionary will be selected next to the word "doctrine" in one object. Then, we will count the frequency of word usage. This will make it possible to establish the most frequent, dominant understanding of the term "doctrine" in the objects of study. In addition, it is possible to compare the understanding of the "doctrine" by types of objects: dissertations, abstracts, academic publications, court documents, and official documents. There are three stages in the process of vocabulary and vocabulary vector formation: 1) the words around the word "doctrine" are established (revealed); 2) variants of combinations of words from the dictionary with the word "doctrine" are established (revealed); 3) the frequency of words and vectors is set.

Given the above, content analysis is an adequate method for researching all texts, including normative legal acts. Content analysis has counterbalanced the well-known shortcomings of traditional methods used in legal research. Applying the method requires additional qualifications from the researcher, with an emphasis on computer technology and philological knowledge. The reliability of the result is predetermined by a representative sample of the objects of analysis. Scholarly publications on doctrine include dissertations, abstracts, textbooks, articles, lectures, and other written works, all subject to contextual analysis.

The developed research model can also be applied to other objects. However, each type of research object is unique. Previous research tools cannot be mechanically transferred to a new object. Correction (significant) is necessary for the purposes and objects of another research.

Computer Programs for Content Analysis

Various computer programs for text analysis have been created and successfully used in the modern world. Programs can be unique, that is, created for the content of text analysis; for example, frequency metering programs consider the purity of a fragment of speech. Programs can collect and count words and sometimes phrases. Such frequency accounting is designed to determine the dominance of some units, such as words.

Some programs divide texts into semantic blocks based on dictionaries. Dictionary units are given semantic meaning. Programs can read a directional vector of words. An essential tool of programs is the selection of words around a keyword – before and after – in a sentence, in a paragraph, or in the number of words (for example, three words preceding and five following a keyword). Such opportunities give the researcher a tool for analyzing words in semantic groups. Some programs can create their own accounting of analysis objects based on groups of words, phrases, and topics. As for texts, substantial grounds for accounting are data about the author (last name, first name, patronymic, academic degree, place of work) and the work (genre, date of publication, type of publication). Even better programs combine data about the author object and the text object itself, and perhaps additional information, into a single database.

Programs for collecting information and technological support for applying contextual analysis in applied analytics are diverse. We have classified them on different grounds.

Based on "the existence of a psychological assessment analysis":

1. with psychological analysis,
2. without psychological analysis.

Based on "type of files, types of documents to be processed":

1. .txt format,
2. documents of any format (.dox, PDF, etc.),
3. voice input of information, including analysis of video and audio sources.

On the grounds of "the need for initial preparation":

1. required,
2. not required.

Programs can also be classified on the following grounds:

- built-in expert evaluation, visualization of results,
- availability of additional philological options, for example, search for synonyms, cognate words, differences in parts of speech (for example, prepositions and adverbs, etc.,
- availability of a topic analyzer, a grouping of objects, often called coding.

User-friendly services connect the object of analysis with the original sources in other storage locations, for example, through Zotero. In the absence of such access, the data about the unit is considered by its ID. There are programs with and without chronological and geographical tools, respectively.

There is a problem with the multilingual nature of the software toolkit. An important quality indicator for comparative legal research is a multilingual interface and the ability to replace the language of the texts under study. The American English language dominates among the programs used for content analysis. There are multilingual services and two types of programs: monolingual and multilingual. The multilingual nature of the service sometimes reflects the peculiarities of the problems to be solved, for example, cross-cultural and comparative problems. In addition to language, there are cross-cultural features of the loss of meaning in translation, untranslatable idioms, and national, State, and legal terminology. For example, the translation or transliteration of the terms "ordinance" or "decree" does not help us understand the instrument's position in the legal system of the countries where these legal instruments are issued. It is even more challenging to compare documents from different States. In this case, it does not matter whether the forms of these documents are named the same or differently. They can be used in the same way and have a completely different place in the system of legislation. I can have the same position and a different name.

A researcher needs a software product that works with the languages necessary for his work with the languages of his research. However, almost all the world's well-known software products have American English as their primary language. As a result, such programs can produce distorted results in other languages, including Russian.

A wide range of software tools are available to study legal phenomena. There are many computer programs, and we need professional navigation to work with and make choices within this variety. Some programs have similar functions and tools but can be fundamentally different upon closer inspection. A set (package) of computer tools may be required if the study is complex. Comparative legal studies with a long observation period impose additional program requirements.

The following software tools can be used for content analysis: 1) Text Date Mining; 2) ABBYY Compreno; 3) IBM Watson Natural Language Understanding; 4) Amazon Comprehend; 5) Microsoft Azure Text Analytics; 6) Natural Language API; 7)

Shepardizing; 8) Provalis (QDAMiner, WordStat and SimStat); 9) Istio.com and others. We do not present all the tools:

1. Text Date Mining[36] automatically retrieves structured data from an unstructured source, such as entities, entity relationships, and attributes that describe entities. The program performs natural language processing and is proficient in the technology of neuro-linguistic programming.

2. ABBYY Compreno is a natural language analysis tool for extracting information represented by entities and their attributes.[37] This product is not sold to individual users. Individuals and independent researchers can only purchase ABBYY FineReader. The intended use of ABBYY FineReader is not directly related to content analysis. The program converts text from PDF format to TXT format via DOC. Converting files to various formats is used in this study to pre-process files in the preparatory stages.

3. Artificial intelligence has provided new possibilities for data processing. The most well-known tool is the IBM Watson Natural Language Understanding application. The tool provides advanced text analysis capabilities. It extracts entities from texts, establishes relationships between keywords' semantic roles, and solves other problems. The service performs an analysis of emotional coloring and tonality. Its most important feature is the identification of general concepts that are not directly addressed in the text.[38] This is a kind of tool, the capabilities of which are much more comprehensive than the needs of this study.

[36] "Text Data Mining | Data Mining Tutorial - Wikitechy" (available online).

[37] "Алгоритм извлечения информации в ABBYY Compreno [Algorithm for Extracting Information in ABBYY Compreno]," Хабр, 2021 (available online).

[38] T. Koreshkova, "Семантический анализ для автоматической обработки естественного языка [Semantic Analysis is an Important Subtask of Natural Language Processing]" (2021) (available online).

4. Another popular tool, Amazon Comprehend, is a natural language processing service with machine learning (AI) technology. Amazon Comprehend detects the language of the text and extracts "key phrases". The program has psycholinguistic capabilities: positive, negative, neutral, or mixed text tone. It defines parts of speech.

5. Microsoft Azure Text Analytics is an AI tool that detects sentiment and entities. It also identifies "key phrases" in unstructured text. This tool evaluates sentiments as negative, neutral, and positive. The following way is to establish a confidence quotient. The first assessment, for example, is positive or percentage-based. The same object can be rated 50 % positive and the other 50 % negative.

6. The Natural Language API analyzes: 1) sentiment (AnalyzeSentiment Choreo); 2) entities (AnalyzeEntities Choreo); 3) parsing (AnalyzeSyntax Choreo). It is a tool for professional philological analysis to identify morphological properties and grammatical relationships.

A significant obstacle to using these tools is the language of the texts with which they can work. Often, programs are positioned as multilingual, but they do not give a significant result when working with texts in Russian. The DeepPavlov[39] campaign promises a breakthrough, but the finished product has not yet been presented.

Provalis has created a state-of-the-art, multifunctional content analysis toolkit.[40] The company's three main products are most suitable for this study: QDA Miner, WordStat, and Simstat.

QDA Miner is a qualitative data analysis software for organizing, encoding, annotating, extracting, and analyzing document collections. The QDA Miner qualitative data analysis tool can analyze various documents, computer coding, and

39 "Research at DeepPavlov" (available online).

40 "Text Analysis & Mining Software I Easy to Use Content Analysis I Wordstat" *Provalis Research* (blog) (available online).

subsequent analysis. Seamless integration of QDA Miner with WordStat, content analysis and text mining software, and SimStat (a statistical tool) provides flexibility in analyzing text and correlating its content with structured information, including numerical and categorical data. QDA Miner provides high-quality data analysis.

The advantage of the program is its integration with other databases and types of documents. Programs of the Provalis family can take data from other sources, for example, from bibliographic systems (Cited, Zotero, Mendeley, etc.), databases (Access, etc.), files of different types, programs (SurveyMonkey et al.). Excel spreadsheets are a universal platform for the mutual transfer of data.

Provalis works with almost all languages and even recognizes the possibility of entering data in spelling languages. The researcher should use the computer language and region settings and the dictionary functions for optimal language settings. However, the program malfunctions when using Russian texts. Some windows do not recognize the Russian language, so they must be filled in English or with Latin characters (transliteration). Transferring data from Excel or World to Russian is converted into symbols. However, through repetition, the user can accustom the programs of the Provalis group to work with Russian-language texts.

The advantage of Provalis is that the system loads any files and images. However, real efficiency is ensured by the pre-processing of texts.

Istio.com is a service that analyzes semantics. The researcher can use the program by pasting a text fragment into the form or dragging the page URL to the desired field. Then, the text will be added automatically. When switching between tabs, scholars can take advantage of additional features. For example, the scholar can specify a list of the necessary search queries, and the service will highlight all their occurrences in the analyzed text.[41]

[41] "Назад к микросервисам вместе с Istio. Часть 1 [Back to Microservices with Istio. Part 1]," Хабр [Habr] (available online).

AntCons is a free tool that performs various types of work on the text for its preparation, processing, and analysis. It selects a set number of words preceding and following the keyword and provides much analytical information, statistics, and philological analysis. This service creates real competition for expensive and hard-to-access programs. It is beneficial at the stage of testing working hypotheses. At this point, the researcher needs to substantiate the hypothesis at the lowest cost. The researcher will then look for those programs that will provide subsequent, advanced opportunities.

For the content study of textual objects according to the legal doctrine, the most appropriate products are the products of Provalis: QDA Miner, WordStat, and Simstat. This set of programs provides the entire necessary range of tools. Migration between programs is carried out while maintaining a common database. Considering that we have conducted sociological surveys, this block of programs is convenient and optimal. It allows scholars to combine text analysis and processing of sociological surveys. Suppose a participant in a sociological survey has worked on legal doctrine. In that case, the programs make it possible to combine all the information into a single whole. At the same time, data about the author of the publication about the doctrine, personal information about them from the questionnaire or collected additionally, the publication's texts, the author's answers to the questionnaires, and so on are processed.

Provalis has additional capabilities due to seamless integration with Zotero, MonkeyServey, and Excel. Easy data transfer in an orderly form creates a single information database, in our case, about legal doctrine. If Provalis does not interact directly with a program, Excel can be used for inner balancing. For example, Google Forms does not transfer data directly to Provalis. However, uploading data from Google Forms to Excel allows scholars to load it with Provalis.

Chapter 4
Sociological Methods of Doctrine Research

Expert Questioning and Questioning as Method of Studying Attitudes to Forms of Doctrinal Expression and Doctrinal Bearers

Sociological research methods open new opportunities for studying forms of law and significantly supplement the existing methodology. We see the particular importance of this group of methods because the officially proclaimed (including legislative) status of doctrine and its actual impact on legal relations differ significantly. In this connection, we consider it necessary to apply the methods of the sociological collection and analysis of data on doctrinal forms. Sociological information captures the attitude of society and a professional group to the phenomenon. The surveys show how the phenomenon is perceived and provides information on the legal regulator's application assessment (positive, neutral, negative), which is the legal doctrine in this study.

The methodological basis of sociological methods is based on the publications of V. A. Iadov,[1] V. I. Dobrenkova, A. I. Kravchenko,[2] V. S. Katashinsky,[3] M. Bulmer,[4] and

[1] V. A. Iadov, Социологическое исследование: методология, программа, методы [Sociological Research: Methodology, Program, Methods] (1995); Iadov, Стратегия социологического исследования [Sociological Research Strategy] (2003).

[2] V. I. Dobrenkov and A. I. Kravchenko, Методология и методика социологического исследования [Methodology and Method of Sociological Research] (2009).

[3] V. S. Katashinsky, Методы сбора социальной информации [Methods for Collecting Social Information] (2017).

[4] M. Bulmer (ed.), *Sociological Research Methods* (2d ed.; 2017).

Émile Durkheim (1858-1917).[5] The peculiarities of applying sociological methods to legal research are analyzed in the works of Matthew C. Stephenson[6] and Sarah Gotschall.[7]

Sociological research has a different object from legal research. Jurisprudence has normative legal acts as its object, and its subject is the social relations that develop in the sphere of operation of the normative act. In legal research, attention is first paid to the normative legal act, then to the relations regulated by these norms. These legal relations may be adequately, insufficiently, or excessively regulated by law. If some social relations have not yet become the subject of legal regulation, then the need for such regulation can be justified. Sociology is the study of the behavior of groups of people in society.

In writing this study, quantitative and qualitative sociological methods were used: questionnaires, expert surveys, interviews, and embedded observation.

A questionnaire is analytical, searching for interrelations and regularities between the object and the author's predetermined variables.

An expert inquiry is a reconnaissance study aimed at gathering additional characteristics of an object. The survey is conducted based on the concept of "Persona-Doctrine". The reconnaissance nature of the survey is predetermined by the fact that this term was introduced into academic circulation for the first time. This predetermines the absolute novelty of the term and the social group to be identified and studied.

In part, the questionnaires for our study can be classified as continuing because we studied the same subject (civil servants and judges) and the same issues from 2003 to the present. In the total number of questions, three questions are repeated

5 É. Durkheim, et al., *The Rules of Sociological Method* (8th ed.; 1938).

6 M. C. Stephenson, *Standing Doctrine and Anticorruption Litigation: A Survey* (2016).

7 S. Gotschall, *A Survey of Arizona State Legal and Law-Related Documents*, CXVI, no. 3 (2021).

verbatim in the 2003–2006, 2007–2008, and 2022–2023 surveys. Not verbatim, but close in meaning, repetition concerns 50 % of the questions. The period between studies was twenty and fifteen years respectively. Such an continuing study makes it possible to assess the dynamics of changes in the same views and values in different generations.

Continuing (Longitudinal Studies of Legal Doctrine)

This study is based on empirical data collected through surveys that form continuing studies:

1. 2003–2006 – a survey of judges (SJ code – 2003 – 2006), the respondents of this survey are referred to as *judges* in the text;
2. 2007–2008 – a survey of civil servants (SCS code 2007 – 2008), respondents – *civil servants;*
3. 2022–2023 – a survey of scholars researching legal doctrine (SSLD code 2022 – 2023); respondents are *specialists;*
4. 2022–2023 – a Persona-Doctrine survey (ESPD code 2022 – 2023), respondents are *experts.*

In the study text, we use the indicated survey years, codes, and names of respondent groups. All four sociological surveys are linked through the elements of the subject matter. The unifying principle of research is the concept of the form of law. Each of the sociological surveys focuses on some form of law. For example, a survey of judges (SJ 2003 – 2006) focused on precedent and jurisprudence. We have collected data on the attitudes of judges toward different types of legal doctrine. The influence of judicial practice on law-making and, as a result, on legislation is investigated.

A survey of civil servants (SCS 2007 – 2008) was aimed at investigating the sources of service law. Much attention was paid to normative legal acts, State, and ideological doctrines.

The survey of legal doctrine researchers (SSLD 2022 – 2023) identifies respondent attitudes toward all forms of doctrine, the features of legal doctrine, and the factors influencing the position of doctrine in the system of sources and forms of law.

The Persona-Doctrine Expert Survey (ESPD 2022 - 2023) focuses on the circumstances that ensure the ascent to Persona-Doctrine status.

Thus, all studies have an overlapping object – legal doctrine.

Visualization and analysis of repetitive (comparable) questions has two dimensions:

1. *temporal* – 2002 – 2008 (specify). We take the description of the result and the diagram for 2007 and overlay its result for 2022 – 2023. The differentiation is probably given by color. If there were too many indicators (answer options) in 2007 – more than three, we divided one diagram into several. In the legend, we indicate the years of research.
2. *by groups of respondents*:

- 2022 – 2023 – experts,
- 2022 – 2023 – specialists,
- 2007 – 2008 – civil servants,
- 2003 – 2006 – judges.

We refer to them in the text by the names of the respondents. We can give comparative results to up to two groups, civil servants and judges, as the representatives of these groups were in all studies. Some defects in representativeness may arise due to the small number of respondents representing these groups. For example, 5 % of judges and 5 % of civil servants are experts. Among the experts in 2022 – 2023, 3.4 % were civil servants. Another risk factor is that in 2002 and 2007, we verified respondents by their status at the time of the survey. In both 2022 – 2023 studies, we considered the presence of status at any period of life, including in the past tense, as an experience.

Because of the reservations made, the comparison is permissible and relevant. For some questions, the comparison can be considered entirely reliable. This is a question of recognizing the works as "absolutely correct" and acknowledging the authorities that have personally influenced the respondents. In this way, it is possible to compile lists of (1) permanent authorities, (2) authorities who have lost their status, and (3) those who have reappeared. For newly emerged authorities, it is necessary to establish the date of birth (years of life) and the dates of significant publications. These may be new publications after 2003 and 2007 (the dates of previous sociological surveys). This will be an "increment" of doctrine. The most significant results can be obtained for judges and civil servants when compared with other categories of respondents, as well as the change in the opinions of these groups over time.

There is also a nuance in staffing the target groups of judges and civil servants. In 2003 and 2007, we selected respondents for this core position without additional requirements. In 2022 – 2023, the requirement to have experience in legal research in a particular subject area was added to the questionnaire group to the official status. The experts selected persons with additional achievements: a doctoral degree – outstanding merits, authority, and recognition. Accordingly, a comparison distortion is triggered due to the increased requirements in the 2022 – 2023 studies. Nevertheless, we accept that the comparison of these three studies is acceptable.

2003 – 2006, we surveyed judges at various levels (SJ 2003–2006).

1,737 judges from seventeen subjects of the Russian Federation (Moscow, Moscow Region, St. Petersburg, Stavropol Region, Saratov Region, and others) participated in the study. Interviews were conducted directly at the duty station. The study was also conducted among newly appointed judges and students of advanced training courses for judges at the Academy of Justice and the Russian Academy of Public Administration attached to the President of the Russian Federation.

Of the respondents, 33.3 % were men, and 66.7 % were women. The age categories of judges were as follows: the most representative (48.9 %) is the age category from 40 to 49 years;

25.2 % of respondents are aged 30 to 39 years; 23.0 % were from 50 to 59 years of age; the age group of 60 years and older is represented by 2.2 % of respondents; up to 30 years old – 0.7 %. That is, most of the sample comprises respondents at the age of full bloom, including professional life.

In terms of seniority, judges were distributed as follows: up to two years of service, 22.6 %; from one to five years – 15.3 %; from six to ten years – 23.4 %; from ten to fifteen years old – 19.0 %; more than fifteen years – 19.7%.

79.7 % of the judges surveyed served in the court of first instance, 19.5 % – in the court of second instance, and one person – in the Supreme Court of the Russian Federation.

It was found that 96.9 % of the respondents had no academic degree, 3.1 % had a candidate of legal sciences degree, and none of the judges surveyed had a doctorate (habilitation).

The survey aimed to determine the judicial attitude to the state of the forms of domestic law and to the prospects of the system. The practical purpose of this survey is to assess the readiness of the judicial community to transform the system of forms of law in the context of globalization and the integration of different legal systems.

The questionnaire contains questions about the role of scholars' law and doctrine in law enforcement, the possibility of citing academic literature in court hearings, the recognition of academic publications as equal to the law, and the availability of absolutely correct books.

In 2007 – 2008, a survey of civil servants was conducted (SCS code 2007 – 2006) to study the phenomenon of legal doctrine in the system of forms and sources of public service relations.

The choice of civil servants as respondents was based on their understanding of the law, which is, to the greatest extent, the basis of law-making and law-enforcement activities. It is in the legal consciousness of civil servants that the foundations of the ideology of the system of Russian legislation are laid and reflected. This group has experience interacting and often creating state and ideological doctrines.

The survey was conducted among civil servants of the various federal legislative, executive, and judicial branches from ten subjects of the Federation. Law enforcement officers and military personnel were among the respondents. The study sample is reasonably representative regarding gender, age, length of public service, and other indicators. Thus, 56.7 % of the respondents are men, and 43.3 % are women. Among the age categories of respondents, the age group from 40 to 49 years old (34.9 %) is the most represented in the study sample, that is, a third of respondents are at the age of the peak of their abilities and capabilities, including professional ones (the age of "acme"+). The distribution of civil servants according to the length of service is increasing. 4.2 % of respondents have candidate or doctor of legal sciences (habilitation) degrees.

To allow for a comparison of studies, we asked questions from previous studies in the 2022 – 2023 surveys. In addition, we posed some of the same questions in the 2022 – 2023 SSLD and 2022 – 2023 ESPD surveys to compare the responses to the same questions from different groups of respondents. The ratio of new and recurring questions of the 2022 – 2023 SSLD to the 2022 – 2023 ESPD 2022 – 2023 is twenty-four questions, and the ratio of the 2003 – 2006 SJ and 2007 – 2008 SCS is three recurring questions.

A sociological survey of specialists involved in the study of legal doctrine was conducted in 2022 – 2023 (SSLD code 2022 – 2023).

Regarding the level of education and the availability of academic degrees, the distribution of specialists is as follows: 30.8 % of specialists have a doctor of legal sciences (habilitation) degree, and 43.2 % have a candidate of legal sciences degree. 19.7 % of specialists have the title of professor, and 23.9 % have the title of docent. 16.7 % are masters.

19.2 % of specialists have the honorary State titles of Honoured Jurist, Honoured Researcher, Honoured Worker of Culture, and others.

All age groups are represented. Up to 30 years old – 10.7 %, 31–40 years old – 22.2 %, 41 – 50 years old – 35.9 %, 51 – 60 years old – 15.4 %, 61 – 70 years old – 12.4 %, 71 – 80 – 3 % to 81+ – 0.4 %.

The number of specialists in the field of research is as follows: 39.2 % in theoretical and legal research, 21.6 % in public law, 15.8 % in private law, 8.5 % in criminal law, and 14.9 % in other specialties, including political research, philosophy, sociology, and history.

Specialists represent all types of localities: small towns – 41 %, cities of one million or more – 20.5 %, capitals – 19.2%, other localities – 10.3 %, and villages – 9 %.

The type of understanding of the law by specialists is of great importance. 28.6 % do not share any clear type of legal understanding. Of those who have decided on the type of legal understanding, the most common is the natural law type (18.4 %), followed by the supporters of positivism (17.5 %) and the sociological type (8.5 %). The remaining 27.3 % of specialists show a rather motley picture of the types of legal understanding (integrative, synthetic, eclectic, and others). The rest of the specialists were divided among other types of legal systems.

The type of legal system to be shared is essential for this study, as we are examining the geographical (country) or personified distribution of legal systems. 68.4 % of specialists consider themselves to be part of the Romano-Germanic type or family of legal system; 20.5 % do not share any clear type. 4.7 % of specialists are supporters of the Anglo-Saxon legal system. 1.7 % of specialists consider themselves to be ideologized, and 1.3 % to be undifferentiated.

Professionals were asked to identify themselves in one leading activity. 43.2 % are engaged in educational activities, 38.5% are engaged in academic activities, 6.4 % are civil servants, and 11.9 % are employees of practical jurisprudence, including advokats, notaries, jurisconsults, and others.

In 2022–2023, we conducted the Persona-Doctrine Expert Survey (2022 – 2023). By type of activity, the experts were distributed as follows. The largest group represented educational activities – 39.4 %. This is followed by a group of expert researchers – 36.4 %. A significant group of experts comprises civil servants – 18.2 %. Other activities represent a total of 6 %.

Because of the importance of the comparative legal dimension of this dissertation, the experts identified themselves as belonging to the types of legal systems. 66 % of the experts identify themselves as belonging to the Romano-Germanic family of legal systems, 31 % do not share any legal system, and 3 % – to the Anglo-Saxon one.

Experts identify the types of legal understanding. 24.2 % are normativists, 21.2 % are supporters of the natural law theory. Supporters of positivism and natural law doctrines took 18.2 % each, and supporters of the sociological approach to the essence of law comprised 9.1 %. Undecided experts amounted to 9.1%.

The distribution of experts in the fields of study is as follows. 30.3 % are representatives of the theoretical and legal specialty, 30.3 % are representatives of public law, and 9.1 % are representatives of research in private law. The experts also presented criminal law and international law specialties. 30.1 % of the experts self-identified in other fields of knowledge, such as comparative law.

For the purposes of this study, the presence of honorary State titles is essential as an indicator of a positive public assessment of the activities of the Persona-Doctrine: 56.7 % of experts have various honorary State titles, including the titles of Honored Researcher (20 %), and Honored Jurist (20 %).

Respondents are divided by age. 45.4 % are aged between 61 and 70 years, 21.2 % are 71–80 years old, 51–60 % are 13.1 %, and 12.1% are in the 81+ and 51–60 age groups. The youngest experts are between 41 and 50, while the oldest are 80+.

Experts are selected based on the following criteria:

- belonging to a professional group (politician, civil servant, teacher, researcher, advokat, judge),
- a bearer of an influential opinion that is likely to influence law-making and law enforcement,
- doctoral (habilitation) degree,
- for teachers and researchers, the H index is greater than 30; for other categories, more than 15,
- opinion (nomination) of other experts by extracting data from previous studies,
- citation in court documents,
- citation in the abstracts of doctoral dissertations,
- participated in all Russian legal events as a speaker at the plenary session.

The *subjective prerequisites for* the selection of experts include:

1. the bearer of the Doctrine is alive and well,
2. the individual is available for our survey,
3. personal relationships allow scholars to ask them to participate in a survey,
4. an expert can work with a computer remotely independently or with assistance,
5. mutual trust between the expert and the author of the study.

Objective prerequisites for the selection of experts:

1. highly cited author,
2. member of expert professional groups (institutions, courts, legislatures, and so on),

3. relevance of works in practical jurisprudence (practice-oriented),
4. participation in law-making, law enforcement, and other legal activities with specific academic priorities,
5. inclusion in the qualification commissions of public authorities,
6. academic degree (habilitation), honorary academic titles,
7. a significant number of students,
8. membership in the expert community, organizations, councils, and other organizations, councils, and other organizations of expert activity,
9. work experience in dissertation councils, academic, research, educational organizations,
10. high academic and public authority.

A selected candidate for nominee may have several of these characteristics, but not necessarily all of them.

We have formulated the characteristics of experts that, as we suggest, could be the cause or result of a person's doctrinal status.

Markers-prerequisites: leadership of the Academic Council, the leadership of the organization, and so on, legal family, presence of authority in official activity, type of activity.

Markers-results: honorary State titles (Honored Jurist, Honored Researcher, and the like (c. 56)), academic (academic) titles (Academician of the Russian Academy of Sciences, Corresponding Member of the Russian Academy of Sciences).

Thus, the selection of experts is based on a set of objective and subjective assumptions.

Judges of the Constitutional Court, judges of the Supreme Court, chairpersons of courts of the subjects of the Russian Federation, members of the qualification board of judges, and authoritative representatives of the academic community of doctrinal status were interviewed.

Guarantees of the professionalism of research are provided by an independent evaluation of the program by E. Nazarova, Doctor of Sociology. The results of the surveys were processed with the participation of applied specialists in applied mathematics (N. Ia. Ivushkina) and social psychology (G. G. Vasiuta).

The theoretical purpose of the study is to elucidate the regularities of the formation of the Persona-Doctrine and the awareness of the Persona-Doctrine of itself as a person of such status. The practical objective is to form criteria for selecting Persona-Doctrines for subsequent use in selecting Persona-Doctrines.

Objectives of the study:

- to study the social cross-section of Persona-Doctrine, we have developed a system of indicators: academic degree, experience, a central area of work, and other indicators,
- identify and systematize the factors influencing the formation of a doctrinal Persona,
- verify the subjective and objective factors of the formation of the Persona-Doctrine,
- to form a typified social portrait of the Persona-Doctrine,
- to identify the properties of the Persona-Doctrine, their correlation, and the possibility of managing the doctrinal status.

We have encountered various difficulties in building a base of doctrinal experts. It was logical to look for experts among legislators with academic degrees. This approach is explained by the idea of our study: the impact of proposals or suggestions made by legal scholarship on the formulation or adoption of legislation. In this case, we are not talking about the influence of someone else's ideas, but the author's, our own. We mean a situation when an experienced researcher implements his ideas about desirable changes or reforms in his legislative work as a deputy of a representative body. We consider the legislator's option of regarding something to be the result of legal scholarship. However, we consider this variant of the influence of the doctrine to be a personal achievement of the researcher. In search of doctrinal experts, we analyzed information about deputies and senators from the official websites of the chambers of the Federal Assembly of the Russian Federation. The picture turned out to be very striking, but useless in our work. The State Duma, VIII convocation, has nineteen deputies with the degree of candidate of legal sciences and three with the degree of doctor of legal sciences (habilitation). For selecting experts, among other indicators, the Hirsch index of 31 was considered. Accordingly, we checked the indexing of current doctors of legal sciences who were legislators"

- Viacheslav Viktorovich Volodin – there is no information in the Russian Science Citation Index;
- Pavel Vladimirovich Krasheninnikov – 31 h,
- Rizvan Danialovich Kurbanov has no information in the Russian Science Citation Index.

The Soviet of the Federation consists of thirteen candidates of legal sciences and four doctors of legal sciences (habilitation):

Irina Valerievna Rukavishnikova -11 h,

Andrei Aleksandrovich Klishas – 11 h,

Alexander Bogdanovich Karlin – 1 h.

Thus, out of both chambers of the Federal Assembly, only one, Krasheninnikov, meets the requirements for experts and is only within the lower limit.

In fact, this non-doctrinal composition of the legislative chambers indicates the demands of the political system, the state of the electoral system, and society as a whole. Accordingly, the position of modern legislator among experts turned out to be vacant. As a result, we selected outstanding representatives of doctrinal scholarship with the necessary indicators from former legislators.

Difficulties have arisen in the selection of experts from among the advokats and jurisconsults. We used different models to search for candidates in this group and selected experts. The main result of the observation of this category of experts is their low interest in any non-monetary or otherwise non-contentious cases. They ignore all offers unless they are the client. This category is generally characterized by a low citation rate and actual detachment from research. The selected experts are multi-professionals: researchers – advokats – teachers. That is, among their types of professional occupations is advocacy. Suppose a particular respondent was only an advokat or jurisconsult and has never worked as a researcher or teacher. In that case, an academic degree is not an indicator of his involvement in the research process. Unethical behavior is possible.

Another group of experts – judges – was also selected with difficulty. We foresaw these difficulties due to our experience surveying judges from 2003 to 2006. During this survey, we found that the judicial caste is closed, self-sufficient, and self-centered. Judges have unreasonably high self-esteem compared to jurists working in other activities. Judges were asked, "Which activity requires higher professional training"? According to 65.4 % of respondents, the work requiring higher qualifications is practical. Only 6.9 % of judges believe that theoretical activity requires higher qualifications. We concluded that judges consider their work to be the most critical and challenging, contributing to the formation of group and individual egocentrism.[8]

Nevertheless, the judiciary has some experts with doctrinal characteristics. Due to personal long-term observation and communication, the author of this study has an established circle of judges-researchers. They are available in the Constitutional Court, the Supreme Court, and the courts of the subjects of the

[8] S. V. Boshno, "Прецедент, закон и доктрина (опыт социолого-юридического исследования) [Precedent, Law, and Doctrine (Experience of Sociological and Legal Research)]", Государство и право [State and Law], no. 4 (2007), pp. 72-78.

Russian Federation. At the level of the district or city court, not a single expert was identified.

An exciting category of respondents is civil servants of the legislative and executive branches. They are difficult to identify, as they are likelier to not name their State positions when affiliating. As in the previous groups, the experts were selected based on the author's personal acquaintance with specific experts. The most significant number of refusals to participate in the expert survey concerning official restrictions is found in this category. In the case of anonymous surveys, such a refusal shows the expert distrust of confidentiality. We have drawn this conclusion from the correspondence of invitations. The main topic of the talks was the protection of the anonymity of their personal data.

It is not easy to separate the two groups of experts – teachers and researchers. A combination of these two activities is prevalent. It is artificially supported by the requirement of publication by university personnel. Annual reporting is a stimulus for this work. To acquire the status of Docent and Professor publications are also required. To occupy certain teaching positions, it is necessary (desirable) to have academic degrees and titles.

In reality, these are two different professions: the researcher and the teacher. To a small extent, they are related. However, the topic of academic publication is always narrower than the object of teaching. In legislation and practice, there is no connection between the academic specialty and the subject of teaching. On the other hand, there is a factor of reducing the number of dissertation councils and the transfer of the right to award academic degrees to some universities. All this objectively reduces the number of people with academic degrees, as personnel are not trained in the same number. Indirect data is the statistics of the decrease in the number of legal protections. In fact, today, we see a trend: a decrease in the percentage of teachers with academic degrees.

Application of interview methods. Most expert surveys were conducted in the form of interviews. In addition, the peculiarity of an interview in comparison with a survey is that both the interviewer and the respondent can go beyond the question and reformulate it. Scholars can add any information at the respondent's request. Interviews as a data collection method were chosen due to the possibility of obtaining detailed answers to open-ended questions. It is difficult for experts to print extensive texts. Respondents have trouble submitting the form. Filling out the electronic form together is faster. During the conversation, there is an opportunity to clarify this question, reminisce, and look for interesting facts.

Use of personal information for doctrinal research (interviews, memoirs, observations).

The sources of this study are personal memoirs – the memoirs of the Persona-Doctrine. The *memoirs* of the participants of the expert survey and persons who did not participate in the surveys have been drawn upon extensively. Encyclopedias and biographical data of prominent jurists were also used. Our markers can be used to select experts for nomination for Persona-Doctrine status.

Memoirs are an essential source of personal information about doctrinal figures. Answers to many of the questions of the expert survey can be found in the memoirs. Through this source, we learn about events in the life of the Persona-Doctrine and can better understand the time and place of these events. The most interested group is young researchers, for whom memoirs are a way to become involved in significant events in the academic community. Memoirs are an authentic source of information about prominent researchers. People who do not have their own experience of being a member of undiscovered communities and, as a result, have a built-in observation of prominent personalities are more likely to need such experiences. Someone else's experience can partially compensate for the lack of one's own. By our own example, we can only marvel at our happy fate, which allowed us to see nearby, observe the work, and even talk with Gennadii Vasil'evich Maltsev

(1935-2013), Oleg Stepanovich Kolbasov (1927-2000), and Veniamin Fedorovich Iakovlev (1932-2018). We could go on with this list, but in fear of missing someone and giving the false impression of disrespect to other senior colleagues. Our department and the Academy of Public Administration attached to the President of the Russian Federation as a whole were unique places for observing Persona-Doctrine. A decade after the closure of the Academy, and in the light of doctrinal research, we see the distinctive features of the Academy in the combination of faculty, academic, and governmental principles in one place. Of course, in those distant 1980s and 1990s, there were many worthy institutions for education, protection, and cooperation. However, no single university combines all these principles. The Academy provided an opportunity to write a dissertation on constitutional institutions, make theoretical generalizations, and, at the same time, to see and even interact with the judges of the Constitutional Court of the Russian Federation. The Civil Registry Office provided a resource to survey judges with the support of all the country's highest courts and secretaries of plenums nearby. And they were genuinely interested in the results of this work.

The Academy encouraged a mutually interested dialogue among senior officials, legislators, professors, and researchers. We must admit that no more such sites exist, and it is impossible to recreate them mechanically. Today, the doctrinal bearers of different species are disunited, and their professional environments are not friendly to each other. Perhaps these memories are inspired by the question of the memoirs of the Persona-Doctrine of the modern world. They have seen and know exactly what kind of world surrounds them. The life of the Persona-Doctrine was necessarily filled with events and encounters that made them doctrinal personalities, and the memoirs will provide information about these facts.

Of course, every person has the right to privacy and will not want to admit people who may dispose of this information differently. But we are more interested in the facts of doctrinal formation, emotions, and sensations of the Persona-Doctrine of one's time, contemporaries, mentors, authorities, and colleagues. Our interviews and observations of the biographies of the Persona-Doctrines show that some knew each other, cooperated for a long time and correctly, competed, were friends, and even lived next to each other. It is difficult to overestimate the factor of synergy in this complex matter. Still, if we deny it completely, we must abandon the influence of academic schools, the team, and the environment. In the journal Право и современные государства [Law and Modern States], we created the rubric "And the Portraits Spoke," using the book by Academician Iurii Kirillovich Tolstoi (b. 1927) as a title. This is not a memoir, not a single work, but a collection of his publications selected by the academician, capturing the time and events that have special significance for him. This is the most significant value, verified facts about the Persona-Doctrine. This person is interesting not only because he has outstanding academic merits but also because the results of his pedagogical activity are beyond the usual practice. A large part of Russia's political and oligarchic elite from 2000 to the present has been nurtured with his direct participation. In this regard, we can consider Tolstoi as the bearer of many doctrines in one person. It includes academic, judicial, and ideological doctrines. Of course, we do not presume to identify the ideas of the academician himself and his students (including the President of the Russian Federation). Still, most likely, there is a connection. But this, as they say, is a topic for a separate study.

In the expert survey, the Persona-Doctrine was asked: "Is writing a memoir a right or an obligation"? This question was intended to induce the Persona-Doctrine to think about the meaning of its fate, its specific facts, and feelings in general for those who have not had and will have such an opportunity.

The overall preponderance – 53.4 % – is on the side of the Persona-Doctrine freedom of decision on writing memoirs. 20 % of experts consider writing memoirs an obligation, which is a significant percentage of self-obligated individuals. However, it should be noted that the question may be posed incorrectly or ethically. Indeed, we perceive memoirs as reflections and summaries. It can be perceived as depressing.

A total of twelve interviews were conducted during the preparation of the present study, most were fully recorded. An interview with Vladimir Il'ich Lafitsky (1957-2023) has been published.[9] Published interviews were used.[10]

Based on these sources, we have formed personal, professional, and public characteristics of the Persona-Doctrine. The availability of information about the same issue from different sources made it possible to verify the data and typify the data obtained. For example, because of the analysis of the questionnaire questions on the role of the academic community, the labor and academic community, and the labor and academic team in the process of the formation of the Persona-Doctrine, it is established that relations in professional and organizational structures are, as a rule, unfriendly, antagonistic. Persona-Doctrines do not trust their colleagues to evaluate their work and personal data. Analogous facts are contained in memoirs and recorded in interviews. Accordingly, the unfriendliness of the academic community has been confirmed by various sources.

A significant amount of personal information is located on the websites of organizations in which Persona-Doctrine works or cooperates. Biographies, reports on personal and professional events, and participation in events provide information about the personal and professional experience of the Persona-Doctrine. From such sources, we draw demographic data (date,

[9] V. I. Lafitsky and S. V. Boshno, "Беседа Президента Клуба Правовой Доктрины С.В. Бошно с профессором В.И. Лафитским [Conversation by the President of the Legal Doctrine Club S. V. Boshno with Professor V.I. Lafitsky]", *Law and Modern States*, no. 6 (2022), pp. 9-23. This Study also is based on autobiographical publications: Iu. K. Tolstoi, Из прежитого [From Experience] (2d ed.; 2013); N. S. Bondar, Публичное и личное: Поиск баланса продолжается ... Мемуарная юриспруденция [Public and Private: The Search for Balance Continues ... Memoir Jurisprudence] (2020), and others.

[10] N. S. Bondar, "Единство теории и практики одинаково важно как для маститых профессионалов, так и для студентов юридических вузов [The Unity of Theory and Practice is Equally Important for Both Venerable Professionals and Students of Law Schools]", Судья [Judge], no. 12 (2022), pp. 4-9.

place of birth, family), educational data (where and when he studied, what specialties and qualifications he received), professional and public statuses, achievements, and awards.

A tendency to reduce personal information and professional experience about members of the chambers of the Federal Assembly of the Russian Federation has been revealed. There are facts of the lack of data on researchers-parliamentarians in the RSCI, which could result from the decision to self-exclude.

Personal websites and profiles in social networks also provide information to clarify the social and professional portrait of the Persona-Doctrine. These resources are not very rich and informative, as Doctrine Personas, as a rule, do not actively use these resources to post personal information.

Programs for Collection and Processing of Sociological Research Data

Modern computer tools for conducting and processing sociological surveys are diverse. There are programs with considerable application experience, such as SPSS. The American *Monkey Survey* and Russian *Questionnaire* programs are extensively used. There are multifunctional tools that, along with other application areas, can be used to conduct sociological surveys.

Instruments for sociological surveys differ in functionality, the number of services available, and accessibility. The most popular, Google *Form tool,* is a tool only for collecting information with some elements of generating statistics on questions.

MonkeyServey and the *Questionnaire* collect and process data. Behind such resources are professional sociologists, marketers, statisticians, and other specialists who can process the data and provide standard questionnaires to their correspondents. They can create a questionnaire, collect data, and analyze the results. This multifaceted cooperation was impossible due to the questionnaire's main complexity – the respondent attraction and motivation. *SPSS* is an analysis system, not a research tool.

Another difference between instruments is their cost. They are divided into paid and free. Some resources are partially accessible. Questions can be included in a free questionnaire, whereas others require a fee. This study contains various question types, yet this combination is available on Google Forms without charge.

The period of the survey affects the choice of questionnaire tools. If the study period is short, there are many possibilities. If the resource charges for use time and the study is lengthy, then the choice is significantly reduced. A free resource for collecting any information of any length is Google Forms. On his workstation, the user independently opens and closes access to his profile for any period.

The disadvantages of Google Forms include a straightforward built-in method of processing data by generating diagrams based on response statistics, which is insufficient for professional research. Questions in tabular form with variables and open-ended questions are not processed. The advantage of Google Forms is the ability to output Excel and Google Docs data. Automatic notifications on Google Email linked to the respondent accounts about respondents who have completed the questionnaire are useful for organizing survey management. Experience shows that many researchers working in jurisprudence do not have experience using Google Forms for questionnaires. They have difficulty in filling out and submitting the survey form. Scholars can overcome this obstacle by generating a Google Form application form as a PDF. File. In fact, this is a transition from an electronic form to paper appearance.

There are significant disadvantages in filling out the questionnaire on paper: 1) the organizer enters the answers received manually, and 2) respondents omit questions or elements of questions, which leads to the rejection of such a questionnaire. Scholars can obtain the missing answers by communicating with the respondent, if possible. To prevent the rejection of questionnaires and the impossibility of filling out the questionnaire in electronic form, we used a combined sociological survey: a survey plus an interview. Questionnaires were sent to the respondent. Using audio or video equipment, the researcher contacted the respondent and filled out the questionnaire in his own words. This combination of non-contact and contact techniques enabled efficient data collection.

Provalis provides excellent opportunities for processing the results of sociological surveys. This program is synchronized with various research tools. It can export a database from sociological programs such as SurveyMonkey, SPSS, and others. Provalis also takes data from citation generators such as Zotero, Mendeley, and the like. It works with Access as a database and exports the information correctly. Sociological survey data can be transferred to Provalis through Excel.

Synchronization with passwords can ensure the automatic transfer of new data to Provalis if they appear in these programs later. For example, the form of the survey with results was transferred to Provalis from SurveyMonkey and other sociological tools. And respondents continue to complete the questionnaire. The Provalis user can update the data, and the new answers will be uploaded automatically. The same can be said about any other files that can be incorporated into an existing project.

The Provalis system has tools for processing the results of sociological surveys that are unavailable in either Google Forms or SurveyMonkey. The system allows scholars to search for dependencies between several variables, compare absolute and relative values results, and see proof (or refutation) of the value or significance of comparisons. These results of comparisons are visualized in tables, diagrams, and figures. Charts are also proof (the presence/absence) of a trend. Of course, any survey must study the influence of objective variables (age, work experience, dominant type of occupation, and so on), which may or may not be significant. At the same time, the Provalis program can assign a value to a variable on any issue, check the indicator value with this variable, and assess its informative value. For example, we can consider the age of respondents to be a variable. The program will allow scholars to check this variable impact on all other questions quickly, for example, how the age of respondents is related to the understanding of the form of law.

The professional processing of sociological survey data was carried out with the help of a consultant, mathematician, and data processing specialist. Data from Google Forms can be transferred through Excel to data processing programs with statistics functions. We used Provalis. The results of the sociological research have been published.[11]

[11] Boshno, "Прецедент, закон и доктрина (опыт социолого-юридического исследования) [Precedent, Law, and Doctrine (Experience of Sociological and Legal Research)]", Государство и право [State and Law], no. 4 (2007), pp. 72-78; Boshno and G. G. Vasiuta, "Доктринальные источники служебного права [Doctrinal Sources of Service Law]", Государственная служба [Civil Service], no. 2 (2010), pp. 44-47; Boshno and Vasiuta, "Отражение в правовом сознании государственных служащих судебной практики (по итогам социолого-юридического исследования) [Reflection in the Legal Consciousness of Civil Servants of Judicial Practice (Based on the Results of Sociological and Legal Research)]", Государство и право [State and Law], no. 10 (2010), pp. 37-46; Boshno and Vasiuta, "Представления об обычном праве в правовом сознании государственных служащих [Perceptions of Customary Law in the Legal Minds of Public Servants Law and Management]", Право и управление. XXI век [Law and Management. XXI Century], no. 1 (2010), pp. 13-19; Boshno and Vasiuta, "Система нормативных правовых актов: современное состояние и потребности в развитии (по итогам социолого-правового исследования) [System of Normative Legal Acts: Current State and Needs in Development (Based on the Results of Sociological and Legal Research)]", Современное право [Contemporary Law], no. 11 (2009), pp. 11-18.

SECTION II

APPROACHES TO THE STUDY OF LEGAL DOCTRINE

Chapter 5
The Space-Time Continuum and the Comparative Legal Approach

COUNTRY APPROACH TO LEGAL GEOGRAPHY: DIFFICULTIES OF COMPARATIVE LEGAL RESEARCH

The comparative legal approach is of great importance for this study. The hypothesis of this study is based on a possible connection between the understanding of the term "doctrine" in publications and the author's belonging to a specific legal system. The comparative approach is based on the work of René David (1906-1991). His book on major legal systems of the world appeared more than seven decades ago and was revised and reprinted many times after his death.[1] Even though there have been significant changes in the legal map of the world since its publication, many of his conclusions have retained their value. The methodological basis of the comparative part of this dissertation is laid by the publications of W. E. Butler,[2] F. Parsons,[3] Eltjo J. H. Schrage,[4] M. N. Marchenko,[5] A. Kh. Saidov,[6] and V. E. Chirkin.[7]

[1] R. David, *Major Legal Systems in the World Today: An Introduction to the Comparative Study of Law* (1985).

[2] W. E. Butler (ed.), International Law in Comparative Perspective (1980); Butler (ed.), *Justice and Comparative Law: Anglo-Soviet Perspectives on Criminal Law, Evidence, Procedure, and Sentencing Policy* (1987), followed by a half dozen or so works based on Anglo-Soviet symposia.

[3] F. Parsons, *Legal Doctrine and Social Progress* (1982).

[4] E. J. H. Schrage, "Sources of Law, the Comparative Legal History of a Concept", *Fundamina: A Journal of Legal History*, no. 1 (2005), pp. 275-284.

[5] M. N. Marchenko, Сравнительное правоведение [Comparative Law] (2d ed.; 2013).

[6] A. Kh. Saidov, *Comparative Law*, transl. W. E. Butler (1999).

[7] V. E. Chirkin, Сравнительное правоведение [Comparative Law] (2021).

The typology of legal systems is based on differences in understanding forms of law. Different legal systems recognize doctrine as a form or source of law. That is why the concept of a legal system is a backbone for the study of doctrine. The place of doctrine in the system of sources (or forms) of law and the legal system is important.[8]

Cross-sectional cross-country studies are of great academic value. For example, Russian scholars analyze the American legal system, legislation, and doctrine. There are publications by American researchers on the United States legal system and doctrine. Russian and American researchers have published studies on the Russian legal system, legislation, and doctrine. Various dissertation sources, their international origin, and different ways to collect and analyze information contributed to the objectivity of the study.

Comparative legal research inevitably faces difficulties in translating into another language. It is not just a translation, but a process of conveying the meaning of legal terms that have the same name and different meanings. The problem of conveying meaning exists in translating the terminology of doctrine research. Avoiding small details, we will show the most fundamental problem. In Russian legal culture and terminology, legal theory is a science. Literally, this object is called Legal Science. In Russian language dictionaries the word "academic" is most often found. In American legal culture, as in other countries of the Anglo-American legal system, jurisprudence is not a science.

This is of fundamental importance for our study since, in the Russian theory of law, doctrine is understood as a legal science. We have renamed Legal Science in this study as Legal Theory or Jurisprudence to overcome terminological untranslatability. Often this renaming is permissible and does not distort the meaning of the concepts. However, there is difficulty translating quotations. The words in the quotation belong to a specific

[8] Marchenko, Курс сравнительного правоведения [Course of Comparative Law] (2002).

researcher. We do not have the right to change the words in the text. In this case, we have retained the words "jurisprudence", the name of jurisprudence as a science, and other authentic words and phrases.

There is a problem conveying the meaning of academic degree names and titles in the United States and Russia. Academic research degrees in the Russian Federation are called "Candidate of Legal Sciences" and "Doctor of Legal Sciences". The correlation of these degrees is set out in Table 3.

Table 3. The Ratio of Academic Degrees, Titles, and Positions in the Russian Federation and the United States

RUSSIA	USA
There is no analog.	Paralegal
Bachelor of Laws	There is no analog
There is no analog.	J.D. (first degree of legal education)
Magister	LLM
Candidate of Legal Sciences	PhD, SJD
Doctor of Legal Sciences	
Doctor of Legal Sciences	LL.D. (British)
Professor (academic title)	*There is no analog*
Professor (position)	A position in any educational institution unrelated to degrees
Corresponding Member of the Russian Academy of Sciences	*There is no analog*
Academician of the Russian Academy of Sciences or Russian Academy of Natural Sciences	There is no analog.
There is no analog.	Doctrinal Professor
Docent (academic title)	Associate Professor

The table shows that many educational and research statuses have no analogues in other countries. Suppose it is necessary to provide information about a specific holder of such an unverifiable title or academic degree. In that case, a translation uses transliteration or a title in the original language.

For example, verifying his status by transliterating a Doctor of Legal Sciences is necessary when describing the highest doctorate from Russia. We do not even presume to assume that the bearer of the Anglo-American legal culture will understand the meaning of the academic degree of Doctor of Legal Sciences (a literal translation of the Russian term). A Russian user will be disoriented by the degree J.D. A letter "D" can be construed as a doctorate, but it is a professional, not a research, degree. The title *doctor juris* means having a first law degree and graduating from a Law School; it is a pjjostgraduate degree fro m a jprofessional school. But the literal translation would be "Doctor of Law". These examples demonstrate the complexities of comparative studies and the value of embedded observation for researchers.

This study compares the understanding of legal doctrine in Russia and the United States. This choice of jurisdictions is justified by the practical tasks we have addressed, combining objective and subjective factors. We do not touch upon the undifferentiated and religious legal systems in this work because of the significant differences in the sources of law of these legal systems. There are several aspects to this problem.

The first aspect is the typology of legal systems and the determination of the type of legal system of each country (United States and Russian Federation). We examine the essence of doctrine and its interaction with other forms of law in the Russian Federation and the United States. Obviously, the United States represents the Anglo-American legal system. The Russian Federation has undergone various stages in the development of legal systems. While experiencing difficulties in translating the historical and modern names of the types of legal systems, we proceed from the fact that in the period 1917 to 1991 there was a socialist (ideologized) legal system. In post-Soviet Russia, the most common assumption is that the Russian Federation represents a Romano-Germanic legal system.

Significantly simplifying comparative studies as an independent field of knowledge, this conclusion is based on the official approach to the forms of law and the identification of the leading form of law. Following this approach, the Anglo-American system is associated with precedent, and the Romano-Germanic system is associated with law (normative legal act) as system-forming forms of law. Studying doctrine is essential to determine which forms of law are officially recognized as forms of law in State documents and are openly used in decision-making by the authorities. It also matters what forms of law are applied latently, even though official documents do not allow it and sometimes even prohibit it.

The second aspect is that each country has its unique way of collecting, storing, and communicating legal information to citizens. In the study of doctrine, we needed to compare databases, library resources, and the storage of academic research in law dissertations. Methods of conducting rankings and citation (indexing) of academic publications and personal researchers were significant for studying doctrine. The conclusion that the databases differ significantly is based on user experience and the expert status of the author of this study in the information databases Lexix+ Ambassador, Consultant+, and Garant.

The third aspect consists of the peculiarities of the positioning of jurisprudence in the system of knowledge (or sciences), the peculiarities of legal culture, legal consciousness, the educational system, and academic terminology.

The comparative legal approach is essential for studying doctrine. We proceed from the hypothesis that there is a connection between the understanding of doctrine and the author belonging to a specific type of legal system. The concept of a legal system for doctrinal research has another meaning. Indeed, most scholars are looking for the place of doctrine in the system of sources (or forms) of law. However, there are also works on doctrine in the legal system, which is obviously a different vector of research and methodology.[9]

[9] S. A. Baturina, "Правовая доктрина как элемент российской правовой системы [Legal Doctrine as an Element of the Russian Legal System]", Юристъ – правоведъ [Iurist – Pravoved], no. 4 (2008), pp. 31-35.

The software used in this study is diversified. The most progressive and high-quality programs have been selected. This study showed the difficulties of applying the tools created in the mentality, legal experience, and culture of the United States to the Russian material. They do not give an entirely correct result when applied to Russian circumstances. In the text, explanations are given (including in the form of tables) to unify objects and make them comparable:

1. with different names and the same meaning, for example, PhD – between Candidate of Legal Sciences and Doctor of Legal Sciences for Russia,
2. with duplicate titles and different meanings, for example, "article" – there is practically nothing common in the requirements for American and Russian academic publications in the form of journal articles,
3. with different names and meanings but needing comparison: citation, a combination of PhD and SJD.

There is a chronological aspect, as objects were created at different times and have different performance methods during operation.

Let us demonstrate the influence of these circumstances on this study's results by one example: we asked respondents to provide biographical information in a sociological survey, including the respondent's academic degree. Russia has a Candidate of Legal Sciences and a Doctor of Legal Sciences. In the United States, the PhD or SJD unites "Candidates of Legal Sciences" and "Doctors of Legal Sciences" in the Russian hierarchy. The American reader does not understand the distinction between these degrees. For the Russian Federation, this distinction is essential and fundamental. The expenditure of labor for the preparation and defense of the PhD in the United States and the Doctor of Legal Sciences in Russia are incomparable. Thus, the comparison of American and Russian academic degrees may be incorrect.

The comparative legal approach is of fundamental importance for the study of doctrine. We proceed from two hypotheses: 1) there is a connection between the understanding of doctrine and belonging to a specific type[10] of legal system (personal approach), and 2) the country is the unit of typology of the legal system (geographical approach).

The concept of the legal system for the study of doctrine has another meaning. Indeed, most scholars are looking for the place of doctrine in the system of sources (forms) of law. However, there are also works on doctrine in the legal system, which is obviously, to a large extent, a different vector of research and methodology. The difference is seen in the system of forms of law. Doctrine is compared to other forms of law, such as a regulatory legal act, precedent, and others.[11] The search for the position of doctrine in the legal system is the inclusion of the doctrine in the system of forms of law, legal consciousness, and legal technique. Accordingly, doctrine can be considered an element of the system of forms of law, which coincides with the first approach. But doctrine can be an element of legal consciousness. It undoubtedly has a unique creation procedure compared to legislation and precedent. However, for most types of doctrines, the technique of its creation does not matter.

Different legal systems exhibit different doctrinal understandings, and countries change their approach to doctrine over time. Understanding the meaning of adopting the term "doctrine" in legal systems may vary. This requires a combination of temporal and spatial approaches.

We implemented the comparative-legal approach using sociological methods. The most valuable results were obtained from questionnaires, expert surveys, interviews, and embedded observation. The surveys contain many questions on the topic of comparative law to solve the following problems:

[10] A sociological survey does not confirm this hypothesis as unambiguous or axiomatic.

[11] Baturina, note 9 above.

1. establishing a standard and different understanding of legal doctrine in the United States and the Russian Federation,
2. verification of the presence/absence of a relationship between the understanding of legal doctrine and the type of legal system,
3. the influence of the type of legal system on the authors-researchers,
4. the possibility of changing the subjective self-identification of the legal picture of the world of research in the context of academic mobility, movement between legal systems, and so forth. The author's affiliation with a particular legal system was used as a variable in the analysis of many questionnaire questions. This method made it possible to analyze the influence of the respondent's type of legal system on his or her attitude to legal doctrine.

9.3 % of experts acknowledge the possibility of borrowing from one legal system to another. Such borrowing is "rather impossible", according to 14.1 % of experts, and categorically impossible – 1.3 %. 75.3 % of specialists chose the uncertain option – "can happen". Accordingly, the overwhelming % of the surveyed specialists – 84.6 % – admit the possibility of borrowing legal ideas and legislation from one legal system to another.

For our study, the comparative legal method is applied in several planes and directions:

1. typification of the author of a work on doctrine,
2. typification of the results of content analysis as a characteristic of the work,
3. peculiarities of the position of the doctrine in the legal system,
4. the interaction of doctrine with other forms of law,

5. the system of normative acts and the possibility of recognizing doctrine as a normative legal act,
6. peculiarities of codification and other types of systematization in different countries (United States and Russia),
7. peculiarities of maintenance of reference legal databases,
8. peculiarities of consolidation, division of elements of the system of law,
9. peculiarities of legal culture, ethics of legal behavior,
10. library databases (formation and filling),
11. collection and storage of the results of academic activities,
12. the collection of judicial practice and its synchronization with the system of normative legal acts are based on the theory of judicial precedent,
13. legal ideology in the system of forms of law,
14. legal education: concept, content of training,
15. theoretical and methodological basis for teaching the doctrine.

Indeed, the type of legal system is both a country and an individual characteristic. There is reason to classify works according to the country and its type of legal system. Uncertainty and difficulties in identifying the author's position occur when publications are translated into other languages. They retain their content and original typology, for example, when translating a Russian publication into English. However, in terms of worldview, such publications remain Russian. Accordingly, the works of American scholars translated into Russian are labeled as Anglo-American. The same solution is implemented in labeling translations of Russian researcher works into English. However, such automatic labeling will not always be adequate in today's mobile world. Indeed, some researchers have moved to a country with a different legal system for a long time, may have received an education there, and have professional (legal practitioner, teaching, research, and other) practice. Counting such authors according to their original country is problematic because this author may already be a "pure" representative of this system. It is no coincidence that data on long-term internships and education abroad are essential. They likely give reason to assume changes in a particular researcher's concept and legal picture. In this study, we did not set out to observe behavior, writing style, or other personal characteristics. We have noticed this fact, and we state its presence.

On large arrays of content analysis, it is possible to identify ideas that deviate from the dominant type of legal system more accurately. For example, it is well known that the Romano-Germanic legal systems do not include judicial practice and doctrine as forms of law. Suppose an author, labeled herein by country of origin and language as Romano-Germanic, deviates and attributes these phenomena to forms of law. In that case, he shares the concept of Anglo-American law. In this regard, it would not be erroneous or distort the study's overall results to label authors by country and language (En, Ru). Accordingly, the content analysis method can trace the prevalence of the actual deviation of the researchers' worldview.

In combination with the content analysis of the functions of the legal doctrine, the words and phrases "source (or form) of law", "judicial practice", and "precedent" made it possible to accurately identify that the content selected publication and its creation are based on the Anglo-American legal model. A broader generalization can be made. If there are deviations within the identified pattern, they should be identified, personified, and considered separately (if necessary). For example, the word "X" is labeled as significant for a type of doctrine and is used next to a keyword in only 10 % of the most frequent ones. It signifies a personal examination of the data about the work and the author. Perhaps he is a representative of a deviant worldview.

The naming of types of legal systems causes considerable difficulties. Of course, the easiest option is to form an adjective based on the country name. However, this does not produce the desired result: typification based on established criteria. It is known that each country uniqueness and the tendencies of separatism and national and territorial identity oppose typification on a planetary scale. However, while acknowledging the uniqueness of each case, we will attempt to classify based on approaches to the system of sources of law.

Moreover, we know which law forms are essential for our study. We focus our research on doctrine, normative legal acts, and judicial precedent. Elements of the legal system, such as legal culture and ideology, are essential. The position of customs and religious forms in the system of sources of law is irrelevant to this study because this study concerns the identification of only two countries, the United States and Russia, which obviously do not belong to religious or customary law. In this regard, we are not interested in the legal characteristics of all legal systems. For us, the name and definition of the type of legal system of the United States and Russia are essential. Based on the requirements for the legal system identified by legal doctrinal scholarship, we call them a specific type. This tests how doctrine manifests itself in different legal systems. In addition, we examine whether the actual content and functioning of the doctrine influence the type of legal system. This is a well-known problem about what is primary and what is secondary: a doctrine depends on the type of legal system, or a doctrine determines the type of legal system. This study is primarily aimed at solving this question.

Forms of law, a system of legislation, and the collection, processing, and storage of legal sources and materials are considered separately and in comparison between the two countries.

Whether a particular doctrine corresponds to a specific legal system remains debatable. We tested this hypothesis using different research methods.

Table 4. Correlation Between the Type of Legal Doctrine, the Type of Legal System, and the Type of the Leading Form of Law

Type of legal doctrine	Type of legal system	Type of leading form of law
State	Romano-Germanic	regulatory legal acts
Ideological	Ideologized	principles, ideas, ideology
Scholars (academic)	Romano-Germanic, Anglo-American	scholars (academic) ideas, works
Judicial	Anglo-American	precedent

The comparative-legal method requires that any legal phenomenon be considered by having regard to the legal system in which it originated, formed, and functioned. This is called the objective context or space-time continuum. Time and historical events are the objective context. We call those facts that the author (actor) cannot influence objective. Objective data exist outside the will of a particular person. These conditions determine the author (actor) as a social group member in specific historical circumstances. Objective factors include the type of legal system of a country, as it does not depend on a particular subject.

Personal (subjective) understanding of the essence of the legal system by a particular person may differ from the officially established type of country. We state the existence of a legal system in the objective sense and in the subjective sense. Objectively, the legal system is a universally recognized, well-known State characteristic. In a subjective sense, the legal system is the subject's understanding of the term. Subjective and Objective Understanding of Type legal systems may overlap or diverge. At the same time, the fact that a person supports an alternative legal system does not affect the official type. For example, a researcher may point to a doctrine as a form of Russian law based on their views. However, officially, in normative legal acts, the doctrine (except State legal acts) is not a form of law; it is an objective legality.

The tendencies towards globalization and separatism and national and territorial identity act oppositely. However, recognizing the uniqueness of each State, we are focused on typification based on approaches to the system of sources of law. Moreover, it is known which forms of law are of particular importance for our study.

Comparative legal research faces difficulties in comparing similar objects from different legal systems. We faced difficulties comparing Scopus and Web of Science data and the Russian Science Citation Index. International databases are in English. They are based on the United States concept in all fundamental matters, including the attitude toward legal research. The United States does not consider legal knowledge to be a science; these databases do not usually index theoretical publications about the law. Some exceptions comprise the legal publications indexed in the Web of Science. Most legal publications come from law reviews, of which only a few are included in Web of Science. We know that the policy of journals is essential to be selected for indexing, as is the presence of practical research using exact academic methods. Applied legal research, such as forensics, can be indexed in the United States. The All-Russian Criminalistic Journal is published in Russia. The publication was included in Scopus but was excluded in 2021. This journal has a problem because it publishes abstract and theoretical articles unrelated to forensics or any other practical field of jurisprudence. Theoretical considerations that contain only descriptions of previous publications cannot be evaluated and indexed as academic.

In the Russian Federation, the practice is entirely the opposite. In Russia, legal researchers are considered scholars, their dissertations are considered academic, and all legal publications are indexed in the Russian Science Citation Index (RSCI). However, there is a phenomenon of "magnificent" lobbying. Based on the RSCI, significant conclusions are made about the ratings of academic and educational organizations, and the Hirsch index for authors is calculated. These indicators directly impact the funding of organizations and the remuneration of authors in research and educational organizations.

Research in the legal field is related to the context of the legal system. The legal culture, law-making, law enforcement, and other indicators of the Russian Federation and the United States differ. Without interpreting this cultural context, one can fall into error.

Specific comparison difficulties arise because "jurisprudence" means judicial practice in some legal systems and legal science in others. As the French lawyer, R. Fabre, noted, the Latin term "jurisprudence" when translated into French, English, and German "has undergone significant changes. And this evolution was not purely linguistic. The concept of 'jurisprudence' has received different philosophical and especially, methodological connotations". In Russian academic and legal literature, "jurisprudence" or "lawyers' law" combines legal doctrine and judicial practice. The concepts of "jurisprudence" and "legal science" were identified, and the concepts of "legal doctrine", "legal science", and "general opinion of lawyers" were also equated.

The theses expressed regarding the combination of doctrine and judicial practice are united by the fact that these phenomena do not coincide, but can be correlated as form and content under certain conditions. At the same time, the court decision is the form in which the doctrinal position is clothed. In this case, the doctrine is indeed the source of jurisprudence.

According to experts, the legal system is a significant factor influencing the formation of legal doctrine. This opinion is supported by 96% of specialists. Only 4 % completely deny such an influence. 55 % of specialists admit a strong influence, and 41 % admit an influence without connotation.

Persona-Doctrine attitude to the legal system's influence on the formation of legal doctrine differs significantly from specialist opinions. Experts have a significantly lower level of trust in the "legal system" category. 23 % of experts categorically deny the influence of the legal system on legal doctrine. 40 %

of experts admit strong influence, and 36.7 % admit simple influence.

Diagram 2. (SSLD 3 - ESPD 5). Comparison of Opinions of Specialists and Experts on Legal System Influence on Doctrine Formation

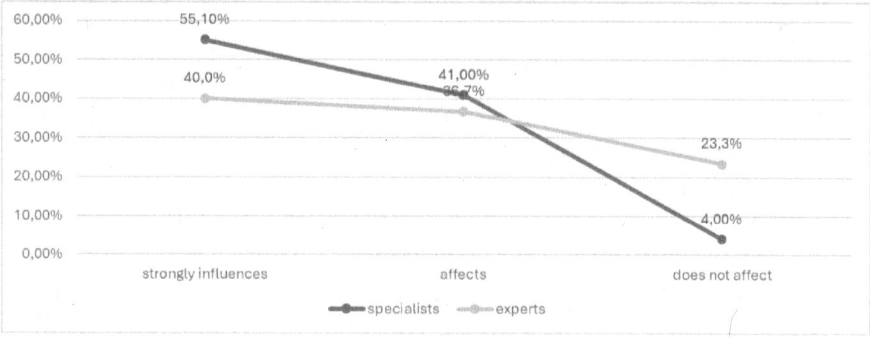

Accordingly, the personal experience of experts of the highest level significantly reduces the legal system's role in the origin, formation, and essence of legal doctrine. This should be interpreted by considering the self-identification of specialists and experts in the legal system.

20.7 % of specialists and 32 % of experts do not identify their affiliation with any legal system. 6.7 % of experts and 0.4 % of specialists do not recognize the importance of the typology of legal systems and do not identify themselves with any legal system. The priority problem is essential in the system of concepts: a form of law or sources of law. The question of what is primary, "understanding the form of law" or "belonging to a certain legal system", has been formulated.

Diagram 3. (SSLD 22). Dependence of the Understanding of Doctrine on Type of Legal System

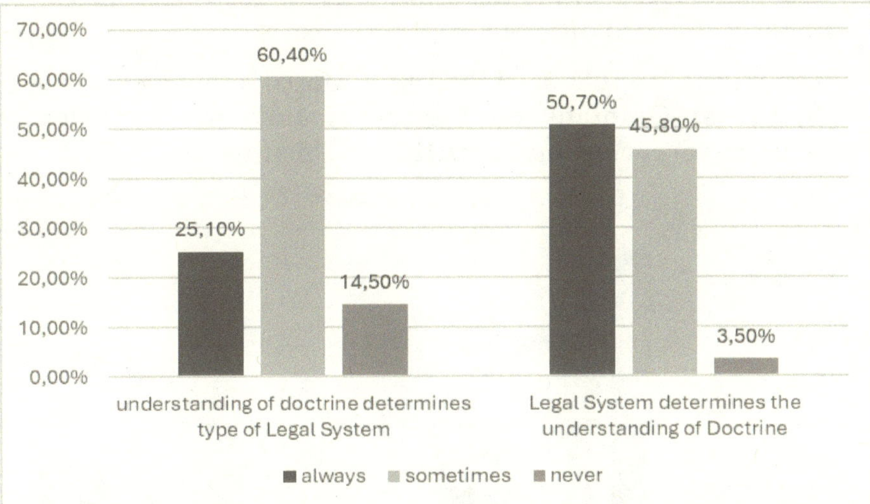

Respondents can choose different academic degrees of certainty for each answer option. There are two variants of the definite answer "always" and "never" and the option of assuming different influences "sometimes". The answer "sometimes" is an option to avoid a specific exact answer. The preponderance of unconditional recognition of primacy belongs to the legal system as the basis for understanding the doctrine. Thus, according to 50.7 % of experts, the legal system determines the understanding of legal doctrine. For example, if the theory of the legal system establishes that a doctrine is not an independent form of law, then this is a hypothesis. In the minority, some specialists consider legal doctrine to be the primary source – 25.1 %. According to this view, understanding doctrine is the reference point; it defines a legal system. Thus, a quarter of the surveyed specialists are open to new approaches to understanding the relationship between doctrine and the legal system. They reject the pre-established, axiomatic dominance of the concept of a "legal system".

The Questionnaire contained questions intended to clarify the status of doctrine in different legal systems. They enable respondents to identify the proposition of doctrine from source to form of law in different legal systems.

Diagram 4. (SSLD 3 - ESPD 6). Comparison of Expert and Specialist Opinions on Degree of Influence of External (Objective) Factors on Formation of Doctrine

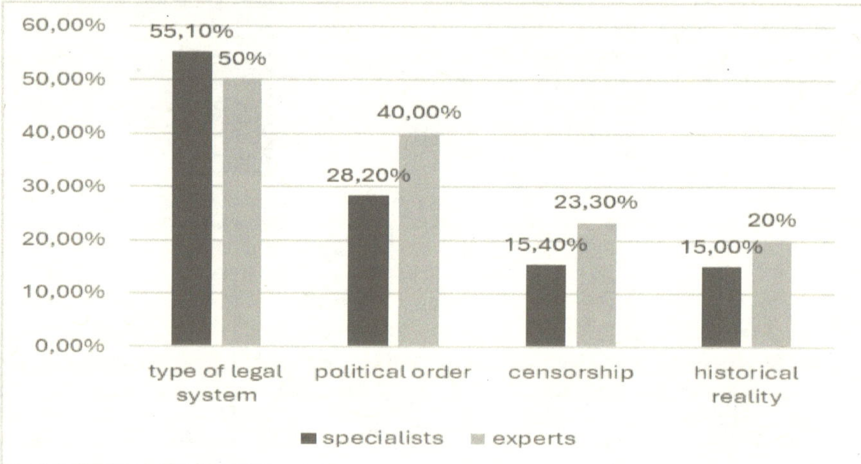

The comparative-legal approach is not axiomatic. Despite its wide distribution, there are criticisms. During expert surveys and questionnaires, it was found that both specialists and experts in the absolute majority recognize the influence of the type of legal system on legal doctrine. The strong influence of the type of legal system on the doctrine is recognized by 55.1 % of specialists and 50 % of experts. Accordingly, these results show the influence of the legal system on legal doctrine. Compared with other external factors (such as political orders, censorship, and historical reality), the legal system has, according to respondents, the most significant influence. Only 4 % of specialists and 10 % of experts denied the influence of the legal system on the formation of doctrine. For specialists and experts, the factors of influence are lined up in the same sequence: the legal system, the political order, the caesura, and the political reality. Attention is drawn to the more significant influence of political orders, censorship, and historical reality in the eyes of experts.

Comparative legal research using ProQuest for American dissertations and the RSL for Russian dissertations encounters significant difficulties when scholars compare the sample. The Russian Federation has introduced official legal regulation for the classification of scholarship, which does not exist in the United States. The naming of academic majors in the United States for legal research is undertaken without an established State system.

In the RSL, the catalog concept is based on the Nomenclature of Academic Specialties for which academic degrees are awarded, which has changed many times[12] and is valid for 2022 in the 2021 edition.[13] HeinOnline and Thomson Reuters (Web of Science) do not have a comparable nomenclature. ProQuest has 28,973 dissertations on law, of which 2,931 are available in full-text access. They are selected by searching for the Subject: Law. Scholars can specify "Main Subject" – "Legal Theory". This is a relatively probable object for comparison with the Russian specialty Theory of Law and State.

Respondents of two sociological surveys self-identified their type of legal system.

[12] Order of the Ministry of Education and Science of Russia dated 10.23.2017, No. 10 "On Approval of the Nomenclature of Scientific Specialties, in which Academic Degrees are Awarded" (available online).

[13] Order of the Ministry of Education and Science of Russia dated 02.24.2021, No. 118 "On Approval of the Nomenclature of Scientific Specialties in which Academic Degrees are Awarded, and Amendments to the Regulations on the Council for the Defense of Dissertations for the Degree of Candidate of Sciences, for the Degree of Doctor of Sciences, Confirmed by the Order of the Ministry of Education and Science of the Russian Federation dated November 10, 2017, No. 1093" (available online).

Table 5. (SSLD 107-ESPD 62). Self-identification of Respondents' Affiliation to the Legal System

Self-identification of the type of legal system by respondents	Specialists	Experts
Romano-Germanic	69,20 %	67,70 %
Anglo-American	4,40 %	
Undifferentiated	1,80 %	
Ideologized	1,30 %	
Byzantine	0,90 %	
Convergence of legal systems	0,40 %	
Slavic legal family, Russian legal system	0,40 %	
I do not share any clear type of legal system	20,70 %	29 %
Mixed	0,40 %	
Legal system of the Russian Federation	0,40 %	
I do not evaluate myself.		3,20 %

Most (69.2 % of specialists and 67.7 % of experts) support the Romano-Germanic legal system.

Despite the established theory of comparative studies, the names of types of legal systems continue to cause difficulties. Of course, the simplest option is to form a name from an adjective based on the name of a country, such as the Russian legal system. However, this approach does not produce the desired result: typification based on established criteria.

Diversity of Geographical Boundaries of Understanding Legal Doctrine

We have investigated the influence of different geographical boundaries on understanding legal doctrine and analyzed the possibility of the doctrine being territorially or organizationally limited.

The first geographical limitation is the borders of the State. A State has territory over which its jurisdiction extends. Within these boundaries State doctrine operates. Judicial doctrine is created by one branch of State power – the court. Accordingly, it is reasonable to expect that there will be State limits to applying judicial doctrine. At the same time, judicial bodies of various interstate organizations, such as the European Court of Human Rights, should be recognized. Some judicial bodies are created to deal only with one case of particular importance, complexity, or planetary significance, such as the Nuremberg Tribunal or the Yugoslavia Tribunal. The planet Earth is the map of the application of such substantive court decisions.

Traditionally, great importance is attached to the territory of the legal system. States belong to a type of legal system, and their boundaries fall within the boundaries of the legal system. States of the same legal system may or may not have a common border (that is, be contiguous). The sum of their territories constitutes the territory of the legal system.

Diagram 5. (SSLD 87). Possibilities to Limit Doctrine (Specialist Opinion)

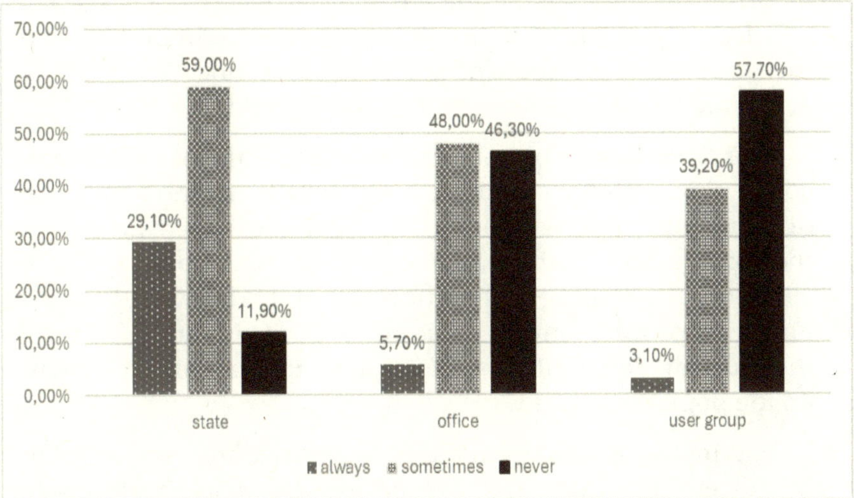

However, there are types of doctrines whose operation may not coincide with State boundaries. For example, a scholar's (academic, academic) doctrine is formed by summing up the people who adhere to this doctrine. They can be in educational or research organizations or schools or work independently. Perhaps the choice of the type "user group" may not seem precise in words. We mean like-minded people, supporters of a particular doctrine.

Objectively, doctrinal scholarship contains a doctrine and ideas without geographical boundaries. With rare negative examples, doctrinal scholarship moves freely with its objective and subjective adherents. The role of the subjective factor as a "group of users" was considered to be insignificant by the survey respondents. The possibility of limiting the doctrine of a group of users is categorically denied by 57.7 % of the surveyed specialists. Restrictions are sometimes allowed by 39.2 % of specialists. Only 3.1 % of respondents admit the possibility of limiting the doctrine to a group of users. Accordingly, the doctrine cannot be limited subjectively.

The doctrine is an achievement of civilization, and this is how the respondents understood it. A group of like-minded people as a limiting factor can become significant. Thus, a particular doctrine may be disseminated and recognized among like-minded supporters of a particular academic school. However, the application of the doctrine has no connection with the academic school and its operation as a form of law.

The office has an option for limitation. This restriction has a connection with the executive body, which can introduce State doctrine through law-making, the ideological doctrine through the formulation of the policy of a particular body, or for all subjects of law falling within the scope of this body. Regulations on ministries are often entrusted with formulating policy in their jurisdiction. In its area of competence, the ministry creates an ideological doctrine.

Estimates of the frequency of restrictions are arranged in descending order and can be expressed in the following formulations: 1) always, 2) sometimes, and 3) never. At the same time, the possibility of territorial or organizational limitations of legal doctrine can be resolved. Each proposed restriction option can be considered territorial and organizational. The number of respondents who recognize the possibility of territorially or organizationally restricting doctrine is significantly lower than those who do not. When scholars drill down into the constraints, it is evident that the constraints are ambiguous.

29.2 % of respondents recognize State borders as a restriction for the movement and application of legal doctrine, 5.7 % recognize the boundaries of departments, and 3.1 % recognize user groups. The respondents prefer the State as the source within the geographical boundaries of the legal system, which determines the status of legal doctrine.

Analysis of Legal Doctrine in the Context of Time and Place

The space-time continuum analyzes an object in the context[14] of time and place. The concept under study should be visualized in measurement systems as time (when?) and place (where?). The space-time continuum includes "the geographical, cultural-civilizational, and other determination of political doctrines that generates their diversity".[15] The term "space-time continuum" originated in the 1930s and became widespread in the 2000s. This conclusion is based on an analysis of n-gram Google Books. In English-language literature, this term appeared no earlier than fifteen years ago. The time is synchronized to the English and Russian segments of Google.

Figure 9. Google Book N-gram «Space-Time Continuum»

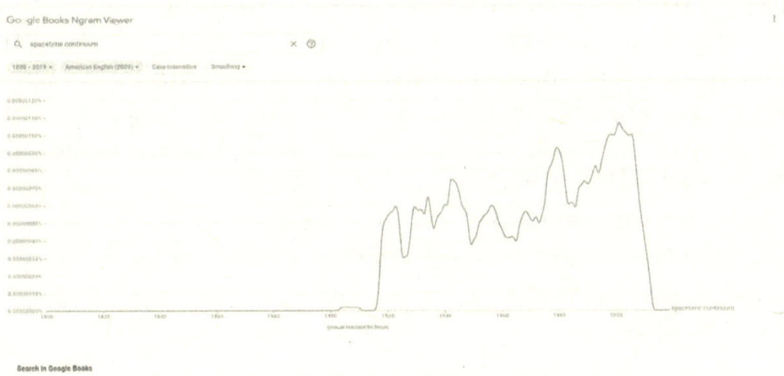

[14] L. Ia. Averianov, Контент-анализ [Content Analysis] (2007). p. 164.

[15] V. K. Belozerov, "Доктрины и идеологии в системе политических институтов [Doctrines and Ideologies in the System of Political Institutions]", Вестник Московского государственного лингвистического университета [*Bulletin of Moscow State Linguistic University*], no. 24 (2013), pp. 31-40.

The spatial continuum is essential for comparative legal research. The time continuum is vital for studying an object over a long period. The researcher should consider the unsynchronized political and legal development of different States, their stages, and different speed of development. Thus, it would be false to assume that if the Renaissance was productive in medieval Italy, then today, Italy is the world's cultural center and the leader of world culture. However, the assumption that all other countries experienced a cultural upsurge and a qualitative leap during the Italian Renaissance is erroneous. The Renaissance from the fourteenth to the seventeenth centuries did not exist in all countries. It was a limited European phenomenon.

Suppose the periods of activity and lull in the development of the object do not coincide in the objects being compared, for example, countries. In that case, this information is likewise valuable for the researcher. In any case, researchers must establish the space-time continuum. Discreteness, the absence of data, is as valuable as its presence.

Any text is created in a particular place, at a particular time, and by a specific author. The totality of these facts is conventionally called the subjective context. The personal characteristics of the author of the work, such as education, country of residence, academic degree, subject of research, and others are essential. The subjective context also includes the following: age, type of legal understanding, and affiliation with a law school. For example, for the study of legal doctrine, the physical existence of the author at the time of citation is essential. Authors are divided into living and deceased. This classification may seem redundant or far-fetched. We see the meaning of the classification in the fact that a deceased author cannot influence the citation and authority of his Works. Accordingly, doctrinal status is established more reliably for deceased authors.

The study has shown that the cult of deceased authorities has noticeably faded from the nineteenth to the twentieth centuries. 81.9 % of specialists do not attach importance to this factor, and only 1.3 % recognize deceased masters as doctrinal persons.

The long active operation of the legal doctrine – more than 100 years – testifies to its stable authoritative position. But this period is more extended than the life of the Persona-Doctrine.

For qualitative analysis, it is necessary to collect data on publications. Such characteristics of the work, such as the date of publication, genre, language, and others, are essential.

We have developed a sophisticated and detailed way of encoding data on texts and their authors. This method establishes the objective and subjective context as accurately as possible. Information about objective and subjective factors is entered into Zotero. The factors of objective and subjective influence will be analyzed at the stage of qualitative content analysis.

This study uses paper and virtual publications created at different times. All information resources, including computer resources, have a short history. For those resources about which this information is known, we indicate from what date the resource exists, how it is filled, and how many documents it stores on a specific date. Based on the diagram, comparing database information will be comparable and reasonable from 2000 onwards.

Diagram 6. History of Creation of Databases

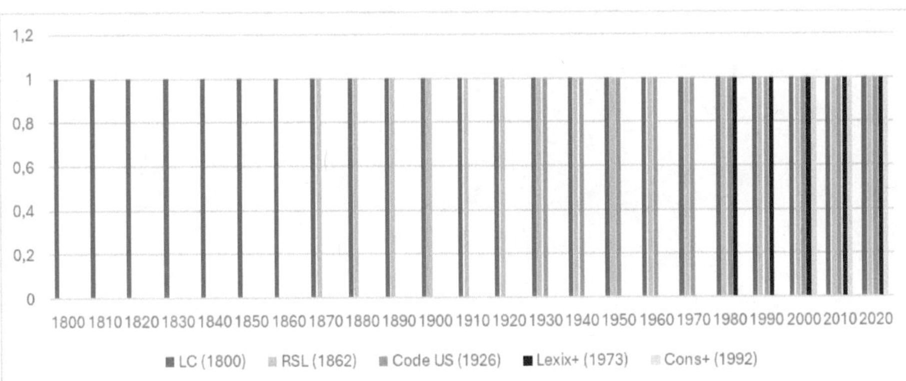

In fact, any historical study of databases will be recurrent if the sources in the different systems being compared are collected over the same period. Accordingly, for our study, it is preferable to determine the beginning dates of the collection of sources in comparable legal systems, compare these data on the timeline, and take the period where they coincide, visualized in the diagram. Scholars can take different periods within the same database without synchronizing these time limits with other databases.

Chapter 6
Doctrine as a Source and Form of Law

GENERAL PROVISIONS OF DOCTRINE OF FORMS AND SOURCES OF LAW

Source Theory and Form of Law

The intensive disputes regarding the essence of the concepts, forms, and sources of law is to some extent explained by the following circumstances: (1) the vagueness of each concept separately, and (2) these concepts are not isolated from each other but tend to various forms of interpenetration.

The various positions of researchers of the forms and sources of law are subject to some systematization. It is possible to distinguish certain tendencies in understanding the problem of form and source of law, depending on the answers to the fundamental questions: 1) whether the concepts coincide (or diverge), 2) which of the terms is preferable.

In doctrinal literature, the following positions have developed regarding the relationship between the terms "form of law" and "source of law":

1. identification of form and source:
    a. complete identification,
    b. equalization of concepts to replace one term with another,
2. separation of concepts into different variants, whereby:
    a. one meaning of the term source coincides with the form or,
    b. one value of the form is equalized with the source,

3. a complete separation of concepts without intersection with other terms that compare form and content.[1]

Despite the wide range of opinions, the terms "source of law" and "form of law" have their own specific meaning. The use of both concepts significantly expands legal research. Criticism of the term "source of law" does not seem convincing. Ambiguity cannot be considered a disadvantage because it only complicates the work of a scholar but does not interfere with it. The deep meaning and varied nuances of the word "source" concerning legal matters could not be more consistent with the sociological type of legal understanding. To a certain extent, the term "source" should oblige the legislator not to write laws randomly but to draw his rules from life. That is, the source of law is people's lives.[2]

We have examined the mutual influence of the type of legal system and the doctrine of forms of law based on our sociological surveys. These are questions about whether a doctrine is a form of law in different legal systems. We have left it to specialists to show the relationship between the source, the form of law, and the legal system.

It is clear from this diagram that the recognition of doctrine as a source or form of law does not depend much on the type of legal system with which respondents associate. This is because in the same type of legal system, with a slight difference, it is possible to recognize doctrine as both a form of law and a source of law. Such a relationship can be: doctrine is a source of law, but it can sometimes become a form of law. The structure of the question in the questionnaire required choosing one categorical answer – this is a source and form of law. Accordingly, those respondents who chose that within the framework of the Romano-Germanic legal system doctrine is a form of law cannot simultaneously choose the option "sources of law".

1 S. V. Boshno, Форма права: теоретико-правовое исследование [Form of Law: Theoretical-Legal Research] (2005) (dissertation doctor of legal sciences).

2 What has been said is only a conclusion that is declarative in nature and requires careful refraction to all the meanings of the term "source".

Diagram 7. (SSLD 23-26). Status, Sources or Form of Law in Different Legal Systems (Specialist Opinion)

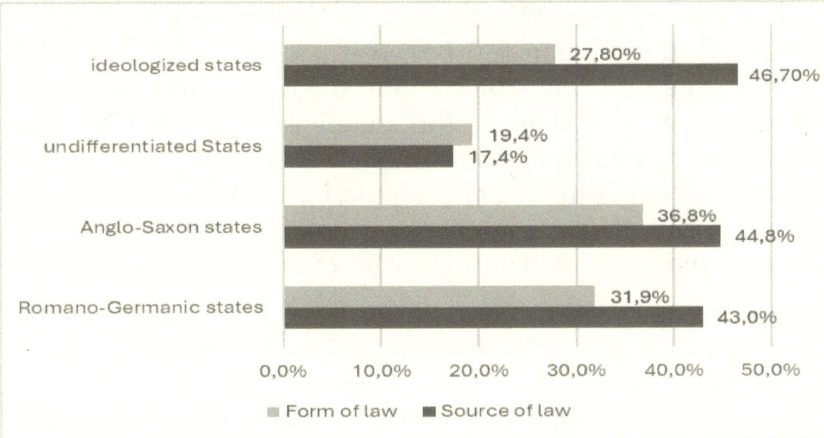

In all legal systems except the undifferentiated one, the recognition of doctrine as a source of law is greater than the adherents of the status of a form of law. The most significant gap in opinions is evident for ideologized States, in which there are significantly more supporters of the status of the source of law (46.7 %) compared to supporters of the status of the form of law (27.8 %).

Respondents indicated that only in undifferentiated States did the status of doctrine as a form of law (19.4 %) prevail over the status of a source of law (17.4 %). Such an understanding generally fits into the general theory. In undifferentiated States, the religious and customary doctrines of law are forms of law. These forms of law regulate relations directly, without intermediaries.

Most respondents avoid precise answers, preferring the median non-informative option. At the same time, there is a certain tendency towards the status of doctrine as a source or form of law. Recognition of doctrine as a source of law dominates in ideologized legal systems (46.7 %). A doctrine is a form of law in Anglo-American States, according to 36.8 % of respondents, which is the highest rate among all types of legal systems.

In Anglo-American states, the role of judicial and academic doctrines is excellent.

Doctrine as a source of law. For Russian legal studies, the debate on the relationship between source and form of law has remained relevant for a century. Many academic studies consider this problem as the main, system-forming issue. These well-known works are titled "Source of Law" or "Form of Law". The present writer's doctoral dissertation in 2004 was called "Forms of Law". Twenty years later, I argue that the form of law is the outer shell of the existence of law.

Regarding content, "form of law" and "law" coincide. The term «form» makes it possible to divide the outer shell of law into types, such as legislation, precedent, custom, and other forms, including doctrine. The term "source of law" describes, in scholarly terms, a precursor, a precondition of law – its attitudes, ideas, models, even conditions. We will not resist identifying the concepts of source and form of law as far as these phenomena coincide. That is, if someone, including the legislator, calls the forms of law sources, this indicates the equivalence of the core of these concepts in the part where they contain law. This is not an assumption or an idea; it is a right in the form of regulatory or protective prescription containing a model of human behavior.

This agreement on identity does not exclude the fact that, on one hand, there are sources that have not become a form of law. On the other hand, some forms of law do not have organic sources, that is, prerequisites of an objective nature. The expectation that all officially recognized legislation should reflect the social needs of all is a utopia imposed by the ruling group to appease the poor, the inactive, and the powerless. This illusion keeps them in a controlled state. Suppose the form of law does not regulate relations but declares models for non-obvious addressees. In that case, this is not a right. This thesis is painful for doctrines consisting of slogans, appeals, and statements not addressed to specific subjects. They do not transform into a model of lawful behavior. Of course, there is no legal responsibility for such doctrines and declarations. In this case, "doctrine" is a name, not a form of law. They are replaced by vague threats such as "adequate response" to non-listed entities (anyone who violates an undefined right). The law cannot exist outside the model of human behavior with a hypothesis, a disposition, or a sanction. Thus, doctrinal declarations do not contain a right. These are documentary doctrines, but not law, legislation, or a form of law. This is how the Constitutional Court defined the military doctrine of the 1995 period.

The word "sources" has a range of meanings. The versatility of this word is encountered in various facets of the meaning of the phrase "source of law" in legal terminology. Most often, the word "source" is interpreted as where certain phenomena come from, where they originate. We are talking about social, economic, and political phenomena, relations, processes, and prerequisites that precede the law. In this sense, the following problem arises: this historical source is social relations or ways of regulating, organizing, and protecting these relations. It seems that both the relations themselves and their regulators can act as a source of law. It is more common to see the source of law in the rules that describe the behavior of subjects. This is because regulatory legal norms create a pattern of behavior. The source's transition into the form of law occurs by obtaining additional features while preserving the essence. However, such apparent positions cannot be confined to such prominent positions. The oldest form of ordering relations is expressed in the actual implementation of patterns of law. The behavior itself is its model, and the transmission of the rule is carried out through forming a habit of such behavior. Custom, just as other unwritten legal forms, is reproduced, exists, and preserved only through appropriate practice. It is the actual conduct that is the source of the law. Thus, the source of law can be both relations and ways of regulating them.

Law absorbs the properties of its sources and acquires unique characteristics. The law does not merge with the sources, nor should it be separated from them. These are the roots of law: the life-giving force, its effectiveness, its social recognition, and the condition of its effectiveness.

Historically, the sources of law predate legislation and other forms of law and continue to exist in the presence of positive law. In other words, there is always a source of law because the law increasingly establishes new relations. In this sense of the word, its source can be replaced by the words "foundation", "forerunner", and "basis" of law.

Thus, the sources of law are the "mononorms of primitive society, morality, ethics, custom, ritual, taboo, myth, and other forms of regulation". It can be said that any established rule of conduct is a source that can give a right.

The source of law in jurisprudence traditionally has several meanings. The most common reference is to the formal meaning of the term "source of law". It is well recognized that there is an ideal source. There are conflicting opinions about the material source. Some researchers speak of the existence of a legitimation and social source of law. Thus, the range of meanings of the term "source" is quite diverse. In general, it can be noted that in any of the above senses, the source of law is not the law itself but its predecessors, factors, ideas, relations, conditions, and resources that determine the emergence of the corresponding forms of law.

The formal meaning is rightly objectified in a certain way. Material meaning is all the various social relations that precede formal law or mediate the process of its formalization. Thus, the material sources are quite diverse. These are law-making procedures (legitimation sources), the practice of social relations, and legal consciousness – in a word, all social factors that affect the content of law.

Legitimation is giving rules State status through direct creativity or sanctioning.[3] The *legitimation of a source of law* acts as a force that gives something the properties of a form of law. Law-making bodies and procedures act as legitimation sources for a normative act. For customs, the source of legitimation is society

[3] S. A. Karapetian, Источники конституционного права Российской Федерации [Sources of the Constitutional Law of the Russian Federation] (M., 1998) (dissertation candidate of legal sciences).

and its practice; for doctrinal forms of law, ideas, concepts, theories, and the conquest of their regulative properties are the source of legitimation.

The *material meaning* of the term "source of law" is the supreme organ of power,[4] the law-making activity of the State.[5] The material source of law is sometimes not explicitly referred to as such in academic literature. Still, judgments are made about it.

The *social source of law* has the following properties: 1) the theoretical elaboration of the question of the participation of the phenomenon under assessment in the process of law formation; 2) its place in the legal process of development of normative acts; 3) theoretical and organizational aspects influencing the interaction of the first two factors.[6] These theses apply to assessing any phenomenon for the possibility of its attribution to sources of law.

Thus, the collective term "*social* source" encompasses all the senses of the term "source" except the formal one. It is a comprehensive concept designed to unite all the diverse conditions and causes, factors, and actions that result in the decision to create a formal source of law. Such an approach allows the study to move from the results in the form of, for example, a normative act to the sources that led to its adoption. These latter constitute the social source of law. The apparent role of a phenomenon in the process of law formation makes it a source of law.

The *ideal meaning of the source of law* corresponds to legal consciousness, the desire, which is the relation to the existing

[4] N. N. Razumovich, "Источники и форма права [Sources and Form of Law]", Советское государство и право [Soviet State and Law], no. 3 (1988), p. 21.

[5] D. A. Kerimov, Источники советского социалистического права [Sources of Soviet Socialist Law] (1950), p. 261 (dissertation candidate of legal sciences).

[6] A. Nashitz and N. Feodor, "Роль судебной практики в формировании и совершенствовании норм социалистического права [The Role of Judicial Practice in the Formation and Improvement of the Norms of Socialist Law. State and Law]", Советское государство и право [Soviet State and Law], no. 5 (1965), p. 22.

natural law, the activities of the law enforcer and legislator, and the desired law. Regardless of the form of law, it has ideal foundations. Nonetheless, they are irrational, unsystematized, arise spontaneously, and exist in different forms. A book, a concept, an idea, or emotions in the form of dissatisfaction with the status quo can act as an ideal source of law.

The most subtle observations in the sphere of ideal sources of law belong to the historical and psychological schools of law. Representatives of these trends are inclined to exaggerate the role of the subjective factor in the formation of law. Only the law corresponding to the ideal sources is used by them. That is, ideas and other intellectual-volitional factors perform a dual function. On one hand, they are the source of law in the ideal sense. On the other hand, positive law that does not correspond to ideal sources does not become a form of law.

A legal precept is doomed to be effective if it conforms to the notions of just law, to the sense of justice, or, to use the terminology of the supporters of the historical school of law, to popular belief. The above does not exclude the possibility of adopting a normative legal act that does not have ideal sources. In this case, the legislator must find other reserves for its effectiveness. The simplest and most sought-after is State coercion, designed to compensate for the lack of internal persuasiveness.

Thus, the source of law in the material sense is a set of ideas, relations, and procedures that determine the social necessity, determinism, and value of law which precede and mediate law in the formal sense (forms of law). The source of law in the formal sense is the form of its expression, the shell in which the law is objectified, the form of law.

Doctrine as Form of Law

In academic literature, the following features of the form of law are traditionally distinguished: obligation, formal certainty, and general knowledge. It is necessary to supplement this list of properties of the form of law with normativity, State support, and "the legality of the source of law as the legitimacy of its emergence and functioning".[7] From the linguistic and logical points of view, the following requirements are imposed on the forms of law: linguistic standardization, systematic structure of law, and graphic certainty of legal norms.[8]

Researchers have accumulated many arguments against recognizing doctrine as a form of law. The most frequently emphasized lack of jurisprudence is the lack of *uniformity*. Indeed, "scholars often differ in their views on certain controversial questions of law".[9] This diversity has been interpreted as an obstacle to accepting doctrine as a form of law.

The most apparent recognition of the form of law is in a legislative act. Indirect proof of the correctness of this thesis was when, in Roman history, the works of five jurists were equated with the law by imperial decree. Such recognition is a rare (if not the only) historical example; therefore, its significance should not be absolutized. Many forms of law acquire this status on the spur of the moment by gaining authority and recognition. Khvostov saw two ways to the development of jurisprudence: (1) if "it is illuminated by the sanction of the legislature"; that is, if it becomes law, and (2) "through long-term practice, it has become a custom".[10] In fact, the problem of switching from one source to another is a common phenomenon.

There is a position in which legal doctrine is not tasked with developing into forms of law. Thus, for example, the influence of legal doctrine can be exercised by advising the legislator on problems directly posed by legal practice. Reutov has spoken out against the practical significance of legal doctrine. However, he does not deny its practical regulative role. He distinguished the

[7] Karapetian, note 3 above, p. 26.

[8] N. A. Vlasenko, Проблемы точности выражения формы права (лингво-логический анализ) [Problems of Accuracy of Expression of the Form of Law (Linguo-Logical Analysis)] (1997), p. 12 (dissertation candidate of legal sciences).

[9] D. D. Grimm, К вопросу о понятии и источнике обязательности юридических норм [On the Question of the Concept and Source of Binding Legal Norms] (1896), p. 26.

[10] V. M. Khvostov, Общая теория права: элементарный очерк [General Theory of Law: An Elementary Essay] (6th ed.; 1914), p.107.

following functions of academic research: a) informational, b) theoretical-critical, and c) applied.[11] The possibilities mentioned above of jurisprudence boil down to the fact that jurisprudence is not only not a form of law, but it is not always a source of law.

It was in this vein that P. F. Puchta spoke earlier. He saw the task of legal doctrinal scholarship as "to know legal propositions in their systematic connection, as conditioning each other and deriving from each other, so that it may be possible to trace the genealogy of individual legal propositions".[12]

The question of legitimacy is relevant to the forms of law. Legitimacy means the existence of a form of law, the authorization of authority. The question of legitimacy is truly relevant only for normative legal acts. Indeed, for them, creating the competence of the publishing body is not a complete list of requirements for legitimacy. The absence of this feature for a regulatory legal act entails the possibility of its repeal. It is not easy to question the legitimacy of other forms of law. For example, the legitimacy of creating a scholar's doctrine cannot be assessed because it arises independently, without special procedural rules.

It is evident that at critical historical moments (for example, revolutions or profound reforms), obsolete legal norms are abandoned when new rules emerge in the depths of social practice. This process is illegitimate, as it requires the rejection of the existing rules in the State. This is precisely what Iakov Mironovich Magaziner (1882-1961) wrote about in 1919 when he proposed the term "non-law".[13] This is an illegitimate form.

[11] V. P. Reutov, Юридическая практика и развитие законодательства [Legal Practice and Development of Legislation] (1968), p. 199 (dissertation candidate of legal sciences).

[12] G. F. Puchta, Энциклопедия права Г.Ф. Пухты [Encyclopedia of Law], transl. P. Karasevich (6th ed.; 1872),, p. 34.

[13] Ia. M. Magaziner, Лекции по государственному праву: (Общее государственное право) [Lectures on State Law: (General State Law)] (1919),, p. 50.

Forms of law have the following characteristics:

1. *clear external expression* on stable materials (stone, paper, and so on, reliable data carriers) in compliance with the requirements for the style of the language. Clarity seems sufficient if the subjects of the law understand the rules and apply them uniformly,
2. *the certainty of the content,* that is, the form of the law must contain provisions that are uniformly understood by the subjects, the addressees of the norms,
3. *duration of existence,*
4. *general knowledge,* that is, the subjects of law must be able to know the law,
5. the *binding nature of* the form of law means that one's conduct must conform to the legal precepts. It may be a duty to perform an action or to refrain from it,
6. *universality means* that the right acquires social value and can be equal to the scope of freedom. The law is a measure of the behavior of different persons,
7. *normativity* means that the forms of law apply equally to all law subjects. The right does not have a personified addressee. It is addressed to all subjects,
8. *reasonableness, justice. This attribute is of the most significant importance* for doctrinal forms of law. The principle of presumption of reasonableness and fairness applies to legislation,
9. *recognition by the subjects of law.* Doctrinal forms of law often do not have formal signs of their legitimacy. They acquire regulative force due to their authority, recognition, and repetition by a reasonable part of society.

Given the above, the form of law is the outer shell in which the legal precept exists. *A form* of law is a duly objectified legal institution that corresponds to the ideas of morality, ethics, reasonableness, and justice accepted in each society, impersonated, long-term, and uniformly embodied in the behavior of subjects of law, guaranteed for execution by the force of authority and (or) State coercion, recognized by subjects of law as a regulator of social relations.

Application of the General Theory of Forms of Law to Doctrinal Forms of Law.

Academic work in the field of law is carried out by professional jurists. This right of jurists has been known since ancient times. In 1914, D. C. Grimm spoke about the possibility of academic doctrine becoming a form of law. He associated a positive solution to this problem with the quality and validity of the academic proposition. These provisions must be explicitly and unequivocally recognized as binding by the State authorities.[14]

The term "lawyers' law" is often used in academic literature. Puchta believed that the law of lawyers is the law of legal doctrine. Legal doctrine is not based on an external authority, but on an internal authority of its own. The law of lawyers is based on the unanimity of the most famous lawyers and courts, who have long and uniformly applied the law of research origin. Acknowledging the role of like-mindedness, which allows the formation of academic schools and trends, we consider it necessary to consider one more facet of the concept of lawyers' law. This feature was noticed by Ia. Gambarov. He stressed that the law of lawyers or jurisprudence comprises theory and practice. Whether individual or aggregate, theorists developed court decisions.[15] He distinguished three forms of expression of lawyers' law: 1) judicial decision, 2) judicial practice, and 3) legal doctrinal scholarship.[16] This helpful model sees the combination of academic research and practice as necessary. Authority comes from the legal professional community, represented in academic research and politics, with all public authorities. An essential component of the authority of lawyers'

[14] Grimm, note 9 above, p. 26.

[15] Puchta, note 12 above, p. 42.

[16] Iu. S. Gambarov, Курс гражданского права [Course of Civil Law] (1911), I, p. 336.

law is the elitism of the legal profession and, as a rule, the high social status in society combined with wealth.

It should be noted that a little later, L. I. Petrazhitsky used the quantitative recognition criterion as a basis for classifying academic views. Overall, this approach seems to be extremely promising. In this regard, we attribute Puchta's opinion on practical and valuable unanimity to the pinnacle of academic law – doctrine.

In the Survey of researchers on legal doctrine, a question was formulated to address the fundamental problem of whether the doctrine is an independent form of law or embodied in other forms of law. The answer options list the different shells in which the doctrine may exist: legal customs, normative legal acts, judicial precedents, religious texts, and ideology. Each of these phenomena can exist outside the concept of doctrine. For example, for a large part, normative legal acts are not a form of expression of the doctrine or related to it. However, there are normative legal acts called doctrines. In addition, the presence of objects of a doctrinal nature (such as, for example, the edict of the President of the Russian Federation on military doctrine or a message of the President of the Russian Federation) strengthens the importance of the discussion of normative legal acts having the status of doctrine. The legal reference system Consultant+ marks the Addresses of the President of the Russian Federation as legislation. In our typology, messages are not normative legal acts. They are part of the ideological legal doctrine.

A survey found that 17.2% of specialists believe that doctrines are never an independent form of law. "Always" doctrine is an independent form of law according to 33% of specialists and "sometimes" – to 49.8% of specialists. Thus, with varying academic degrees of categorality, 82.8% of specialists admit recognizing doctrine as an independent form of law.

Such statistics indicate a high recognition of legal doctrine as a form of modern Russian law. For a State with a dominant (according to textbooks) Romano-Germanic legal system, this is an unexpectedly high level of approval recognition of the status of doctrine as a form of law.

Diagram 8. (SSLD 63). Possibility of Expressing Doctrine in Different Forms (Specialist Opinion)

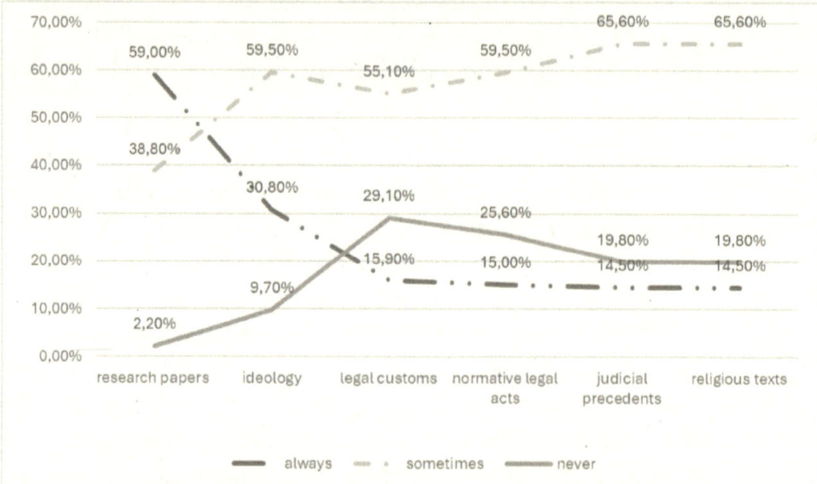

The variants "always" and "never" seem logical and consistent. The option "always" for academic research is 59% versus 2.2% against. This is followed by expressing doctrine as ideology – 30.08% against 9.7%. After ideology, the ratings sharply decline. All other proposed forms (legal customs, regulations, judicial precedents, and religious texts) have a total approval rating ranging from 15.9% to 14.5%. Accordingly, legal customs, regulations, judicial precedents, and religious texts are considered non-doctrines.

If we combine the answer options "always" and "sometimes," then such a variant can be called "maybe".

Such an association of groups forms the following sequence of the implementation of doctrine in various forms: (1) scholarship, (2) ideology, (3) judicial precedents, and (4) normative legal acts.

In analyzing the data of a sociological survey, we take affiliation in a particular legal system as a variable. Experts have identified themselves by the following legal systems: 1)

Romano-Germanic, 2) Anglo-American, 3) undifferentiated, and 4) ideologized. Some respondents did not choose any types of legal system.

Diagram 9. (SSLD 18 – 107). Relationship Between Type of Legal System Shared by Specialists and Recognition of Doctrine as Form of Law (Specialist Opinion)

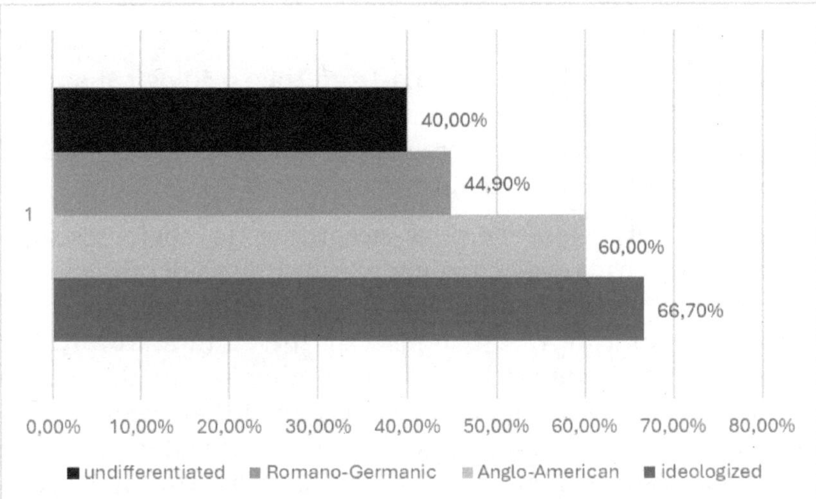

Representatives of the ideologized form of law show the most significant recognition of doctrine as a form of law (66.7%). This fully correlated with the understanding of this type of legal system. Representatives of the Anglo-American legal family are in second place, with 60% of representatives of this legal system considering doctrine as a form of law. 44.9% of the supporters of the Romano-Germanic legal system and 40% of the supporters of the undifferentiated legal system consider doctrine a form of law.

An analysis of respondents to a sociological survey using a significant variable clearly shows the influence of the type of legal system on recognizing doctrine as a form of law. The data for supporters of the ideologized and Anglo-American legal system coincide with the well-known approaches. By a wide margin, representatives of the Romano-Germanic legal system demonstrated a decline in support for doctrine as a form of law. They showed the same level of support as respondents who did not identify as supporters of a particular legal system. They show less than 50% support, which indicates that they are indifferent to the status of the doctrine since, for them, it is not a defining issue. At the same time, the attitude of the official approach recorded in textbooks shows that 30% provide information about doctrine in the section on sources (forms) of law (Diagram 1).

The correlation between data from the sociological survey and the qualitative content analysis of a sample of educational literature shows that the average approval rate of doctrine as a form of law ranges from 30 to 50%.

Respondents were verified according to their research interests, which allowed us to analyze the impact of professional interests on understanding the status of doctrine. We have obtained significant results regarding the attitude toward the status of doctrine depending on the academic specialty. At the program's development stage, we assumed that theorists and international relations specialists are more inclined to recognize doctrine as a form of law than industry experts. This hypothesis was partially confirmed. The highest level of recognition of doctrine as a form of law was demonstrated by representatives of public academic research – 39.4%. This result is based on the theory of constitutional law and constitutional justice. Indeed, the acts of the Constitutional Court of the Russian Federation are understood as normative legal acts and judicial doctrines simultaneously.

As expected, representatives of scholarship devoted to criminal justice are in first place supporting doctrine among industry specialists, accounting for 29.8%. The hypothesis about international relations specialists ultimately failed; they showed 0%.

Public law scholarship recognizes the critical role of decisions of the Plenum of the Supreme Court of the Russian Federation. The recognition of doctrine as a form of law will be primarily connected with judicial doctrine. Procedural civil and arbitrazh law openly recognizes judicial practice and doctrine as a form of law. But only 1.9% of private law scholars recognized doctrine as a form of law. Specialists in criminal law answered this question in complete opposition to their branch legislation. 28.9% confirmed the status of the doctrine as a form of the law. We believe that this result of a sociological survey shows that criminal legislation does not recognize the existence of judicial doctrine, the influence of generalizing acts of the judiciary, and even decisions on specific cases on the adoption of decisions resulting from criminal proceedings. It is difficult to say whether this is a "hidden influence" or "lawless justice".

We have analyzed the correlations between the age of specialists and their attitude to the status of doctrine in the system of forms of law. Age shows a correlation compared to other factors.

Diagram 10. (SSLD 18 – 103). Influence of Age on Recognition of Doctrine as Form of Law (Specialist Opinion)

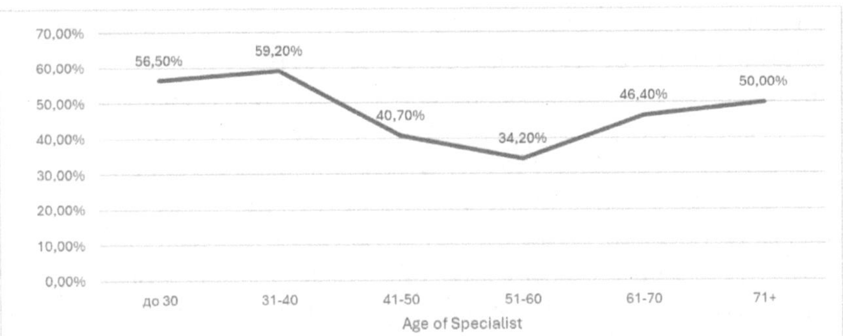

Respondents under 40 (59.2% in the 31 to 40 age group and 56.5% under 30) showed the highest (significant) acceptance of the doctrine as an independent form of law. This is followed by a drop to 34.2% (the lowest rate) in the 51 – 60 age group and an increase to 50% in the 71+ group. Professionals aged 41 to 60 do not express significant support for doctrine as a form of law. This is the most active age group in the creative process.

Based on an analysis of the influence on attitudes towards doctrine and the possibility of its recognition as a form of law, it can be concluded that belonging to the type of legal system is greatly exaggerated, but nevertheless, this influence exists. The analysis has shown that belonging to a specific legal system does not decisively affect the recognition of a doctrine as a form of law. Perhaps this is indirect evidence that the boundaries between types of legal systems are blurring, or at least no longer very clear-cut. Another explanation is that the status of a legal doctrine is not a fundamental issue based on which a particular researcher can be classified as a supporter of a particular legal system. That is, neither does the legal system determine the attitude to the legal doctrine nor does the attitude to the legal doctrine determine the affiliation to a particular legal system.

The treatment of doctrine in a legal system is an independent problem that has little to do with the typology of legal systems. Accordingly, the application of the methods of comparative law to the study of legal doctrine is unlikely to be effective.

The continuing study confirms the increase in the number of supporters of doctrine as a form of law from 2003 to the present, and there are prerequisites for an increase in the future. However, a qualitative breakthrough is not yet expected. In 10-20 years, the rating of trust in doctrine as a form of law will not exceed 50%. Nevertheless, for a State that officially positions itself as Romano-Germanic or Anglo-American, the rate of recognition of about 50% of any form of law other than normative legal acts and judicial precedent is an indicator of the crisis of 1) the traditional forms of law or 2) the comparative legal classification of types of the legal system, considering the understanding of the hierarchy of forms of law.

Chapter 7
Theoretical and Practical Foundations of the Doctrine

LEGAL DOCTRINE AS THEORY (ACADEMIC, JUDICIAL, IDEOLOGICAL)

Most often, doctrine is identified with *legal theory*. However, the social value of academic creativity differs significantly from work to work, and therefore, equalization is impossible. In addition, some works have no applied significance. That is, their implementation in life does not occur, which excludes the possibility of their perception in social practice. For example, historical and descriptive works.

The constructive interaction between theory and practice is manifest in the fact that theoretical developments serve as a source of knowledge to fill in gaps in legislation by analogy. Doctrine makes it possible to clarify the legislation and "hear" judicial practice, if any, on a specific issue or to assume previously unknown institutions, arguments, and so on.

Legal doctrine makes it possible to eliminate difficulties that arise in law enforcement (gaps in existing legislation and its inconsistency). Academic validity is manifested in the research, elaboration of legislation, and legal practice materials by sociological, historical, and comparative legal empirical methods. Legislation and law enforcement practice are the objects of research. Based on their analysis, theoretical generalizations are made, and the regularities of the development of objects are revealed.

Doctrine is influenced by the developments of researchers and practitioners and the dominant social relations on which it is based. In this regard, a scholar's doctrine may be less detached from reality than, for example, an ideological doctrine.

A doctrine is formed in the academic processing of existing legislation and law enforcement practice. It involves many scholars, making it possible to identify the best ideas for developing legislation and practice (involvement of researchers).

There is also *a cyclical approach* to the interaction of theory and practice for doctrine. Researchers analyze practice, process its results, and develop ways to improve legislation. They embody their ideas in new works that affect practice. An idea's first occurrence can occur in theory and practice (for example, legislation). But then, starting from the initial experience, the idea proceeds: from theory to practice and vice versa. Such a mutual transition can take place not just once, but in many cycles.

Doctrine addresses the interaction of theory and practice and supports the existence of these hypotheses. However, transforming a scholar's doctrine into legal practice, gibrn the peculiarity of its form, causes difficulties. Usually, the form of objectification of academic research is monographs, academic articles, and so on. These genres are challenging to understand. Monographs, as a rule, have are substantial in size. Only a researcher can be interested in monographs and understand them. This is exceptional literature for the target reader – an academic worker.

In the 2007 – 2008 study, I asked questions to determine the preferences of civil servants in legal literature. 0% of civil servants were interested in monographs. For most subjects, studying and working through such sources is difficult. The study found that reading a multi-page academic text to solve a single issue for civil servants looks like a waste of time. A survey of civil servants (2007 – 2008) found that commentaries are the most helpful literature. In general, 21.5% of civil servants expressed a lack of interest in legal literature and found it difficult to answer the question of what literature is helpful to a civil servant. 45% of respondents dodged the question: they said all the diverse literature is helpful. That is, 66.5% of civil servants have no particular interest in literature. Textbooks are read by 0.5% of civil servants, and academic articles by 1%.

Accordingly, the meeting of academic legal doctrine and the legal consciousness of civil servants is unlikely.

Perhaps researchers should be able to make their products accessible to different readers. The opposite is true. Excessive detail and a scholarly style complicate the understanding of academic material for the mass reader. Accustoming civil servants to legal monographs would enable them to study doctrines of legal scholars. This assumption sounds attractive and optimistic, but neither side is motivated for rapprochement.

The chief defect of doctrine is its isolation from practice. A doctrine should not be based only on academic and theoretical conclusions or views, theorems, or considering the structure of the State and the form of government. It should be based on links with law enforcement practice. A valuable observation is a doctrine's combination of theory and practice because it is developed by researchers and then confirmed or refuted by practice.

It is essential to establish the origin of an idea to compare legal theory and doctrines. Some ideas are created in a library (in this context, a physical or virtual place for the researcher's creativity) through reflection and logical inference. However, not all the ideas that determine the development of social relations are of armchair origin. Ideas can arise from law enforcement, case law, and other practical legal work. Some do not have an exact, let alone a sole author, and do not have a definite, formal location. A semi-mythical ancestor or several figures may be competing for this title.

On the other hand, such ideas have many interpreters, including in the academic community. It seems helpful to identify narrow and broad approaches to the term doctrine. In this case, we are talking not only about the scope of the concept of doctrine (more broadly, narrower) but also about authorship, about the place of its creation and location. In a narrow sense, the creators of the doctrine are experts. In a broad sense, they are different people (a relatively wide circle of people, all people who have lived and are still living). A broad approach to understanding doctrine changes the role and significance of this phenomenon in society, putting its essence far beyond academic boundaries.

The theoretical sources of doctrine are evident in identifying the activities of the persons who have created and are creating doctrines. Conventionally, the types of activities can be divided into theoretical and practical. In our questionnaire, theoretical activities include the work of teachers and researchers. They are the most promising for reaching the doctrinal level. This conclusion is based on an analysis of the opinions of experts who believe that researchers (44%) and thinkers (36.3%) have the prospect of ascending to the level of doctrinalism. Experts showed a similar result: researchers 45.2% and thinkers 48.4%. Representatives of practical jurisprudence, represented by politicians and judges, lose by a wide margin to theoreticians. Experts admit that 3.5% of politicians and 2.7% of judges predict success. Experts believe that the contribution of 16.1% to the statistics of doctrinality can be given by politicians and 12.9% by judges. Thus, two surveys showed that judges make up the smallest share of doctrinal sources.

We have compared the opinions of specialists and experts on the possibility of becoming a Persona-Doctrine of each of the listed representatives of different types of activity. The data showed a coincidence in the assessments of the possibility of creating a doctrine by different categories of promising Persona-Doctrine.

Diagram 11. (SSLD 44 - ESPD 13). Comparison Specialist Opinions and Expert Opinions on Likelihood of Doctrine Being Created by Different Groups

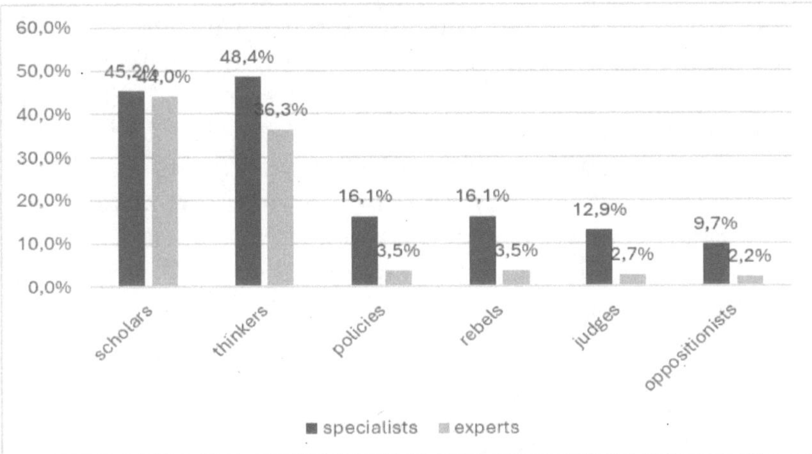

On the basis of sociological surveys, the possibility of thinkers becoming founders of legal doctrine has been investigated. According to 48.4% of specialists and 36.3% of experts, doctrines are "always" created by thinkers and "most often" by 35.5% of specialists and 58% of experts, respectively. Doctrines are "rarely" (6.5% and 4.9%) and "never" created by thinkers (9.7% and 0.9%).

We are aware of the ambiguity of the term "thinker". In this context, we understand *a thinker* to be a person of intellectual pursuits who reflects on the essence of state-legal phenomena, including international law, in writing. This generalizing figure does not reflect the profession, education, occupation, or field. We could associate it with lawyers with academic degrees engaged in academic work. However, we intentionally gave a more multifaceted personality with different interests in law, politics, philosophy, sociology, and other fields. Thinkers may not have academic degrees, which is partially compensated by personal authority, which allows them to communicate their ideas to an indefinite circle of people.

Rebels are persons who actively oppose the official legal conscience. They have an alternative opinion compared to State doctrine and legal policy. They engage in open actions to bring their alternative opinion to the attention of an indefinite circle.

Overall, the opinions of both groups of respondents on the possibility of doctrine being created by rebels are very close. The most excellent convergence of opinions is in the answer options "rarely" and "never". Thus, doctrines are "rarely" created by rebels, according to 54.8% of specialists and 62.8% of experts; "never" is created by rebels – 22.6% of specialists and 19% of experts. The most significant gap in support is for "always" and "most often" answers. Experts support the "always" answer more strongly than experts, indicating they have more hopes for rebels than experts.

Doctrines are "always" created by rebels, according to 16.1% of specialists and 3.5% of experts, and "most often" by 6.5% of specialists and 14.6% of experts, respectively. Thus, most respondents do not see the rebels as promising Persona-Doctrine. They do not see rebels as possible authors of doctrine. Nevertheless, a favorable prognosis for the rebels' doctrinal status was given by 22.6% of specialists and 19% of experts. Rebelliousness, disagreement, and alternativeness can become a growth point for new, different views. The overall intellectual background can stagnate without alternative and perhaps contradictory ideas. Like-mindedness and uniformity do not create prospects for qualitative leaps. The good can be improved, which is a noticeable movement towards stagnation. However, the need for conservatism (uniformity) and innovation differs significantly between doctrines. But in general, the dynamics and innovation align with the legal doctrine.

The antipode of rebels is a person who is loyal to the authorities, the State, and the law. Refusing to trust rebels increases the chance of supporting ideas proposed (developed) by authors acting in sync with State policy and ideology. This is a kind of service and commentary of the legal profession in the service of the State, the ruling elite.

Doctrines are "always" created by the oppositionists, according to 9.7% of specialists and 2.2% of experts, and "most often" by 12.9% of specialists and 14.2% of experts, respectively. The doctrines of "rarely" (51.6% of specialists and 62.8% of experts) and "never" are not created by oppositionists or dissidents (25.8% of specialists and 20.8% of experts).

Of course, it can be assumed that researchers and thinkers by occupation may be oppositionists and rebels regarding political correctness. However, since respondents were not given such diversification, we consider researchers and thinkers to be a category that does not contradict government guidelines. Such figures who are loyal, or at least do not actively contradict the dominant ideology, are more likely to become doctrinal authors than those who are oppositionists and rebels.

The respondents were ambivalent about the possible authorship of doctrine by politicians and judges. "Always" doctrines are created by politicians, according to 16.1% of specialists and 3.5% of experts, and "most often" – 38.7% of specialists and 37.4% of experts, respectively. The doctrines of "rarely" (38.7% of specialists and 50.7% of experts) and "never" are not created by politicians (6.5% of specialists and 8.4% of experts). Generally, the trust connotation of "always" is slightly lower than the negative one. However, experts are more critical in assessing the possibility of politicians creating a doctrine.

Accordingly, the probability of the ideas of politicians being indoctrinated is lower than that of thinkers. Indeed, there is no reason to call modern politicians, including representatives in the chambers of the legislature, doctrinal thinkers. It is noteworthy that experts see the authors of doctrine even less than experts in politicians. It turned out that political power and doctrinality are not related.

Surprisingly, citizens authorize politicians to decide on their vital issues (for example, war and peace) by voting. Nonetheless, it is clear to experts that they cannot think systematically and produce a predictive, well-grounded product. Politicians do not engage in systems thinking, innovation, and methodology. A deficient rating of politicians as possible founders of doctrine is based on Persona-Doctrine opinions, among whom there are many political figures. Former and current legislators and civil servants in senior positions also do not see intellectual power in politicians and more often identify themselves as researchers and researchers.

Doctrines are "always" created by researchers, according to 45.2% of specialists and 44.9% of experts, and "most often" by 48.4% of specialists and 52.4% of experts. Doctrines are "rarely (3.2% and 2.6%) and "never created" by scholars (3.2% and 0%). Thus, according to respondents of the two surveys, the potential probability of scholars acting as the creators of doctrine is much higher than other professional groups.

"Always" doctrines are created by judges in the opinion of 12.9% of specialists and 2.7% of experts, and "most often" by 25.8% of specialists% and 37.2% of experts, respectively. The doctrines of "rarely" (54.8% of specialists and 52.7% of experts) and "never" are not created by judges (6.5% of specialists and 7.5% of experts). In the aggregate of positive and negative perspectives, judges are close to politicians and generally do not see them as active figures of doctrinal creativity. Content analysis of academic texts has shown that judicial doctrine occupies an essential place among the types of doctrines. At the same time, respondents do not see judges as authors of doctrines. Such a comparison of the results of doctrinal studies by different methods (questionnaires and content analysis) allows us to conclude that the respondents do not consider judges to be the authors of judicial doctrines. This conclusion seems to be quite viable. Most often, judicial doctrine refers to works of academic origin cited in court documents openly or latently. Judicial doctrine in the United States is based on legal doctrinal scholarship, theory, and citations from doctrinal writings.

The judicial system is highly politicized in both the United States and Russia. Political pressure may be exerted through the appointment of judges or the election of judges. Both ways of forming the judiciary are political in nature. Casuistic, murky ethical requirements give politicians incredible power over judges. The preceding allows us to see a political component in judicial doctrine. In this regard, references are not academic research, but an embellishment covering the essence of judicial doctrine.

The question of how to qualify judicial citations of academic publications is debatable. It is an academic doctrine in origin and judicial in sanctioning it. In its pure form, there will be doctrines in the form of decrees of the Plenum of the Supreme Court of the Russian Federation. Such documents may have no academic sources and may be created directly by the judiciary. These are official documents without a personified author published under a particular procedure. These examples show that judges are most likely not the authors of judicial doctrines.

From the diagrams presented, it is possible to see a general synchronization of the opinions of specialists and experts about the various authors of doctrine. According to the academic degree of probability of success, in the view of experts, the possible authors are distributed as follows: 1) researchers, 2) thinkers, 3) politicians, 4) rebels, 5) judges, and 6) oppositionists. Specialists build the rating of occupations slightly differently, putting thinkers in the most promising place (48.8% of specialists compared to 36.3% of experts).

Doctrine as Practice (Judicial, Ideological, State)

Doctrine combines theoretical and practical principles. These properties oppose each other, support each other, and create space for each other.

The academic character is often contrasted with the practical orientation, value, and possibility of application in practice. Theory and practice, categories in different forms of interaction and reaction, determine each other. Creative cooperation between theory and practice means that legal doctrine results from the interaction of scholars and practitioners.

The thesis that practice is the criterion of truth seems reliable (at the very least, this applies to doctrinal scholarship). Legal doctrinal scholarship origins are tested by practice. One does not remain on bookshelves, in libraries, and in professional discussions. Scholars' doctrine enters the world of practice in various ways, from consideration in other forms of law to the independent regulation of relations.

Doctrine must be the theoretical basis for practical action. It is possible to identify competition between academic validity and practicality (for example, political). Politicians believe they are inherently empowered to decide all issues based on their understanding. They can make and implement decisions directly. The range of their freedom can be limitless. They will always seek to subordinate legal doctrinal scholarship to their interests.

In search of a balance between theory and practice, we asked respondents an alternative question: "Do you think doctrine results from theory or practice"? It is difficult to argue against the flexible position that doctrine combines theory and practice, which 43% of specialists favored. The choice of their two alternatives showed that most supporters of the dominance of theory in doctrine. According to 16.7%, this is only a theory, 3.5% believe practice dominates, and 6.2% – only practice.

Diagram 12. (SSLD 17). Assessment of Interaction of Theory and Practice in Legal Doctrine (Specialist Opinion)

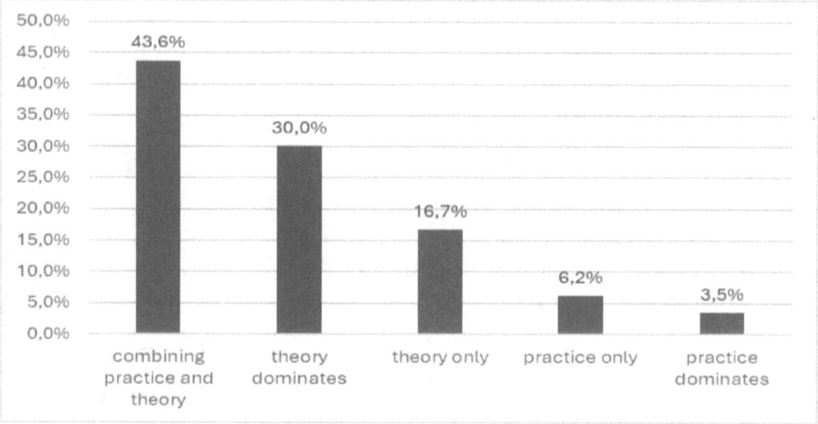

The confrontation between theory and practice is a global problem for many spheres of human activity. Its manifestation probably differs depending on the subject area. In jurisprudence, the distinction between theory and practice can be demonstrated by the term "practicing lawyer". This is a person who gives legal advice and draws up documents of an individual nature for clients. Traditionally, lawyers are not called practicing lawyers. Lawyers are said to have a practice most often understood as an established client base. They represent client interests, consult, and draft documents. Practicing lawyers include judges and other law enforcement officers. This whole body of practitioners is opposed to theorists-researchers and teachers. Researchers should develop new ideas and offer solutions to unresolved problems in legislation. Their works interpret legislation, give academic commentary, and predict the development of law.

In contrast to practice, "ideas" do not exist in the material world. The creators of doctrine create ideas and then impart them in written form. This is the theory of jurisprudence. I would like to see a harmony of theory and practice, which has not been observed in the real world and is not observed now.

The teaching sphere in jurisprudence is even stranger. Professors are neither theorists (researchers) nor practitioners. As a rule, they do not have experience in practical jurisprudence; they are engaged exclusively in teaching the legal profession. Their skills include knowledge of the subject, techniques, and methods of transferring knowledge about jurisprudence to the trained contingent. Some faculty members have academic degrees, probably used to impart research skills to students. Otherwise, academic degrees and research skills are not in demand in teaching. Depending on the level of the education system (bachelor, specialist, magister, postgraduate, and so on), the trainees write independent works in the form of diploma projects and other works. Having research experience will undoubtedly help the teacher. Notably, the presence of experience or status in practical jurisprudence (for example, the status of a lawyer) is not required for teaching legal subjects in the Russian Federation. In modern conditions, the presence of an academic degree is gradually being squeezed out of the qualification requirements for teaching positions.

Our question is addressed to a doctrine that is supposed to be evaluated as the result of theory or practice. However, the relationship with practice or theory differs significantly for legal doctrines. For example, academic doctrine tends toward theory, while judicial doctrine tends toward practice. At the same time, we usually use the term "legal doctrine" as a collective for all kinds of doctrine, which reduces the possibility of understanding the nuances of the discussion.

Proponents of greater practical importance believe that scholars' doctrine is the methodological and legal basis for reforming and improving the effectiveness of legislation. Therefore, the undoubted merit of the doctrine is its close connection between theory and practice, which is why "viable" and "useful" legal postulates for society are formulated.

Cyclical Development of Doctrine (Theory ↔ Practice)

Cyclicity as a mutual transition with conditional repetition within the cycle framework organically fits doctrine. Cyclicity is seen in the possibility of mutual transition of doctrine from one type into another. At the end of the cycle, it is natural to expect to move on to the next cycle. A new cycle may begin with the injection, maturation, or objectification of a new idea, separating the new cycle from the previous ones. It seems that innovation in the real sense of the word is inherent only in academic doctrine. These new ideas result from the work of researchers and have evidence obtained by using reliable tools. If State doctrine accepts a derivative status, it gives legal form to the rules generated by scholars' doctrine. Accordingly, judicial doctrine also applies. It combines the answer to social relations challenges and the solution's academic justification. A part of scholars' doctrine can become part of a new ideology. The content is preserved, but the ideological doctrine's form, style, and connotation are significantly edited. It should be simplified and transformed into theses and positions. In an ideological doctrine, there must be a motivation for the followers, which is irrelevant to a scholar's doctrine. An ideological doctrine should be able to motivate and formulate understandable goal-setting for heterogeneous, numerous groups of followers. The victory of a new, different ideology leads to a reformatting of State ideas and bodies.

A free, independent academic doctrine in a new cycle assimilates new data and develops according to the old formula. The ability of legal scholars to set problems and solve them independently depends on many factors. If the State is the customer of academic research, it already programs the result. The country's political leadership is not interested in free academic research, especially jurisprudence. The State has full, almost divine, power over legislation. In formulating an order for a doctrine, the State simultaneously orders the result.

The relationship between jurisprudence and precedent has not changed in the past twenty years. Overall, the discussion of a hundred years ago continues without definite progress. Judicial practice still does not have a clear legal form. No one knows what is included in judicial practice and where it accumulates. The problem of removing the judiciary from law-making has not been resolved. Consistently, the judiciary introduces less than one percent of legislative initiatives in Russia.[1] The judicial community is satisfied with its elitism. Lifetime judges harass society and the participants in the process. They are entirely invulnerable and have no need for self-development. A system of non-case law recognizing judicial practice as a form of law does not stand the test of pure case law. Ambitious, uncritical, lifelong judges and the closed nature of the system suggest that the fate of case law in its classical form in the Russian Federation is unlikely.

Over the past forty years, the number of laws and regulations adopted in Russia has increased considerably. More than 500 federal laws are passed every year. A new negative external factor has appeared: a quantitative assessment of the effectiveness of the legislative activity of deputies and senators. For various purposes, including their own productivity, legislators introduce bills in large groups of up to half the size of the House. This group form of exercising the right of legislative

[1] SOZD GAS "Zakonotvorchestvo" (available online).

initiative does not make it possible to keep adequate records of the results of the work of deputies.

Even though researchers and legislators are infinitely different, they are united by a typical style of blasphemy of their professional activities with elements of playing with quantitative indicators. For comparison, collective monographs without division of authorship are reflected in each author's profile in the Russian Science Citation Index for each author as one work according to the formula: 1 author – 1 work. Each team member is given one point for citing the book. As a result, when a collective book is cited, each of the authors of the fragments has a quote. For example, if there are 100 authors in a book, then 100 citations will be counted, although the whole book is cited only once. The same is true of legislators and, accordingly, of the statistics of the legislative process. Each legislator from the group of subjects of the right of legislative initiative numbering N receives one point for the draft law in his statistics. In the general statistics, when added together, these are N bills. The solution gives each co-author 1/N of the project, where N is the number of co-authors.

We rejected the definition of doctrine entirely in my 2004 doctoral dissertation because this definition is only partially consistent with scholars' doctrine. Considering that we distinguish four types of doctrine respectively, the definition is correct by one-fourth. Our hypothesis that significant political shifts lead to a decrease in the role of doctrinal forms of law is fully confirmed today. In modern conditions, ideology is becoming the leading form of doctrinal law. Legal nihilism flourishes in the form of non-law. The denial of a right has become the basis of the new legal order. What seemed right and unconditional yesterday was legal. Today, it has become impractical and has been abolished or frozen. An example of uncertainty in the form of a de facto freeze on the publications of Russian researchers in Scopus and Web of Science.

No breakthrough by scholars has been made in eighteen years because descriptive methods still dominate, and there are no powerful tools capable of creating a new original theory. An analysis of the legislator's activities and the results of his work show that they are unrelated to legal scholarship. The legislator knows everything by the fact of his election. The legislature no longer has significant scholars, with a few exceptions. Following the threshold of 30 units of the Hirsch index, it has been established that no single legislator has such indicators. The aggressiveness of the relationship between legal scholarship and the legislature has reached a significant point. Scholars have distanced themselves from this process, which means there is no reason to foresee an increase in the influence of scholars' doctrine on legislation. There are also no streams of influence of the scholars' doctrine on judicial activity. As a result, all forms of law and doctrines are separated, operating in isolation.

Chapter 8
The Subjective Approach and Personal Dimension of the Legal System

We proceeded from the hypothesis that country and language are the basis for the assumption that an author with these characteristics has a presumed type of legal picture identical to a particular legal system of his country. However, this hypothesis may not be supported by specific deviant examples or may be refuted by mass deviations.

Country of residence is essential (30.2%), while 21.7% consider this characteristic subjective. According to respondents, the country the researcher studied in is less critical (14.6%) than the country of residence. 22.1% of experts believe that the legal system is a subjective characteristic and has nothing to do with geography.

The purpose of this question is to identify factors influencing the identification of the legal system. Subjective factors (personality, views of the work's author) or objective factors (geographical boundaries of the type of legal system) are considered. The Questionnaire creates a hypothetical situation of a researcher moving from one country to another with the same or a different legal system. The factors of study and geography (place of birth, place of study, and place of long-term residence) in the life of a researcher in the context of this question may seem far-fetched.

A situation is proposed in which a person in a particular country has received an academic law degree and then moves in another direction. He may have returned to his home country, from which he had temporarily left to study law. Alternatively, he moved to another country after training in the legal profession. In this hypothetical example, the country of residence and the country of instruction belong to different legal systems. A chain of events could be developed, supposing multiple moves between legal systems.

The purpose of these moves may also be research since the researcher uses the method of embedded observation. We assumed that this was not a short-term tourist visit. The time limit should be reasonably long and sufficient for the possible impact of the new legal system on the displaced researcher. Presumably, a period of at least 3 years is considered since the period should be comparable in duration to the study period. Training is singled out as a fundamental stage because the professional legal consciousness of a lawyer and his picture of the world is being formed. Naturally, an educational institution acts based on legislation, following the ideology and traditions of the legal community of this State.

The formation of the individual in his youth before his legal education is undoubtedly essential since, in this period and the following years, the formation and maturing of ordinary legal consciousness occur. Nevertheless, this is a haphazard process that does not imply the purposeful formation of a legal picture of the world following the guidelines of the type of legal system.

Two leading directions are evident in the variants of answers. The first direction is the recognition of the influence of the environment, the objective factors of the distribution of the legal picture of the world of a specific type of legal system. The following answers correspond to this first direction: a) the researcher retains the type of legal system he studied, and b) the researcher acquires the type of legal system of the country of residence. The second direction is the denial of objective external influence, the denial of objective external influence, the denial of the geographical factor, and the recognition of only the subjective factor – the opinion of a particular study. The following options correspond to this direction in the Questionnaire: a) the country of residence does not matter, 2) the country of study does not matter, and 3) the type of legal system is a subjective characteristic unrelated to geography.

The country of residence is where the researcher permanently or predominantly resides. Scholars had never lived outside the country for a long time. He (she) did not receive a systematic education in a country with a different legal system. According to our hypothesis, a person is the bearer of the country's legal system in which he is permanently located. Such identification or marking is automatic. This can happen due to country marking. Alternatively, neither country nor education matters, as this is a subjective understanding that does not change automatically.

The answer option in the questionnaire is that the researcher retains the type of legal system they studied throughout life and focuses on the importance of the country of study of law. Proponents of this opinion proceed from the fact that during the study period, a worldview corresponding to the type of the country's legal system is implanted in the student's mind.

The answer "the type of legal system is a subjective characteristic unrelated to geography" is opposed to all other presented and suggested answers. Following this approach, external factors greatly influence the formation of the researcher's views. Professional consciousness no longer depends on external influences because external factors inevitably cross-pollinate the researcher. This approach, like the others, has its own logic. For example, it makes it possible to understand how the bearers of the views of different legal systems are formulated in different educational institutions in the same country. That is, there is no predetermination that a specific external influence axiologically produces a result. It should also be considered that some respondents do not identify themselves with any legal system, so for them personally, the movement, as it were (the opinion of experts), does not matter.

Diagram 13. (SSLD 86). Impact of Researcher Movements on Identifying Their Affiliation with Legal System (Specialist Opinion)

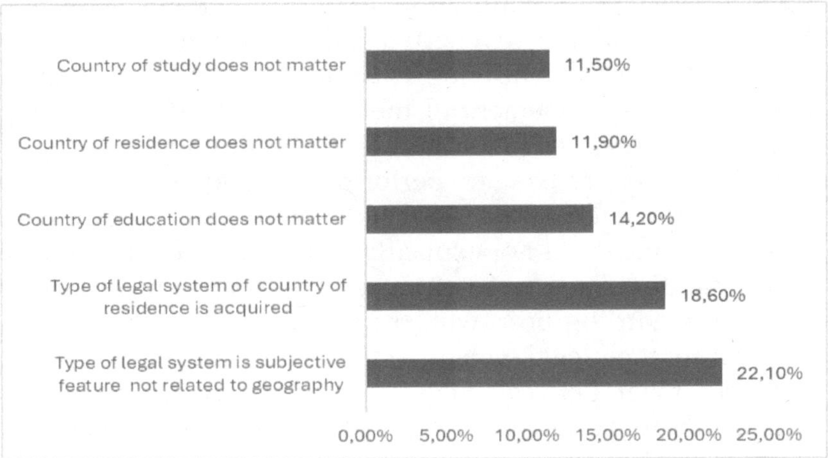

The answers to this question were as follows: 14.2% of specialists recognized the decisive influence of the country of study. 18.6% of specialists unequivocally recognize the country of residence as a decisive factor in forming views. This is a strong influence as a determining factor. In the Questionnaire, the option "may affect" was presented. A combination of confident and influential specialists gives us statistics that follow the same pattern: the country of residence influences more than education. But this difference is not significant. In fact, they have almost the same effect.

The analysis has shown the importance of geographical factors and personal characteristics in understanding and accepting the type of legal system. Accordingly, this instructs researchers who carry out comparative research: it is necessary to clearly declare one's position through self-identification. We have a well-established expectation that Russian legal scholars base their research concept on the ideas of Romano-Germanic law and American jurists on Anglo-American law. According to the hypothesis, they act according to country affiliation and based on geographical factors. However, our sociological research has refuted this hypothesis.

The recognition of the subjective factor as significant, as well as the different self-identifications of the respondents, show that there are grounds for diversity in this matter. In comparative legal research, self-identifying as belonging to the legal system is necessary as an element of methodology. Naturally, being a part of the legal tradition and legal culture, the bearer of a worldview, the researcher performs an evaluative function about other legal systems since he compares each other with his own implicitly, if not explicitly. It is also essential because in comparative legal research, researchers make proposals or forecasts regarding borrowing norms, institutions, and ideas into or from their legal system. At the same time, the movement of a researcher between States with different legal systems for teaching, research, active legal practice, or other personal motives implies the possibility of legal mobility by default. At the same time, long-term residence in a country with a different legal system can impact the researcher, who may even perceive it as his own. This possibility is recognized by 95.1% of specialists. Studying in another country is also an influential factor, according to 93.8% of specialists. The results show that geographical reference to a country and its educational system, and therefore to the type of legal system, together with other factors, affects a person. This is the influence of objective factors that have an external impact on a person.

69% of specialists consider the type of legal system to be a subjective matter of the researcher, which is formed by the researcher. Such respondents deny the influence of the country of residence (70%) and the country of study (73%). Moving from State to State, such motivated and self-organized specialists remain unchanged in their views despite the influence of external circumstances.

Those respondents who consider the factor of the country of study irrelevant assume that a lawyer educated in one type of legal system can integrate into the legal profession in a country with a different legal system. Our experience and observations give a rather negative answer to this question about possible mobility. It is not easy to make such a transition without a long process of retraining and assimilation, including nostrification of documents and additional training.

Theorists who abstract themselves from current legislation have a better chance of successful adaptation. Members of legal professions that are based on unique national legislation have fewer prerequisites for mobility. Accordingly, this observation raises the importance of the personal rather than the geographical factor. What matters is the qualifications and specialty of a particular researcher and adaptive capabilities.

There is a strong view that the system of sources and forms of law in general, and doctrine in particular, depends on the type of legal system. This kind of objective approach predetermines how the legal system determines the system of forms of law. This category appears as transpersonal, not personified. But, works are created by people not tied to the boundaries of the legal system as a geographical division of the world map. Using sociological methods, we tested the hypothesis that the bearers of the type of legal system act according to the typological qualifications of the State in which they are located. In this approach, the type of legal system operates within its geographical boundaries. All people within these geographical boundaries represent this type of legal system. Accordingly, whatever position or opinion they represent, according to the geographical criterion, is part of the general opinion of the legal system about a particular object. The totality of the opinions of all persons within the boundaries of a type of legal system is made up of the content of legal knowledge in that legal system. The status of a doctrine is determined by the type of legal system or vice versa – this is a topic of independent research. In the questionnaire, we proposed to confirm or deny the existence of a relationship between the types of doctrine and the type of legal system in the given feedback force: 1) they are directly related, 2) they are somewhat related, 3) most likely there is no dependence, 4) there is no dependence. We compared the most clearly articulated attitude. According to 33.6% of respondents, the recognized type of doctrine and the type of legal system are directly related.

0.9% of respondents are of the opposite opinion, as they believe there is no dependence. Suppose we add to the respondents with a clear position those whose opinion is not definite but admit such influence. In that case, it turns out that 92.9% of respondents generally recognize (admit) the connection between the understanding of legal doctrine and the dominant legal system. 7.1% of specialists generally deny the interdependence of these concepts. We can assume that the respondents, who recognize the interconnection of the concepts under study, believe that the legal system is an objective given within geographical boundaries. Respondents who do not see this dependence are apparently inclined to believe that the doctrine concept is not predetermined by the type of legal system in which the author finds himself. Primarily, the personal (subjective) factor is influenced.

Let us compare only the definite positions on the connection between the doctrine concept and the legal system type. The conclusion will be as follows: the number of those who admit dependence is higher (92.9%), and the number is lower (7.1%). However, suppose we summarize the categorical and soft answers. In that case, the picture changes: 50% admit, and 40% deny the connection between the doctrine and the type of legal system. The second picture seems more reliable since lawyers avoid extreme assessments. Soft supporters can transform into clear followers of a particular position.

Responses to the question on influence factors were distributed as follows: 73% of specialists recognize the determining influence of the country of study. 95.1% of specialists unequivocally recognize the country of residence as a decisive factor in forming views.

Thus, geographical boundaries are essential in comparative legal studies using the spatio-temporal continuum method.

SECTION III

THE ESSENCE OF LEGAL DOCTRINE

Chapter 9

General Approaches to the Essence of Legal Doctrine

Doctrinal forms of law are diverse, making it difficult to search for features inherent in all or most legal doctrines. Nevertheless, doctrines possess several features that make it possible to distinguish this specific legal phenomenon from similar ones, including other forms of law.

Doctrinal forms of law have several standard features:

1. the doctrine is more stable and conservative than many other forms of law,
2. doctrines do not have a definite form of expression,
3. not all types of forms of law are directly related to the activities of law-making bodies of State power,
4. there is no single center for the emergence, formulation, and maintenance of the doctrine, which makes it difficult to cancel or terminate it,
5. there are no procedures for adopting (publishing) most doctrinal forms. They are created in the absence of prescribed law-making and other procedures. Their emergence, formation, and improvement often occur over a long period and outside specific procedures.
6. doctrines, in some respects, are superior to normative legal acts,
7. their written presentation may not meet the requirements of legislative technique for official legal texts. They may not be structured at all, or their structure is different from the structure of a normative legal act,

8. the vagueness of the content is manifested in the fact that the verbal form of expression of the doctrine does not allow for a uniform determination of its content,
9. doctrines may contradict each other and other forms of law, including normative legal acts,
10. understanding the doctrine requires active intellectual activity from the user. It is up to users to discover this elusive doctrinal right, formalize it for their own purposes, and then draw the appropriate conclusions,
11. the doctrine has a general, universal character on a global, civilizational scale; it may or may not have traditional boundaries, such as a State doctrine.

We asked the survey respondents to evaluate some features of doctrine that we recognize as significant and whether these features are an advantage or a disadvantage.

Diagram 14. (SSLD 19). Properties of Doctrine (Specialist Opinion).

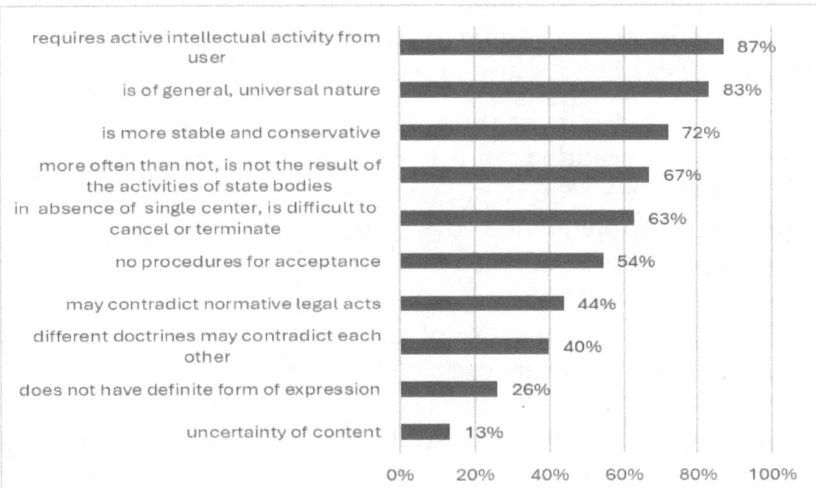

In the opinion of the surveyed specialists, a clearly identified *advantage* of the doctrine is that it "requires active intellectual activity from the user" (87.2%). Other advantages include the following properties: 1) "has a general, universal character"

(83.2%), 2) "it is more stable and conservative" (72.1%), 3) "more often it is not the result of the activities of public authorities" (66.9%), 4) "in the absence of single center, it is difficult to cancel it or stop" (62.8%).

The apparent *shortcomings* of the respondents were: "uncertainty of content" (86.7%), "does not have a definite form of expression" (73.9%), and "different doctrines can contradict each other" (60.2%).

Some properties offered to the respondents were *ambivalent,* that is, there was a minimal difference between positive and negative evaluations. Thus, the ambivalent property is evaluated as an advantage and disadvantage with a close degree of probability. Respondents had reasonable difficulties assessing the property, which "may contradict regulatory legal acts". 52.6% of specialists consider this a disadvantage, and 43.8% an advantage. The development of the same trend fits the respondent answers with an assessment of the doctrine's lack of an acceptance procedure. For 54.4%, it is an advantage; for 45.6%, it is a disadvantage. Indeed, some State doctrines are normative legal acts and have adoption procedures. Academic doctrine does not have any procedure; it results from creativity.

A significant part of the respondents used an open-ended question. They added additional properties to doctrine. We processed these expert suggestions as doctrinal properties proposed (supplemented by respondents). Analysis of the expert proposals confirmed our hypothesis that one and the same property can have negative and positive connotations. Such properties form pairs of properties that may appear to be opposites. However, each element of the pair is perfectly acceptable. Because this study is longitudinal, it will be helpful from a research point of view to conduct a survey on these complemented properties of the same respondents in the next cycle of sociological surveys.

The essence of a doctrine is that most of its properties are their opposite. This dual nature is embodied in dialectical pairs of properties, each of which is, at the same time, the negation and development of each other. For example, flexibility is the opposite of conservatism. However, both properties are characteristic of the doctrine. Each property can be interpreted as both a disadvantage and an advantage. This is dialectics, a mutual transition of opposite properties. Respondents of sociological surveys recognized the following features of the doctrine as essential: 1*) conservatism (stability) and dynamism, 2) State – non-State, and 3) general accessibility – elitism.*

Chapter 10
Properties of the Form of Expression of Doctrine

OBJECTIVE – SUBJECTIVE DOCTRINE HAS BOTH OBJECTIVE AND SUBJECTIVE DIMENSIONS

The subjective dimension of doctrine. A doctrine can be based solely on subjective opinion corresponding to its genesis. Authors have created many types of doctrine alone, naturally reflecting their subjective opinions.

Subjectivism is an extension of individuality. In academic research, it is customary to express the author's opinion on the issue under study. Subjective opinion is the researcher conclusions. However, the researcher position should be founded on the database. A researcher must apply research methods that make his opinion well-grounded and reasoned.

The negative side of subjectivity can create conditions for bias and lack of objectivity. Indeed, doctrine often reflects group interests. The formation of ideological and State doctrines with the direct participation of the leading political group has, as a natural consequence, been expressed in the relevant documents and in the agenda of this particular social group. Another non-State doctrine will be dissident and oppositional if its ideas do not follow in the wake of State ideology, the official State ideological doctrine. Group scholar doctrine may also result from the subjective preferences of research groups.[1] Subjective preferences in the form of "like or dislike" are harmful. They are not so much subjective as anti-academic.

[1] L. A. Alekseeva and A. B. Kasakov, "К вопросу о роли правовой доктрины в правоприменительной деятельности [On the Issue of the Role of Legal Doctrine in Law Enforcement Activities]", Международный журнал конституционного и государственного права [International Journal of Constitutional and State Law], no. 1 (2019), pp. 48-51.

Conjuncture is often referred to as a flaw in legal doctrine. Conjuncture is a form of subjectivism. Here, too, truth and authenticity suffer. Research researchers can act subjectively following a political order. This order can be legislative or unwritten, depending on the capabilities of the political system and the form of political regime of the State. The desire to place this order can be imposed and organic, that is, following the researcher opinion.

Authoritative and well-known researchers in narrow circles can create prerequisites for stagnation precisely through their closed-mindedness behind the scenes. This creates the prerequisites for subjectivism and pseudo-science. Such conservative groups can be formed in academic councils, where dissertations are defended before a group of experienced members who are not in sync with social relations and legislation. They tend to be people with academic careers, do not practice law, or are self-sufficient in the most negative sense. In this case, doctrine may be artificial and pseudo-academic.

Doctrine is indeed subject to the influence of the selfish ambitions of those who have achieved great success. This is subjectivism of non-State origin. Established academic opinion is often complex and challenging to change, whether outdated or wrong. This substitution of obsolete subjective interests for doctrine exhibits subjectivism and leads to stagnation.

Doctrine depends on the authority of its founders, authors, and followers, which is a distinctive form of its subjectivism. But this subjectivism emanates from collective opinion. The movement's founders, the academic school, set the main parameters of their academic results. It is assumed that the group members, as followers of the founder, will develop the doctrine based on his methodology. This is creativity limited by the coordinates set by the founder.

On one hand, this model is advantageous because ideas develop in a single methodological way, with subjective boundaries set by the theory's founder. On the other hand, the restrictions have drawbacks, such as the lack of freedom of creativity. These shortcomings are not an insurmountable obstacle. New ideas not consistent with the subjective approaches of the doctrine's founder can create offshoots or develop into a wholly or relatively autonomous idea, theory, or school.

RELIABILITY – FALSEHOOD

Presumption of certainty. Compared with other forms of law, doctrine is presumed credible based on the academic tools for developing an idea. Credibility is also presumed based on the author's authority. Suppose the author is a judge of the Constitutional Court of the Russian Federation or the Supreme Court of the Russian Federation, or an adviser to the President. In that case, his words are respected solely on this basis. Perhaps this does not preclude these doctrines being substantiated by academic tools. It is likely that the proposals of talented, educated people turn out to be helpful and are acted upon. But this is more a probability than a 100% predictable outcome. However, despite the doubts expressed, there is a presumption of certainty based on authority. In assessing credibility, we must consider the innumerable restrictions imposed by law, corporate and group norms, and self-control. This is no longer the opinion of a particular person, professor, or citizen. This is the opinion of his position.

Attitudes toward doctrines are not stable. Some doctrines questioned contemporary ideas, including State ideas. They struggled for recognition, became dominant, and then were later rejected outright. The presumption of doctrinal certainty is exaggerated and cannot be applied recklessly. This is predetermined by the heterogeneity of works and ideas. Jurisprudence does not have any specific academic tools that guarantee the receipt of a reliable, verifiable result. Studies in the field of jurisprudence are essentially descriptions, at best, interpretations.

The highest achievement of legal doctrine without tools is foresight based on divination, assumption, the expression of an idea slogan, or an idea prediction. All this is done in the absence of calculated mathematical and statistical patterns. In terms of the form of expression, these are words and tools – vision, assumption, and opinion. Thus, doctrinal certainty is an untestable property. "Marx's doctrine is all-powerful because it is true",[2] the famous words of V. I. Lenin. This is an example of ideological taboos. Instead, we can speak of credibility as proven by practice. In the past tense, it is possible to assess the credibility of legal doctrines if they have led to the promised result. However, it is more valuable to offer reasoned foresight that can be tested by a quantifiable toolkit.

Erroneousness. A doctrine may contain erroneous theses, ideas, and propositions. Ideas can be inherently wrong. They may lose their credibility and realism over time. Thus, errors and inaccuracies may be embedded in a doctrine from the beginning or revealed later. An existing doctrine may be re-evaluated from positive to negative or vice versa. This means that the doctrine does not change, but its evaluation does.

Thus, the fallaciousness of a doctrine is highly probable. A doctrine based on subjective observation can quickly become erroneous. It may be mistaken in good faith, which damages public legal consciousness. An author can create a knowingly wrong theory to order or out of his own motivation. Selfish, well-paid ideas are replicated by clients or other beneficiaries. Any change in the researcher's position to the opposite of the actual or intended order provides material for analysis. Now, thirty years later, this has become apparent.

An error may be identified during a subsequent assessment. For example, one expert shared that the idea of an irrevocable deputy mandate, expressed by him in co-authorship with a respected corresponding member of the Russian Academy of Sciences, but it proved to be erroneous. However it was implemented and violated some rights.

The Constitutional Court of the Russian Federation sometimes gives examples of disappointment with its own legal doctrine;

[2] V. I. Lenin, Три источника и три составные части марксизма [Three Sources and Three Component Parts of Marxism], Просвещение [Enlighten-ment] (1913).

for example, it is known that it is looking for an alternative between two possibilities: 1) appointment and 2) election of the heads of the subjects of the Federation – nomination by the legislative body of the subject of the Russian Federation. Rejecting its legal position, the Constitutional Court of the Russian Federation pointed out that "the Russian Federation at each specific stage of the development of its statehood independently adjusts the state and legal mechanism established by it".[3] Accordingly, the previous obsolete provision should be abandoned on the grounds of expediency in the interests of the present day. Thus, the Constitutional Court of the Russian Federation allowed the correction of the fundamental state-legal ideas (to appoint or elect the heads of the subjects of the Russian Federation) at each specific historical stage. In fact, it was not a question of correction, that is, clarification. In fact, a complete revision of the legal provision was introduced. So too the United States Supreme Court has changed its stance, for example, on abortion, educational benefits for the diversity of color, and other issues. Thus, the fallacy can be embedded in a doctrine or in the understanding and interpretation thereof.

ACCESSIBILITY – ELITISM

Universal accessibility is inherent in doctrine in all its

[3] Постановление "По делу о проверке конституционности отдельных положений Конституции Республики Алтай и Федерального закона "Об общих принципах организации законодательных (представительных) и исполнительных органов государственной власти субъектов Российской Федерации" [Decree re: the Case Concerning the Verification of the Constitutionality of Individual Provisions of the Constitution of the Altai Republic and the Federal Law "On the General Principles of the Organization of the Legislative (Representative) and Executive Agencies of State Power of Subjects of the Russian Federation"], No. 10-P (Конституционный Суд Российской Федерации [Constitutional Court of the Russian Federation] 7 June 2000); Постановление "По делу о проверке конституционности отдельных положений Федерального закона 'Об общих принципах организации законодательных (представительных) и исполнительных органов государственной власти субъектов Российской Федерации' в связи с жалобами ряда граждан" [Decree "Re the Case of Verification of the Constitutionality of Individual Provisions of the Federal Law 'On the General Principles of the Organization of Legislative (Representative) and Executive Bodies of State Power of the Subjects of the Russian Federation' in Connection with the Complaints of a Number of Citizens", No. 13-P (Конституционный Суд Российской Федерации [Constitutional Court of the Russian Federation] 21 December 2005).

manifestations in a certain sense. The general accessibility of a doctrine consists in the openness of its external forms of expression, which differ depending on the type of legal doctrine. The general availability of official State legal doctrine is ensured by the official publication of legal acts. Ideological sources reach their potential users by different means. They become a mass ideology thanks to active propaganda. In general, these methods apply to other types of legal doctrine, which is confirmed by sociological research.

However, we cannot expect all types of legal doctrine to be universally accessible. The general availability of academic research is ensured by its publication, requirement of the legal copy, and other mechanisms for preserving and ensuring the availability of intellectual achievements. Dissertations are available to the public. There are many mechanisms for ensuring the general availability of electronic versions of academic publications, including DOI. Libraries provide access to paper and electronic publications. Obstacles may arise because some resources are available only on a paid basis. However, this is overcome in public or specialized libraries, corporate access, and other tools.

The accessibility of doctrinal sources should be distinguished from the accessibility to be understood. The simplest to understand are the rules of conduct that contain models of actions (or failure to act). Law in the form of legislation is addressed to the subjects of law. Their most prominent group is people, individuals, and citizens. Legislation should be understandable by these actors. The above also applies to ideological State doctrine, which takes the form of legal acts.

The complexity of legislation is justifiably criticized by almost everyone. However, the more general the prescriptions, the less easily they can be understood. In terms of the style of presentation and, accordingly, accessibility, judicial doctrine is close to State doctrine. Its peculiarity lies in the fact that the most likely readers of this type of document will be professional lawyers. A doctrine of this type is difficult to understand without special education.

Still further from the standards of obligatory understanding are ideological and scholar doctrines. Ideological doctrine has an accessible version for promotion and propaganda. Its sources can be multi-volume political, philosophical, and economic works. Marx's "Capital" was read by a select few, and the majority of the citizens of the USSR considered themselves followers, along with many people worldwide. Sixty years later, the masses who supported Marxism abandoned it without ever becoming acquainted with the original source. The version of Marx's outstanding political and economic theory, processed for mass consciousness, was propaganda. However, primary sources are available in almost any library. However, the linguistic complexity, the author's high professionalism, human laziness, and other obstacles make the Work inaccessible to the mass consumer.

In its organic form, academic doctrine is not accessible to everyone; it is accessible to a select few. It does not have a particular simplified version. However, in this kind of doctrine, the interaction of accessibility and elitism is apparent.

Elitism. Doctrine has a specific style of external expression, presentation style, objectification, and a special contingent of creators and consumption subjects. However, it is not always accessible to understanding and is often abstract. Some types of doctrine are characterized by excessive theorizing, detachment from legal and social practice, and armchair character, contributing to the closedness of law to society and indifference to ordinary legal consciousness. These elements can be combined under the single name of elitism.

In the questionnaire, the respondents were asked to assess the attribute of the legal doctrine – that "requires active intellectual activity from users". 87.2% of specialists considered it a virtue of legal doctrine, the highest indicator of support for the doctrine feature. We combined the answers to this question with respondent suggestions from the open-ended question. As a result, active intellectual activity was transformed into elitism and inaccessibility. Respondents must support two opposite properties: accessibility and elitism. Active intellectual activity will be a positive fact if a person is looking for such an occupation. He is interested, educated, and optimistic. For all other users, this requirement will be redundant.

Scholar doctrine has an original style of presentation. It can be abstract and even figurative compared to other types. Academic doctrine can be descriptive, debatable, interrogative, and even exclamatory. Moreover, genuine academic research such as a monograph or doctoral dissertation is understandable only to specialists with high research qualifications.

For legislation, there are requirements of style which should ensure clarity of the law. However, even at the level of laws, this cannot be ensured. The higher a document is in the hierarchy of normative legal acts, the more general it is (for example, a constitution). It abstracts from behavior and moves on to ideas, such as principles and other generalizations. The lower the position of the document in the hierarchy system, the more precise it will be in content. As scholars move down the hierarchy, the specificity of normative texts and the level of detail increase. Such documents as, for example, an instruction, are designed to provide step-by-step guidance for the executor's actions, who does not necessarily have a legal education.

It is difficult to assess the level in the system of legislation where the norms that regulate mass behavior are located. Such acts must be composed clearly for all citizens. We conditionally put a marker for a mandatory, understandable form of presentation at the level of federal laws. Codes deserve special attention, as they have a significant impact on citizens. For example, the Criminal Code should clearly explain to citizens what must be done, what may be done, and what cannot. Accessibility requirements relate to the structure of the document, its style, and its content. Everything should be directed toward an unambiguous understanding by all those to whom the criminal law affects.

Applying this reasoning about accessibility to scholar doctrine, we argue that the level of complexity of the textbook (manual) is not addressed to citizens. Educational literature is cognitive and has a uniform and predictable structure. As a rule, the textbook does not contain discussions and original (subjective) views of the author. For an advanced educational level, the textbook titles include the words "problem" or "topical problems", being intended for people without a legal education, which means that a potential textbook reader is someone with a secondary education interested in law. Such printed material seems to be a legitimate point of reference for the level of everyday legal consciousness.

However, textbooks are not scholar doctrine. They are not a study, not an original study, of a topical issue of jurisprudence. That is why publications that claim to be academic, based only on textbooks, are criticized. Academic publications must correspond to the professional level of legal creation.

Ascending the hierarchy of types of publications, there are articles, dissertations, and monographs. In this context, articles can be considered an element of scholar doctrine if they result from the research. Descriptive commentary articles are not academic.

In the questionnaire for experts, we asked about the age and academic status of t hose who produce the most significant academic research. It was ascertained that the main result that can become a doctrine is a monograph or a doctoral dissertation. Based on this determination, scholar doctrine, as a rule, is created by the Doctor of Sciences in monographic literary forms based on creative research initiatives.

Scholar doctrine does not aspire to be simple and easily understood. Accordingly, elitism and the inaccessibility of scholar doctrine obviously exist, and there is no tool to cope with them. This is an organic aspect of this type of legal doctrine. Indeed, the sources of the doctrine lie in academic activity, and its bearer is an educated, creative person with an original creative mind.

The elitism of doctrine is confirmed by a sociological survey. It has been established that active intellectual activity is necessary to establish, clarify, and implement the doctrine as a form of law. 87.2% of specialists positively assess that searching for and understanding the creation of doctrine "requires active intellectual activity from the user". A high level of user intellectual activity is a prerequisite for the discovery and establishment of the content of doctrine. These efforts are several times higher than the labor costs of working with the texts of normative legal acts. For example, scholars can read the provision of the Constitution of the Russian Federation on the separation of powers. In this case, the user extracts the meaning from the normative legal act, which is set out as clearly as possible. One can turn to primary sources, such as Charles de Montesquieu (1689-1755) and J. S. Smith, to understand the separation of powers or John Locke (1632-1704). However, in the vague expressions of philosophers and other non-juridical works, it is not easy to ascertain the formal content of the principle of separation of powers. Legislation and scholarly publications have different styles and lengths (in this example, one article in the Constitution compared to thousands of pages of reasoning) and other differences.

The elitism of a doctrine is a natural continuation of its creator, its bearer. Doctrine does not try to be understandable by different social groups with different educational levels. It is sublime, unattainable, and magnificent precisely in its elitism. The bearers of legal doctrine have little interest in cooperating with the bearers of the ordinary legal consciousness. Even professional legal consciousness cannot stand on par or claim to be understood at the same level as doctrinal legal consciousness. As sociological research has shown, doctrinal status is often associated with a specific position of the author in the social hierarchy. Often, this status of the Persona-Doctrine is combined with prestigious positions and high material well-being. In any stratified, let alone class, society, elitism is an element of status, of belonging to a specific social group. Legal doctrine has a general elitism and a special legal one. The second is that legal language differs from ordinary language. Learning and accepting this language is possible only during an extended, expensive legal education.

Within the private international law framework, foreign family law may become part of national family law. Following Article 166 of the Family Code of the Russian Federation, the courts of the Russian Federation or civil status authorities must possess the skills to apply official interpretations, practice of application, and doctrine in the relevant foreign State.[4] These qualification requirements, unjustifiably inflated by the law, are (veiled, not directly) addressed to judges and civil servants who do not possess such skills. These requirements are not included in their qualifications and administrative regulations.

The Family Code of the Russian Federation recommends implementing this atypical law enforcement. It can involve experts and apply for comments from other state authorities. The situation is generally complex and clearly beyond the qualifications of persons charged with the duty to correctly establish, interpret, and apply foreign legal doctrine.

An additional difficulty arises from the diversity of doctrine. Regarding foreign doctrine, it is more challenging to determine which is sufficiently authoritative and admissibly applicable. Deciding on the official State doctrine and how to bring it to an indefinite circle of people is difficult for domestic sources to make. It is much more challenging to decide about a foreign legal doctrine written in another language in an innumerable unstructured number of sources. This problem of diversity of doctrine and different languages exists for any doctrine. However, only in family law is it placed on par with other forms of law, including legislation. The implementation of accessibility is complex for the doctrines of foreign States. Obstacles are at least linguistic and organizational.

Elitism can be understood as a high level of theorization of a textual object. A high level of generalization is inherent in legal doctrine, an organic property. However, theorization must be well-grounded, academic, have research tools, and produce verifiable results. Contrived theorizing of armchair origin, unrelated to legal and social practice, is detrimental to doctrine.

[4] See W. E. Butler, *Russian Family Law* (2015), pp. 289-208

Such groundless abstract scholarship empty in content does not lead to authoritative and, most importantly, practical academic publications.

According to one respondent, academic doctrine is a rare diamond in an endless series of non-academic rubbish. Another survey respondent said the scholar doctrine is "a hard-to-reach mineral". Respondents also spoke about the intellectual impotence of modern scholarship. Indeed, the convergence of term papers and candidate dissertations by lowering the latter's quality does not create prerequisites for forming imaginative legal theory.

Linguistic elitism results in the doctrine being misunderstood by untrained users. A subject with an ordinary level of legal consciousness cannot understand doctrinal law and, as a result, cannot embody it in his own behavior. Professional interpretation occupies a middle position between doctrinal and ordinary legal consciousness.

An extreme form of confrontation between doctrines and ordinary legal consciousness is the rejection of everything academic as too complicated, lifeless, and useless. Mass misunderstanding of doctrinal forms alienates citizens from this form of law, which leads to legal nihilism. A kind of indirect result, a side effect, is a dislike of the bearers of the academic doctrine – the researcher. An ambiguous relationship develops between professional and doctrinal legal consciousness. Professional legal consciousness belongs to people with legal education. The elitism of academic doctrine does not correspond to the level of understanding of the bearers of professional consciousness. And, of course, ordinary legal consciousness cannot understand academic doctrine.

UNCERTAINTY – FORMAL CERTAINTY

The vagueness of the content is manifested in the fact that the verbal form of expression of the doctrine does not allow for a uniform determination of its content. This feature of legal doctrine is the leading shortcoming in the opinion of the respondents of the sociological survey. This negative opinion is shared by 86.7% of specialists. A few survey participants (13.3%) consider this property an advantage. Here is an example from other textual matters: the difficulty of comparing a poem and an instruction for television is not apparent. It may be expedient to compare the text of a scholar doctrine with a normative act. In case of uncertainty of the content of the Doctrine, it is not uncommon to abuse the application of the Doctrine for purposes both contrary to current legislation and aimed at actions contrary to the results of the application of the Doctrine intended by the author(s) of the Doctrine.

The content vagueness has many manifestations: insufficient formalization, lack of clear criteria and requirements for the doctrine, ambiguity, abstract or superficial nature, lack of a specific addressee, and room for interpretation and interpretation (except judicial doctrine). This is facilitated by the lack of legislative consolidation of most doctrines. Unclear limits of doctrinal interpretation are challenging to establish, which can lead to an expansion of the discretion of the law enforcer in each specific situation.

Formal certainty. Doctrine contributes to the legal certainty of social relations, the formation and development of a legal glossary, legal technique, and general legal principles. In addition, doctrine helps ensure the uniformity of legal activity and structures the legal sphere.

SINGULAR AND TYPICAL

The second most supported feature of doctrine was its general character, its universal character. 82.2% of experts consider this feature a virtue of doctrine. Indeed, doctrine is the most generalized, typified, and abstract compared to most forms of law. It may be supposed that some customs and religious regulators may surpass doctrine in the degree of abstraction of their precepts. In additional personal interpretations of the properties of doctrine, specialists in open-ended questions, along with the general, universal character, emphasized typification as a path from the singular to the multiple, the repeatable, the general, the typical, and the universal. The one and the plural are the endpoints that mark the ends of a line: the beginning and the end. Accordingly, the singularity of the source of the legal doctrine, or rather its basis on a separate case, is perceived as a drawback. The opposite of singularity, diversity, is evaluated positively.

Typification is a complex thought process that requires high professional qualifications, skills, and abilities. Accordingly, it is inexpedient to disperse the qualification (most often expert) forces into isolated cases without repetition. Typification connects the singular and the plural. This term is often used in legal language within the framework of the theory of law-making, legal formation, norms of law, forms of law, and so on, as well as typification in distinguishing types of an object, such as legal understanding, legal system, and states. Although we need not explain this vocabulary for this study, it is essential to define the meaning of "type" and, accordingly, the "typification" of the object we are studying.

Doctrine creates rules for the future and foresees and forecasts the development of law. Doctrine can set new goals not provided for in political and normative acts, thus changing the political and legal situation. It has a programmatic character and puts forward ideas for the future. Typification is mental activity in which, analyzing a large amount of data about an object(s), its repetitive properties are revealed.

However, typification can also be carried out in single or a few cases if there is reason to assume this is the first or early case out of a predicted or foreseen set. This logical technique is called synthesis. Typification without the possibility of applying to similar cases in the future has no practical value. In jurisprudence, the singular is usually irrelevant and too costly. However, there are cases of single regulation, such as laws in Russia on the Sochi Olympics. The United States has official private laws, such as those on a state reserve. As a rule, the singular is not typed. But there are exceptions. For example, a judicial precedent is an isolated case. This is the nature of the precedent, its organic property. In a court decision, precedent as a form of law consists of a model, analysis, and decision-making method. Such a combination can be called typical in the singular.

Typification is a meaningful way of forming a doctrine. It is typical in that it is the result of generalization and abstraction. On one hand, doctrine in the future will be a measure, a type, for the subsequent relations that will arise based on the doctrine. However, doctrine is significantly different from other forms of law. Certain forms of law arise from one specific source; for example, normative legal acts are adopted by legislative or executive authorities, and judicial precedents are adopted by the judiciary.

On the other hand, doctrine has multiple sources of origin, and sometimes maintains a fixed relationship with its pre-source or merges with it in such a way that it is difficult to distinguish between the two. However, there are differences. Consider the correlation between judicial precedent and judicial doctrine. A precedent is a specific case referred to in the future by courts considering similar cases. Suppose there are several cases. In that event, there will be many repetitions. Each situation in the pattern has unique elements. Accordingly, the consideration of cases with some diverse elements based on the initial precedent is clarified and expanded to cover all the diversity that has been identified. This is typification in the form of identifying and assimilating significant elements in their repetitive variety.

Courts may refer to one specific case or a set of cases, indicating each. Nonetheless, the expression "following the doctrine" is fixed.[5] However, references to cases typed in doctrine may remain in parentheses for some time. In the future, due to multiple repetitions, there is a high probability that the reference to the original cases will disappear. Most likely, only the name of the doctrine will be used; often, it is unrelated to previous cases in a generalized anonymized form.

[5] R. Barrick, "The Ministerial Exception: Seeking Clarity and Precision Amid Inconsistent Application of the Hosanna-Tabor Framework", *Emory Law Journal*, LXX (2020), pp. 465-519.

For example, in the United States, the case of *EEOC v. Hosanna-Tabor Evangelical Lutheran Church* considered the dismissal of a teacher from a religious school.[6] The legal basis was the First Amendment to the United States Constitution. Subsequently, several cases were heard concerning this matter, which later became part of the judicial doctrine known as the "ministerial exception".[7] This expression captures the subject-matter of the claim, the name of the participant, or some event in a memorable form. For example, "Rico" is a figurative name for organized crime cases. "Megan", "Lemon", and other well-known names have stuck to a whole class of cases.

"Ministerial Exception" legalized a simplified procedure for dismissing employees from religious organizations if their activities are related to religious ceremonies. Religious organizations based their position on the principle of freedom of worship, religion, and non-interference of the State in the activities of religious organizations. This leads to the conclusion that the state secular court cannot accept and consider the claims of employees of religious organizations. As a result, labor laws do not apply to employees of religious organizations because their rights cannot be defended in state courts. In this generalized form, the courts have repeatedly applied this typified conclusion from the Hosanna-Tabor Evangelical Lutheran Church case. It has created the doctrine of "ministerial exclusion".

Judicial doctrine in the Russian Federation is more often enshrined in generalizing documents. However, the courts have created rules that were not in the legislation. This may be an expansive interpretation or even an interpretation outside the norm. In fact, it is an add-on. These new judicial norms have not been developed or tested. Indeed, the decrees of the Plenum of the Supreme Court of the Russian Federation never indicate

[6] Hosanna-Tabor Evangelical Lutheran Church and School v. EEOC, 565 U.S. 171 (2012) (N.J. Supreme Court 2012).

[7] W. C. Duncan, "Colorado Religious School Asks Supreme Court to Take Case on Ministerial Exception", *Sutherland Institute* (blog), 16 March 2023 (available online).

in which cases the generalization was made. In fact, this is the direct law-making by the courts, the results of which are not called normative legal acts.

But it does not matter what this is called. This must be a new right of judicial origin, not provided for in normative legal acts. As a rule, the reasons for its adoption are the expedient abuse of gaps in legislation. The court issues rules for the case and applies them itself. The peculiarity of this model in Russia is that the legislation does not allow these rules to be challenged. It is possible to challenge most normative legal acts, but it is not possible to challenge the decision of the Plenum of the Supreme Court of the Russian Federation. In fact, this document cannot be appealed within the judicial system by appeal or cassation. It is possible to appeal against documents issued by the courts in specific cases in accordance with procedural legislation. However, it is impossible to challenge the generalizing documents of the judiciary in court, such as, for example, decrees of plenums and reviews of judicial practice. It is an entirely invulnerable form created by the highest judicial body.

Whether this decree of the Plenum of the Supreme Court of the Russian Federation is a form of law remains relevant. More likely, no than yes. But if it contains a right that is then applied by the courts, it is a form of law. It can be called a judicial doctrine, or it can be called a legal provision. Legal status is given to ideas formulated by the court based on legislation as an idea and not on a specific rule. This is abstract reasoning about the meaning of law and the purpose of legal regulation. Although it does not contain an explicit rule, its strength lies in this vagueness and uncertainty. It can be applied as a principle to various situations. But it cannot be asserted that these situations are resolved directly based on a legal provision without legal norms. Nonetheless, specific ideas, principles, and rules are moving from the individual to the general in the Russian judicial system. Typified forms are doctrine.

Doctrine can be assessed as uniform and as diverse. Combining the individual and the collective consists of doctrine formed by many individual and group subjects. It crystallizes in academic disputes and discussions. Along the way, the idea gains support, which enhances its authority. As a result, legal doctrine can be positioned as a collective result.

"Singular" and "plural" with respect to doctrine can be understood as "single author" – "plurality of authors". The author can come from a single object or from many objects. The singular can be interpreted as subjective, self-centered, and insignificant to doctrine. Fallibility can also be regarded because of the subjective, the singular.

Proponents of the position of movement from the individual to the general believe that a doctrine arises from a single episode (an academic discovery belonging to a single author). In support of this position, we may note that doctrine is often based on the idea of a particular individual. Sometimes we can implement or act upon it, sometimes we cannot.

A doctrine may relate to one specific legal phenomenon. Perhaps it will be interpreted and applied more broadly in the future. However, at the stage of its creation, such a broad understanding was not foreseen. The singular transformation into the plural shows that the author has found or created a single but typical object.

A distinction should be made between the number of authors of a legal doctrine. Consequently, a doctrine can be created individually or by a group of creators. According to the degree of individualization of the author(s), legal doctrine is divided into personified and non-personified.

Sole authorship is sometimes clearly established; proven authorship takes place. A sole or personified doctrine may be created by an eminent, well-known, authoritative person, whom we call the Persona-Doctrine, the doctrine founder. At the same time, it can be considered a general non-personalized achievement over time, considering the spread of the doctrine. The more acknowledged, obvious, and axiomatic a doctrine becomes, the more plural and general it becomes. As a result, the doctrine belongs to the country or even the whole world and not just to its author.

Various opinions can have different manifestations: 1) a multitude of phenomena and different sources of the same content, 2) a multitude of different, including contradictory, opinions from different sources, and 3) a multitude of opinions of different content from one source. All these forms of diversity are represented in legal doctrines.

Doctrinal diversity must be overcome, as application requires an unambiguous choice from various sources. Vague criteria such as authority, dominance, and other excellent but useless guidelines exist. The authority and power of one researcher over another are associated with an attempt to build a hierarchy of doctrines by analogy with the ordering and systematization of normative legal acts. For doctrines, however, the foundations of the hierarchy are irrational, incalculable, and evaluative. We do not have straightforward tools for verifying doctrines in their hierarchical organization. In this study, we tested the admissibility of applying scientometric indicators to doctrine.

The citation hierarchy of cases is being tested for the judicial system. Thus, the Chairman of the Board of Directors of "Garant", D. V. Persheev, in a speech at the VII All-Russian Legal Forum on 20 September 2023, said that about 10% of court decisions contain such references. The decisions of the Constitutional Court of the Russian Federation are most often referred to, followed by the Supreme Court of the Russian Federation. The third place is occupied by the Supreme Arbitrazh Court of the Russian Federation, which was abolished in 2014. In the GARANT system, such court decisions are noted if they are mentioned in more than a hundred other judicial acts. The leader in terms of citation is the Ruling of the Constitutional Court of the Russian Federation of 21 December 2000, No. 263-O, referred to in more than 290,000 court decisions. The top 500 includes decisions of higher instances, but there are also decisions of lower instances. For example, 438th place was taken by a decision of the Federal Arbitrazh Court of the Volga Region. It is mentioned in more than 4,000 judicial acts. A decision of the Federal Arbitrazh Court of the Moscow District was cited in 1,800 rulings of arbitrazh courts.

Proponents of the plurality of sources of doctrine (as if scattered co-authorship) believe that the doctrine is multifaceted, not constrained by the framework of the opinion or idea of one author. Multiplicity, creative cooperation in working on a common idea, and other descriptions of a non-single-handedly created legal doctrine are essential. These can be academic schools, labor and creative collectives, and other forms of organization of joint creativity. Purposeful, deliberate cooperation with an organizational structure (for example, an academic institution) may be a platform for joint work on legal doctrine.

General work on the idea can also be done outside the official organizational forms. Moreover, a doctrine can be created by the collective efforts of people who have lived at different times, have never crossed paths, have never known each other, and have never experienced any unity, much less deliberately organized a collective. It is possible that many years later, other researchers, because of the analysis of their absolutely individual creativity, united into a group of like-minded people. Researchers have combined their works (ideas) into a single puzzle. They formed a common doctrine (a kind of diffuse cooperation). For example, a collective of founders, continuers, and supporters of normativism clearly demonstrates the possibility of diffuse cooperation. These groups lived in different times and countries and may not have known each other personally.

These individuals were unified into a group by followers and researchers of types of legal understanding. They typified them, united them into a group of like-minded people, and the ideas from different works made up a doctrine.

Research teams can be represented by schools, universities, law faculties, groups, corporations, and a professional community of lawyers. A reference to a group of authors who are part of the legal profession may describe a doctrine as the result of the work of scholars, judges, and lawyers. It is a form of diversity.

Multiplicity can be emphasized by the fact that a doctrine is not the subjective opinion of an individual researcher. A doctrine can be the result of a consolidated opinion, which is emphasized by the following verbal expressions: "established", "well-known", "stable", "dominant", "united", "universal", and other epithets of collectivity. It is not collective, like the sum of the opinions of the members. It is an established opinion, an idea, a concept.

Only those provisions of a doctrine that have multiple (if not universal) support can perform an actual normative function. If we consider a doctrine as a source of law, then it can be singular authorial. If doctrine is regarded as a form of law, it needs multiple support and typified content. The universal, generalizing character of doctrine correlates with multiplicity.

Some provisions of legal doctrine can be interpreted in multiple ways, reducing the specificity level. This is another form of diversity: multiple interpretations or ambiguity of position. However, laws are also understood and applied in different ways. This variety of interpretations generally does not abolish the legislation or its application.

In the Questionnaire, a question was formulated to study the relationship between the individual and the collective in creating doctrine. We added a time factor to the quantitative factor: if it is a group of authors, they are contemporaries, figures of the same period, or figures of different times who worked at different times but in the same thematic area. The quantitative approach contains the possibility of creating a doctrine individually or collectively.

Naturally, the concentration of like-minded people and the place of work may not coincide. However, if they do not correlate, this may indicate disharmony: the researcher does not have like-minded people in his work collective. A way out can be found by searching for associates outside the organization (workplace) or individual creativity. At the same time, it should be noted that the absence of like-minded people in the organization indicates the unfavorable state of the team, especially if the organization has a dissertation council, educates its graduate and doctoral students, and claims to form an academic school.

Diagram 15. (SSLD 2). Possible doctrine authors (Specialist Opinion)

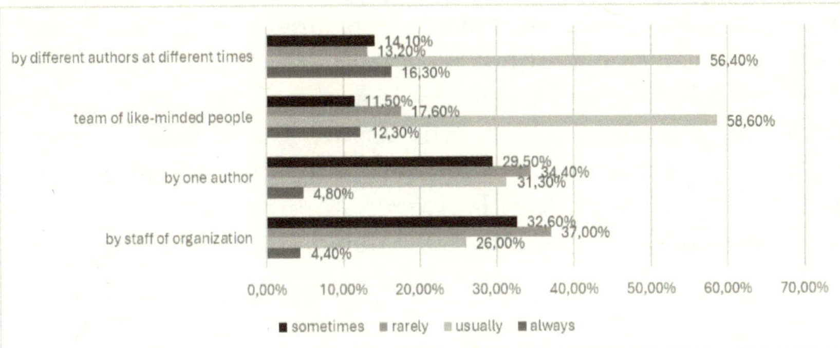

The survey showed that specialists prioritize collective forms of doctrine creation. Doctrines are "always created by one author", according to 4.8% of specialists. The level of trust among the teams of organizations is even lower – 4.4% of specialists see this team as the place where the doctrine was created.

Doctrine is an organizational unity of authors who have the same views, concepts, and ideas and develop them in a specific direction in the form of an academic school. In the opinion of 12.3% of specialists, a team of contemporaries working together could provide a doctrinal product. A dispersed group of contemporaries is more promising –16.3 %.

With the enlargement of answers, the priority of collective forms of creativity within the framework of a voluntary academic "collective" increases. A team of like-minded people was supported by 58.6%, and the possibility of creation by different authors at different times was supported by 72.7%.

The diversity of authors' opinions is often emphasized as a virtue of doctrine. This property is an organic continuation of its academic origin. Academic freedom is a prerequisite for the independent creativity of researchers. As a result, opposing ideas claim the status of doctrine, and each may be true. For example, in the academic sphere, ideas that justify democratic and tyrannical ideas are expressed. Researchers can justify public and private ownership and theological or atheistic States. Creative freedom goes a long way in creating doctrine. The principle of pluralism of opinion results in various forms of expression. A deliberative environment is a prerequisite for free discussion without regard to criticism or censorship. It is possible to give this property a name – an academic and debatable nature – which will ensure that the diversity of opinions is considered while preserving the individual ideas and beliefs of the author. However, "multiplicity" can have a negative connotation as quasi-debatable, controversial theories.

Thus, a doctrine can arise from a single fact and a collective one.

UNIVERSALITY – LOCALITY

Universality is an organic property of doctrine. Its authority and effectiveness are based on its general recognition. Universality means the acceptance of doctrinal ideas by leading jurists and public consciousness as an imperative for establishing order in social life. The degree of dissemination, recognition, and prominence geographically or prolifically may be blurred. Worldwide, a group of States, one State, and other shrinking borders are well-known.

General recognition can have a global, universal character, that is, be recognized by everyone. On the other hand, the reduction of a loyal group can go down to one person.

Universality is the operative part resulting from broad popularity and axiomaticity. Beyond the original work, the doctrine gains acceptance among an indefinite number of people. Universality is directly related to the practical side of the doctrine. The authority of some doctrines is so great that it cannot be revised. This is especially evident for religious doctrines, but is beyond the scope of this study. The term "universal" also demonstrates the broadest possible distribution of the doctrine territorially, organizationally, and personally.

The antipode of universality is localism. It means a limited operation of doctrine, which is also the case. Limitations can be subjective (depending on the author or the group of supporters). This means that a group of subjects or persons create a doctrine. A doctrine can be known, appreciated, and accepted by a group. However, depending on the type of doctrine, the ratio of common knowledge and localism may differ significantly. State doctrines are presumed to be well-known as any legal act. Non-state ideological and academic doctrines can be well-known as well as local. Judicial doctrine tends to be a State doctrine, with some significant differences from it. Documents from the judicial system are partially publicly available, such as the decrees of the Plenum of the Supreme Court of the Russian Federation. Other documents of doctrinal significance, such as reviews, are not published in official sources. Often they can be found in electronic legal reference systems, the entrance to which is not free of charge. These documents are also available on the website of the Supreme Court of the Russian Federation.

Chapter 11
Procedural Properties of Doctrine

PROCEDURAL – ABSENCE OF PROCEDURES

Procedurality. Because of the diversity of the doctrine concept, it is impossible to speak unequivocally about the presence or absence of procedure with respect to all types of doctrine simultaneously. State ideological doctrine is characterized by the presence of a procedure for adoption, which is known as "law-making". Judicial doctrine arises from various procedures, such as rulings, reviews, and decisions on specific cases. However, legislation does not regulate the transformation of a specific law enforcement document in judicial practice. The law only states the result – to recognize the admissibility of arguing a court decision by some act of the judiciary.

Academic and ideological (non-State) doctrines are created without prescribed law-making and other procedures. Their emergence, formation, and improvement often occur over a long period and outside specific procedures. They have a long process of formation and recognition.

The peculiarity of doctrine (except State doctrine) lies the complex or impossible procedure for its amendment, repeal, or replacement. This is true for many doctrines unless legislation embodies the doctrinal idea. The exception is the ideological State (official) doctrine, a legal act issued by an agency of State power. Such a doctrine does not contain norms or rules of conduct but gives general ideas of behavior in some way. Following the position of the Constitutional Court of the Russian Federation, we do not consider these documents to be normative legal acts. They are legal acts because of their origin. Such documents are easy to change, repeal, and replace, which has been done many times. This simplicity is due to the fact that this activity has a regulated procedure. It is a single document issued by a specific body. Accordingly, this body has full authority over such a document within the framework of its creative activity. These documents are unrelated to legal science or judicial practice. Doctrinal State documents are autonomous.

Other types of doctrine may be found in different sources. Their creation, repeal, and amendment are not regulated by normative enactments and do not have any procedural forms. They cannot be changed by any action from a particular center. However, the methods of their repeal are periodically applied in the form of censorship. It can be a ban on certain books, some authors, or an ideology of a specific content. This prohibition may be officially imposed by public authorities. There may be latent prohibitions in the form of State support for a specific or opposing doctrine at the State level. A view, an idea, or a thesis may not be welcome. An element or the entirety of doctrine can be fundamentally replaced. It is also possible that a doctrine loses its relevance, a well-reasoned criticism of the doctrine, and the academic community voluntarily renounces it.

In a sociological survey, we formulated a particular question to clarify the issue of the actual withering away of a doctrine or the generally recognized denial of a doctrine. If a doctrine has been refuted over time, today it (1) continues to be a doctrine, (2) has somewhat lost its status, (3) may retain its status, or (4) is no longer a doctrine.

Diagram 16. (SSLD 43). Status of Refuted Doctrine (Specialist Opinion)

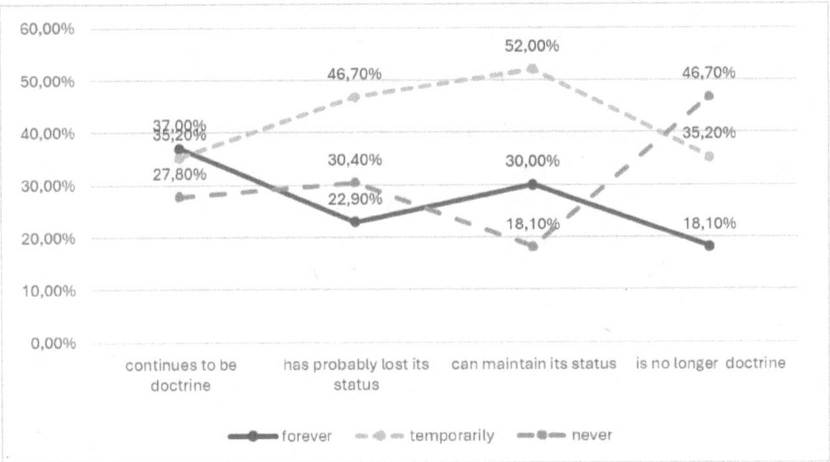

This question determines whether a doctrine retains its doctrinal status if its provisions, theses, and ideas are refuted. The answer options gave a choice from "continues to be a doctrine" to "is no longer a doctrine", with half-tones of answers. The results showed that the most significant number (52%) of specialists chose a relatively specific version of the future of such a doctrine – it "can maintain its status". This is followed by a group of specialists (46.7%) who believe the doctrine has irrevocably lost its status. The exact number of specialists (46.7%) admit the possibility of the doctrine's return because the loss of its status is temporary. 37% of specialists believe denying the doctrine does not affect its doctrinal status. It forever retains the achievements of authority, recognition, and value. It seems to remain in the doctrinal treasury of humanity.

The double-negative answer "is no longer a doctrine", which 46.7% of specialists chose, needs to be decoded according to the double-negative rules. Accordingly, if we remove the two negations, we get a doctrine forever. As a result, more than 67% of specialists categorically support the constancy of the status of the doctrine. This indicates that the doctrine has a relatively large margin of stability. It is primarily protected from subjective assessments, including negative ones. To some extent, this is due to the location of academic doctrine in different books, countries, and languages. This makes it difficult to physically destroy it.

GAP (CHAOTIC) – CONSISTENCY (COMPLETENESS)

Gaps. Doctrine is criticized for being incomplete, conflicting, illogical, and contradictory. Gaps exist because doctrine is scattered in various materials and publications which results in controversy and contradictions among different points of view. Consequently, it can be understood in different ways and may contain incomplete necessary information.

Doctrinal works are a heterogeneous totality. They are not comparable in depth, scale, and authority. These can be works of different lengths. An idea may be expressed in a single line or in many volumes of significant authoritative works, and a doctrine may produce heterogeneous and contradictory results. Accordingly, we return to the question of measuring quality and credibility.

Let us consider the problem of citations of publications, such as court documents. As a rule, citations, arguments, and references are of a single, one-off nature, and they cannot fully show the quality and authority of the idea embodied in a particular publication. Does this mean other similar cases will use the same idea from the same publication? More likely no, than yes. We propose to create a single portal of legal doctrine, which will reference both individual and collective, but in any case professional expert Persona-Doctrines. The antipode of the gap is completeness, consistency, orderliness, and inconsistency.

The systematic nature of doctrine has different manifestations. Doctrine is systematic, an ordered collection of theses, ideas, and propositions. Another dimension of consistency is the systematic comprehension of law. Law is viewed as a system. For theoretical and legal researchers, "systematic" is a trendy property, term, and idea. There is a system of views, a system of law, a legal system, a system of legislation, and many other "systems". On closer inspection, several "systems" turn out to be aggregated. However, this does not affect the frequency with which the term "system" refers to various legal phenomena.

The system-forming nature of doctrine is manifested in the fact that legislation, law-making, and law enforcement can be developed on its basis. Doctrine is a concentrated expression of the existing system of law and the system of prevailing views on the peculiarities of implementing legal norms in this system.

The objects of influence of the doctrine are law-making, law enforcement, norms of legislation, the mechanism of legal regulation, the legal system, the legal life of society, political culture, legal consciousness, and others. These objects form a system of legal phenomena. The system of the academic development of this object is a legal doctrine.

Doctrine influences a significant number of legal phenomena. Some are influenced by acting from the outside (for example, doctrine affects law-making and law enforcement as a process). Doctrine interacts with other phenomena and often passes into them, losing its independence and dissolving in them. For example, rules of legislation can absorb doctrine by incorporating precepts of doctrinal origin into their fabric. Another form of influence (interaction) is doctrinal forms of law and the object of influence coincide under certain circumstances. For example, legal consciousness can be seen as a doctrinal form of law. There may be another influence of doctrine on various legal phenomena.

The degree of influence of a legal doctrine differs significantly, depending on the environment in which it operates (groups of people), the forms of its expression (for example, State ideology or academic research), the methods of its protection (State sanction or self-defense), and others. It influences public authorities and officials. The most numerous objects of influence of the legal doctrine are the subjects of law in all their diversity. The legal picture of the world's value legal guidelines differs among the bearers of professional and ordinary legal consciousness. That is why we recognize the stabilizing effect of legal doctrine.

Legal doctrine performs the following: 1) interprets the rules of law, 2) fills gaps in the law, 3) coordinates and disciplines legal understanding and law enforcement, 4) has a valuable impact on the consciousness of subjects, their value systems, including legal consciousness.

Doctrine acts as a legal value, being the value basis of any legal regulation, understanding, and behavior. Legislation is the embodied will of the economically dominant class. Political power uses a set of democratic façades and manipulates the concept of public interest. However, it acts only in the interests of the economic beneficiary. All reliance on solving social problems and achieving the common good in the capitalist economic model is compromised. The socialist model has defects in the same area, substituting the common good for the prosperity of the Soviet party leadership, which had become a separate class (not workers, peasants, or working intelligentsia).

Legal doctrine contains value guidelines for any socio-economic system in the most ideological form. Perhaps that is why legal scholars (more broadly, social researchers) are often portrayed as disembodied individuals concerned about the common good. Although it sounds humiliating, this soft power of legal doctrine is the most potent weapon for social development. It presupposes, motivates, and educates an indefinite circle of people to strive for the highest values of freedom, equality, and justice. Descendants take answers to their queries from it and often distort them for their own purposes (as with the ideas of sovereignty, self-determination, and others). However, their manipulations do not change doctrine as a general cultural value. Over time, any political frenzy fades away. Often it becomes its opposite. The next generations of politicians draw ideas from the same reservoir of values for subsequent distortion in the interests of new beneficiaries. In this sense, it is perfect that politicians cannot create new ideas at the doctrinal level. They cannot do without the great names and ideas of the doctrinal piggy bank of the past. They return to it, meaning that doctrine again enters natural social relations. Then politicians get punched in the nose and return to scholar doctrine. Current issues, such as global climate change, green economy, international law, State sovereignty, and other striking examples are unsuccessful attempts to radically renew political ideology. In the wake of their failure, politicians are returning to their roots: democracy, common interest, values, and the like. This is a new cycle of the return of State ideology to academic doctrine.

CONNECTION WITH LEGISLATION (DERIVATIVENESS) – FREEDOM FROM LEGISLATION (PRIORITY)

Primacy and derivativeness are difficult to refract from the correlation of doctrine with normative legal acts. Doctrine is derived from the normative legal act because we constantly look for definitions of doctrine in legislation. We also persistently try to determine the place of doctrine within the system of forms of law based on a normative legal act. Thus, we assume that doctrine will be what the law defines, and its place will be as it will establish. Such expectation means that doctrine is recognized as the subject of legal legislative regulation. This is followed by recognizing that a doctrine exists by virtue of having achieved recognition as law, which is also a false thesis.

Doctrine is a self-sufficient phenomenon. It does not need to be legitimized by legislation. In general, the comparison of legislation and doctrine is somewhat contrary to the laws of logic because we are comparing phenomena that partially coincide. Indeed, some doctrines are not normative legal acts, and there are normative legal acts that are not doctrines. In the middle, at the intersection of these groups, there will be legal acts that call themselves doctrines. For example, comparing a doctrinal book with federal laws is incorrect.

Doctrines have advantages in comparison with normative legal acts. They are often the source, precursor, and foundation of the last. Doctrine also serves as the basis for adopting, amending, and repealing normative legal acts.

It is possible to find instances of contradiction between the doctrine and normative legal acts. In fact, this inconsistency, disclosed by critical analysis, is embedded in the nature of legal research. Suppose we simplify the meaning of legal research: it comes down to identifying problems of legal regulation and proposing ways of resolving them. Suppose the researcher is completely satisfied with legislation and does not see the need to supplement or change it. In that case, it remains to draw a conclusion about its merits. It is difficult to imagine the conclusion: "The legislative analysis showed its completeness and excellent quality. It does not need to be changed, as everything has been done and considered. It is perfect". We deliberately exaggerated the researcher degree of satisfaction and admiration for normative legal acts to show the absurdity of such a conclusion. This proves that the rationale for the study is precisely the shortcomings in the legislation or its application.

If the author is satisfied with the law and agrees with it, then the law does not need to be changed. A more politicized version of the confrontation between the researcher and the normative legal act is also possible.

The law is created by a large group of elected people, such as deputies, or members of Congress. This collective legislator is, by default, the representative of society, the people. Accordingly, the scholar who criticizes the law speaks against the people's representatives and, therefore, against the people themselves. In some periods of Russian history, such individuals were called "enemies of the people".

The questionnaire asks respondents to assess the contradiction between the doctrine and the legislation. The respondent votes were almost equally distributed in assessing contradictions between the doctrine and normative legal acts. From the point of view of 56.2% of respondents, this is a disadvantage, and for 43.8% is an advantage. Respondents indicate that the doctrine can perform some regulatory functions, an implicit recognition of doctrine as a form of law. Doctrine can regulate relations that are not regulated by the rules of law at the level of axiology.

These features make doctrinal forms of law competitive compared to normative legal acts and other traditional forms of law. Arising from a distributed source, which is difficult or impossible to influence, dramatically increases the viability and self-sufficiency of doctrine in comparison with legislation.

The lack of a legal definition is a drawback of doctrine. A legal definition is a definition established in a normative legal act. There has never been a general definition of legal doctrine in legislation of the Russian Federation. However, suppose we are talking about forms of law that regulate social relations and are applied by public authorities when considering juridical persons. In that case, a legislative definition is unequivocally necessary.

There is no law on any form of law in the Russian Federation. No one knows what a normative legal act is because legislators have been evading the adoption of laws on normative legal acts for more than 35 years.[1] There is no reason to expect the adoption of a law on normative legal acts in the near future. However, some elements of legislative definitions of certain types of doctrines still exist, among them, specific State doctrines. However, this is not a generalized definition of State ideological doctrine as a legal doctrine.

There is no legal and, at the same time, universal definition for all types of doctrine. This gap could be eliminated by adopting a law on normative legal acts of the Russian Federation if there were to be a reference to legal doctrine in it. This is the only suitable form. However, not all doctrines are normative legal acts. In this sense, the doctrines that are not normative legal acts are formally outside the scope of such a law. For all the recognized regulators of social relations to be covered in such a law, it seems more appropriate to use the title "Federal Law on the Sources (or Forms) of Law of the Russian Federation". However, we do not see any real prospects for a legislative act on definitions.

POLITICIZATION – NEUTRALITY

Politicization. Doctrine can have a solid connection to politics and ideology. For an ideological doctrine, this connection seems natural and logical. The legislature is formed primarily along party political lines. State doctrines issued in the form of legal acts are, on one hand, an external form of expression of a political decision.

On the other hand, these are documents of a general nature, ideological in content and method of influence. Suppose the State is a one-party State with a single dominant ideology. In that case, all forms of legal regulation are synchronized: the party State issues legal acts based on a (sole or dominant) legal ideology. Political conditionality is understood as a disadvantage for academic and judicial doctrines but is not

[1] S. V. Boshno, "Закон о нормативных правовых актах: прошлое, настоящее и перспективы [Law on Normative Legal Acts: Past, Present and Prospects]", Право и современные государства [Law and Modern States], no. 2 (2015), pp. 7-22.

excluded. Researchers should draw conclusions based on data analysis. These should be reasonable, objective, verifiable results, free from external influences, including political and ideological. The interaction of legal science with political actors is indeed inclined to see the political factor as predominant. Legal scholars in the service of the State follow the guidelines formulated by political circles.

Academician Sergei Sergeevich Alekseev (1924-2013) was a well-known political weathervane in Russian jurisprudence. Surprisingly, to this day, his publications have a high citation level. With rare exceptions, these are textbooks of the Soviet period. His notable books are on the general theory of law[2] and problems of the theory of law,[3] almost the only educational material clothed in a seemingly academic shell at the time of their publication. His colleagues and students, scattered from the Sverdlovsk (Ekaterinburg) community at one time (end of the 1960s), just as the those from St. Petersburg in the 2000s, found positions in State agencies and continue to hold them (geographical nepotism). For example, P. Krasheninnikov, a deputy, former Minister of Justice, professor, Doctor of Legal Sciences, belongs to the Ekaterinburg school.

St. Petersburg University and some other St. Petersburg schools (among them, St. Petersburg State University, Mining Institute) forged political cadres who supported the communicative theory of Poliakov (a candidate for the post of judge of the European Court of Human Rights and now a judge of the Constitutional Court without a doctoral degree), Bushev, Salnikov, and others. There is no reason to expect new legal developments when there is nepotism and the merger of science and politics. Being well acquainted with one another, they created a science-ideological-State doctrine to achieve their goals. The dominant attitude has become that if a researcher or teacher is on the staff of a State institution or otherwise receives

[2] S. S. Alekseev, Общая теория права [General Theory of Law] (1981).

[3] Alekseev, Проблемы теории права [Problems of the Theory of Law] (1973)

funding from the State, they agree to act only in the interests of the ideological or political guidelines of the State.

In the face of increasing political pressure, there is no possibility for originality and creativity except in the status of a free thinker. This is what we asked the respondents of the sociological survey: who most often creates doctrines? A total of 20% chose a "free thinker", an oppositionist, or a dissident. Jurisprudence, in the context of restrictions on freedoms and academic freedoms, is becoming an ideological, political sphere. Indirectly, this is due to the lack of standards, analysis, and statistical methods to measure scholarship.

There is an original management of freedoms and creativity in jurisprudence compared to other sciences found in a provision of the Criminal Code on public calls for a violent change of the constitutional order. As a result, States have become police officers who repress opinions, which naturally prejudices academic creativity. All possibilities for creating a new legal doctrine are blocked, except for the one preferred by the current government.

Relations between politics and doctrine may be unfriendly. The confrontation between politics and doctrine can be expressed in the actions of political and State institutions taken against legal doctrine. As a result of direct and indirect persecution, doctrine can go underground to a hidden, illegal level.

Political institutions representing State power serve their own interests and their beneficiaries. Those concerning the common good attract illiterate marginalized individuals. It is impossible to believe that wealthy people spend all their energy on resolving the affairs of the poorly protected groups of the indigent and the sick.

Representatives of legal doctrine close to political institutions act not only under the influence of punishment for dissent. They may be guided by different desires, such as the desire to please, be on the ruling team, curry favor, advance, and not be excluded from the inner circle. This is a relatively common condition among researchers and educators. They can, if necessary, join the systemic ideology. But it is more promising and profitable to lead by following in the wake of at least an ideological doctrine supported by the State.

In non-democratic political circumstances, science can be more important than politics only if this serves the intentions, ideas, and desires of politicians not yet embodied in legislation. This is a custom science. The influence of academic doctrine in the opposite direction, that is, on the State, is impossible. With a ban on other ideas (immediately labeled undemocratic), the impact of the authority of academic research disappears. Unless ideas are in the mainstream, they are opposed. These are grounds for the destruction of the work, the alienation of the author.

A politically dependent doctrine can be used to preserve the existing State order. The stagnation of ideas glorifying the existing State as the best, and leadership as the wisest, are properties of a stagnant order. Policy and doctrine protect each other from development and change in such a situation. As soon as authoritative works praise the existing legal order, relying on the words of the incumbent leader as the only true and far-sighted one, we have an example of stagnation, which, as a rule, is a justification for the established practice. Doctrine is often tied predominantly to official public policy rather than civil society interests.

Legal doctrine may have a regulatory impact but constantly uses its recommendatory potential. Scholars can turn to it not under compulsion but at will, proactively, and interestedly. We have noted that the assimilation of doctrinal sources requires qualification and considerable intellectual effort, which is not characteristic of the State machine on its own initiative. It is not easy to imagine a State order developing and using doctrines that are not loyal to the existing State order.

Doctrine is the most challenging source for elected officials, who often do not have and are not required to have a legal education. The career of an athlete, an artist, and many others offers no help in mastering legal doctrine. From the point of view of typology, these persons are the bearers of ordinary legal consciousness with all the obvious consequences. Even if incumbent legislators decide to attend law school, it probably will not change anything. As practice shows, deputies, senators, and other power figures use their public potential to evade training, falsifying their reporting results in exams, and finding other ways to avoid real training and assessment.

Legislators and law enforcement personnel do not always use doctrine. This is due in part to its advisory status. In addition, they may not be aware of or interested in it. These deficiencies can be partially compensated by academic councils attached to State agencies. However, these are consultative bodies that have no power. In the relevant sections of this study, we examine expertise and expert law in more detail and draw reasoned conclusions.

Neutrality (independence). Academic doctrine is more effective without the pressure of official State ideology. Ideally, the academic version of doctrine should develop independently of external economic, class, and ideological factors. However, working groups and expert councils of State agencies aim to solve problems already known to and resolved by legal science. Independent researchers with their own positions are not invited to these cells of the ideological doctrine under the roof of the State. That is why an independent doctrine develops outside State institutions. The absence of an all-pervasive official State ideology contributes to developing a different legal doctrine. The State attitude to ideas that contradict its own ideas is an indicator of freedom in any country.

In this study, we consider such phenomena as wrongness and anti-law as forms of denial of law, especially legislation.

Wrongness is the negation of legislation. In the absence of explicit new norms, this negation becomes the basis of the future legal order in the abrupt transition between different models of legal regulation. Injustice accompanies obsolete, outgoing legislation. However, the form is most often the legal consciousness of the victorious group, for example, the workers and peasants in the socialist revolution. In the post-revolutionary period of Russia, the wrong persisted until the adoption of the legislation of the new order.

Anti-law is current legislation that does not correspond to the law, prohibits, or significantly restricts, a right. Anti-law is a constant companion of the legislation of the positivist State, according to the supporters of the libertarian understanding of law.

The revolutionary etiology of wrong, revolutionary, and socialist legal consciousness is only one aspect of the question. Another side is of exceptional relevance. "By non-law", wrote Magaziner in 1922, "one can also understand any formally unlawful act in general, which in its content is a law, a decree or a judicial act, if, despite its illegality, it is carried out and acts as a lawful act; for example, a law contrary to the Constitution, or a decree contrary to the law".[4] Legislation that has been declared not subject to application by the courts because of failure to conform to the Constitution and other normative legal acts is also a non-right. This is no longer the domain of legal consciousness. This type of injustice, which has the form of a document issued by legitimate State authorities, is a normative legal act.

Doctrine in the legal consciousness of civil servants is not an organic part of the forms of law. They do not perceive it as a phenomenon on which legislation is based and develops. They do not trust academic sources of legal information, and they do not see any prospects for arguing their position with scholarly works. They are not interested in this source, which was established due to a survey of civil servants: 0% interest in monographs, 0.5 % in textbooks, and 1 % in articles.[5]

[4] Ia. M. Magaziner, Лекции по государственному праву: (Общее государственное право) [Lectures on State Law: (General State Law)] (1919), p. 75.

[5] SCS 2007–2008.

In general, doctrinal forms of law do not significantly impact public law relations because the motives of quality, authority, persuasiveness, and fame in these relations are inferior to political expediency.

Mutual respect, the desire of academic community members to meet each other as bearers of the appropriate type of doctrine and the State apparatus, high standards of science, and genuine academic preferences of civil servants should contribute to recognizing doctrinal phenomena as effective forms of law. However, this ideal State has not yet been reached. What can be demanded of legal doctrine if obvious, physically tangible, and visible facts, measured by exact sciences, are denied by the leadership of States? It could be melting glaciers or a flying meteorite. And yet, these theses of politicians consider all objects to be managed according to their will for money and interests.

STATE – NON-STATE

A doctrine can be of State and non-state origin. Moreover, the State supports some doctrines of different origins through its various organs. Other types of doctrine do not have such support.

The State principle in the doctrine. The State authorities issue State doctrine in the form of documents. Doctrinal documents (strategies, concepts, doctrines, and others) are not normative because they do not directly regulate social relations. They have a legal nature, as they are issued by public authorities. We have no information on how they are used in the judicial system. It is only known that they cannot be challenged in court because these are neither normative nor individual legal acts.

An ideological doctrine can be linked to the State. Such a combination forms an ideological doctrine of a State (official) character. This doctrine may be created or maintained by public authorities. In their constitutions, some States openly recognize a particular ideological doctrine of the State, as did the former Soviet Union. Article 6 of the 1936 Constitution of the USSR provided that the core of the political system was the

Communist Party of the Soviet Union. The ideology of the State was based on Marxist-Leninist ideological doctrine. In the 1977 Constitution of the USSR, the modern version of the Soviet State was the Program of the Communist Party of the Soviet Union. In fact, as a State-ideological document it was stronger than the constitutions. The strength of the Program was that the CPSU was a limitless divine power, according to the taboo model.

Many States do not enshrine an official ideology in the constitution but adhere to it or, on the contrary, prohibit a doctrine (for example, communist or slave-owning).

Doctrines related to the State arise, are amended, or repealed by State authorities. Judicial doctrines are mentioned because their source is the State represented by the judiciary and the organs of justice. This introduction and operation sanctioned the recognition of academic publications as judicial doctrine. The State can also commission or engage scholar doctrines. It is widely opinion beliieved that if a researcher receives a salary from the State, he is paid, *inter alia*, for his loyalty to the political State order.

Extra-State. Academic and ideological doctrines can be non-State if they are not directly related to the activities of State authorities. 66.9% of respondents see this non-State status as a virtue of the legal doctrine, whereas 33.2% see it as a disadvantage.

Independence is a property of only those doctrines that arise without State involvement. Such doctrines are created and developed without the protection of the State. When academic freedom is restricted, free thought is possible only to a limited extent. In a sociological survey, we called this group of unbiased doctrinal authors "independent thinkers". In addition to the unbiased authors of doctrinal works, others oppose the State with varying degrees of openness. Their ideas may not correspond to the State ideological line and may actively oppose public policy. Their writings can provide an ideological platform for the opposition. In the survey, we asked respondents to assess the prospect of creating a legal doctrine by dissidents and oppositionists.

A feature of legal doctrine is the absence of a single center of emergence, formation, and support, which makes it challenging to abolish or terminate. This makes the doctrine a more stable form of law. 62.8% of specialists see this as an advantage of doctrine and 37.2% as a disadvantage.

Chapter 12
Properties Related to the Operation of Doctrine

CONSERVATISM (STABILITY) AND DYNAMISM

Doctrine is dynamic despite a certain conservatism. Constantly developing, its core is stable and little changeable as a legal dogma.

Conservatism. The traditional dimension of doctrine is ensured by the fact that it undergoes a lengthy path of crystallization from an idea to an influential factor. It ensures continuity in understanding legal categories and forms a vector of development. It is doctrine that shapes the corporate traditions of lawyers.

The stability of a doctrine can be regarded as its conservatism. This property can be positive and negative. In a negative sense, conservatism can restrain development and progress. The correlation between stability and dynamism is perceived differently, depending on the stage in the State and legal history. Suppose a State develops progressively, without leaps, in a linear manner. In that case, the stability of doctrine is a positive factor. However, in non-linear abrupt movement conditions, the previous period's stable doctrine may be inadequate under the new conditions. In the epoch of the dominance of the outgoing doctrine, ideas of wrongness could be pursued which destroyed previous legal theories.

In transitional historical periods, a stable (conservative) doctrine may not be able to cope with new social challenges and demands. Slow change and the inability to respond to new realities reduce the credibility of legal doctrine. For example, today the deterioration of such well-known doctrines as democracy, sovereignty, human rights, and many others is evident. These doctrines did not withstand the test of new socio-political relations. However, creating new doctrines requires active work over a long period. The negation of the previous one itself looks like an innovation during the period before the formation of a new doctrine. In this study, we have referred several times to the phenomenon of anti-right, wrong. These ideas of negation create the prerequisites for the new by negating the previous.

Doctrine creates a stable basis for the development of law, economic stability, and observance of the rights and legitimate interests of the subjects of legal relations. It is inherently stable; it cements the existing legal picture and enhances its value within the professional community of lawyers and citizens.

The stability of a doctrine is seen in the fact that ideas accumulated therein are preserved in their original form, while simultaneously being developed, including through interpretation. The momentary understanding may change significantly when interpreting doctrinal ideas about the current situation. Doctrine is not overturned by a court and cannot be withdrawn, destroyed, or banned. In this sense, it is stable and self-sufficient. The primary defense mechanism of legal doctrine is the lack of unity of forms of its existence. Divided into different forms of expression, it does not have a single source (body) of control that allows or prohibits its presence and operation. This distribution guarantees its stability, permanence, and irreducibility in a certain sense.

The questionnaire included a question about the importance of stability and conservatism of doctrine in comparison with other forms of law. According to 72.1% of experts, this property is an achievement. 27.9% of specialists see this as a flaw in legal doctrine.

Doctrine is formed over a long period, distinguishing this form of law from normative legal acts. Doctrine ensures the continuity of legal ideas and prescriptions because of its conservatism and long-term development.

Sometimes, doctrine can be an ossified structure that does not correspond to the natural development of relations. This is the flip side of conservatism and traditionalism. Excessive conservatism leads to the severance of ties with the political, legal, and cultural realities of society.

Content analysis of a sample of textbooks showed a high frequency of the use of markers of conservatism in definitions of doctrine: archaic, conservative, constancy, predecessors, past, past, retrospective, older, ancient, old-fashioned, centuries, and traditions.

Academic research also uses certain words: classical, development, general, century, historical, identifying, tradition, preexisting, Germanic, glossators, Italian, and age.

Dynamism. Simultaneously with conservatism, a doctrine can be flexible, developing, and dynamic. Flexibility allows the doctrine to adapt to changing conditions. Doctrine links official flexibility, positive law, and a society's "living" law.

Doctrinal flexibility is the opposite of stability. Many doctrinal ideas have a centuries-old history; in this case, they are the basis of legal values. However, stability should not stagnate, where a generally positive property becomes negative. Lack of development transforms into stagnation, followed by destruction. Nevertheless, flexibility may well coexist with the stability of legal doctrine. Flexibility means that it can be changed without formal procedures and without the involvement of public authorities. A thinker who can inject new ideas into an established legal doctrine develops it. New ways of assimilating traditional and even ancient legal doctrine to new and changing relationships can be suggested. For example, the theory of dividing law into private and public still relies on Ulpian's authority. There is modern content that is adequate for contemporary legislation.

Due to the evolving nature of the doctrine, it most adequately responds to the challenges of the time and meets the current needs of the society within which it was formed.

PRIMACY IS DERIVATIVE

This feature makes it possible to establish the relationship of doctrine with other forms of law. It is often assigned a subsidiary role as an interpretation of other forms of law. Such a function can also be referred to as an *auxiliary* function. Filling in gaps is also often a property of doctrine, but a derivative activity. Commentaries can be academic or academic-practical, doctrinal, or practical. All types of commentaries are united by a derivative of an object's interpretations of nature. Most often, the object of interpretation is normative legal acts and judicial practice. Commentaries are a sought-after genre of creativity. The prospects for the commentary to become doctrinal are rather high, as was confirmed by survey results. Commentary ranks fourth among the doctrinal genres selected by respondents, following a dissertation, textbook, and article. 25% of specialists and 16.2% of experts voted for the likelihood of success of a commentary.[1] In the genre preferences of civil servants, commentaries take first place (chosen by 30% of respondents).[2] Thus, a commentary has at least two connective forms with doctrine: 1) a commentary can interpret forms of law, including jurisprudential doctrines, and 2) a commentary can become a doctrine.

OBLIGATORY – DECLARATIVE

An *obligation* is an organic property of doctrines associated with State power. This refers to State, ideological, and judicial types of doctrines. They are binding because they are issued as legal acts adopted by public authorities. It is the authority of power supported by a State. The obligatory nature of academic doctrine is an exception to the rule. It is characterized by soft power and soft commitment, manifested in self-imposition by the subjects of the right on themselves of the obligation to obey such a form of law. Respondents indicate that the doctrine can justify the adoption by courts and authorities of unlawful

[1] ESPD 2022–2023.

[2] SCS 2007–2008.

decisions and violate formal procedures to protect against judicial errors. The ideological dominant doctrine has almost unlimited power in a party-State when there is one party, and the other parties are banned.

Declarativeness. Doctrine at the law enforcement stage is of a recommendatory nature due to the absence of a normative legal fixation of punishment for a violation. It does not have a structural and organizational mechanism. The reason for the recommendatory nature of doctrines follows from its norms not containing sanctions.

Doctrine as a form of law can be understood as the basis for forming the discretion of the law enforcer. Courts are officially (legislatively) allowed to exercise discretion. Discretion is "the power given to a person who can choose between two or more alternatives when each is lawful".[3] In general, discretion appears to be a legitimate authority. However, this is relative legality. An excessive discretion called "breadth of discretionary powers" and "determination of competence according to the formula 'right'" is regarded as a corruption-causing factor.[4]

A binding or declarative nature is essential in recognizing a legal doctrine as a form of law. It is wrong to say that a doctrine is non-binding or obligatory without referencing the fundamental question of what types of doctrine we are discussing. A broad approach, which identifies any legal doctrine with academic doctrine, essentially removes the question of obligation and responsibility for failure to comply with its provisions. However, legal doctrine of certain types is built into the system of forms of law and constitutes legislation. In such circumstances, it is binding, and penalties are inevitable for its violation. In the relevant sections of this study, the different types of doctrine and the forms of their expression are

[3] A. Barack, Судейское усмотрение [Judge's Discretion] (1999), p. 13.

[4] "Методика проведения фнтикоррупционной экспертизы нормативных правовых актов и проектов нормативных правовых актов [Methodology for Conducting Anti-Corruption Expertise of Regulatory Legal Acts and Draft Regulatory Legal Acts] (available online).

examined in depth. Accordingly, certain types of legal doctrine are protected by the State in the same way as other recognized forms of law. Legal doctrines that are not a form of law can be self-binding, as they are elements of the legal consciousness of subjects of law and law enforcers. They operate in a paradigm like a taboo. Judicial doctrine in countries with different legal systems stands apart from other types of doctrine in terms of binding nature and State protection.

Significantly simplifying a complex, multifaceted problem, it can be said that State doctrine is always obligatory. Judicial doctrine can be binding if it is expressed in legitimized State forms. The part of ideological doctrine that expresses the order of the State is binding. In some cases specified by law, academic doctrine is binding. Binding and non-infringing doctrines are directly related to the State. Doctrines that are not supported by the State are implemented through voluntary self-assignment on the part of the subjects. There may be doctrines that are contrary to binding norms and officially banned by public authorities. Doctrines not welcomed by State authorities gravitate towards the forbidden. In this sense, doctrine tends to be a custom sanctioned by the State. However, the absence of authorization does not invalidate the custom of its validity. Customs and doctrines not sanctioned or formally binding can effectively regulate social relations and retain their competitiveness in comparison with normative legal acts. Doctrines not supported by the State through sanction may be more effective and enduring than obligatory doctrines. Changes in the tastes and assessments of the State under the influence of objective and subjective factors cannot be discounted. In the history of the Russian-Soviet-post Soviet State, the assessment of Marxism has changed many times. And these are not isolated examples. The law of the philosophy of negation is negation and, as a result, going in circles.

TERRITORIALITY – EXTRATERRITORIALITY

We understand the territoriality of a doctrine as the presence of a territory within whose boundaries it is applied, manifests its authority, and influences social relations. The territory has boundaries that are traditionally significant for forms of law. The following types of borders are generally recognized: State, confederation, legal system, subjects of the State, local self-government bodies, and organizations. The recognition of these types of boundaries is based on the possibility of publishing legislation that will be in force within these boundaries. These geographical approaches can be understood with respect to doctrine.

An important issue is the boundaries of the validity of a legal doctrine (recognition) and application. To a certain extent, the formulation of this geographical question in a sociological survey is predetermined by the concept of a legal system and a legal map of the world. The doctrine of the typology of legal systems is widely shared. Legal systems are recognized, and the idea of their existence is replicated through teaching in law schools. However, sociological studies have found that 29% of the experts and 20.7% of specialists do not identify themselves with any legal system. There are differences in the naming of specific types of legal systems. Different bases for the classification of legal systems and legal families are assumed.

Nevertheless, there is no doubt as to the need for a typology of global legal space. Comparative jurisprudence (comparative legal studies) has developed from a legal research method into a science with its own tools.[5] Almost all dissertation research is based at least partly on the comparative-legal method. This is often understood simplistically as comparing some countries with the main object. Such primitivism was a natural consequence of mass incompetence and the lack of special training and qualifications of people trying to apply the comparative legal method. The simplification is due to applying this method as any simple comparison. In fact, selecting objects

[5] M. Van Hoecke and M. Warrington, "Legal Cultures, Legal Paradigms and Legal Doctrine: Towards a New Model for Comparative Law", *International and Comparative Law Quarterly*, XLVII (1998), pp. 495-536; D. LaVon Roberts, *The Representation of Law Student Information Literacy Definitions in Legal Research Textbooks: A Comparative Content Analysis* (2012).

and assessing the admissibility of comparison are the most labor intensive professional tasks in comparative legal studies.

A survey of the respondents to the questionnaire showed the distribution of their choices according to specified types of boundaries.

According to 25.7% of specialists (they chose the option "crucial"), the most effective limitation of legal doctrine is the boundary of a legal system. This indicates that the dominance of any form of law depends on the type of legal system.

According to 14.6% of specialists, State borders are decisive. The option "maybe" for the State border was chosen by 33.2% of specialists. 16.4% of specialists indicated that State borders do not matter. For a more unambiguous decision on recognizing the role of State borders, we added up all the shades of positive recognition (decisive, matters, can matter). We compared the resulting number with categorical non-recognition ("it does not matter"). Respondents were distributed as follows: 83% of specialists recognized the State border as an active factor, and 16.4% did not recognize the influence of State borders on the understanding, recognition, and application of doctrine.

Diagram 17. (SSLD 16). Impact of Boundaries on Doctrine (Specialist Opinion)

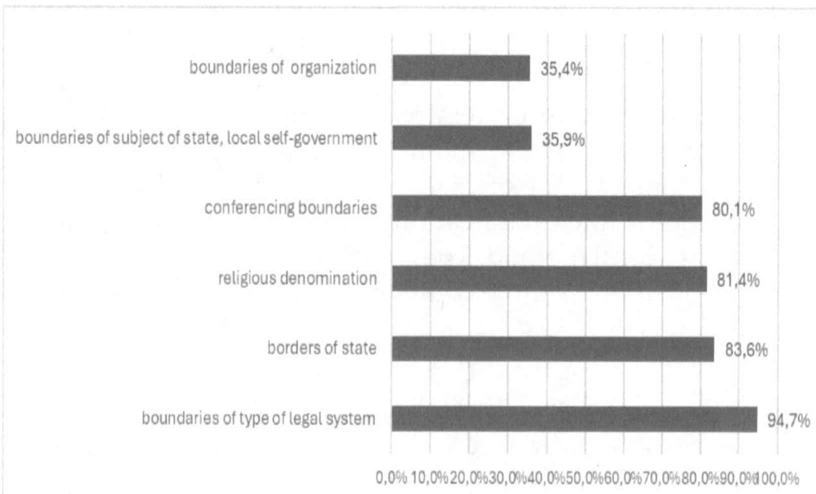

The reason for the study of the influence of the State border and its elements (internal borders) on the operation of the legal doctrine is predetermined by the State nature of legislation – the primary form of law. Normative legal acts are valid for national documents within State borders. Legal acts are issued within the subjects of the Federation and municipal bodies. There are examples of supranational parliaments, as well as international law. Many boundaries prevent legislation from working.

As can be seen from the diagram, most popular among specialists was the boundary of the legal system, which was recognized as an active factor by 94.7% of specialists. 83.6% of specialists consider the borders of the State to be an active factor, the borders of a religious confession – 81.4%, the borders of a confederation – 80.1%, the boundaries of a municipality – 35.9%, the boundaries of the organization – 35.4%. Thus, the sociological survey demonstrated the recognition of the territorial limitations of the doctrine, which, however, does not exclude the discrete action of the doctrine, the carriers of which are people books. They move in their logic, carrying ideas and representations that tend to doctrine.

A doctrine may be transformed into a normative legal act and lose the status of an independent form of law if the legislator rewrites the essence of the rule developed by the doctrine into the document text. In addition, the legislator authorizes the use of doctrines and establishes a particular procedure. In the positivist legal understanding, this activity is called sanctioning (permitting) without absorption.[6] To implement the permit, the legislator refers to other forms of law, such as custom (Article 5, Civil Code RF)[7] in a normative legal act or doctrine (Article 166, Family Code RF).[8]

6 S. V. Boshno, "Санкционирование обычаев государством: содержание и классификация [Sanctioning of Customs by the State: Content and Classification]", Юрист [Jurist], no. 3 (2004), pp. 11-14.

7 See W. E. Butler (ed. & transl.), *Civil Code of the Russian Federation* (2021), I, p. 6.

8 W. E. Butler, *Russian Family Law* (2015), p. 391.

In the Questionnaire, specialists were offered a question with a choice of answer options: "If a normative legal act embodied the developments of researchers, then it is: "scholar doctrine", "State doctrine", "a normative act, not a doctrine".

It is evident from this diagram that most specialists (78%) believe that when an idea passes from a scholar doctrine to a normative legal act, it becomes a normative act and ceases to be a doctrine. 11.5% of specialists indicated that, in this case, the type of doctrine to which the idea belongs changes. It passes from scholar doctrine into an ideological State doctrine.

10.6% of specialists favored retaining the status of scholar doctrine. Thus, it is recognized as a scholar doctrine and a normative legal act. Suppose we classify the form of a legal phenomenon depending on where it is located. In that case, such examples are preserved in two forms: they continue to be preserved in books, but are also included in normative legal acts. However, for practical application, it is essential to draw a conclusion, and it is obvious: a normative legal act will be applied in law enforcement practice. The original source (academic publications) will not be cited. Sanctioning remains the only way to enforce the rule.

However, strange metamorphoses can take place. Thus, the propositions transferred from doctrine to law are later perceived as law. Accordingly, they can be changed as a law. And suppose it is impossible to change Montesquieu's doctrinal principle of the separation of powers. In that case, it is easy to change the legislative form of this principle. It is noteworthy that the original source looks erroneous thereafter because it contradicts the law. It is difficult to resist the astonishment of a legislator making changes to his own creation, the law, without regard to the author of the doctrinal idea. Sometimes, legislative innovations are significant. They completely change the essence of the principle, the idea that gave rise to the law.

Given the above, it can be noted that jurisprudence, legal theory, and doctrine are related concepts. However, this is not a 100% overlapping: not all research is doctrine, and not all doctrine is research. However, in specific examples, these concepts may coincide.

DIRECTIVE – REGULATORY NATURE

Orientation (principles of law). In the theory of law, the rules of law are classified as relations and norms, rules of conduct. Rules of conduct regulate or protect social relations. The precepts do nothing: they do not regulate or protect. They ascertain, affirm, determine, and set goals. This classification can be induced into scholar doctrine linearly. It primarily contains policy norms. They are direct, tangible, and visual. They do become part of the rules of behavior. These are the conceptual apparatus, definitions, goals, and objectives. However, the non-obvious practical value of the guidelines is more important than the rules of conduct. They are the basis of the rules of conduct.

A doctrine is a statement of the most general precepts with the broadest possible application. These are ideas and attitudes of a general nature. According to the formula hypothesis – disposition – sanction, these are not specific rules of conduct. Accordingly, doctrinal ideas (mainly) create the prerequisites and conditions for subsequent detailed regulation. This is apparently what the Constitutional Court of the Russian Federation had in mind when it said that doctrines do not contain norms regulating social relations.[9] In this study, we see an opportunity to compare doctrine with the principles of law.

[9] Постановление «По делу о проверке конституционности Указа Президента Российской Федерации от 30 ноября 1994 года No. 2137 "О мероприятиях по восстановлению конституционной законности и правопорядка на территории Чеченской Республики)", Указа Президента Российской Федерации от 9 декабря 1994 года N 2166 "О мерах по пресечению деятельности незаконных вооружённых формирований на территории Чеченской Республики и в зоне осетино-ингушского конфликта", постановления Правительства Российской Федерации от 9 декабря 1994 года No. 1360 "Об обеспечении государственной безопасности и территориальной целостности Российской Федерации, законности, прав и свобод граждан, разоружения незаконных вооружённых формирований на территории Чеченской Республики и прилегающих к ней регионов Северного Кавказа", Указа Президента Российской Федерации от 2 ноября 1993 года № 1833 "Об Основных положениях военной доктрины Российской Федерации" [Decree "Re: the Case Concerning the Review of the Constitutionality of Presidential Edict No. 2137 of 30 November 1994 "On Measures to Restore Constitutional Law and Order in the Territory of the Chechen

Some *principles of law* (we can call them normative principles) are enshrined in legislation. Some are set out at length (for example, the principle of freedom of contract), others briefly (the principle of the presumption of innocence). Most are merely named in legislation (humanism, autonomy, self-interest). These normative principles constitute a subset of basic legal norms. They do not directly impact behavior subjects of law (neither regulatory nor protective). As a rule, they serve as a basis, a condition for implementing influence on the part of norms – rules of behavior. Their natural regulative effect can take place in the event of a gap in the law when using the mechanism of analogy. That is, it is causal.

Several principles are not enshrined in law, but their existence is confirmed by legal science and practice. Some are well-known. Of course, they appeared from someone's pen or because of the development of a series of events. Their origin and authorship are no longer significant or have been lost over time. They do not have a personified addressee and operate indefinitely, which allows them to claim the status of a form of law. However, they are not protected by State coercion, their location is unknown, and their outer shell has not been clearly defined.

Thus, despite the disputed status, the principles not enshrined in normative legal acts still have a particular impact on the mechanism of legal regulation. However, this is not enough to classify them as forms of law. The direct regulatory impact of principles is more often spoken of in international legal relations.

Republic", Presidential Edict No. 2166 of 9 December 1994 "On Measures to Suppress the Activities of Illegal Armed Groups in the Territory of the Chechen Republic and in the Zone of the Ossetian-Ingush Conflict", Government Decree No. 1360 of 9 December 1994 on Ensuring State Security and Territorial Integrity of the Russian Federation, the Rule of Law, Rights and Freedoms of Citizens, and the Disarmament of Illegal Armed Formations on the Territory of the Chechen Republic and Adjacent Regions of the North Caucasus, and Presidential Edict No. 1833 of 2 November 1993 on the Basic Provisions of Military Doctrine of the Russian Federation], No. 10-R, Конституционный Суд Российской Федерации [Constitutional Court of the Russian Federation], 31 July 1995).

The position of identifying doctrine and principles of law as synonyms is widespread. There is also a diametrically opposed view that there is no reason to identify normative principles and their academic interpretation with doctrine. Norms-principles are an element of a normative act with all the corresponding consequences. A legal science that follows the description of existing legal constructions cannot claim doctrinal status. A doctrine is not a commentary on legislation but a developed innovative theory.

In addition to the principles enshrined in law, some have not yet received such a form. These principles tend to be academic doctrine.

Regulatory capacity. Doctrine has a regulative potential that is sometimes badly implemented. The ability of a particular doctrine to unleash its regulatory potential depends on many factors: recognizing doctrine as a form of law or only as a source of law. As a form of law, doctrine regulates relations directly, without intermediaries. It is an ideological, State, and judicial doctrine. These regulate relations by being embodied in other forms of law. The issue remained controversial: "Do such phenomena retain the properties of doctrines, or are they already fully incorporated into the system of the corresponding forms of law?" A corresponding question is included in the questionnaire for specialists using sociological tools.

For example, State doctrines confirmed by edicts of the the President of the Russian Federation are part of the legislative system. However, other types of legal doctrine – ideological, non-State, and academic – are applied in their original form – different works of the respective genres. Other forms of law, such as precedents, may refer to academic doctrine and identify specific publications and authors. However, academic doctrine continues to exist outside this reference. An ideological doctrine as a system of attitudes of a primarily political nature can be injected into judicial practice with the use of specific works or not; this is what the confrontation between supporters and opponents of abortion looks like. At the heart of this continuing confrontation between social groups with little support for various academic (primarily medical research) arguments is the ideological tolerance or religious intolerance of abortion in the United States. It is based on a system of values and social attitudes. Relying on legislation and judicial precedents has not yielded results because both State-dependent regulators have shown instability, have changed several times, and are no longer a source of arguments in the confrontation. In this matter, it is evident that judicial doctrine follows non-legal arguments and reflects the relevant political forces and social groups at each moment. And they rely on their doctrinal values.

RATIONALITY – ARBITRARINESS, VOLUNTARISM

Mind is the mental faculties, the mental experience of the human, presupposing self-consciousness, free will, thought, and subconscious processes. The principle of reasonableness in law means the correspondence of individual behavior to social experience, awareness, and motivation of his actions. Rational actions are purposeful, typical, and, in this sense, performed every day in a given society.

Reason or the principle of reasonableness may also be referred to as one of the sources of law. The role of the principle of reasonableness in the formation of law will vary from one legal family to another. Under certain historical and legislative conditions, reason can claim the status of a form of law. This concept was rejected in the Romano-Germanic States during the nineteenth century with the triumph of the doctrine of legal positivism, which identified the concepts of law, rights, and rule. Generally, the idea of the supremacy of reason has a proud, solemn sound, positively affecting citizen legal consciousness. Even though the presumption of the inviolability of legislation of the Romano-Germanic States narrows the sphere of the regulatory influence of reason, the domestic legislator makes blanket references to reason in local matters. For example, to act reasonably or within a reasonable time.

There are many gaps in open systems, and reason is recognized as an independent source of law to fill them. A decision is made based on reason when no statutory rule, precedent, or binding custom exists. Reason manifests itself in the search for a solution most consistent with the rules of the law in force and, therefore, most satisfactorily ensures order in conjunction with justice, which is the basis of law.

Reasonableness as a criterion is universal and, therefore, essential for most forms of law. This attribute acquires special significance in doctrine. Other forms of law (especially normative legal acts) are presumed reasonable, often becoming a source of confrontation between legality and practicality.

Voluntarism is the negation of the objective, socially conditioned. It is opposed to reasonableness, reasonableness.

It cannot be ruled out that doctrine may be voluntaristic, based solely on the will and desires of a person. Vanity, indifference to other ideas, and the lack of fundamental academic research tools create the prerequisites for voluntarism. Voluntarism breaks the link between the form of law, social context, and social needs. For legal doctrine, voluntarism would mean that the State is the sole source of will in the person of its officials and the State. Only its will may be embodied in legal doctrines.

ACADEMIC – NON-ACADEMIC

An academic doctrine has an academic origin. Other kinds of doctrine may have academic roots, but arise from other sources. Legal science may create other kinds of doctrines to a greater or lesser extent. Academicity is positioned as a virtue of the doctrine. Accordingly, if certain types of doctrine do not have stable ties with legal science or conflict with it, this may be a reason to diminish their authority and detract from their validity.

Other types of doctrines, such as State doctrine, do not directly derive from academic publications or ideas. We do not rule out the possibility of creating a State doctrine with academic and expert support. However, there is no reason to see the influence of legal science on the development and publication of State doctrines. The same is true for other types of normative legal acts.

Doctrines without academic roots have the tools and experience to simulate a connection with legal science. State, ideological (perhaps), and judicial doctrines have power based on the powers of the bodies that created them. They discuss their decisions with researchers to make them more academic. Thus, they recognize the importance of academic participation, or at least presence, but are not prepared to base their acts on an academic basis. The authorities feel self-sufficient. They need only embellishment and the appearance of academic elaboration.

Academic validity can be expressed in various studies, examinations, and other academic methods. Actual academicity indicates quality, authors' qualifications, rationality, validity, and conceptuality.

The academic nature of the doctrine is evident in the development of academic terms, concepts, and definitions. Researchers develop, generalize, and systematize the conceptual and categorical apparatus. Academically elaborated definitions can compete with the conceptual apparatus of legislation. For example, there are doctrinal dictionaries.[10] Developing definitions, categories, approaches, and essences of legal phenomena is one of the achievements of legal doctrine.

Scholar doctrine is heterogeneous in quality and authority. It has a methodological basis; it is methodologically verified. As a rule, the academic character of a doctrine is associated with legal science. However, a significant foundation of legal doctrine was created long before the advent of jurisprudence. Legal ideas were developed in treatises on philosophy and politics. However, the doctrine of legal scholars dates to the late nineteenth century. In the narrow sense, legal law is created by lawyers, an emerging legal science. Under a broad approach, these are not only lawyers working in the academic field, but also representatives of other components of the legal profession.

[10] A. V. Malko and D. A. Lipinsky (eds.), Юридическая ответственность. Доктринальный словарь [Legal Responsibility. Doctrinal Dictionary] (2019).

The collective term "corporation of lawyers" refers to lawyers involved in various activities. The positive connotation suggests that such collective professional creativity is the key to professionalism, high-quality doctrine, and legislation. Legal doctrine should be the conventional opinion of the professional legal community, represented by different legal specialties and areas. It also means a plurality of authors, a collective creation of a legal doctrine.

The importance of the academic concept of the development of legislation and law enforcement is indirectly proved by the fact that personnel of State agencies at all levels strive to obtain academic degrees and titles. This is often perceived as a good qualification for the position and enhances (perhaps) the authority of the official position. For example, on the Constitutional Court of the Russian Federation there is a judge who does not have an academic degree, with a citation index of "0". Judges of various ranks and degrees left the court for various reasons. This judge has been sitting since 1997. The judge did not defend either a candidate of legal sciences or doctoral dissertation. This is an anti-example of the bureaucratic approach to academic jewelry.

Most civil servants must be convinced that they are *ex officio* omniscient authorities. Nevertheless, they simulate academic research and obtain evidence of established (subjective) official authority by obtaining academic degrees. Surprisingly, dissertation councils and academic community members are not immune to this harmful movement. Out of fear or command, they vote for falsified dissertations.

Judges of higher courts and legislators with degrees in jurisprudence should be the legal community's most qualified and highly professional representatives. However, this presumption is refuted by numerous examples. The peculiarity of doctrine as an academic phenomenon is that it is an object of self-study; that is, doctrine studies itself. Scholars examine doctrines by extracting their substance from other academic research. At the same time, however, doctrinal works are themselves doctrine.

AUTHORITY – COERCION

Authority is the key word for understanding doctrine. This aspect of doctrine is transmitted mainly from significant researchers and authors of works on jurisprudence. We substantiate the term Persona-Doctrine to designate the founders of doctrines. The personal authority of these persons is both the basis and the result of respective legal doctrines.

On one hand, the authorship of doctrinal works is the basis for the academic authority of the creator of this product. On the other hand, the author's authority draws attention to his works. It increases their citation, which increases the work's authority. This general observation is modified for collective works. René David's 1964 book *The Major Legal Systems of the World* is one example. This book has been translated into ten languages. The revised and enlarged edition is published under the names of two authors: C. Jauffret-Spinosi and David, the latter considered to be the founder of approaches to the legal map of the world. It seems that over time, the authorship of these two people will be perceived as equal.

The question of personal authority has been investigated herein by sociological methods. The questionnaire included a question about the motives for choosing academic literature. We have found that Persona-Doctrines are more likely to read the work of a familiar author. Questions were raised about the authority of the author's position. The brief conclusion is that it is possible to recognize all kinds of authority, including author, work, office, and other types of authority that contribute to the emergence and dissemination of doctrine.

The analysis of educational literature has shown a high frequency of the use of word-markers of authority (authoritative, influence, will, recognition, persuasiveness). Words are markers of authority in English-language literature: authority, common, influence, important, power, significance, significant, and substantial.

Coercion as an external influence on doctrine has its own peculiarities. Usually coercion is perceived as the impact of a

State mechanism that enforces the execution of a right. Doctrine is often criticized for the lack of State support in the form of coercion. However, the problem is more significant because the State protects some types of doctrine, does not support others, and may prohibit others.

SECTION IV

TYPOLOGY OF LEGAL DOCTRINE

Chapter 13
Classification of Legal Doctrines

In legal theory, there are various classifications of legal doctrines. The variety of classifications results from the application of different grounds to justify each. We have provided as many classifications as possible and will continue to work on increasing their number:

1. By the number of authors:
- individual, personalized,
- collective (countable, known number of authors),
- eternal, well-known (an unknown, incalculable number of authors).
2. By the presence (or absence) of connection with the State:
- related to the activities of public authorities,
- not related to the State.
3. By the State authority that created the doctrine:
- judicial
- law-making (created by legislative and executive power).
4. Concerning a specific legal fact:
- related to a specific legal fact (precedent),
- not related to a specific legal fact (regulatory).
5. By constancy of reproduction:
- occur continuously,
- occurring in non-traditional, stressful circumstances.
6. By prevalence:
- local (geographical and numerically small),
- common (in a large group over a large area),

- State (valid throughout the territory of the state),
- universal (international),
- interstate (operating in several States).

7. According to the degree of prevalence in the system of law:

- general law,
- cross-sectoral,
- industry,
- special (for institutions in law and groups of legal norms).

8. By degree of obligation:

- mandatory (with sanctions),
- optional/voluntary.

9. By degree of certainty:

- abstract, figurative,
- defined to a significant extent,
- precisely defined.

10. 10) By form of expression:

- have a strictly defined form (most often a document),
- they do not have a specific form, or the forms are diverse but not unified.

11. Assessment by the State:

- are protected by the State,
- are not protected by the State,
- sanctioned by the State,
- prohibited by the State,
- not supported by the State.

12. By the form of external expression (where are located):

- academic, academic,
- judicial,
- ideological, including the State,
- usual,
- religious.

13. By prescription of occurrence:

- modern,
- past years, starting from the previous generation – 30 years),
- ancient (100 years or more).

14. According to the author's status:

- living contemporaries,
- departed masters.

15. By method of legal regulation:

- imperative,
- declarative,
- dispositive.

16. As recognized in modern conditions:

- fully operational,
- declared inactive,
- acting in fragments.

17. By the degree of connection with the State:

- created by State authorities,
- established by supranational bodies,
- not related to State.

18. By correlation with State guidelines:

- actively cooperating,

- loyal,
- confronting the State.

19. By the number of sources:
- located entirely in one source,
- located in multiple sources.

20. By the form of statements, the features of the text:
- figurative, not legalized,
- descriptive but legalized,
- clear, normative.

21. By degree of structure:
- designed, structured,
- Ideas without a specific structure.

22. By obligation:
- indisputable,
- controversial but permissible (fighting for authority),
- controversial and inadmissible.

23. By source of power:
- have their own power from their authority (power of authority),
- have an external force (authority of force).

The prevalence of types of doctrines was measured during a sociological survey, the results of which were processed by the content analysis. The Questionnaire and the Expert Survey ask the same question about what types of doctrine scholars accept. This is a multiple-choice question, that is, respondents could choose any number of acknowledgments or doctrines and even add their own types.

Diagram 18. (SSLD 1 - ESPD 1). Comparison of Expert and Specialist Opinions on Recognition Types of Doctrines

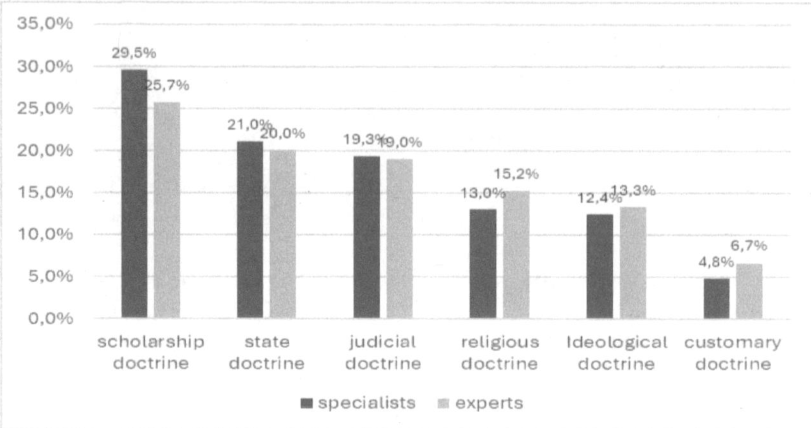

Predictably, the most recognized type of doctrine was the scholar doctrine. It is recognized by 29.5% of specialists and 25.7% of experts. State doctrine is recognized by 21% of specialists and 20% of experts, and the judicial doctrine is recognized by 19.3% and 19%, respectively. Ideological doctrine is recognized by 12.4% of specialists and 13.3% of experts.

These main types of doctrine have almost identical support in two different groups of respondents, which proves the existence of a confident attitude to the typology and support of the corresponding types of doctrines.

Respondents also support other types of doctrine: religious – 12.4% of specialists (13.3% of experts), ordinary – 4.8% of specialists (6.7% of experts). These results demonstrate that these types of doctrine have a foothold in legal circles. They also need to be researched following appropriate approaches and methods.

The official doctrine received a lot of support from the respondents. It is noteworthy that the name "State doctrine" was chosen verbatim by 21% of specialists and 20% of experts. An ideological doctrine can be official or unofficial, depending on the support of the State and unity of purpose. In any case,

32.4% of specialists and 33.3% of experts supported the doctrine of an ideological nature in one form or another.

Respondents also named the types of doctrines we divided into groups. The first group is *sectoral doctrines*: constitutional, civil, criminological, pre-trial, and disciplinary. The second group consists of *doctrines of non-legal origin:* social, philosophical, economic, ethical, spiritual, philosophical, and methodological.

As a result of processing the questionnaire questions, a list of marker words was compiled, distinguishing the type of legal doctrine from the total number. For example, the author uses the words "an established trend in science that enjoys the protection of public authorities", and others. In this definition, there is one marker of scholar doctrine (science) and three States (bodies, State, and power). In addition, satellite words refer to any doctrine (established, current, protection). Accordingly, the author understands doctrine to be an academic or State phenomenon. In mass content analysis, it is possible to conclude that some legal doctrine dominates or subsides in the studied space-time continuum. It can be assumed that in modern Russian conditions, there is a transition from the dominance of a scholar doctrine to an ideological one in the form of an official State.

Content analysis of academic publications on different types of doctrines yielded the following results.

Diagram 19. Priority of Types of Legal Doctrine in Russian Legal Academic Literature (Content Analysis of Publications)

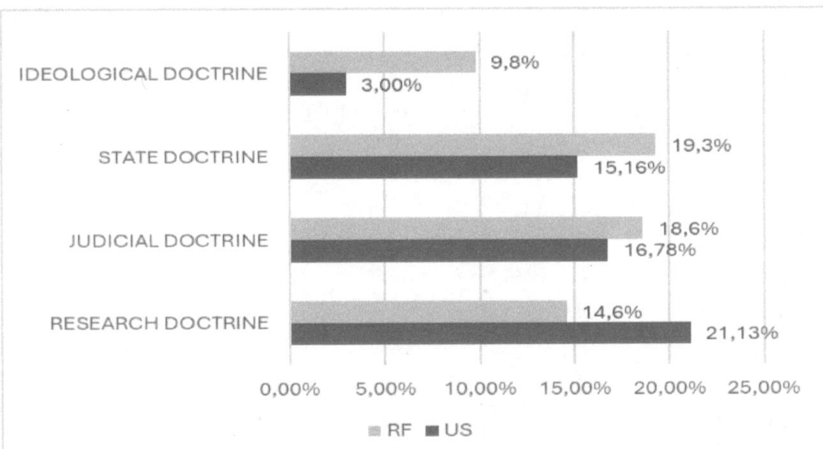

This diagram reflects the prevalence of types of doctrines in academic literature determined by the satellite words of the types of doctrines.

All words in the dictionary should be divided into thematic groups. We call this marking vocabulary words to typify doctrine. An author's affiliation and the work thereof to a specific type of doctrine is determined by the number of marker words (for example, three markers in one text). For example, the author included marker words in the definition of doctrine: "idea", "established", "science", and "scholar". Three words are markers of a scholar doctrine (an idea established by scholars). Respectively, a given researcher accepts a scholar doctrine.

From 1905 to 1968, the dominance of academic doctrine in textbooks was in a state of growth, and it achieved the most significant role in Soviet jurisprudence from 1929 to 1968. From 1968 to the present, there has been a pronounced decline in scholar doctrine.

Chapter 14
Scholar Doctrine: Concept, Essence, Features

CONCEPT OF SCHOLAR DOCTRINE

Scholar (academic) doctrine gravitates towards jurisprudence as legal science research but is the same. What matters is the form of expression of scholar doctrine, that is, the works, genres, and publications that can move from academic research to the next level and become an academic legal doctrine. For a scholar doctrine, the problem of personification or preservation of authorship is relevant because doctrines can be personified and impersonal, and they can also be collective or individual.

As a first approximation, there are differences between legal science and doctrine in the degree of recognition of these phenomena. The authority of doctrine is higher than that of legal science. A doctrine is an authoritative academic study. We see another difference in their efficacy and regulative properties. Academic research is created because of general research. They do not have a direct regulatory impact. In this sense, the works of legal science are the source of doctrine. Some ideas born in offices and libraries become part of public life, are perceived by subjects of law, and have a direct regulatory impact on natural social relations.

Compared to other forms of law and types of doctrine, academic doctrine loses out by reason of uncertainty and is rarely protected by State coercion.

Doctrines, unlike academic research, are usually not personified. They are more often represented by school ideas but not by individuals, which in other respects does not exclude the preservation of Persona-Doctrine. Several authors compete for the authorship of most of the recognized ideas. In this regard, the view of doctrine as an accepted opinion in legal science seems to be justified.

The great Russian jurist Nikolai Mikhailovich Korkunov (1853-1904) proposed to see the differences between legal science and doctrine in the degree of their obligation and the possibility of being embodied in practice. Legal science must be translated into practice.[1]

Because of the above, it can be noted that research and doctrine are related but not identical concepts. Not all legal science is a doctrine, and not all doctrine is legal science. Legal science and doctrine can coincide to form a scholar doctrine if professionals accept the academic idea. A higher level of acceptance is achieved if doctrine serves as the foundation of the appropriate school, meets with the support of society, and, under its authority, directly regulates social relations. A scholar doctrine may be incorporated into, or at least influenced by, other forms of law, such as ideological, State, or judicial doctrine.

In academic literature, a classification of academic research is proposed from the point of view of being recognized by doctrine: 1) the law of lawyers, the direct consolidation of such a fact in the legislation; 2) the right of academic opinions (*communes doctirum opinio*); 3) the right of training of groups (schools); 4) the teachings of some great jurists. The regulative role of these phenomena depends on time, which can be divided into the present and the past.[2] The question of the correlation between scholar doctrine and legal, jurisprudence, and systematized opinion about law is debatable.

Expert law gravitates towards the scholar doctrine. Experts are people who have unique knowledge in the field of jurisprudence. They do not always have academic degrees and publications. Expert testimony may be oral and used in court in its verbal expression, having been entered into the record.

[1] N. M. Korkunov, *Лекции по общей теории права* [Lectures on the General Theory of Law] (3d ed.; 1894), p. 298.

[2] L. I. Petrazhitsky, Теория права и государства в связи с теорией нравственности [Theory of Law and the State in Connection with the Theory of Morality] (1907), II, p. 587.

This oral expert testimony may not always be regarded on a par with written reasoned opinions. However, if the court accepts this oral evidence, it will become the basis for a court decision. That is, it will be applicable next to the law.

Experts are a heterogeneous group. They can be members of the academic community with academic degrees and publications. Or, an expert can be someone outside the legal corps. An expert can be a ballistician, a chemist, and almost any field of activity. These specialists, heterogeneous in terms of educational and academic experience, are united into one group because there is some reason to trust their opinion in particular matters more than others. This may be based on 1) the license or other certification of authority or authorized organization, 2) the method of calculation, the method of conducting the examination, and 3) the reliability and verifiability of the results.

We distinguish expert law as a separate type of scholar doctrine. It cannot be fully identified with published materials, much less with the generally accepted opinion. The expert proves his right to testify in a particular matter. Personal achievements (education, experience, publications, place of work, and other significant markers) are essential. The testimony (conclusions) of an expert in a trial is evidence that the court evaluates and can consider when deciding. It is not a form of law based on which a decision is axiomatically made. A form of law exists; it is given. Evidence, including expert opinions, is provided by the party's participants in the process and may be requested by the court.

Forms of law exist independently of a specific case, arise before it, and are not in any way dependent on it. Evidence in the form of expert opinions is given about a specific case, and outside of it, it does not have an independent value, but it can be given greater importance by legislation and judicial practice.

In the context of academic expertise, we are only interested in examinations related to law and its various manifestations. This can be a connection through the object – expertise, legislation, and other forms of law, for example, anti-corruption expertise of normative legal acts. A link may arise in law enforcement, such as forensics. Lawmaking can also involve experts in jurisprudence (assessing the form of the project from the technical and legal side) or legal regulation (for example, a specialist in demography and beekeeping).

Experts have unique knowledge and evaluate facts, events, and phenomena. Their position ceases to be a subjective opinion due to their personal authority. It becomes a law-forming fact. Experts are significant participants in the legal process, especially in interpreting terms and principles, applying foreign law in other countries, customs of certain groups, and other issues.

Expert opinions are essential in various spheres of legal activity and periodically activate the discussion on the registration of experts. A proposal is made to maintain a roster of experts. Data on them in a systematized form can be included in information systems and reference publications. Assigning experts to issues most relevant to their qualifications is possible. Such State accreditation experience is used in anti-corruption expertise. The registry of independent experts is posted on the official website of the Ministry of Justice of the Russian Federation.

Petrazhitsky believed that the right to legal expertise is one type of source of law. He proposed an original approach to assessing this phenomenon. The researcher rightly noted that expert opinions have a force proportional to the academic authority of the author and the success of their content.[3]

The historical roots of expert law are found in Roman practice, more precisely in the decision of Emperor Augustus to give the expertise of outstanding lawyers imperial sanction and authority. In addition, the authority of experts and the trust of the addressees of opinions played a significant role in the emergence of expert law. Petrazhitsky singled out the stages in forming expert law. The first stage consisted of recognizing

[3] Ibid., II, pp. 591-592.

the examination as mandatory for the decision of a particular case. The second stage of the expert opinion is its application to resolve other similar cases. In the second stage, the expert opinion is applied as a law.

Assessment of the role, significance, and effectiveness of legal expertise in the modern mechanism of legal regulation is a significant academic problem that researchers have not sufficiently developed. Despite their controversial status, many acts of current legislation use this tool. For example, the reglaments of the State Duma and the Soviet of the Federation of the Federal Assembly of the Russian Federation mention examining (internal and independent) draft enactments at different stages. State agencies, primarily the Ministry of Justice of the Russian Federation, act as legal issues experts. Many public authorities have academic advisory bodies or expert advisory councils.

There are recognized expert centers, such as the Institute of Legislation and Comparative Law attached to the Government of the Russian Federation and the Institute of State and Law of the Russian Academy of Sciences. Some scholars are authoritative experts in certain branches of law; they are accepted by the Constitutional Court as specialists and speak at sessions.

The diversity of expert actions makes it difficult to unify the results of this activity. Most examinations are of a recommendatory, auxiliary nature. The uncertainty of their legal status, the lack of State protection, and transparent regulatory properties do not allow us to recognize all examinations as a form of law. However, their role as a source of law may transpire if the legislator considers the results of expert opinions.

Most effective are preventive opinions, that is, those that precede the legislative process. Such examinations include the opinions of the Government of the Russian Federation prepared and based on Article 104(3) of the Constitution of the Russian Federation. The reglaments of the chambers of the Federal Assembly of the Russian Federation provide for various examinations. In fact, these are permissive opinions.

The above is true for modern Russia, whereas in some countries the role of expert materials collected during the legislative process is much higher. The interest in preparatory documents and verbatim records of meetings is explained by the fact that some facets of the norm were not adequately highlighted. At the adoption stage, they secured the support of legislators.

There is an opposite tendency: experts involved in developing significant doctrines are ignored (not invited, not asked), or invited but not listened to. This thesis was confirmed during interviews with Personas-Doctrines. For example, Lafitsky, an authoritative researcher, cited many facts about his own experience and other Personas-Doctrines clearly not in demand in matters in which their knowledge is indispensable.[4]

In the current legislation of the Russian Federation, however, there are examples of the recognition of expert law, that is, of the actual validity of expert opinions. Such examples include urban planning and environmental expertise. Several laws regulate different types of expertise, such as the Federal Law "On Environmental Expertise". The role of expert opinions in procedural legislation is well-established. However, these episodes belong to the first stage of the formation of expert law because they are given in specific cases, and their role is most likely limited to the first stage.

Expert law gravitates towards a scholar doctrine if the expert is an authoritative law researcher. This is the practical part of doctrine because, often, an expert opinion is a documented response of a representative of the academic community to a practical request from a public authority. This can be a request from the legislative (law-making), judicial (law enforcement), and executive authorities.

Objective and subjective factors influence expert law applicability and effectiveness. We note the presence (or absence) of a real need for the requesting authority to obtain

[4] V. I. Lafitsky and S. V. Boshno, "Беседа Президента Клуба Правовой Доктрины С.В. Бошно с профессором В.И. Лафитским [Conversation by the President of the Legal Doctrine Club S. V. Boshno with Professor V.I. Lafitsky]", *Law and Modern States*, no. 6 (2022), pp. 9-23.

an independent expert opinion. Instead, it is the need to cover up the decision made. In fact, omniscience by reason of office is characteristic of civil servants and elected officials. Qualifications and knowledge in all fields come to such people simultaneously at the second appointment or election. Such an attitude does not create a positive mood in obtaining objective, independent examinations. The personal distrust and hostility of the two groups, "the authorities" and the "academic community", is growing with time, and there is no solution.

In general, there is an apparent order for decorative conclusions to academically justify a political (and therefore the only correct, in the opinion of the authorities) decision. A group of researchers who are always whining, begging for money for research, and personally impoverished are sharply opposed to the well-groomed layer of power. Between them is a fluttering academic and educational management of people who once served research or attached themselves to it but have sold themselves out. They must provide the necessary academic opinions of their wards for a fee hundreds of times higher than the payment of the research freaks.

The questionnaire asks whether the payment for expert activities is sufficient. Suggested answer options include extremes ranging from "not paid" to "it is a high-paying job". In the middle are several intermediate assessments.

Accordingly, the assessments of expertise in public authorities, measured by various special tools, showed that the largest group of respondents consider the remuneration of experts to be low. It is no coincidence that we offered a variant of the "paid humiliatingly" answer, which is common in State authorities.

59.1% of specialists voted for the "pay score". The option "not paid" was chosen by 22.9%. In the opinion of 47.6%, the remuneration for expert activities is insignificant, and 11.5% is insufficient to be humiliatingly chosen. Some respondents are optimistic. 16.7% of respondents believe that the pay is sufficient. According to 1.3%, this is a high-paying job.

The situation is identical in many television programs. Presenters grimace at fees, and experts share unique knowledge for free. Moreover, experts who are eminent researchers act to their own detriment because they create a problem for their professional activities.

Volunteering is the performance of activities gratuitously that are usually paid. The idea of this institution is to involve broad masses of participants in socially valuable activities. This gives such activity a pretentious appearance due to its social usefulness and a semblance of public support. Socially harmful or illegal activity cannot be considered volunteering. It is not possible to assess the professional work of highly qualified specialists, such as experts in the legislative process, as being mass and requiring evaluation as socially beneficial. However, the established norm is free of charge, that is, volunteering is welcomed by the authorities. For example, anti-corruption expertise by experts accredited by the Ministry of Justice is free. Perhaps this is one reason why this tool is ineffective.

In several questions, we discussed *the cost of academic* expertise (the expert remuneration, to be more precise). Pricing and deciding on the cost of any work is essential. Many objective and subjective factors impact the cost of academic expertise in law.

Objective factors include the current cost of the service, the labor intensity of work, complexity, and the qualification characteristics of the expert. The cost should mirror of the social value of the work. Expertise is inseparable from the expert as a unique specialist in some issues. An expert has the knowledge and skills that create the prerequisites for such work. Often, contracts for expert services are concluded with an institution (academic, educational, expert, or others). Then, the institution's brand plays a significant role in comparison with the personal characteristics of the expert – the direct executor. The institution must ensure that the contractor work meets the level of quality generally provided by the institution. However, there are cases where, in the application for the competition for the examination of the institution, they indicate that they have

600 Doctors of Sciences on their staff. The opinion, however, is written by a postgraduate student.

In the questionnaire, we provided various factors that affect the cost of the examination:

1. subjective nature as expectations from the achievements and properties of the expert (status of the expert, personal value of the expert),
2. objective nature is a characteristic of the object of the contract – an expert opinion (expertise must be of high quality, be socially valuable, and be in demand to solve the problem that created the prerequisites for requesting an expert opinion).

In the questionnaire, no distinction was made for examinations performed by personified specialists or ordered by the institution (without personalization of the contractor). We now regret the absence of such a gradation in the questionnaire.

Expert work can be 1) permanent (in an institution), 2) systematic (repeated without a schedule or periodicity), and 3) one-off. An expert may be invited to a one-off meeting of a legislative body (for example, a committee). He may be a permanent expert council member or other advisory body working group. An expert can participate in several thematic events (round tables, parliamentary hearings). The body concerned may order a thematic expert opinion or even a study with expert recommendations. In court, the parties can involve specialists and petition the court for the appointment of a forensic examination. It is impossible to cover the variety of methods of attraction and the results of examinations, and we do not set ourselves such a goal.

For all types of examinations, the *strength of the opinion* is essential. Hypothetically, expert opinions can be 1) mandatory, 2) generally mandatory, 3) optional rather than mandatory, and 4) not mandatory. Questions give the respondent the opportunity to choose only one option. It is essential to clarify our position on the meaning of "mandatory" concerning legal expertise. Obligation as an imperative obligation to follow the expert opinions may be established by law. There have been such examples in history, and they gave Petrazhitsky the basis to include expert law among the non-traditional forms of law. In modern conditions, we cannot cite a single example of legal expertise whose results are mandatory for a public authority. In this context, we do not consider forensic and other related examinations. Their toolkit is based on precise methods and tools of exact research. They have a verifiable or maybe patented examination method. This is the knowledge of other sciences (for example, the DNA test in determining paternity) applied in the legal field.

There is a traditional half-measure: conducting an expert examination is imperative, and the customer applies the result. The most effective might be the anti-corruption examination of normative legal acts and draft normative legal acts carried out by Procuracy. The result is binding, but this obligation is implemented during the judicial process. Anti-corruption expertise conducted by other entities, including experts accredited by the Ministry of Justice, is treated as information for the law-making body. It must inform the expert of the decision based on the results of the expert opinions, but is in no way bound by the expert opinion.

Examinations with a controlled (pre-ordered) result will not be implemented. The strength of such expertise lies in following the customer requirements. Excellent examinations have a closed cycle from conception to acceptance of results. The one who writes the object of expertise (draft normative legal act) also acts as an everyday customer of examinations; he pays for them and accepts the results. There are such examples in the legislative process.

Forensic examinations concerning legislation are rare, except for types of legal proceedings with specific normative legal acts as their subject. Instances are known of challenging normative legal acts.

Nevertheless, we allowed the respondent to assess the effectiveness of an expert opinion, including as binding. Only 4.4% of the surveyed specialists believe that experts give instructions that are not otherwise binding. According to 38.3% of respondents, an expert opinion is "as a rule, it is mandatory". Two other options are closer to an unfavorable prognosis regarding the binding nature of opinions. An expert opinion is "optional rather than mandatory". This is the opinion of 49.3% of specialists. The remaining 7.9% categorically do not believe in the binding nature of the examination. 92.1% of respondents admit the effectiveness of legal expertise in one form or another, and 7.9% do not see such a prospect.

We have examined the influence of specialist expert experience on their attitude to the power of legal expertise. The use of the variable "own expert experience" made it possible to assess its impact on the assessment of the impact of expert opinions.

Only specialists without experience in court cases (100%) are recognized as always authoritative. There is a pronounced tendency to reduce the assessment of the status of examinations in proportion to examiner experience. Specialists who regularly participate in the expert litigation practice chose only one option for assessing the examinations: "optional rather than mandatory". Not a single expert with experience recognized the results of the examination as useless. The categorical variant of the non-bindingness of examinations (not mandatory) was chosen by specialists with no experience and with unsystematic experience. Thus, personal expertise significantly impacts the recognition of the role of expertise.

The position "can be taken into account" received the greatest approval. The opinion of specialists who systematically act as experts in legislative bodies dominates. 76.9% of specialists took the position "can be taken into account". There is a tendency to increase the possibility of considering expert opinion depending on personal experience. Specialists with no experience gave 56.8% of the "can be taken into account" option, and 69.5% with a single experience. A frank answer about embellishment status or a complete lack of meaning is supported slightly but still has supporters.

We have formulated a hypothesis about the possible assessment of examinations in different State authorities. To test it, we asked respondents about their personal expert experience in court, in a legislative body, in an academic organization, in an educational organization, and in an executive body and the degree of satisfaction with the payment.

Diagram 20. (SSLD 72 - SSLD 75). Influence of Type of Body on Remuneration of Experts (Specialist Opinion)

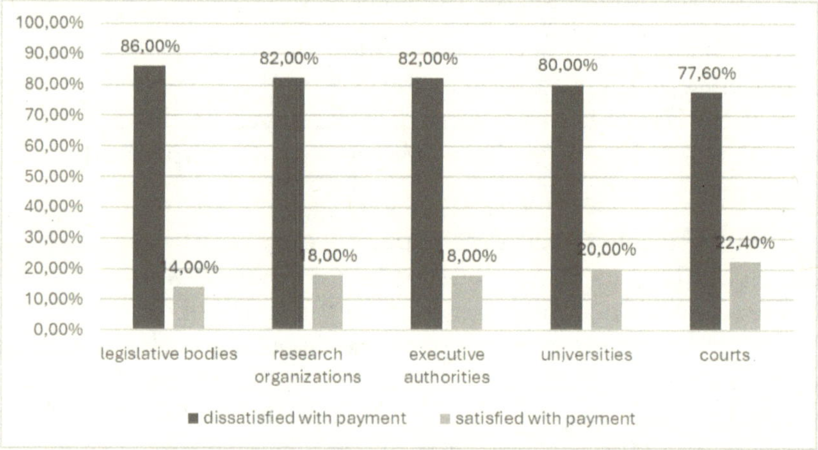

We correlated the bodies where the experts prepared their opinions and the degree of satisfaction with the remuneration. The following were named: court, legislative body, academic organization, educational organization, and executive authority. We have found that the type of customer is almost irrelevant.

The percentage of specialists who are dissatisfied with the remuneration of experts ranges from 86% to 77.7% for different customers. According to 86% of experts, the legislature was the least remunerative. The judiciary has shown itself to be the most generous among the tight-fisted (77.4% of experts think so). The degree of satisfaction with the pay ranges from 14% to 22.4% of specialists.

Thus, the meager remuneration of experts is apparent, and this assessment is not significantly influenced by either the respondent personal experience or the type of customer. The material factor has a strong demotivating effect on those who could hypothetically do this work. The notoriousness of low pay almost immediately eliminates the opportunity to interest a significant, authoritative, well-known specialist. The lack of financial motivation can be partially compensated by positive emotions about high recognition from public authorities. This attraction is akin to *pro bono publico* when experts give opinions free of charge for advertising purposes. In this way, they hope to gain notoriety and capitalize on their investment in other cases.

The questionnaire contains questions about experts in various proceedings (or bodies). Question 76 clarifies the status of an expert opinion in the law-making process. The second clarification is the doctrinal level expert compared to heterogeneous experts in general. Thus, two clarifications make it possible to separate the status in such exceptional circumstances. We did not give the status an imperative meaning – "It will always be axiomatically taken into account". Legislation does not recognize an empirical status, even for forensic examinations.

As with all other forms of legal doctrine, the power of expert law lies in its authority or the customer's indifference in case of a negative result. It can be not only the expert authority but also the addressee state, his readiness to accept the expert opinion as the truth or to ignore it. There is absolutely no reaction from the addressee. He agrees in advance with any conclusion.

Perhaps such an answer could be assumed. The distribution of respondents was as follows. According to 12.8% of respondents, the opinion of the Persona-Doctrine is that "the conclusion is more likely to be taken into account", and 62.6% say "the conclusion can be taken into account". Usually these options demonstrate an upbeat assessment of the cooperation between the doctrinal expert and the law-making body. 75.4% of experts admit the possibility of using the opinion of a doctrinal expert regarding a normative legal act.

20.7% of experts believe that despite the doctrinal level of an expert, his opinion is merely information that will be evaluated by the law-making body at its discretion. The disinterest of the law-making body increases in the following: it does not matter – 1.8% of specialists, it is used as an embellishment – 2.2%. All variants of a negative forecast for expert opinions together total 82.8%.

Particular attention should be paid to assessing doctrinal-level expertise as an embellishment. This answer was chosen by 2.2% of specialists. This assessment is much higher in actual expert practice. It is difficult to identify and prove due to its latent nature. The practical implementation of the thesis about embellishment is as follows. Of course, before the discussion begins, there is an expert document (for example, a draft normative legal act) and a position taken on it (i.e., an explanatory memorandum or draft decision of a legislative committee). This may be followed by a discussion with doctrinal experts, although the results are not recorded in the final documents. However, it was established that a discussion was held with experts on the draft, indicating the full name, positions, and additional statuses. The discussion result is not considered or needed. The legitimacy of the final decision is inevitably increased by the names of the persons who participated in the discussion. We are not suggesting that anyone intentionally conceals discussion documents (that is, transcripts of meetings). However, these sources are not readily available, as were transcripts of meetings of the constitutional commission that drafted the 1993 Constitution. Moreover, these materials are not included in such resources as the Russian Science Citation Index.

Normative enactments provide that candidates for experts satisfy high requirements, including higher education, possession of special knowledge, recognized reputation, and authority. As a rule, it is prohibited to involve those who prepared the draft enactment being evaluated as experts (Law of the Briansk Region No. 28-Z of 3 November 1997, "On Laws and Other Normative Legal Acts of the Briansk Region"). Many subjects of the Russian Federation provide for the work of an external (outside the structure of the parliament) specialist (expert) on a reimbursable basis (Decree of the Legislative Assembly of St. Petersburg, No. 462, of 20 September 2000 "On the Procedure for Financing Legislative and Expert Work in the Legislative Assembly of St. Petersburg"). In some subjects of the Federation, the subject of the right of legislative initiative is obliged to reimburse the costs of conducting a legal examination (Law of Sakhalin Region No. 168, of 3 April 2000, "On Legislative Activity in the Sakhalin Region"). Free expertise is widely used (Decree of the Riazan Regional Duma, of 22 March 2006). In the literature, examinations provided on a *pro bono* basis is assessed negatively: "It leads to the complication of the law-making process and a decrease in the quality of laws".[5]

In general, the unwillingness of researchers to serve on expert communities reflects the low status of this activity for all reasons: 1) the results are not realized, 2) the payment is from miniscule from symbolic or zero, 3) the form of participation in the events is as a guest, 4) it requires that one pay own expenses for self-development, and 5) it distracts from other activities.

UNDERSTANDING OF SCHOLAR DOCTRINE BY RESPONDENTS OF SOCIOLOGICAL SURVEYS

In the questionnaire, specialists were asked to compare doctrine and research (academic studies). The need for such a comparison is the organic connection between these concepts.

42.3% of specialists believe that research and doctrine are different concepts. The smallest number of supporters of recognizing doctrine and research as synonyms is 7.5%. The heterogeneity of academic research is the argument against recognizing research and doctrine as synonymous. Their value

[5] O. A. Fomicheva, "Экспертиза как форма законотворческой деятельности специалистов в реализации законодательного процесса [Expertise as a Form of Legislative Activity of Specialists in the Implementation of the Legislative Process]", Российское право: образование, практика, наука [Russian Law: Education, Practice, Science], no. 5 (2019), p. 54.

for the development of knowledge, and even more so for the development of society, law, and the State, differs significantly from work to work. Another argument is the diversity of doctrine. There are several types of legal doctrine, and scholar doctrine is only one of many.

Traditionally, much attention is paid to academic schools in the description and study of doctrine. The academic school includes the following elements:

1. the founder of an academic school,
2. research program (academic direction),
3. interrelated pedagogical and research functions, dialectical unity of the processes of cognition and transfer of knowledge, skills, and abilities of research work, samples, and shared traditions;
4. academic and pedagogical work style, including a unique moral atmosphere.[6]

There are external attributes of recognition of a team of researchers as an academic school: 1) duration of existence, 2) a stable team of members, 3) tools for the education and growth of school members, 4) periodic events of an academic nature, and so on. Such teams are not structured and do not have permanent and sometimes even periodic academic events.

The survey proposed that the role of academic schools in forming doctrine be considered. The suggested answers are divided into semantic groups – factors: 1) human factor, 2) functional character, and 3) material factor.

Table 6. Activities of Academic Schools

1. Set goals	Functional factor
2. Solve problems	
4. Present solutions	

[6] V. V. Kvanina, "Понятие и признаки научной школы [Concept and Characteristics of an Academic School]", Вестник Университета имени О. Е. Кутафина [Herald of O. E. Kutafin University], no. 11 (2016), pp. 37-42.

3. Form teams of like-minded people 6. Ensure the continuity of generations 7. Accumulate Knowledge	Human factor
5. Consolidate funds	Material factor

These groups of factors are conditional because each interacts with the other and can have points of contact. Each factor can be rated on a scale: a) always, b) often, and 3) never. These assessment options allow respondents to set expectations of academic schools. The need of the State and of research and educational institutions to form, develop, and support academic schools is argued. As a rule, this reflects an intention to elevate academic life to a higher level. One gets the impression that the expectations of organizational and power structures from the academic schools are greatly exaggerated.

The desire of the State to exert an organizational influence on researchers is manifested in the propaganda of academic schools in normative legal acts. Funds, for example, are being consolidated. We clarify this because many forms of researcher self-organization in the name (most often informal) imply the mentor's name. For example, the followers of O. E. Kutafin, V. S. Nersesiants, and G. V. Maltsev. It is expected to have functioning leadership if it is a structured school of thought. In addition to State and grant funding, there may be sponsorship and donations to the activities of the academic school. However, it seems there are not many active academic schools in jurisprudence. We have yet to determine the reason for the academic community's low trust or lack of action in responding to a relevant State proposal. The listed properties of academic schools in terms of the strength of their influence and areas of activity are arranged as follows: 1) accumulate knowledge – according to 61.7% of specialists, 2) form groups of like-minded people – 48.5%, 3) ensure the continuity of generations – 44.%, 4) set tasks – 41%, 5) solve problems – 39.6%, 6) present solutions – 26.4 %,7) consolidate funds – 20.3%.

Respondents showed a high level of negative assessment based on "accumulating knowledge". A record number of specialists disagree with this – 22%. The ability of the academic school to consolidate funds was also negatively assessed (18.1% of specialists). The factor of efficiency of the economic activity of the academic school is the lowest in two respects. On one hand, this factor enjoyed positive assessments by the smallest number of specialists – 20.3% and many negative ones – 18.1%.

Table 7. (SSLD 88). Assessment of Effectiveness of Activities of Academic Schools (Specialist Opinion)

The Human Factor			Functional factor			Material factor
accumulate knowledge	form groups of like-minded people	ensure the continuity of generations	set goals	solve problems	present solutions	Consolidate funds
140	110	101	93	90	80	46
		351			263	46

The most significant effect of the academic school is revealed in the human factor. This result corresponds to understanding an academic school as a virtual place where like-minded people connect. The effectiveness of schools is low, demonstrating the respondent low scores on the functional factor. The material factor is practically non-existent.

In the variant of the answer "always", it is evident that there is a concentration of answers on the factors of influence on legal doctrine on the part of the academic school. Thus, the primary value of academic schools is ensuring the unity of approaches to academic knowledge. Like-minded people at different times and in different spaces ensure the preservation and development of the academic school. Academic schools have little functionality, which apparently reduces their attractiveness. Some attempts by the Russian leadership to revive academic schools by registering them and providing targeted grant support have not yet yielded tangible results.

Based on the survey results, we analyzed the criteria for evaluating the works of researchers. When selecting sources for study, specialists make an input (deciding on familiarization) and final decision (after completing the assessment according to the listed and other criteria).

Using sociological tools, we studied the criteria by which specialists select academic materials for review. In fact, academic research has several markers of their outer shell of a bibliographical nature (for example, the year of publication) and the degree of relevance (the Hirsch index). We have formulated criteria groups: quantitative, titular, qualitative, and evaluative.

Quantity criteria: 1) citations in the Russian Science Citation Index, 2) year of publication, 3) several co-authors, 4) circulation, 5) several citations, 6) several views (downloads). Indicators of this group are quickly established by the external properties of the work and available Internet resources for general free use. This indicator is expressed as a number and can be easily compared with other work indicators. The ranking (ratings) procedure by quantitative indicators is simple. These criteria can be used by anyone and do not require any special education or degree.

Title criterion – titles of the work or author: 1) publisher, 2) reviewers, 3) genre of publication, 4) place of work of the author, 5) academic degree of the author. These indicators are found in the publication and relate to the characteristics of the work as printed products or are established from external sites (for example, from the author's biography). Establishing these criteria also does not require professional knowledge and an academic degree. They are easily accessible to any observer and do not require special knowledge and skills.

The quality criterion characterizes the work as the result of academic activity. This criterion includes the following elements in the text: 1) visualizations (by visualization, we mean diagrams, tables, artistic illustration, and the like), 2) statistical data, 3) a unique empirical base, and 4) writing style. This criterion makes it possible to determine the content of appraiser activities and the requirements for their professional characteristics. Applying the quality criterion requires familiarization with the text of the work. Evaluation of research methods, ways of using the results in work (for example, tables, graphs, diagrams), and the author's style require professional education and an academic degree. This is a complex and informative assessment of a specialist in the subject of research who has research skills.

The evaluation criterion is based on an opinion about the object. It includes 1) the author's reputation and the reputation of his works to the evaluator, 2) personal characteristics, and 3) the opinions of colleagues and like-minded people. These indicators are united by a common condition for their implementation: the appraiser's involvement in the academic community knowledge of specialists in their subject area. The expert gives a personal assessment of the publication, considering the author's personal characteristics, which can be done based on direct contact, acquaintance, personal and indirect, and the opinion of academic community members. Such impressions can be obtained in the work collective at the place of work, at professional events (conferences, hearings, forums), in a narrow circle of experts, for example, among members of a dissertation council. To apply the evaluation criteria for an included observation, the evaluator must be a member of the specified groups (all or several). The peculiarity of this criterion is that it can only be implemented by experienced researchers involved in professional and academic information flow professional groups, where they can become a subject of monitoring. To conduct a qualitative analysis, the examiner obtains information, as a rule, using methods of built-in observation.

Accordingly, for each criterion, the respondent is provided with options for choosing the degree of their attention to the listed characteristics: "always", "often", and "I do not pay attention". We hypothesize that more professionally trained respondents with research experience and academic degrees do not apply the criteria of groups 1 and 2. They focus more on criteria 3 and 4, emphasizing criterion 4.

When evaluating empirical data and visualizations, it is necessary to consider their insignificant use in legal research. They are more applicable in applied legal research, less in branch legal research, and are rarely used in theoretical and legal publications.

The rating of effective characteristics always taken into account when evaluating the research is as follows: 1) writing style was supported by 35.4% of respondents, 2) unique empirical base – 34.1%, 3) author's reputation – 30.5%, 4) academic degree – 23.9%, 5) genre of publication – 22.6%, 6) year of publication – 20.8%, 7) statistics – 14.2%, 8) author's place of work – 13.7%, 9) reviewers – 11.9%, 10) some co-authors – 10.2%.

Even less influential are the following characteristics: publisher, size of publication, personal characteristics of author, affiliation with an authoritative institution, opinion of colleagues, number of views, visualizations, citations in the Russian Science Citation Index, circulation, and number of citations.

Accordingly, the following characteristics are not crucial for the evaluation of the study: 1) circulation – 52.7%, 2) the number of citations – 36.2%, 3) personal characteristics of the author – 34.5%, 4) number of views – 31.4%, 5) visualization – 31.4%, 6) number of co-authors – 27.9%, 7) citation in Science Citation Index – 25.2%, 8) size of publication – 23%, 9) affiliation with reputable institution – 22.1%, 10) place of work of the author – 22.1%, 11) publishing house – 20.8%.

The presence (or absence) of the influence of the respondent academic degree on his assessment of indicators was checked. In general, it can be stated that the academic degree does not significantly influence the choice of research objects. For all three categories of respondents, indicators such as style, unique database, reputation of author or works to the respondent, and academic degree are first in importance. Accordingly, these criteria are credible indicators of validity when rechecked in various ways. It is these indicators that creative researchers should pay attention to concerning their own works.

Diagram 21. (SSLD 41). Influence of Presence/Absence of Academic Degree on Criteria for Selection of Literature (Specialist Opinion)

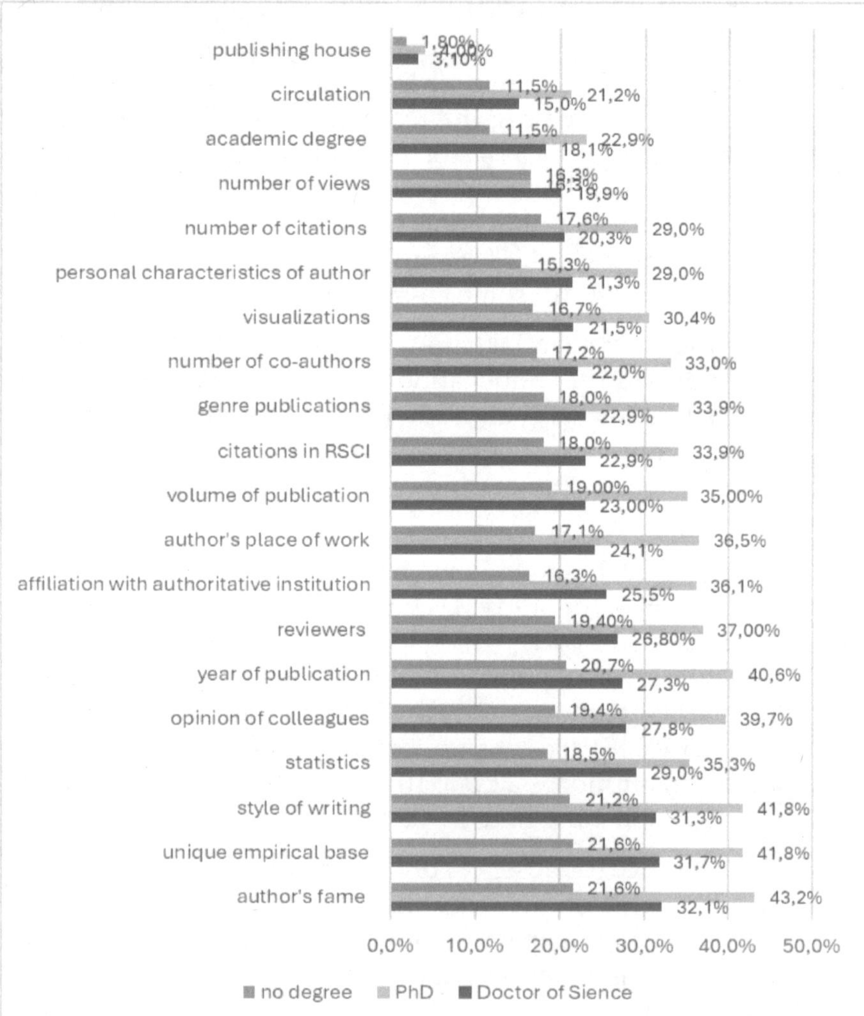

There are differences between representatives of various groups of respondents. For example, a Doctor of Science pays attention to the publishing house and the personal qualities of the authors.

Diagram 22. (SSLD 41). Influence of Doctoral Degree of Respondent on Attitude to Characteristics of Works (Specialist Opinion)

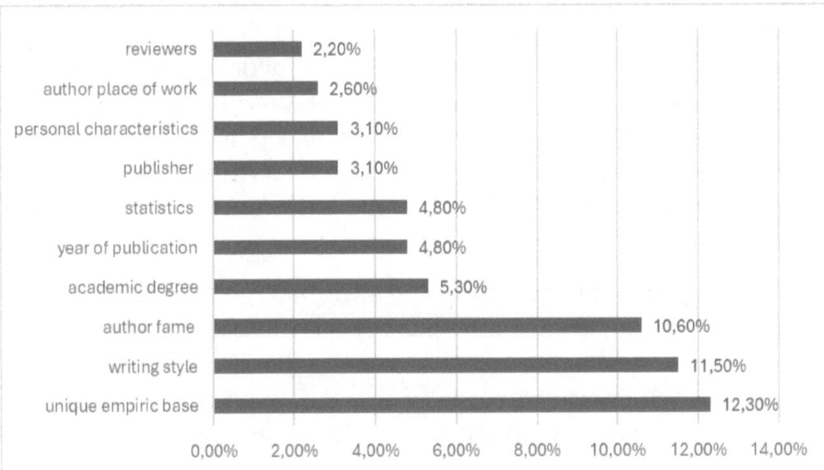

Publishing houses are divided into prestigious, ordinary, metropolitan, regional, professional, multidisciplinary, or printing houses. Considering the personal qualities of the author when evaluating the work is more of a doctoral refinement. Eminent, honored, prominent lawyers make up a small group whose members often know each other personally, which affects their attitude toward their work. Moreover, the connotation concerning this category of authors may be different. Of course, in priority, one would like to see the positive impact of the author's reputation as a reason to read and use his publication. The highest admiration for a particular study can be expressed in the expectation of an innovation or the discovery and introduction into academic circulation of an inaccessible publication by an outstanding master. However, there is likely an indifferent and negative reaction to persons who are formally part of a senior circle of experts but do not enjoy academic authority. A thousand monographs on a new topic from the owner of a publishing house or any work by a pseudo-academician will only strengthen the negative reaction.

Respondents with a candidate of legal sciences degree additionally pay attention to the number of co-authors of the study. Specialists without a degree pay attention to the presence of visualizations. We did not specify whether a large or small size of a work is more motivating and attracts readers. Indeed, there is a fashion for huge books, the size of which is often supplemented by normative legal acts. There are works of 1000+ pages. There is an antipode of such large-scale works – "cheat sheets" and concise books of up to 100 pages that attract readers without a degree. It can be assumed that the size should be reasonable – 250-500 pages. Extremes tend to be less attractive.

When formulating the questionnaire, we understood visualization as diagrams and typed images of some legal phenomena. We have a textbook on the theory of State and law in which each chapter begins with a professional drawing, for example, rules of law, forms of law, and offenses. [7]

As a result of the survey, the attractiveness of visualization for a particular reading contingent has been ascertained, which means that this method can be used in educational works or to promote legal knowledge. However, as sociological research has shown, visualizations attract readers without degrees, and vice versa, scare away more qualified readers. Candidates of legal sciences and Doctors of legal sciences deny the attractiveness of visualization for evaluation (13.7% and 11.5%, respectively). Thus, pictures and artwork are more likely not to be accepted by readers with advanced degrees.

Doctrinal recognition in modern conditions, in the short and long terms, will be based on the opinions of candidates of legal sciences and doctors of legal sciences, respectively, and visualizations in academic publications are inappropriate at

[7] S. V. Boshno, Теория Государства и Права [Theory of State and Law] (2003).

this stage. In the long term, with the possibility of professional growth for people without a degree, we can expect an increase in the value of visualizations in the overall treasury of doctrinal merits of publications. Another explanation for the low acceptance of visualizations is the traditional formatting of legal publications. There are practically no figures, diagrams, or tables in them. Of course, there are no entertaining visualizations, although caricatures are allowed. For example, V. B. Isakov places a caricature for each topic of the theory of law and State.

Figure 10. Caricatures as Way of Visualization[8]

Respondents were provided with a list of relevant, relatively new ways to promote the results of their academic research in the form of publications. To the question: "How do you assess such methods of promoting ideas?" the following answers were offered: 1) video interpretations, 2) reviews in print media, 3) public recommendations of politicians, 4) direct advertising, 5) posting on library platforms, 6) social networks.

[8] The man says: Constance! The woman answers: What kind of Constance!? My name is Constitution!

Among the promotion methods, there are rather conservative techniques: reviews in printed publications. Direct advertising is more of a method implemented by publishers for high-volume publications. This contributes to book sales but is not acceptable for articles.

Methods of promotion using the Internet (video presentations, social networks) are more advanced and technological. Most methods require the use of Internet resources. Some are complex, such as direct advertising. We did not include in this questionnaire the apparent methods of promoting researcher ideas in the research community, such as the publication of research presentations at conferences. Expert activities, including those in public authorities, are considered elsewhere. These can be a way to promote ideas and, as a result, increase the authority of a person as an expert and as a researcher in general.

We call the recommendations of politicians unique methods. This method is not widely used and not easy to implement. Consider the influence of the President of the Russian Federation, V. V. Putin, on enhancing the authority of Ivan Aleksandrovich Il'in (1883-1954).[9] Paying for the reburial from Switzerland and a new tombstone on Il'in's grave at the personal expense of the head of State undoubtedly promoted the reputation and ideas of that legal philosopher. In addition, the head of the Russian State has repeatedly quoted Il'in,[10] especially noting his work "What the Dismemberment of Russia Promises the World".

The N-gram clearly shows how the actions of the President of the Russian Federation (possibly in conjunction with other factors) concerning Ivan Ilyin influenced the growth of mentions

[9] "Путин возложил цветы к надгробиям деникина, Ильина и Шмелева [Putin Laid Flowers at the Tombstones of Denikin, Il'in and Shmelev]", Вести [News], 24 May 2009 (available online). AFor a thorough account, see I. A. Il'in, *On the Essence of Legal Consciousness*, ed. & transl. W. E. Butler, P. T. Grier, and Paul Robinson (2d rev. ed.; 2023), pp. 53-54.

[10] "Путин закончил «Георгиевскую речь» цитатой русского философа Ильина [Putin Ended the 'St. George's Speech' with a Quote from the Russian Philosopher Il'in]" (available online)

of the philosopher in publications. Until 1997, it had a modest number of mentions. They peaked in 2007 and fell by 2015, confirming the unnatural, politicized origin of the increase in citations.

Figure 11. The Reaction of Google Books Ngram Viewer to Political Factors, to Mentions of I. Ilyin

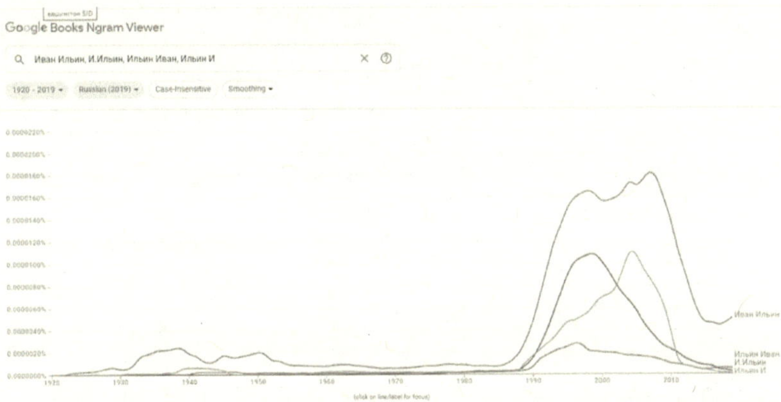

Public recommendations may give a negative message to the research community, such as the President and the Prime Minister's participation in appointing a person without a degree and with substantial anti-academic compromising material as the rector of the Russian Academy of Public Administration. In 2014, the candidate for this position, Komissarov, was refused his academic degree due to accusations of plagiarism. He was an acting rector from 23 January 2023, until the moment he defended his thesis. This is the first time that an aspirant with a questionable academic biography has been appointed to the post of rector of a leading state educational and academic institution. It is like an indulgence: the main thing is to repent, but a "scholar" can commit a sin. A "good chap" with an anti-academic reputation as a rector is a public recommendation to politicians not to care about their academic reputation. Considering this example, the topic of administrative resources and personal connections becomes important for identifying points of doctrinal growth.

Diagram 23. (SSLD 90). Evaluation of Methods for Promoting Author's Ideas (Specialist Opinion)

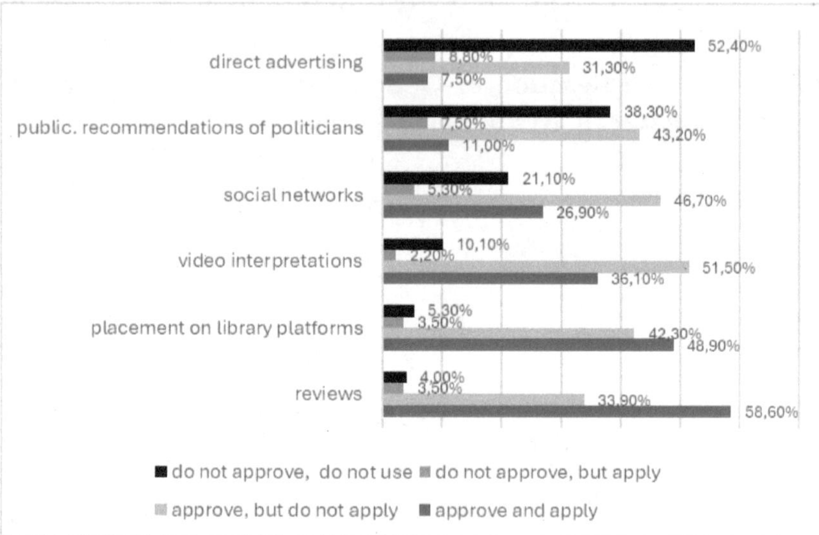

The most approved and used reviews were reviews in print, placement on library platforms, and video interpretations. Promotion types such as social networks and public recommendations from politicians are approved but not applied. The most conservative method received the highest approval level – placement of reviews and reviews in printed publications. Placement of reviews on library platforms is a modern tool that makes a work available electronically. As a rule, this is not an initiative of the author, but of the publisher. This is a new form of advertising. Recognition of the usefulness of video presentations has been exceptionally high. This method of promotion may or may not be used, but has been highly praised. 36.1% of specialists use video presentations, and 51.50% do not use them, but in any case, they are viewed positively. If we consider those who disapprove of video presentations but nonetheless use them, the popularity of this method reaches 89.9%. The reserve of this method comprises respondents who approve but do not apply it due to the high technological complexity and lack of appropriate skills among the researchers themselves.

Methods not approved by specialists: direct advertising (52.4%), public recommendations of politicians (38.3%), and social networks (21.10%). It may be assumed that other researchers will use these methods to express a negative assessment of a work. If specialists consider these methods unacceptable, they may not support those authors who use such methods, and this may affect citation of the work.

Concerning how ideas are promoted, we traced the correlation between the age and academic degrees of specialists.

Diagram 24. (SSLD 90A_6 - SSLD 103). Influence of Age on Use of Social Networks to Promote Author's Idea (Specialist Opinion)

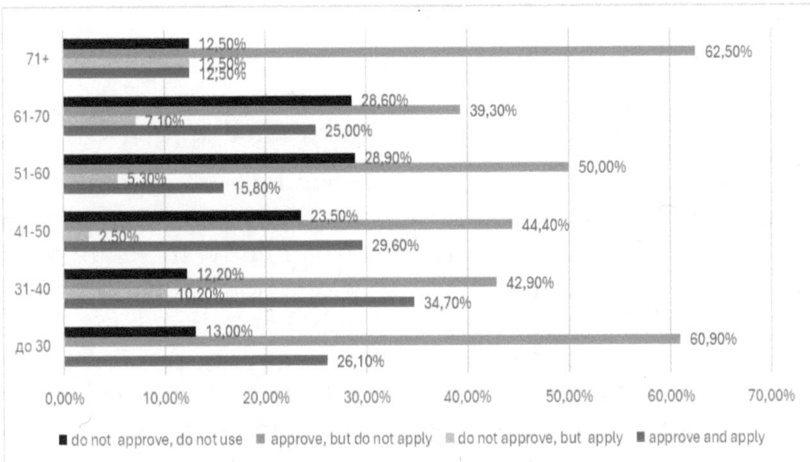

Correlation with age was carried out for different age categories. The group of 31-40-year-olds is the most active and works with social networks. The low activity of the youngest group may be due to the lack of facilities for them. Accordingly, they are more represented in the "approve, but not applying" group, which has 60.9% support. This is a promising group of young people with education, many of whom are already masters or other postgraduates. From the peak after the age of 40, the activity of social media use has been decreasing. However, there is a high interest in social media among this 40+ group. Notably, among researchers aged 71+, it is as high as among young people under 30. Unlike specialists under 30, they have access to facilities and an academic degree. The reasons for not using social media in this age group may lie in lacking skills to use this tool.

We have enlarged the groups. The group of "active researchers" included specialists who chose the options "approve and apply" and "disapprove but apply" social networks as a way to promote their ideas. The group of "passive researchers" includes specialists with the positions "I approve, but do not approve" and "I do not approve, do not apply".

The most active group social network users are specialists aged 31–40 years, of whom almost half (44.9%) use social networks to promote their ideas.

Respondents were asked to assess their involvement in using the video interpretation method. The application of the video interpretation method by age was distributed as follows:

Quite an exciting category of respondents chose the option "I approve, but do not apply". It would be interesting to know the motivation behind that choice. Apparently, there are some obstacles to the application of promotion. Such obstacles include engaging in a core gainful job. These may be material limitations because the employee must pay for services if it is impossible to do it himself. Perhaps the lack of knowledge and skills in the production and placement of video content hinders specialists.

The interpretation of the high acceptance of video presentations in the 70+ age group led us to interview such researchers. Having reached the peak of their academic degrees and achievements, they have reached a mature age and receive prestigious offers, including the creation of video products.

FREQUENCY AND VECTOR ANALYSIS OF THE CONCEPT OF SCHOLAR DOCTRINE (CONTENT ANALYSIS)

Marker words of scholar doctrine: item, aggregated, citation, citations, creating, define, defining, distinction, foundational, fundamentally, generally, identified, identify, importance, meaning, original, suggests, systematically, validity, interpretation, subsidiary, classical, development, approach, base, concept, idea, issue, opinion, point, research, statement, term, though, treatise, theory.

Prognostic Functions of Scholar Doctrine, Foundation of Other Types of Doctrines. The influence of academic work on lawmaking undoubtedly exists. However, we lack evidence because the legislator does not keep records of borrowings from legal research into the texts of normative legal acts. Indirect evidence of borrowing (influence) can be: 1) the coincidence of the text of the normative act with academic work; 2) documents accompanying the draft law (explanatory note with theoretical justification of the draft, expert opinions, and other texts), 3) materials from parliamentary hearings, round tables; 4) proactively directed proposals, conclusions, and the like.

Consider an example from our own academic work. In 1997, S. V. Boshno defended her candidate of legal sciences thesis on "Legislative Initiative in the State Duma of the Federal Assembly of the Russian Federation". The study concluded that it is necessary to exclude the legislative proposal from the permitted forms of initiating the legislative process (Article 95, Rules of Procedure of the State Duma of the Federal Assembly of the Russian Federation). Boshno pointed out that Article 95(3) of the Rules of Procedure

> significantly complicates the law-making process. The current normative legal acts do not provide the procedure for transforming a legislative proposal into a draft law. There are no formal rules on the execution of proposals or the procedure for their submission to the legislative body.[11]

[11] S. V. Boshno, Законодательная инициатива в Государственной Думе Федерального Собрания [Legislative Initiative in the State Duma of the Federal State Duma of the Russian Federation] (1997) (dissertation candidate of legal sciences).

Until the constitutional amendments of 2020, senators were called members of the Soviet of the Federation, p. 81.

Thus, the dissertation contained a reasoned conclusion about the need to amend Article 95 of the Reglament. The results of this study were sent to the State Duma in the form of an abstract with an explanatory letter. These materials were made available to the Committee on Legislative, Judicial, and Legal Reform of the State Duma of the Federal Assembly of the Russian Federation and were used by the Ministry of Justice of the Russian Federation.[12] In the new edition of the 1998 Reglament of the State Duma of the Russian Federation this norm was included in the wording recommended by Boshno (omitting legislative proposals as a form of exercising the right of legislative initiative).[13] Recognizing the significant contribution of Boshno to the theory and practice of the legislative process, on 13 December 2017, the Soviet of the Federation held a round table "Issues of Improving the Effectiveness of the Use of the Right of Legislative Initiative by Federal Parliamentarians", timed to coincide with the twentieth anniversary of the defense of this candidate of legal sciences thesis. The author was responsible for the elimination of the negative norm from the Reglament of the State Duma of the Federal Assembly of the Russian Federation, which positively impacted the legislative process. Proof of the importance of Boshno's publications, research, and educational activities is the Certificate of Honor of the Chairman of the Soviet of the Federation dated 27 January 2015, No. 4593 (Appendix). However, all the evidence presented is circumstantial, and the actual changes can be explained by chance. It is possible that other researchers presented similar conclusions to the State Duma. Patent certificates are not issued for academic ideas in the form of proposals for improving legislation nor are they protected by copyright.

[12] Ibid., p. 17.

[13] "Постановление ГД ФС РФ от 01.22.1998 No. 2134-II ГД "О Регламенте Государственной Думы Федерального Собрания Российской Федерации" [Decree of the State Duma of the Federal Assembly of the Russian Federation of 22 January 1998, No. 2134-II of the State Duma "On the Reglament of the State Duma of the Federal Assembly of the Russian Federation]", СЗ РФ (1998), no. 7, item. 801.

In the empirical base of our study, respondents, experts, and interviewers provided extensive material from their personal experiences influencing legislation. The examples we have collected can be divided into several groups:

1. work on the draft law and connections with the field of research work. This is a conditional doctrinal form because the law did not include the results of the project research. To some extent, however, it tends toward doctrinal forms. We see this attraction in that the credibility of the project on the part of the law-making body is primarily based on the author's authority as a researcher.

2. the author of the project did not offer his work to the legislator in any way. Information flowed from the author to an indefinite circle of people from publications, public speeches, participation in expert groups, and so on.

3. the author submitted his research to public authorities. A good example was the Soviet and early post-Soviet practice of defending legal dissertations. Submitting a certificate to the Dissertation Council on implementing the research results in practice was necessary. This document reported what proposal was sent by the dissertation author to the law-making agency of State power and the result of consideration thereof (if any). However, even without a recognized official result, this encouraged researchers to inform law-making bodies openly and purposefully about new ideas for improving legislation. It could take the form of a draft normative legal act, idea, concept, or proposal. It should be noted that researchers are no longer encouraged to submit their work or recommendations to public authorities.

4. Researchers may hold public office. Their legal knowledge as legal scholars may coincide with their job duties. This is an ideal option because the State, ideological, and research doctrines, and perhaps judicial doctrine (depending on the position), are combined into a single

whole. We know of one such example – Professor E. V. Taribo.[14]

14 E. V. Taribo, Доктрины Конституционного Суда Российской Федерации в сфере налогообложения: Теоретический и практический аспекты" [Doctrines of the Constitutional Court of the Russian Federation in the Field of Taxation: Theoretical and Practical Aspects] (2005) (dissertation candidate of legal sciences); Taribo, Проблемы эволюционного развития российской модели судебного конституционного нормоконтроля [Problems of Evolutionary Development of the Russian Model of Judicial Constitutional Norm Control] (2019) (dissertation doctor of legal sciences).

Chapter 15
Judicial Doctrine

CONCEPT OF JUDICIAL DOCTRINE

Judicial doctrine is the established opinion of the judicial system or judges, expressed in certain forms, which impacts the understanding and application of other forms of law, including normative legal acts. It is like three forms in one object. In terms of the form of expression, a judicial doctrine can be a law-enforcement act or a generalization of decisions (precedents). In terms of its origin, it may or may not have an academic basis (scholar doctrine). Judicial doctrine is closest to a normative document in respect of its impact on other decisions. However, decisions may or may not have an academic basis. The voluntarism of the judicial system has not been abolished. Without legal grounds, it has been creating a more robust law than legislation for decades. This is a kind of appropriation of power, the seizure of the right to create a normative legal act without the legislator's decision. But suppose for decades no one has prohibited the law-making activity of the courts. In that case, it has been legalized by the actual existence and application.

Judicial doctrine has the most significant impact on the courts. Suppose other courts do not follow the judicial doctrine. In that case, this indicates a lack of unity in the judicial system and deprives the intermediate form – the decision (precedent) – of meaning.

A decision based on a scholar doctrine is more likely to turn into a judicial one. Otherwise, it is a one-off decision without a sequel. The peculiarity of judicial doctrine in comparison with other doctrines is its formulation in the judicial system. It can result from the actions of judicial authorities (for example, decisions on fundamental cases) in the form of their normative law enforcement practice. A judicial doctrine may be created by bodies of the judicial system consisting of judges, for example, by the Plenum of the Supreme Court of the Russian Federation (decrees). Reviews of judicial practice are confirmed by the Presidium of the Supreme Court of the Russian Federation. These are generalizing documents of an evaluative and instructive nature. Moreover, court decisions are a form of judicial practice that directly or indirectly affects subsequent law enforcement. This is an individually created court practice. The sociological base of the study establishes that it is possible to recognize single decisions made in fundamental cases as a judicial doctrine. As a rule, the legal provision formulated in the previously issued law enforcement act is borrowed and continues to be applied. It is to this form that the final decisions of the Constitutional Court of the Russian Federation belong. In cases of their subsequent application, the opinions (legal provisions) of previous decisions are used in other cases.

Publications by judges are at the intersection of judicial and scholar doctrine. Judges of the Constitutional Court and the Supreme Court of the Russian Federation often hold academic degrees, including doctor of legal sciences degrees, and publish articles or books. In form, this is academic work, such as a textbook, an article, or a monograph. However, the author's personality has a robust instructive effect on readers when such works are published in his judicial capacity. This applies to individual and collective publications, such as commentaries associated with the Supreme Court. At academic events, publications emphasize the judicial position of the participant, which affects the perception of his speech or published theses.

The judicial background of retired judges influences the subsequent perception of their works. This is a form of abuse of status or trust. However, the user community gives the re-evaluation, not the judges themselves. Users do not conduct "blind peer review", that is, reading the material without the name and regalia of the author (editor, compiler). In fact, they begin to read with knowledge of the full name and position of the author and absorb the material under the influence of the position. As a result, readers may, inadequately dumbfounded by authorial titles (editors, and so on), overestimate the publication. They perceive it not as the author's opinion, but as the official position of the authority, in this case, the court. This phenomenon takes place in various other situations. It is as if they act as complex figures: 1) a teacher or researcher plus 2) a judge. Two-in-one increases the pressure on the reader's expectations.

Since 2020, judicial doctrine has not been enriched by the dissenting opinions of judges of the Constitutional Court of the Russian Federation. Judges of the Constitutional Court of the Russian Federation are prohibited from publicly publishing a dissenting opinion or opinion referring to it (Article 76, Federal Constitutional Law of 21 July 1994, No. 1-FKZ, as amended 31 July 2023, "On the Constitutional Court of the Russian Federation"). As a result, we have lost an informative source, which remains a form of judicial doctrine in previously published documents.

We are not aware of the official interpretation of the effect of the 2020 rule in time. If we apply general theoretical approaches, this prohibition does not apply to previously published dissenting opinions. This is a form of the judicial doctrine of individual production, and it is always opposite in content or does not fully coincide with the principal final decision in the same case. Thus, the judicial doctrine simultaneously contains several provisions, ideas of opposite or at least different content, emanating from the judicial body as a whole and from an individual judge (dissenting opinion). Many types of doctrine are pluralistic. This diversity is assessed ambiguously. Some researchers consider diversity an advantage, while others consider it a disadvantage. However, in any assessment, we cannot exclude contradictions between different ideas in a doctrine of the same type (in this case, judicial doctrine): significant differences in conceptual nature or partial discrepancies between different doctrines (for example, lack of uniformity between scholars' and judicial doctrine).

For a more in-depth study, it is necessary to distinguish between judicial doctrine and practice; it can be assumed that the difference lies in the degree of relevance in other legal forms.

Judicial doctrine is fixed in court acts. In the Russian legal model and judicial system, the Constitutional Court of the Russian Federation occupies a special place because its activities are often doctrinal. This judicial body often encounters legal problems and conflicts in constitutional law enforcement. However, there is no explicit legislative norm for resolving them. Decisions are based on prevailing opinion, scholar doctrines, and their own legal positions. The final documents of the Constitutional Court of the Russian Federation are primarily in the form of reasoning, discussions about different positions, and evidence. The legal positions of the Constitutional Court of the Russian Federation are binding. But they are not legislation. Accordingly, judicial doctrine is a form of law formed in law enforcement and is not the result of law-making. In terms of content, it is an interpretation of legislation. The interpretations explain the legislation but do not constitute new legislation.

In the questionnaire, we asked the respondents about the legal nature of the decrees of the Plenum of the Supreme Court of the Russian Federation concerning types of doctrine. The respondent was asked to identify decrees of the Plenum of the Supreme Court of the Russian Federation with different types of doctrines: judicial and State. A generally negative answer is assumed – it is not a doctrine. We did not give the option to recognize the decrees of the plenum as a scholar doctrine because it was possible to prove or argue the origin of the decrees of the Plenum of the Supreme Court of the Russian Federation.

The most significant number of specialists – 65% – attribute decrees of the Plenum of the Supreme Court of the Russian Federation to judicial doctrine. 5.3% of specialists consider these documents part of State doctrine, and 29.6% do not consider these documents to be doctrine. Experts were also offered an answer – "ideological doctrine" – not chosen by any specialist.

A large group of specialists (29.6%) who do not consider the decrees of the Plenum of the Supreme Court of the Russian Federation to be doctrine in general is of great importance. Perhaps they distinguish between jurisprudence and judicial

the Supreme Court of the Russian Federation). Other subjects of the right of legislative initiative can also take the ideas of their draft laws from law enforcement acts. Indeed, reviews of judicial practice and decrees of the Plenum of the Supreme Court of the Russian Federation are a storehouse of professional legal information about gaps in the legislation and proposals for their elimination.

The Government of the Russian Federation is obliged to submit draft laws to implement legislative proposals of the Constitutional Court of the Russian Federation. However, none of the official channels (through the Government or directly from the Constitutional Court or the Supreme Court of the Russian Federation) work at a certain speed. There are instructions from the Constitutional Court to amend legislation that have not been implemented for years. Thus, the mechanism for transitioning judicial doctrine into legislation has not been properly debugged. We assume there could have been relevant academic research before judicial registration, then this way: scholar doctrine – judicial doctrine – legislation. The result will be law. There is no legally established information channel between courts and law-making bodies for other types of law-making. However, if they develop in the future, it could improve the quality of normative legal acts.

The transition from judicial doctrine to normative legal acts may be carried out at the request of a judicial body (for example, Constitutional Court) to change legislation in a certain way. Judicial doctrine can interact with normative legal acts – doctrines. Such a case occurred in 1995 concerning the constitutionality of the Military Doctrine. At that time, the Constitutional Court refused to address the constitutionality. It did not recognize the Military Doctrine itself as a normative legal act. However, one cannot be immune to requests to test the constitutionality of any doctrine. The academic literature has not yet formulated a definite opinion on this matter.

As an agency of power, the Constitutional Court of the Russian Federation gives official normative interpretations, formulates legal positions, participates in law-making by addressing general instructions to the legislator on the adoption of current legislation, the recognition of certain norms as unconstitutional ("negative legislator" – G. A. Gadzhiev). Judges of the Constitutional Court of the Russian Federation are doctors of legal sciences and professors, some of whom are bearers of legal doctrine. Their publications constitute a golden legacy of Russian jurisprudence.[2] However, in general, the personnel and, as a result, the Constitutional Court doctrinal potential are declining and reaching a critical level in 2025. Suppose the supreme authority of the State does not make conceptual decisions. In that case, the Constitutional Court will cease to be part of the space of academic legal doctrine.

Diagram 25. Judges of Constitutional Court of Russian Federation

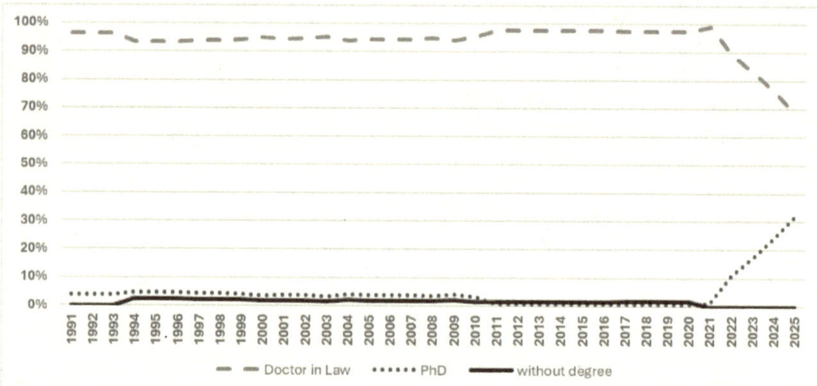

Work with doctrinal sources in the Russian Federation and the United States is organized differently. Some doctrinal resources in the United States are entirely different from those in the Russian Federation. For example, American judicial acts are very academic in form. They extensively cite academic research and judicial acts previously adopted in other cases. The design of court documents tends to be academic; for example, there

[2] G. A. Gadzhiev, Онтология права: (критическое исследование юридического концепта действительности) [The Ontology of Law: (Critical Study of the Legal Concept of Reality)] (2020).

are endnotes to all sources used, including articles and books. Such a judicial-academic approach to formatting makes it easy to search for doctrine in the footnotes of judicial acts. These judicial citations are indexed in the same way as academic citations, such as HeinOnline.

In Russia, there are practically no citations in the court decisions (except for the Constitutional Court of the Russian Federation). We have never seen endnotes in Russian court documents. Available examples of citations are formatted as in-text inclusions in parentheses with a full or partial bibliographic description. There are practically no references to academic research, textbooks, and commentaries that predominate.

Courts are more likely to assess academic works as an inadmissible source of law. Often, judges criticize the content of works not so much as the fact of the citation itself. Courts of general jurisdiction criticize the content of a work less than they deny the possibility of quoting an academic publication and using it as a source of law. This denial is because scholar doctrine and academic works are not officially recognized as a form of Russian law (except for foreign family law). This position of the judicial authorities regarding citation is recorded in a Ruling of the Supreme Court of the Russian Federation, according to which a court's reference in a decision to the textbook on the theory of State and law edited by doctor of legal sciences S. S. Alekseev and to the commentary to Article 116 of the Code of Civil Procedure of the RSFSR (edited by D. A. Sergeev and A. P. Rizhakov) were inappropriate because textbooks and commentaries on legislation are not sources of law and, under Article 10 of the Code of Civil Procedure of the RSFSR, cannot be applied by the court directly as a justification for a court decision. The position of the Constitutional Court of the Russian Federation is entirely the opposite.

There are hundreds of decisions and rulings of the Constitutional Court of the Russian Federation where the main argument is the presence or absence of a thesis in legal doctrine. For example, the Decree of the Constitutional Court of the Russian Federation of 14 July 2005, no. 9-P, "Re: Case of

Verification of the Constitutionality of the Provisions of Article 113 of the Tax Code of the Russian Federation in Connection with the Complaint of Citizen G.A. Poliakova and the Request of the Federal Arbitrazh Court of the Moscow District" contains the following argument: however, neither the Constitution, nor legislation in force, nor legal doctrine provides any basis for such conclusions, but, on the contrary, contradict them. A reference to a provision generally accepted in the domestic legal doctrine is contained in the Decree of the Constitutional Court of the Russian Federation of 27 April 2001, no. 7-P. This indicates that the complexity of assessments and the need for qualification in decision-making differ significantly in administering justice in specific civil (or criminal) cases and constitutional justice.[3]

It is necessary to separate judicial doctrine properly, which originates from the court and is legitimized by it, from decisions and precedents. The diversity of references to previous court cases seems to form an established trend. This practice may eventually acquire its own name, unrelated to the original case. For example, the "ministerial exception" doctrine is used in the United States as a general legal doctrine without reference to a specific case. As a rule, upon closer examination, it is not difficult to find precisely the case that first formed the corresponding vision (idea) in this chain. It can be a decision on some matter of principle.

The high status of the parties, the exceptional importance of the case, and the involvement of the United States Supreme Court ensure citation and perception by subsequent jurisprudence. Despite its singularity, such a decision is quoted and interpreted often, not only directly but indirectly, based on a general meaning. Conventionally, we can say that court documents in the United States have a rating that reflects the meaning and value of judicial texts. This value is not for the parties to a particular case. For them, the decision (another document) is legal and has practical value. In doctrinal terms,

[3] Boshno and G. G. Vasiuta, "Доктринальные источники служебного права [Doctrinal Sources of Service Law]", Государственная служба [Civil Service], no. 2 (2010), pp. 44-47.

we are talking about the expected value for all people and things that will be in the future. It is a universal value.

A decision in a particular case is original in that, without acceptable primary sources, the court makes its own (conditionally new) decision with its own reasoning. The court fills the gap in the law under its own responsibility. Such a solution could create a chain of followers. They will give the original decision the status of a precedent. Suppose in the future, there is a uniform practice that fits the status of a doctrine of the judicial type in content. In that case, it will also be a judicial doctrine in origin (legitimation). Thus, it arose in court and was legitimized by the court as a right.

In Russia, without the official status of judicial precedent, it is impossible to imagine the formation of judicial doctrine through the repetition and citation of earlier decisions on specific cases. In the absence of citations of earlier decisions (prohibition of quotation), tracing this vector is impossible. Court documents are uniform because they are based on the same legislation. In this regard, the Russian doctrine of judicial origin cannot be formed by moving along the line of recurrence. At the same time, there are unique information channels in the Russian legal system through which the highest court – the Supreme Court of the Russian Federation – receives information about how certain norms are understood and applied in different ways. In this case, the Supreme Court of the Russian Federation has two primary forms of response: the publication of a review of judicial practice for the quarter of the year or a decree of the Plenum of the Supreme Court of the Russian Federation. At one time, we studied the forms of expression of judicial practice in the Russian Federation. We came to the following conclusions:

> The forms of expression of judicial practice can be understood, and this is, more correctly, the outer shell in which judicial practice is contained. To identify the forms of expression of judicial practice, we used two

grounds: 1) legislative regulation and 2) recognition and consideration in legal practice by subjects of law.[4]

Time has passed (20 years), affecting the Russian Federation's judicial system and our views. The most significant changes are the abolition of the Supreme Arbitrazh Court of the Russian Federation, the creation of cassation courts, and the reform of the Constitutional Court and the Supreme Court of the Russian Federation. From the conclusions of the 2002 study, it is necessary to exclude the information letters of the Supreme Arbitrazh Court and the decrees of the Plenum of the Supreme Arbitrazh Court. In the system in force for 2025, the information letters of the Supreme Arbitrazh Court of the Russian Federation and decrees of the plenums of the Supreme Arbitrazh Court of the Russian Federation issued in 2002 should be used with greater attention. Even though such documents are not issued now, previously issued ones may continue to operate.

Reviews of judicial practice and decrees of the Plenum of the Supreme Court of the Russian Federation have been retained. The Constitutional Court of the Russian Federation has lost its academic doctrinal status for personal reasons and has lost the public form of dissenting opinions. How judicial doctrine is formed in the Russian Federation and the reasons for the publication of documents in some make it difficult to compare the judicial doctrine of the United States and the Russian Federation.

The reason for interpretations in the form of rulings and reviews in the Russian Federation is negative *signals* from the judicial system that some cases are considered heterogeneous; there is no homogeneity in the understanding and application of certain norms. Review and ruling have different methods of responding to these issues. The reviews address cases in which, in the opinion of the Supreme Court of the Russian Federation, the court "correctly" applied the law, and this example should be followed as instructive. This information resource of

[4] Boshno, "Формы выражения судебной практики [Forms of Expression of Judicial Practice]", Юриспруденция [Jurisprudence], no. 1 (2002), pp. 14-33.

the Supreme Court of the Russian Federation is not official. However, it is authoritative material, placed in legal reference databases, and acquires an instructive character. The decree is an abstract document, not related to any specific case.

Citation of reviews in courts is not welcome. However, they are instrumental in law practice, and lawyers are guided by the cases selected in the reviews. Courts tend to avoid accepting documents with a position rejected in reviews. Instead, they will follow a position the Supreme Court recommends as instructive.

FREQUENCY AND VECTOR ANALYSIS OF CONCEPT OF JUDICIAL DOCTRINE. MARKER WORDS OF JUDICIAL DOCTRINE

We asked respondents to choose markers from the proposed words to identify judicial practice. Respondents could choose any number of words that could be used to define and understand judicial doctrine. It was possible to add new words to the list.

Table 8. Frequency Analysis of Judicial Doctrine

Frequency of mentions	A Word to Define Judicial Doctrine
319	Practice
304	Precedent
292	Decision
184	Judge
183	Presumption
164	Business
154	Court
146	Plenum
135	Interpretation
132	Position
123	Law enforcement

122	Generalization
96	Review
59	legal provisions
58	Comment
43	Special

In American academic space, the following marker words of judicial doctrine have been identified: court, case, decision, judge, judgments, judicature, judicial, justice, precedent, judicially, supreme, and precedents.

Chapter 16
Ideological Doctrine

CONCEPT OF STATE DOCTRINE

An approach to this phenomenon is officially formulated in the Doctrine of the Development of Russian Science, which is a system of views shared by Russian society, the State, and researchers, expressed in the form of programmatic and declarative political attitudes that determine the social status, development goals, principles of organization, and the role of Russian science. Under this approach, a doctrine is a view that has simultaneously won the recognition of society, the State, and researchers. This force unites the mass, professional, official, and academic consciousness, and thanks to the support of the State, such a doctrine becomes a political orientation.

This ideology officially and legitimately operates in each territorial-political organization of society. There cannot be many such ideas. Their strength lies in the unity of these three components. The definition clearly states that the doctrine does not perform a normative function. This is emphasized by "programmatic and declarative political guidelines". Such an approach is logical in a State professing statist positivism. It is used in official documents of a declarative nature. A distinctive feature is the proclamation of agreement between forces in constant confrontation. It is an embellishment, a pact of intent, a strategy for moving in a particular direction.

Content analysis of State acts with the word "doctrine" in their titles has shown that the most common word combinations are the main directions of State policy, a system, the basis of the strategy, and a strategic planning document.

Thus, an eclectic definition of State doctrine can be formulated: a State doctrine is a strategic planning document containing the main directions of State policy, a system of strategic provisions, and the basis for activities in certain areas. It is not possible to transfer this definition to other types of doctrine.

The definition of the doctrine uses the phrase "political attitude", which makes it possible to see in the "Doctrine of Science" not a State official doctrine but an ideological political doctrine. This document is an appendix to the Edict of the President of the Russian Federation. Accordingly, it is not a normative act because it is not adopted as a decree or other normative act. The text of the document is not binding; on the contrary, it is declarative.

State documents containing the word "doctrine" in their titles contain practically no active verbs. The content analysis of all State doctrines revealed the following words, to one degree or another, related to the operation of the doctrine: introduction, achievement, protection, use, located, prevention, ensured, provide, determine, implement, implement, enhance, enhance, support, application, forecasting, dissemination, expansion, implement, recommendations, recommended, improvement, creation, correspond, established, take into account, is, formation. These are words of the passive voice.

It turns out that State official doctrine is a species of ideological doctrine, which, in addition to State ideas, includes ideas of other origins. State ideological doctrine derives from official institutions or seeks to become such.

Official State doctrine is bound by the geographical boundaries of the State. Ideology can be stated, in which case it has State boundaries, but it can hypothetically be applied beyond them.

Ideological doctrine has several forms of expression. State ideological doctrine is objectified into official legal acts. Their names include the words "doctrine", "concept", and "strategy". Of the experts interviewed, 16.6% recognize the existence of a State doctrine as a particular type. The opinion of an expert who claims that this is the only type of doctrine is quite interesting. Experts believe that all the other types we propose (academic, judicial, non-State ideological) can only be called concepts or ideas. But they are not doctrines. We have taken the liberty of calling this view a statist view, which absolutizes the State as the source of doctrine. All subsequent responses by this expert follow in the wake of this initial statement. As a result, they are embedded in the logical line of the ethical understanding of doctrine.

Experts who are proponents of statism think that:

1. State authority and administrative resources support the validity of the doctrine,
2. Experience in public service helps to form a doctrinal status.

Such experts are participants in a consolidated State ideological doctrine. In this regard, they do not see restrictions as obstacles to their creativity but as the natural boundaries of the power stratum. They are involved, responsible, and of one mind with respect to the State doctrine. At least, that is how they position themselves. The names doctrine, strategy, and concept are used interchangeably in government documents. Thus, the State doctrine "is a set of official views on the goals, objectives, principles and main directions", and "the concept is a system of views".

In the Constitution of the Russian Federation, the term doctrine is used in connection with the description of the powers of the President of Russia. He has the right to approve military and other doctrines. Evaluating the Military Doctrine, the Constitutional Court concluded: "That the Military Doctrine does not contain normative provisions". This policy made it impossible to assess the Military Doctrine for its compliance with the Constitution of Russia. Given this judgment, the doctrine has lost its normative significance. Only the declarative role remained. After such an unequivocal negative assessment of the Constitutional Court of the Russian Federation, the interest of law-making bodies in doctrinal works should have dried up. But this did not happen. As of January 2025, five doctrines are in force and placed in the legislation database of Consultant+.

Assessing the relationship between doctrine and the normative legal act, it is clear that the legislator has demonstrated a desire to take into his own hands the formation of fundamental ideas and views to formulate a new State ideology. The Constitutional Court of the Russian Federation categorically declared the symbiosis of doctrine and the normative legal act untenable. Nevertheless, subsequent law-making practice demonstrates the continued and expanded adoption of doctrinal documents.

Official documents are included in the general source coding table. In the database of this study, these documents are assigned ID: ODOC_RU_#, ID: ODOC_US_#, which, as the objects are collected, are supplemented by the number of the document (this is not the number of the normative legal act). For documents, the fields in the Excel workbook are sequence number, document type, document title, date of acceptance, issuing authority, and storage location/document reference.

Official documents are entered into Zotero using the source type "document". Zotero does not automatically store data from Consultant+. The information is entered manually.

UNDERSTANDING OF STATE DOCTRINE BY RESPONDENTS OF SOCIOLOGICAL SURVEYS

In 1995, the Constitutional Court of the Russian Federation considered a case concerning the review of the constitutionality of several normative legal acts, united by the fact that, in the applicants opinion, they had unconstitutionally legitimized the beginning of the operation to restore constitutional order in the Chechen Republic. The Constitutional Court of the Russian Federation refused to assess the constitutionality of the Edict of the President of the Russian Federation dated 11 February 1993, No. 1883, on the confirmation of the Military Doctrine because the document, including the Military Doctrine, had no normative content. The Decree of the Constitutional Court of the Russian Federation dated 31 July 1995, No. 10-R, contained an analysis of the legal nature of the document and examined its possibility to regulate social relations. It was found that the document was very general and did not contain rules of law.

Since this decision by the Constitutional Court of the Russian Federation, the public authorities have continued to issue doctrines, concepts, and strategies. Naturally, the relevant issue concerning the new documents is their status as a normative legal act. To date, it has not been empirically proven that the Constitutional Court of the Russian Federation would decide differently with respect to other doctrines and recognize them as normative legal acts based on their content. Considering the legal nature of each document, they may have different features of normativity. Suppose we do not assess the content of each document and proceed from its type (declarative, non-normative). In that case, it can be assumed that all similar documents are not normative legal acts following the position of the Constitutional Court in 1995. A more probable scenario is that if a new request arises, the Constitutional Court of the Russian Federation will abandon the 1995 position as outdated and not consistent with the new socio-political conditions.

The Constitutional Court of the Russian Federation has rejected previous legal positions openly and procedurally. For empirical verification, a reason must be created in the form of a new request to the Constitutional Court of the Russian Federation with a new document(s). As long as there has been no such case, researchers can express their understanding of Decree No. 10-P and the possibility of its application to subsequent doctrinal documents.

In the questionnaire, we asked whether the legal position of the Constitutional Court of the Russian Federation remained valid today, thirty years after the Decree was issued.

In the opinion of 63.3% of specialists, the position of the Constitutional Court of the Russian Federation has remained valid. 36.7% of specialists believe that the position is no longer valid. The motives and rationale for the answers were left out of this survey. However, several other survey questions clarify this issue.

FREQUENCY AND VECTOR ANALYSIS OF STATE DOCTRINE (CONTENT ANALYSIS). MARKER WORDS OF STATE DOCTRINE

Marker Words Associated with the State Doctrine from Academic Literature in Russian Language: leaders, leader, ideologies, ideology, ideological, quasi-party, class, communism, communist, Communist Party, CPSU, Lenin, Leninist, Liberal, Marx, Marxism, Party, Politics, Political, Post-Soviet, Programmatic, Program, Proletariat, Proletarian, Soviet, socialism, socialist.

State Ideological Doctrine in the Academic Literature of the United States: ideological, ideology, legislation, legislative, legitimate, parliamentary, policy, politics, political, political politics, statute.

State doctrine in educational literature experienced its finest hour in 1999. Interest in it returned in 2003, and since 2009, there has been an upward trend.

State ideological doctrine is a legal document of indefinite normativity.

In the questionnaire, we formulated a clarifying question, which is considered in conjunction with the Constitutional Court Decision No. 10-R: respondents are asked to evaluate modern doctrines, strategies, and concepts without normative prescriptions. Each document needs to be studied, and the subject matter determines the type of rules of law therein. This requires expert knowledge of the typology of legal norms and normative legal acts. The text may contain not only general rules, but also regulatory or protective ones. In this regard, it would be more correct to pose the question not about the document but about each norm separately. The simplified, unambiguous structure of the document being assessed in the questionnaire question is given – it does not have normative prescriptions.

According to 4.40% of specialists, doctrines, strategies, and concepts are "always" normative legal acts. This opinion is diametrically opposed to the position of the Constitutional

Court of the Russian Federation in 1995. Experts were offered an evasive answer, admitting that some documents may be normative acts. It was chosen by 49.60% of specialists. 46% of specialists strictly follow the position of the Constitutional Court. They pointed out that strategies, concepts, and doctrines without normative prescriptions are never normative legal acts.

Thus, the supporters of unequivocal recognition of State doctrines by normative legal acts are represented by an insignificant, absolute minority. Nevertheless, many undecided respondents, ready to individually assess each document for the possibility of recognizing it as a normative act, constitute a significant percentage (46%) for their probable recognition as a normative act. However, experts who avoid an unequivocal assessment may increase the number of supporters of the Constitutional Court's position of 1995.

Regardless of the number of respondents who recognize certain State doctrines as normative acts, the opponents of such a decision will, in any case, be in the majority. There comprise 50 % of the total. However, a distribution of specialists in which 50% of those are confident in the validity of the Constitutional Court Decree and 46% have doubts indicates the insufficient authority of this Decree in the professional legal environment. Most survey participants are doctrinal researchers. They are knowledgeable about these issues and can argue their position, which differs from that of the Constitutional Court. 46% of those who hesitate in a categorical view assume that it is necessary to evaluate not the type of documents as a whole (for example, doctrines) but the content of each object separately. Some can be assessed as normative, while others are declarative and non-normative.

A cross-poll of respondents on the problem of "State doctrine" or "normative legal act" attempts to determine the status of these documents as accurately as possible. Suppose the position of the Constitutional Court of the Russian Federation remains valid. In that case, documents of a general nature (such as concepts, doctrines, and strategies) are not normative acts.

The analysis shows the overall consistency of respondent answers. Accordingly, those respondents who consider the Decree of the Constitutional Court of the Russian Federation to be in force do not recognize the strategies, doctrines, and concepts as normative legal acts. There are 55.6% of such respondents.

Several questions of the questionnaire for specialists are address the status of State doctrines (documents) within the system of forms of law. There are several options:

1. these are normative acts with the same status as the normative legal act by which they are confirmed or in which they are issued, for example, an edict of the President of the Russian Federation;
2. they are not normative acts because they have only declarative and not normative prescriptions,
3. these are not normative acts. They are a particular type of doctrine – State doctrine – a subtype of ideological doctrine,
4. depending on their content, these documents may or may not be partially or fully normative legal acts; they contain a heterogeneous set of norms of a general and normative nature. These documents have been confirmed or signed by officials but do not have a specific normative legal act concerning their legitimation.

There are other options for determining the status of these documents. Suppose a doctrinal document is not recognized as a normative legal act. In that case, this does not negate the possibility of recognizing it as a State doctrine because it is a doctrine of State power, a State policy on a particular issue. If we recognize it as a normative legal act, it is not a doctrine. This assertion is based on the approach that, simultaneously, the same precept is not considered in several legal doctrines or forms of law.

Thus, State doctrine is not a normative legal act but another form of law – an ideological State doctrine. 61/5% of respondents agree that it is a State doctrine. On the other hand, 38.5% of respondents do not recognize documents that have the words "doctrine", "concept", or "strategy" as State doctrine.

The correlation between the attitude to the military doctrine in the position of the Constitutional Court of the Russian Federation, which did not recognize it as a normative legal act, is as follows. About 60% of specialists consistently refuse State documents of this kind to be recognized as normative legal acts. Respondents who do not recognize, for example, the Information Security Doctrine (type – State doctrine) as a legal doctrine may not recognize these documents as a normative act; that is, it is not a doctrine, but it is not a normative act. This type of document is classified as a legal act.

It is essential to establish whether the words "concept", "strategy", and "doctrine" are a type of document or an element of a title from both a theoretical and a law enforcement standpoint.

This contradictory construction contains two contradictory theses: 1) acts of a general, conceptual nature are normative legal acts and, at the same time, (2) they are called concepts or doctrines. The position of the Constitutional Court of the Russian Federation excludes the possibility of documents of a general conceptual nature being normative legal acts. Accordingly, respondents who chose the "invalid name" option followed the position of the Constitutional Court, but only 11.5% of specialists did.

In the same block, a question draws respondent attention to the differences between the document type and the title element. There are many such problems in jurisprudence. Here is a well-known example: the Federal Law "... Code".[1] This

[1] Boshno, "Codification", Право и современные государства [Law and Modern States], no. 2 (2014), pp. 44-51; Boshno, "Кодификационные акты и другие источники права: проблемы приоритета [Codification Acts and other Sources of Law: Priority Issues]", in: Международная научно-практическая конференция "Кодификация законодательства: теория, практика, техника" [International Scientific and Practical Conference "Codification of Legislation: Theory, Practice, Technique"] (2008), pp. 120-142.

construction involves the dispute between scholars and judges, including the Constitutional Court of the Russian Federation. The debate about whether any code equals any federal law has not found an unambiguous solution. It seems that the position of the Constitutional Court of the Russian Federation has been reduced to a simple rule: we will decide on a case-by-case basis. There is no one-size-fits-all solution for all cases. The same can be said about doctrines – documents: There is no one-size-fits-all solution. We will address each individual example.

In this survey, using induction, we transfer the discussion about the type of document as a normative legal act and its name, written in quotation marks from the code, to the doctrinal document. The primary purpose of the title is to orient the subjects of law in the subject of legal regulation of the document. The document type is intended, *inter alia,* to establish its position in the hierarchy of legal acts and determine its effect concerning subordinate documents. The hierarchy also indicates the higher types of documents concerning the one being evaluated.

We asked respondents to identify the words "strategy", "concept", and "doctrine" in government documents as (1) a type of document, or as (2) an element of the title of a document.

Specialist opinions were distributed as follows. The words listed indicate the type of document for 45% of specialists. 55% believe it is an element of the name. Accordingly, this document does not have a legal nature clearly defined by law. The word "doctrine", like "code", is an element of the title. If it is a type of document, then it is an edict of the President of the Russian Federation. The National Security Concept is the Edict of the President of the Russian Federation, No. 1300, of 17 December 1997. Accordingly, this is a normative edict. Following the constitutional hierarchy, the edict must comply with federal laws, and other normative legal acts, starting with decrees of the Government of the Russian Federation, must comply with the edict.

Getting those doctrines and concepts signed or confirmed by officials is more complicated. Because they are not a normative legal act, it is impossible to include them in the hierarchy of normative legal acts.

Referring to the same decision of the Constitutional Court of the Russian Federation of 1995, let us recall that it considered the Military Doctrine of the Russian Federation, confirmed by Edict of the President of the Russian Federation. As a result, the Constitutional Court of the Russian Federation assessed not only the military doctrine but also pointed out: "In this regard, there is no normative content in the Edict of the President of the Russian Federation dated 11 February 1993, No. 1833" (Decree of the Constitutional Court of the Russian Federation, of 31 July 1995, No. 10-P). Thus, the Constitutional Court of the Russian Federation shifted the assessment from a derivative document (in this case, from the Military Doctrine) to the main document – the Edict of the President of the Russian Federation. The Court considered that to determine the type of edict on military doctrine, it was unnecessary to examine its annex containing the text of the military doctrine. Even without this, it was evident that this edict had no content. In legal theory, such documents are called legal decisions. Laws enacting other laws are of the same type.

Until 2020, Article 115(1) of the Constitution of the Russian Federation specified "normative edicts of the President of the Russian Federation"[2] as a type of general type of document. The Constitution of the Russian Federation as amended in 2020 eliminated this reference. Nevertheless, the academic classification of edicts into normative and non-normative has been preserved. Accordingly, not only individual edicts of the President of the Russian Federation but also edicts in which "there is no normative content" can be non-normative. The analysis shows that recognizing these words (doctrine, strategy, concept) as a type of document prevails among respondents who believe in these documents high value and independence. In the opinion of such respondents, they are conceptual, do not merge with other State documents, and stand above them

[2] See Butler, *Russian Law and Legal Institutions* (2d ed.; 2018), p. 455.

because they provide general ideas that should be embodied in normative legal acts. This opens another discussion on the topic of hierarchy. Consideration should be given to the legal status of doctrine, concepts, and policies for federal constitutional laws and federal laws, which, however, is beyond the scope of this study.

An ideological political doctrine is a volatile type of doctrine. The attitude to ideology in the mass consciousness undergoes dramatic changes repeatedly.

An ideological doctrine can not only follow the law, but also operate when there are gaps, or deliberate silence, and even against the law. Strictly speaking, following the Constitution of the Russian Federation, no ideology can be State-owned. All views are equal and equidistant from the agencies of State power. This is what ensures competitive ideological diversity. In the same constitutional approach, State legislation and party norms are separated. At the junction of these phenomena, a party State with a single ideology emerges, which confuses people with skeletons from Soviet historical memory.

After the dissolution of the former Soviet Union and the Communist Party of the USSR, the term "ideology" acquired a negative connotation in Russia. This psycho-emotional perception of the term has led to its being ousted from the political and legal context. However, this was done unreasonably. On its own, the term is entirely neutral. It denotes a whole systematized consciousness. Ideology is the second level of consciousness after the empirical one. The 1993 Constitution of the Russian Federation established a ban on State ideology to overcome the fears of the past – a centralized political system based on one party while banning others. And suddenly, after thirty years of relative indifference to this issue, there was a surge in public discussion about the need for a common State ideology. A quest is underway for both a new definition and a new ideology. The appeal herein to ideological doctrine has little to do with this ferment of social consciousness. We have assumed that ideological doctrine has always existed alongside other doctrines.

The need for an ideological doctrine arises without other effective forms of law. This is part of the wrongness in its formulated form; it is the right of the future that is expected but not yet existing. In this way, gaps in the law are filled. A wrong can become a right after it is legitimized. For example, in pre-revolutionary Russia, the banned Marxist circles propagated ideas that, after the revolution's victory in 1917, became the official law of the new Soviet country. In fact, wrongness rejects existing law as unjust, not corresponding to some ideas or ideology.

CONCEPT OF IDEOLOGICAL DOCTRINE (ANTI-LAW, WRONG, PROGRAM LAW, LAW OF ELECTION PROMISES, AND OTHER IDEOLOGIZED PHENOMENA)

We have identified two forms of ideological doctrine: official, State, and unofficial, political. By defining these two forms as separate and self-sufficient, we do not exclude the possibility of a State ideology. However, this phenomenon in its proper form is beyond the scope of our study.

We separate State and ideological doctrine by origin, which has led us to acknowledge the possibility of combining them. State doctrine is formulated by the State.

Ideological legal doctrine is a set of ideas regarding the organization of State authorities, legislation, and legal policy.

State legal (official) ideological doctrine is a set of ideas shared by State authorities and constituting the basis of State policy. A type of ideological doctrine, it is issued in various legal acts sanctioned by State authorities. State doctrines are not normative acts. They are not published, but are approved by public authorities.

An unofficial ideological doctrine is a set of ideas of State-legal content developed by non-State bodies, organizations, and individuals who do not have State sources and forms. Parties are the main channel for generating, maintaining, and disseminating an unofficial State doctrine. A party with a majority in the agencies of power, a parliamentary majority, has a party ideology that turns into a State line, a State Doctrine.

A State without a legal or de facto multi-party system and pluralism is a party State. The official ideological doctrine of such a party is the only or super-dominant one. It purports to permit or forbid an unofficial ideological doctrine.

Table 9. Comparison of State Ideological Doctrine

Type of Doctrine / Properties	State Official Ideological	Political Ideological
Created by	State	Various sources: researchers, politicians, thinkers, oppositionists, politicians, and State agencies. authorities
where it is embodied, in what it is expressed	legal acts such as strategy, doctrine, concept	books, articles, and programs.
official status	eat	usually not / maybe be
degree of commitment	required	optional
guaranteed by coercion	could be	no
language form (style)	neutral, informative, hidden connotation	energizing, open connotation, motivating, inducing
structured	complies with the requirements of legal technique	it has no structure

If the legal system of a State is typified as undifferentiated or ideologized, then, as a rule, it has a State ideology, which underlies all State documents. We proceed from the hypothesis that the United States and Russia are not representatives of these legal systems. They officially proclaim ideological diversity, no single ideology can be dominant, that pluralism occurs, and that censorship is prohibited. These freedoms are designed to prevent the creation a party State with a single-State ideology.

This hypothesis is based on the fact that we do not exclude the possibility of a doctrine of the State-ideological type, especially because there are historical and modern examples.

According to Marxist theory, law is a superstructure over the base, the economy. The combination of Marxism with positivist legal conceptions asserts the rule of law as the only form of law. In this paradigm, the law is a document that reflects the will of the economically dominant class.

Beginning in the mid-1980s, the Soviet and then the Russian legal system abandoned Marxism as a fundamental ideology. The general boundless "devotion" of the professors to the classics of Marxism-Leninism was abruptly replaced by sharp and later irreconcilable criticism. Subsequently, Russia completely abandoned Marxist ideology. As time has shown, the rejection was just as groundless as the acceptance of Marxism was uncritical. Extremes disrupt the dialectical development of knowledge and make knowledge discrete. Extremes lead to the interruption of academic schools, call into question research based on a previous ideological platform, and sever the connection between generations of researchers. For doctrine, the progressive development is of great importance because doctrine is, *inter alia,* a research school. The school includes a set of researchers who follow a single methodological line and strategy. The change of ideology to a diametrically opposite (from Marxist to liberal) led to a rupture of academic schools and divided generations of researchers.

The year 2022 marked a new ideological upheaval. Now, liberal ideology is under attack. However, the alternative is not yet apparent. The primary trend is rejecting liberal doctrine with a return to the period before 1991, the collapse of the USSR, but based on the capitalist economic model. Proposals for a return to 1991 were made in isolation because the USSR did not recognize private ownership of the means of production. The USSR is impossible without socialist ownership and communist ideology. The other, incomplete, fragmented return version does not have a viable beginning, a functional economic model. Assuming a return to the USSR through the reproduction of some structures, often renamed, will not yield results without a fully-fledged economic and ideological foundation. For example, volunteers are not Timur's followers, and the Young Guard is not the Komsomol. This is a fragmentary borrowing of helpful power in an extreme socio-political situation. It is a renaming with a loss of meaning. But there are many contradictions. Against the increasing Soviet influence on the mass legal consciousness, politicians erected monuments to the White Guards and tsars, but officials and the media began to quote the classics of Marxism-Leninism widely.

The authorities use anything that attracts a social group. For example, Christians get a censer, and atheists can fly into space. But waving a censer at a spacecraft looks unnatural. It is like saying that astronauts in the sky have met a god.[3] Eclectic State ideological models lead to the strengthening of anti-academic theses that deny prominent natural law theories (Darwinism) or revive ideas about the flat Land.

However, the triumph of "wrongness" is evident. There is a denial of the existing law and legal order. So far, the legislator is actively "improving" normative legal acts. However, the concept of law should be abolished, as it is not found in subordinate acts. It is in the Constitution, federal laws, and codes. The number of improvements to the Constitution, federal constitutional laws, and the codes clearly indicates the crisis of the fundamental concept. The demand for a single-State ideology contradicts ideological diversity and freedom of speech.

A concrete example shows the crisis of improvements. For example, expanding privileged categories to incalculable limits in legislation on education contradicts the proper access to education based on achievement. Most importantly, the distribution of responsibility to all members of society, combined with the receipt of profit by an insignificant part of the population, breaks the connection between the State and society, the oligarchy and the people.

[3] V. Korzun, С Богом в космос [With God into Space] (available online).

A doctrine may take the form of an ideology, including a State ideology. In this connection, we have included in the methodology of our study views that refer to ideology doctrinal phenomena. The "legal policy" concept is close to ideology.[4] Researchers refer to ideology as doctrinal forms.

During the past century, Russia has changed its State-forming doctrines several times: imperialist, Soviet, and capitalist. The Russian Empire became a Soviet State in 1917; in 1991, it became a capitalist presidential republic. And every historical turn has had opposing ideological doctrines, from individual to collective decision-making and back to individual, transferable – elected power – and transferred again, capitalist – socialist mode of production – and capitalist again. All ideas and State institutions have come full circle and returned to their original position in less than a century. And these changes took place based on ideas that arose in previous regimes as wrong. These ideas created a platform for eliminating the existing order and became dominant doctrinal at the next historical stage. From the point of view of the typology of doctrines, this period looks like the transformation of a non-State ideological doctrine into an ideological State doctrine. But it is not moving forward. It is not even going in circles. Obviously, this is a backward movement, justified each time by some ideologues who manipulate the mass consciousness using well-known thinkers to solve their own egoistic problems.

At a time that outwardly appears calm, without apparent conflicts and contradictions, without military clashes, State-transforming reforms can be so profound that they replace the dominant doctrine with its opposite. For example, the ideas of perestroika in the USSR, which arose in the socialist State, initially proposed reforms to improve the socialist State doctrine. However, the self-development of ideas eventually led to the complete rejection of the socialist mode of production

4 A. V. Malko and Ia. V. Gaivoronskaia, "Доктринальные акты как основной инструмент правовой политики [Doctrinal Acts as the Basic Instrument of Legal Policy]", Право. Журнал Высшей школы экономики [Law. Journal of the Higher School of Economics], no. 1 (2018), pp. 4-25.

and Soviet social relations and the dissolution of the USSR. An ideological doctrine can be expressed in different forms.

The right of unilateral promises is normative facts and promises that are perceived as binding for objective and subjective reasons. Petrazhitsky gave the following examples: "For example, the promises of monarchs to preserve or grant certain rights to the people or a certain part of it, to preserve and sacredly observe former rights, the constitution, etc."[5] In fact, it is an ideological doctrine.

The doctrinal nature of program law or the right of pre-election promises is seen in their structure, consistency, and wide distribution. Programmatic law is focused on self-realization without coercive State mechanisms. It deserves special attention from the State, as it reflects the public (if not the mass, then the group) consciousness, including in the legal sphere. It is precisely these qualities that should draw legislative attention to ideological doctrine.

Petrazhitsky noted that it is challenging to identify the legal nature of these sources. He stressed the futility of equating them with jurisprudence, laws, or customs because, in his opinion, they are independent sources. Agreeing with Petrazhitsky and continuing his reasoning, we have created a typology of this phenomenon as an ideological doctrine.

In today's social practice, some phenomena are akin to the forms described by Petrazhitsky. So, for example, there are pre-election programs of speeches by officials, often called programmatic. Public promises can be made in interstate communication at the highest level. However, these written and oral undertakings do not have any legal mechanism to ensure their implementation. Implementing these undertakings is not supported by State coercion. For such phenomena, the concept of legal responsibility is unacceptable, but this does not exclude the possibility of political responsibility. Combined

[5] L. I. Petrazhitsky, Теория права и государства в связи с теорией нравственности [Theory of Law and the State in Connection with the Theory of Morality] (1907), II, pp. 598-599.

with the lack of a mechanism for recalling elected officials, the programs do not have any normative impact on social relations. Moreover, the addressees of the programmatic promises themselves rationally perceive them in the same dispositive way but nevertheless actually orient themselves towards them. Citizens are still waiting for the programs and promises generously distributed by politicians during the election period to be fulfilled.

In the history of Russian law, however, there is a very definite (not the only) episode of equating the programs of social organizations with the form of law. We remember the reference to the Minimum Program of the Russian Social-Democratic Party and the Party of Social-Revolutionaries in the Decret "On the Court" of 22 November (5 December) 1917. According to the Note to Article 5 of the Decret, "all laws that contradict ... the minimum programs of the Russian Social-Democratic Labour Party and the Party of Social-Revolutionaries".

Legislation of the USSR was familiar with the "mandate to a deputy", which, to some extent, can be equated with program law. Following Article 103 of the 1977 Constitution of the USSR, a people's deputy had to ensure the implementation of the voters' instructions. The Law of the USSR "On the Status of People's Deputies in the USSR" of 21 December 1989 (Article 1), established that a deputy organizes his work based on such mandates. These are historical examples of Party law. There are no analogues in Russian legislation. Modern legislation no longer has such a rigid and open manifestation of programmatic law. Today, programs are acts of an informational nature. There are some references to program acts in legislation; for example, public access to social association programs is required. In connection with election campaigning, the electoral legislation establishes the procedure for publishing programs. For example, suppose a political party nominates a candidate for the President of the Russian Federation. In that case, it must publish its election program in at least one all-Russian State periodical and place it online.

Although there is no reason to speak of widespread programmatic law, this does not detract from the importance of this legal phenomenon. It cannot be attributed to the forms of modern law because it is not supported by State coercion. However, it existed historically, and its obvious usefulness for the functioning of public power does not allow us to ignore it.

Legal scholars rarely refer to this form of law or even mention it. None of the textbooks published in the USSR and modern Russia mention this phenomenon when addressing the system of sources and forms of law.

"Program Law". "Party Law". and "Right to communicate future actions" regulate people's behavior under certain circumstances. It is difficult to identify the legal nature of these sources. Attempts to equate them with jurisprudence, laws, or custom have proved futile. Perhaps this is evidence that doctrines are an original form of law.

Not often, but there are court cases using pre-election promises as a legal regulator. In particular, the courts assess whether these promises are normative and whether inevitable legal consequences are associated with them.[6] Another case was related to the election of the head of the rural settlement of Erzovka in the Gorodishchenskii district and election promises. The Supreme Court of the Russian Federation assessed the possibility of regarding pre-election promises as bribing voters.[7] The institution of recall of deputies, including for non-fulfillment of election promises, was considered by the Constitutional Court of the Russian Federation and recognized as constitutional.[8] In 2021, State Duma deputy Oleg Nilov introduced and later withdrew draft Federal Law No. 1233926-

[6] Case No. 2-1405/2012 of 28 September 2012 (available on Consultant+).

[7] Ruling of Supreme Court of Russian Federation No. 71-G06-14 of 10 March 2006 (available on Consultant+).

[8] Decree of Constitutional Court of the Russian Federation of 24 December 1996, No. 21-P, "Re: Verification of the Constitutionality of the Law of the Moscow Region of 28 April 1995 "On the Procedure for Recalling a Deputy of the Moscow Regional Duma" in Connection with the Request of the Judicial Division for Civil Cases of the Supreme Court of the Russian Federation" (available on Consultant+).

7, "On Amendments to the Criminal Code of the Russian Federation Regarding the Establishment of Criminal Liability for Failure to Fulfill an Election Promise".

Thus, in history, soft law has been applied as legislation. There is no reason to discuss the extensive application of soft law in today's legal reality. Nevertheless, ideological doctrine is a phenomenon akin to soft law. That is why we include soft law as a kind of ideological doctrine in this study. Under today's conditions of declared pluralism, no party is dominant under a multi-party system. The 1977 Constitution of the USSR provided (Article 6): "The Communist Party of the Soviet Union shall be the leading and directing force of Soviet society, the core of its political system, State and social organizations". The decision of the Constitutional Court of the Russian Federation in 1992 confirmed that "in August-September 1991, the CPSU actually disintegrated and lost the status of an all-Union organization". The Court also found that the dissolution of the CPSU leading organizational structures and the RSFSR Communist Party as an integral part thereof was following the Constitution of the Russian Federation.[9]

The disappearance of the Soviet party-State altered the political landscape. But overall, Party law has been preserved in other forms. Parliamentary parties promote their party ideas in legislation. Members of parties work in the executive and judicial branches. Our sociological research has confirmed party law as a party source of law. The parties different rights are a local form, extending to party members.

Other sources are the law of programs, communication of future actions, and parties law. In the school of psychology, the responsibility for programmatic law in the form of

[9] Decision No. 9-P of the Constitutional Court of the Russian Federation of 30 November 1992 "On the Case of Verification of the Constitutionality of the Decrees of the President of the Russian Federation of 23 August 1991, No. 79, "On the Suspension of the Activities of the Communist Party of the RSFSR», of 25 August 1991, No. 90, "On the Property of the CPSU and the Communist Party of the RSFSR" and of 6 November 1991, No. 169, "On the Activities of the CPSU and the Communist Party of the RSFSR", as well as on the Verification of the Constitutionality of the CPSU and the CP of the RSFSR" (available on Consultant+).

election promises was shifted to the people. Their mass legal consciousness contributed to the understanding of pre-election promises as "the duty to act following this about those for whom it is important to observe what is proclaimed, who had reason to hope for observance, and so on".[10] Programmatic law is represented in the history of Roman law, in particular, praetorian law. It is difficult to identify the legal nature of these sources. Attempts to equate them with judicial practice, laws, or customs have proved futile. Still, it is an independent phenomenon at the intersection of law and politics.

In today's social practice, some phenomena resemble the forms mentioned above. For example, there are pre-election program speeches, often called programmatic. It is common for public promises to be made at the highest level of interstate communication. Legal guarantees and sanctions are not applied for violations of such promises. These are promises of honor and authority of the State. However, relying on such promises looks like frivolous behavior.

The refusal to recognize Party documents as a form of law must be analyzed and investigated in the following context. Ideology, party programs, and official speeches are specific regulators of social relations which only a few scholars openly recognize as forms of law. Excellent attention is paid to them in the psychological school of law (Petrazhitsky). Legal consciousness and doctrine – phenomena of the same order – are recognized as forms of law more often in this line of legal thought.

For example, one expert in the sociological study observed that at one time, he and other prominent researchers proposed to abandon the recall of the deputy mandate. Now, thirty years later, observing the results of this legislative decision, he assessed it as harmful and would not make such a proposal. Thus, he expressed disappointment with the lack of obligation of deputies, who do not fulfill their promises without the threat

[10] Petrazhitsky, note 5 above, II, p. 599.

of recall. His words also confirm the value and effectiveness of party law.

UNDERSTANDING OF IDEOLOGICAL DOCTRINE BY RESPONDENTS OF SOCIOLOGICAL SURVEYS

Ideological doctrine has been investigated herein with the use of sociological methods. Our research began in 2003 and gave us a unique opportunity to have a time continuum through such a longitudinal study.

Respondents to the 2003 survey (SJ 2003 – 2006) were asked whether norms of political parties could be considered forms of official law. This question has a complex structure of suggested answers:

1. the norms of political parties are forms of service law because a civil servant is bound by party discipline;
2. the norms of political parties are not forms of official law because a civil servant is obliged to obey only the law;
3. the norms of political parties are a latent source: they are not directly referred to, but they impact the civil service.

It may seem that only the first option makes it possible to consider party norms as legal norms. But this is too direct an answer, which only 0.5% of the surveyed civil servants chose. The third variant of the answer provided respondents with an excellent opportunity to remain in the legal field without abandoning party norms (17.6% of civil servants). Thus, they consider the norms of the parties to be the norms of law. But they speak of this not explicitly as a kind of illegitimate custom. Thus, 18.1% of respondents, to one degree or another, consider the norms of political parties to be forms of official law. Most respondents (81.9%) believe that the norms of political parties cannot be considered forms of official law since a civil servant is obliged to obey only the law.

We believe that this question, in its deliberate formulation, provoked a reaction of denial as a kind of social order. In fact, it is forbidden to talk about the ideologization, domination of the party, and imposition of its standards and ideas. Interviewed civil servants should not officially proceed from the interests of a particular political party. Out of a desire not to be accused of off-duty behavior, the respondents, as they say, threw the baby out with the bathwater. Out of a desire for personal security, they denied the existence of a particular form of law that was legitimate in its entirety.

By 2023, priorities had shifted, and, in general, respondents had turned to party law and began to recognize it more openly. The number of categorical opponents decreased – to 58.2% in 2023 compared to 81.9% in 2007. The number of recognitions of party law as a latent source of law has almost doubled from 17.7% in 2007 to 31.3% in 2023. In 2007, there was no unconditional recognition of party law. Only 0.5% of civil servants recognized party law. In 2023, 10.7% supported party law.

From 2007 to 2023, the recognition of party rights increased significantly. Respondents who do not recognize the party right decreased from 81.9% to 58.2%. The number of open supporters increased from 0.5% to 10.7%. In 2007, 17.7% of respondents supported recognizing party law as a non-official latent source of law. In 2023, this figure increased to 31.1%.

Diagram 26. (SCS 7). Influence of Age on Respondent Attitude to Norms of Political Parties as Forms of Service Law (2007–2008)

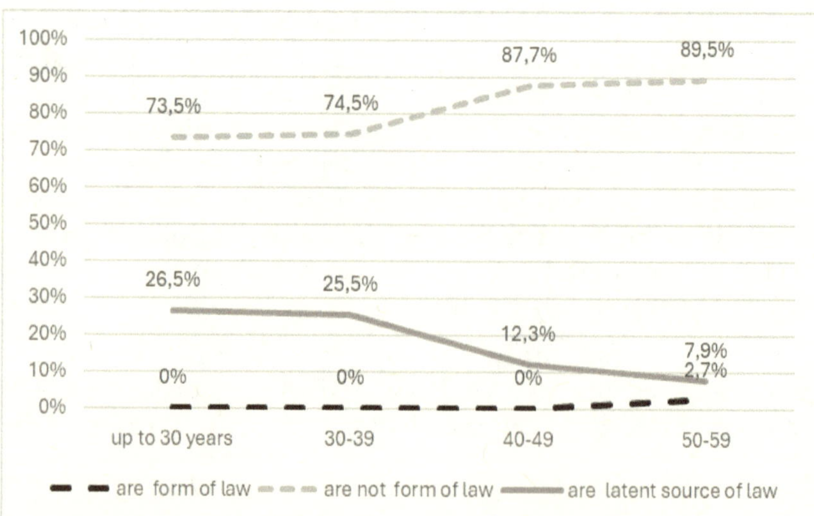

Among those who believe that party norms are a latent source of official law, two-thirds are people under 40. 26.5% of the surveyed civil servants under the age of 30 believe that party norms are a latent source of official law, and 25.5% of respondents aged 30 to 39, while at the age of 40 to 49, the number of supporters of this position decreases: only 12.3% of respondents and 7.9% of those aged 50 to 59.

Diagram 27. (SCS 7). Impact of Seniority on Respondent Attitudes Towards Norms of Political Parties as Forms of Service Law (2007– 2008)

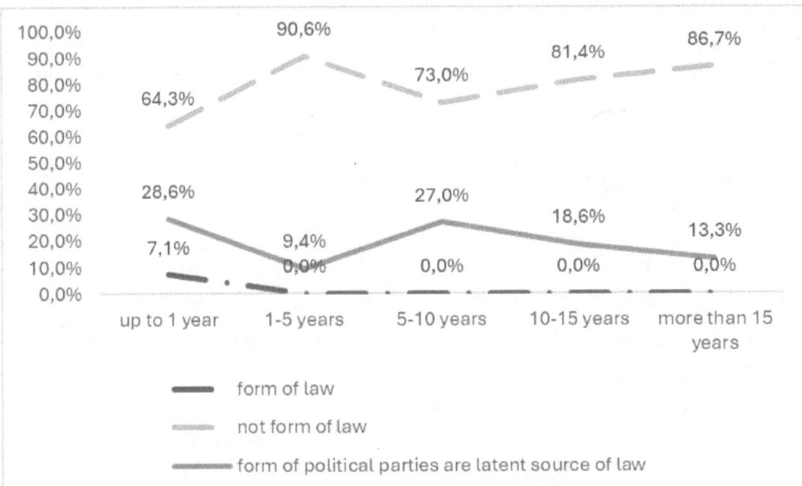

Diagram 28. (SSLD 14 - SCS 7). Changes in Attitudes to the Norms of Political Parties as Forms (Sources) of Law Over Time: A Comparison of Studies 2007– 2008 and 2022–2023

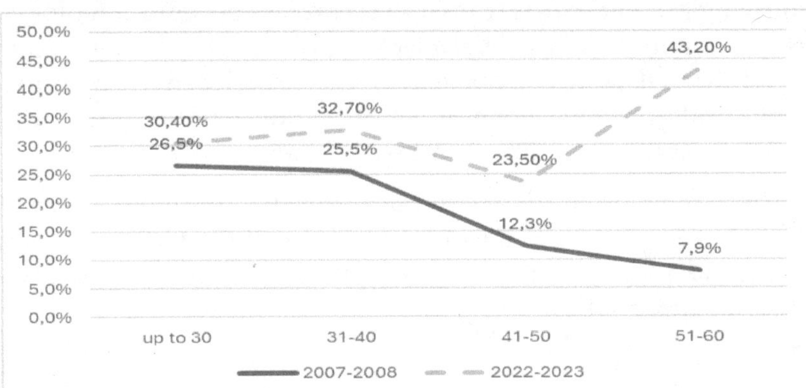

A comparison of the 2003 and 2023 opinion poll results shows that the number of respondents who recognize party law as a latent form of law has increased in all age groups. The age groups of 41–50 years (almost twofold) and 51–60 years (5.6 times) show the most significant growth. Thus, the influence of ideological doctrine in the form of party law has taken a sharp leap in the last twenty years. The vector of attitude towards the party-State has changed with age. In 2003, he was trusted the most by his younger forms and least by his older colleagues. In 2023, the trend is the opposite: with age, support for the party-State increased from 30.4% in the under-30 age group to 43% in the 51 – 60 age group.

Respondents admit the existence of an ideological doctrine: 37.6% are specialists, and 33.3% are experts. This is a relatively high level of support for a country where the Constitution enshrines ideological diversity and effectively prohibits party law.

Concerning the attitude towards ideology in general and ideological doctrine in particular, a revolution was made around the axis, returning to the idea of an ideological State with a single-State ideology.

FREQUENCY AND VECTOR ANALYSIS OF IDEOLOGICAL DOCTRINE IN CONTENT ANALYSIS. MARKER WORDS OF IDEOLOGICAL DOCTRINE

Content analysis showed that the respondents supported the following marker words from the research hypothesis: ideology, program, and anti-law. We selected political worldview from the additional words proposed by the respondents. Thus, the ideological doctrine's general list of marker words *is* ideology, program, anti-law, politics, and worldview.

The analysis of academic publications using content analysis made it possible to significantly supplement the marker words of the ideological doctrine: ideology, policy, ideological, political, and politics.

Ideological doctrine is still poorly represented in educational literature, and its references are sporadic (1979 and 2017). However, the tendency to strengthen the ideological doctrine in scholarly literature will likely affect educational literature.

Censorship, loyalty, unity of ideology

Censorship, in this context, refers to the relationship between publication and certain ideological attitudes. It can be State, corporate, group, or other types of ideology. From the open-ended questions in the sociological study, it was found that some respondents understand censorship not only as the refusal of a print publication to publish an article for non-academic reasons. It may be the author's decision not to submit some politically Incorrect material to the editorial office. In addition, a personal decision not to write about specific topics may be made due to the contradiction of one's views with the dominant political vector. Some experts point to the status of a judge as a source of limitations. They see this restriction as censorship. We can assume that we are talking about restricting the use of materials relating to specific cases.

The emergence of censorship and political orders can be internal and external. External influence can come from legislation, public authorities, and organizations. Internally, the subject of decision-making implements it independently. This is self-censorship.

A significant manifestation of ideological doctrine is the influence of censorship and political orders on forming other types of doctrine. To establish the opinions of experts and specialists, we posed a question in the Questionnaire and the Expert Survey about whether censorship and political orders influence the formation of doctrine. The attitude towards censorship and political orders had to be assessed: "strongly influenced", "affected", and "does not affect".

60.6% of specialists recognize the strong influence of censorship on the formation of doctrine, and 35.8% – recognize the influence without connotation. And only 3.6% believe censorship does not affect the formation of doctrine at all.

Experts feel less vulnerable to censorship and political orders than specialists. This is confirmed by the following data: 36.7% of experts deny the influence compared to 3.5% of specialists. It is difficult to assess the reality of censorship as a ban from the outside or as an external solution. Suppose we proceed from the hypothesis that Personas-Doctrines are people with high social status, wealth, and social position. In that case, these statuses guarantee the free-thinking and independence of the Persona-Doctrine in comparison with a younger, less organized, and less authoritative group of specialists. This hypothesis is confirmed by analyzing the distribution of opinions by the age of the respondents.

Attitudes towards the impact of censorship on the formation of doctrine depend on several factors, including the age of the respondents. Analysis of respondent answers confirms this hypothesis. For specialists, there is a tendency to reduce the influence of censorship on the formation of doctrine with age. With age, the number of specialists denying censorship influence increases.

The youngest professionals under 30 have the highest recognition rate of censorship impact – 86.9%, of which 13.1% find this influence strong. The lowest level of influence of censorship was shown by a group of specialists aged 61 – 70 – 60.7%. Regarding the "strong influence of censorship" on forming legal doctrine, the 71+ age group is in the lead.

During interviews and analysis of textual responses to open-ended questions, examples of specific censorship concerning researchers were recorded. Based on the age category, the recognition of the high impact of censorship is inherent in people who have the Soviet period in their biography (60+). In this regard, it is essential to consider the experience of the Soviet State in presenting the theory of law in textbooks as an example of censorship and the influence of ideology on educational literature. First, the socialist Marxist conception of every question was expounded. It was positioned as the correct one. There was no alternative. At the end of a segment of teaching material (paragraph, chapter, section), there were fragments with titles consonant with this example: "Critique of Bourgeois Doctrines" on this subject. For example, after the official doctrine of the origin of the State and law in a class interpretation based on F. Engels's *The Origin of the Family, the State, and Law,* sections criticized J.-J. Rousseau and J. S. Smith, John Locke, and other representatives of non-Marxist views under the general title of *Critique of Bourgeois Doctrines*. Such a sequence of exposition clearly fulfilled an ideological function. It formed a socialist legal consciousness based on a single ideology. All other views were criticized.

In conditions of proclaimed pluralism and the flourishing of democracy, as well as in the official absence of censorship, a uniform (guideline) ideological and, at the same time, State doctrine should be constrained in its actions. Ideology cannot be straightforward, as in totalitarian regimes and party States. Taking certain risks, we classify textbooks in ideologized States as ideological doctrines.

This issue is topical since freedom, permissiveness, lack of self-restraint, democracy, and ideology are words that often touch, support, or contradict each other in the semantic field. We investigated the relationship between the presence of censorship and the type of legal system. Censorship is always a qualifying feature of an ideologized legal system, according to 54.9% of experts. Censorship is recognized as an essential feature but is not qualified by 31.4% of specialists. A group of specialists who do not consider the presence of censorship to be a sign of an ideologized legal system by a significant margin. Such specialists account for 13.8% of respondents.

Experts were asked to provide examples of their experience in being restricted by prohibitions or publication restrictions. One expert coined "self-censorship", meaning responsible, voluntary, self-limiting behavior. He gave an example of necessary self-restraint when a helpful idea can stir up a social group with unpredictable consequences.

Ideological doctrine is concerned with State and political institutions. The possibility of ideological uniformity or diversity is an important issue. The content and variability of ideological doctrine were assessed by the respondents on a five-point scale: 1) uniform, 2) dominant (relatively uniform), 3) irrelevant, 4) rather diverse, and 5) diverse. 41.8% of specialists acknowledged the existence of an ideological doctrine.

Following the Constitution of the Russian Federation, most respondents should have chosen the option of "diverse" ideology. However, the current (2022 – 2023) social demand for a uniform ideology is apparent. When enlarging the groups of respondents, 35.6% admit uniformity, and 30.4% prefer diversity. This gap is tiny, and 33.9% of specialists are undecided. This is a group that can lean in either direction.

All types of responses show that the transition from pluralism to a single ideology has not yet occurred. Nonetheless, a single ideology no longer frightens the academic community and civil society. In general, the transition from domination in the understanding of doctrine from an academic to an ideological doctrine can return to its position before 1991 (the date of USSR dissolution), and there are prerequisites for this.

In the early 1990s, ideology had an exclusively negative connotation and was associated with the Communist Party of the Soviet Union. When the Communist Party was liquidated, society celebrated the victory of pluralism, which became a fundamental constitutional principle. It is reasonable to assume that under those conditions, only a diverse ideological doctrine would have been supported. After thirty years, 81.1% of experts do not see anything negative in the general State ideology.

This position contradicts the Constitution but expresses the mood of society. 18.9% of specialists support the unity of ideology. Constitutional pluralism is followed by 81.1% of specialists.

In an expert survey, we identified indicators of the impact of censorship (external or internal). Respondents were asked to recall cases where their position prevented them from being able to publish a research paper. We are talking about official censorship. This is the inability to publish any materials related to the position as a ban. 60% of experts completely deny personal experience of being banned from publishing due to their official position.

First, we are talking about Persona-Doctrines in public service. In this type of activity, the ban and restrictions on publication are more likely to happen. We have examples of researchers being prosecuted and fired for their opinions expressed in academic publications. This reaction is censorship but in a different sense. *Preemptive censorship* means checking a work for loyalty before publication. *Subsequent censorship* is an evaluation after publication with conclusions on political grounds. Criticism of the author is not carried out for merits and demerits following the requirements for an academic publication. The novelty and methodology of the publication are not evaluated. Censorship is evaluated based on political and ideological motives, which, as a rule, are described in a very vague, vague, and non-exhaustive way. This assessment is like labeling "us" and "them" in modern political Queries. This is one of the "cancel culture" tools for academic opinion.

The questionnaire identified the most self-dependent (self-censored) activities more likely to be censored in their hierarchical power organization.

6.7% of experts faced direct bans on publishing, and 33.3% faced indirect bans. Thus, a small margin prevails by a group of experts who have not had any clashes with censorship. Overall, 60% of the experts had censorship experience, while 40% had not.

We are cautioned against overestimating the freedoms of civil servants and politicians by comparing experts with the experience of public positions subject to prohibitions (such as civil servants, legislators, politicians, and judges) and without such experience. The indicators for experts with and without experience in censorship restrictions differ significantly. The diagram shows the impact of personal experience of public service on the recognition or rejection of censorship of their works.

We asked experts (open poll) to tell us about their own cases of prohibition or restriction on publication. They gave the following examples:

- the author's vision did not always coincide with the opinion of the publisher,
- service in a departmental police academy,
- political censorship in the USSR on the topic "Theory of Freedom,"
- the publication may harm the planned actions of State authorities,
- ethical constraints,
- the restriction was due to the holding of the position of the head in the judicial system and the status of a judge,
- the status of a civil servant did not allow him to directly express his position on the decisions of State authorities,
- military service involving access to State secrets,
- possession of non-public data,
- when using statistical data in an article on the budgets of municipalities for placement in a foreign publication.

The experts stressed that the civil servant contract stipulates that publications are prohibited. In exceptional cases, they are possible on behalf of the top management (for example, an agreed text of an interview or others to explain decisions of State authorities). One source of the conflict is prohibitions and restrictions, which take place with the author's insufficient justification of positions and high aplomb.

Interviews have shown that experts understand censorship as both external and internal. A ban on publications and other, less severe methods of influence, but to change the publication (opinion) or even get in its way, undoubtedly takes place. The source of censorship can be different governing forces in the State, an organization, or a group. This instruction must come from an authority with sufficient power, including enforcing its decision. Most experts – 60% – deny such an impact on them, and only 6.7% openly admit such facts in their biographies. However, experts suggested another aspect – self-censorship – during interviews. Self-censorship means a voluntary decision not to raise a sensitive issue in public if it is likely to cause chaos and other socially significant undesirable consequences. In this approach to self-censorship, experts recognize the validity of the thesis of the actor's authority. Indeed, an opinion expressed by a non-authoritative person is likely to have little or no impact on public relations than an opinion from an authoritative source.

One expert described an episode where a senior university official advised him to refrain from discussing a sensitive issue at a general staff meeting. The expert agreed with these limitations, recognizing them as reasonable. He implemented restrictions in the form of self-censorship.

Whether internal censorship is helpful if it is done solely for self-preservation but to the detriment of progress arises. For example, we do not criticize the idea of a leader, although it is objectively and obviously harmful. To some extent, this behavior results from internal censorship and is anti-social.

The French comparative lawyer, René David (1906-1990), penetrated deeply into the essence of the ideologized legal system of the USSR. He noted that the doctrine involves fewer legal works than Party programs and decisions. They "do not constitute law in the proper sense of the word. However, their doctrinal significance is indisputable, for these documents contain an exposition of Marxist-Leninist theory".[11]

As a rule, a doctrine has proof of its theses. It is rational and reasoned. Ideology is more addressed to consciousness. It gravitates towards faith and religious ways of influencing society. This, however, does not deny that certain ideological attitudes have doctrinal origins.

[11] R. David and C. Jauffret-Spinosi, Основные правовые системы современности [Major Legal Systems of the World Today] (1999), p. 189.

The form of existence and operation of ideology in the academic field are the citation or quotation by political figures. The ideological theses of political leaders are more often used in relevant dissertations or in the prefaces or introductions of works. This is the reincarnation of Soviet science, in which everything took place only under the all-encompassing leadership of the CPSU and the classics of Marxism and Leninism. Political citation as ideological doctrine is weakly connected with the research subject.

To collect empirical data on this orientation in the development of ideological doctrine, we asked specialists to decide to what type of doctrine the citations or quotations of statements of contemporary politicians in academic research belong. Options to choose were: 1) State, 2) academic, and 3) ideological. Citations in dissertations and other academic research in the form of a hypothesis, a phenomenon of an orientation nature, and political and State ideas are doctrines. The dissertation uses this kind of thesis as an attitude, an indisputable idea not subject to criticism or rethinking. This doctrine is the basis of the dissertation. The indicator is the presence/absence of a connection with the research subjects. Suppose there is no such connection, and a political quotation of a general nature is far-fetched in academic research. In that case, it is obviously an ideology. The author alerts the reader to his loyalty to the authority's decisions.

The specialist answers were almost equally distributed as follows: 29.1% of specialists referred to the statements of contemporary politicians as State doctrine, 33.5% as ideological, and 37.4% as scholar. Thus, experts do not have a uniform opinion about the type of doctrine that is ideological in content, State in terms of the source of authority, and academic in terms of its actual finding. Such quotations are "three in one".

The cited objects are not homogeneous, but the academic level of the authors of the cited works is heterogeneous. For reference, we can assume, for example, the citation of V. V. Putin or D. A. Medvedev as candidate of legal sciences or M. V. Mishustin and V. V. Volodin as doctor of legal sciences.

However, if a citation contains a political or public position and quotes or cites non-academic publications, then this is ideology.

The foregoing does not exclude the possibility that these academic publications may acquire an academic doctrinal status. Administrative resources and position influence doctrinality but do not create or shape it. Politicians can articulate State documents on their own behalf (for example, messages of the President of the Russian Federation), can make presentations at State, academic, and other events (for example, the address of the Chairman of the Constitutional Court of the Russian Federation at the St. Petersburg Forum). The same persons have academic dissertations which could have been written before or after obtaining a high State position, but without an obvious connection with this position. The academic research of some public officials, such as the Minister of Culture, V. R. Medinskii, was strongly and negatively perceived by experts. However, this assessment of the academic community did not affect his position and career.

The motivation for citations of modern politicians in the survey was examined by enumerating the sources of decision-making and indicating the possibility of the influence of this particular factor. Respondents were asked to assess the possibility of the following motives for quoting political figures: 1) shows relevance, 2) demonstrates loyalty, 3) requirement of the dissertation council, 4) requirement of the organization, 5) requirement of the supervisor, 6) personal desire, 7) unconscious adherence to mass behavior.

The possible answers can be divided into groups:

1. in connection with the subject of research:

- related (1),
- unrelated (2–7).

2. In connection with the personality of the author, the influence may come from

- the author voluntarily (1, 6),

- the mass mood in society (2, 7),
- the significant environment of the researcher (3, 4, 5).

An analysis of respondent responses shows that factors related to the subject of the study are considered dominant. Dissertation authors derive the relevance of their research from political citations (33%). This is a form of implementing a political order. The authors are looking for the formulation of problems and topical topics in the political statements of State authorities. Accordingly, the research responds to the authorities demands and is derivative of political ideology.

More explicit is the recognition of loyalty, adherence to State ideology, and acceptance thereof as the basis. Such motives were acknowledged by 22.9% of specialists: "I share all the theses expressed by representatives of State authorities". This is both collective and personal loyalty. The author of the loyal citation articulates his agreement with State authorities, specific leaders, and State ideology.

The third place in motivation is personal desire (20.7%), a voluntary, conscious decision to quote politicians. A tiny percentage of specialists recognize the influence of such external factors as the dissertation council, supervisor, or organization (from 9.7% to 4.4%).

The citation of contemporary politicians in academic research has a cyclical nature for Russian authors. In the Soviet period, quoting the party leadership was necessary for all kinds of work, from school essays to doctoral dissertations. We cannot determine what the basis for such a steady trend was. Several sources for political-party and Soviet-State quotations can be assumed. This requirement was formally enshrined in some documents in the form of an oral directive of governing bodies, a decision of educational institutions or dissertation councils, or others.

Regardless of the source of this rule, quoting political figures has become a custom over a long period. This natural tradition for a party State continues in the academic field. The general trend enshrined in Article 6 of the Constitution of the USSR was the unity of the political system and the guiding line of the CPSU.

Article 13 of the 1993 Russian Constitution enshrined ideological diversity, political diversity, and a multi-party system. All these presuppose the absence of single coordinated political thinking. In general, consolidated legal opinion is formed in a multi-party parliament. It is impossible to assume the existence of party law because it will be a different right for many parties. The return of political citation in academic research in the 2010s is remarkable. Perhaps the same tendency exists in other publications, but we examined only academic ones.

A dissertation differs from other works by reason of the dependence of the dissertation writer. The desire to obtain an academic degree is formalized by the decision of the dissertation council. Through learned secretary, the policy of the dissertation council is carried out. Accordingly, it can be assumed that the source of political-state citation is the decision of the dissertation council.

Analyzing sociological research data from the Russian Science Citation Index on the ratings of political figures and other sources shows the significant role of censorship in forming legal doctrine. Censorship is imposed under the influence of internal and external factors before and/or after publication. In any case, censorship verifies that the ideas expressed in the work are consistent with the political order. Works should be loyal, tolerant, and ideologically correctly oriented. The absence of criticism of the political course is complemented by the requirement to articulate support for ideological decisions or positions or, even better, criticism of other political positions. This is usually inappropriate for the text but is not essential for academic research and doctrine. The most appropriate place is the introduction. Politicization, the assertion of one's ideological position, is an important (necessary) assertion of the relevance of academic research.

Loyalty and tolerance are demonstrated in academic research, for the most part, not by the will of the dissertation author. They are explained by external reasons, such as the desire to defend the dissertation.

Ideological and State doctrines are excluded from the field of criticism. They have become the indisputable basis, the foundation. They have become the measure of other kinds of doctrines.

SECTION V

SUBJECTIVE AND OBJECT DIMENSIONS OF LEGAL DOCTRINE: CURRENT STATE, PROSPECTS, MODELS

Chapter 17

Persona-Doctrine as Subjective Dimension of Types of Legal Doctrine

SOCIAL AND PROFESSIONAL PORTRAIT OF A DOCTRINAL BEARER

The possibility of the personification of doctrine is a debatable issue. The personification and impersonality of legal doctrine are different responses to the personalization of the Persona-Doctrine and, consequently, the admissibility of the term Persona-Doctrine.

Specialists were allowed to determine which types of doctrine can personify the author with the assignment of Persona-Doctrine status: "The term Persona-Doctrine can be used in the following types of doctrines".

Some questions correlate with each other, complement, or clarify. Respondents were asked whether the personification of doctrine is necessary (possible) and about the possibility of personification by endowing the authors with the status of Persona-Doctrine.

The most promising application of Persona-Doctrine is fixed in scholar doctrine. Scholar works are always personified; they have a specific author. However, transitioning from a particular academic publication to a doctrine is not a transition in the same form (as a rule). 60% of specialists consider the term Persona-Doctrine to be adequate for use in scholar doctrine. According to the degree of adequacy of the use of the term Persona-Doctrine, specialists note ideological doctrine (28.3%), then State doctrine (26.5%), and judicial doctrine (17.4%). State and judicial doctrines are formalized in legal acts (normative and individual), and, nevertheless, respondents allow their personification.

The difference between State and judicial doctrine is the possibility of acting as a signatory (or document author). State doctrine is embodied in a document signed by an official. Measured by legal consciousness, law enforcement is the result of the activity of the person who signed the document. In a broad sense, all normative legal acts have a signatory; in this sense, they are personified. However, it is impossible to consider the signatories as authors. This would be contrary to law. We do not exclude. We admit authorship of the idea of the document.

For State and judicial doctrines, the signatories of the documents and the enacting authority may not coincide. For example, a federal law is adopted by senators and signed by the President of the Russian Federation. The Plenum of the Supreme Court is perceived as a collective body. The decrees are signed by the Chairman and by the Secretary of the Plenum of the Supreme Court of the Russian Federation. This excludes authorship in the total sense of the word. Accordingly, the personification of State and judicial doctrines is unlikely. In precedent States, the names of doctrines may be given in honor of Presidents, judges, names of the parties, and the circumstances of cases, and they are also given figurative names.

Elements of personification can be found in scholar and other doctrines. Generally, it is possible to assume Persona-Doctrine status in other types of doctrines, especially the ideological one, which can be verified by appropriate research. The originality of this research lies in the fact that the definition of Persona-Doctrine is introduced into academic circulation for the first time.

The term "Persona-Doctrine" is based on an analysis of academic literature, sociological surveys, expert surveys, interviews, dissertation abstracts and other academic publications, and other data. In academic literature, the question of the Persona-Doctrine has never been raised. However, there is discussion about the possibility of personifying doctrine. Data on personification can be found in reports on specific doctrines, academic schools, currents of thought and teachings, and theories that have preserved the names of their founders, successors, and followers.

The possibility of personification of legal doctrine was investigated by using sociological tools. For example, in the 2022 – 2023 survey, the question was raised about using doctrine in a personified or impersonal form.

Expert opinions on the personalization of doctrine were follows: 50.7% of specialists chose the answer "could be". That is, they admit such a possibility. Personalization was strongly supported by 44.9% of specialists. And only 4.4% would not allow personalization.

14.1% of specialists supported using doctrine of "always" only in an impersonal version. The option "could be" was chosen by 62.1% of specialists. 23.8% of them categorically opposed the depersonalization of legal doctrine.

A personified doctrine has a named founder and may be named after the person. In ideology and political research, the Monroe Doctrine is well-known. In jurisprudence, we do not recall a doctrine with an undisputed founder after whom it is named. Nevertheless, there are specific ways of personifying legal doctrine. There are examples of a clear association of a doctrine with a historical figure. For example, Ulpian is proclaimed the founder of the doctrine of private law, and Montesquieu of the doctrine of the separation of powers. The personification of doctrine is fundamental, system-forming, and significant for the Persona-Doctrine. In fact, when starting a dissertation, every researcher begins with the bibliographic part. The methodological part of the dissertation is the academic basis of persons who have made a significant contribution to this field of research, gravitating towards doctrinal status.

Nevertheless, the presence and frequent repetition of the full name in dissertations and other comparable works does not automatically form a Persona-Doctrine according to a quantitative criterion. However, this is significant information. In combination with other methods of identifying a Persona-Doctrine, citation (indication of full name) can be used to compare lists of Persona-Doctrines. The association in the legal consciousness of specialists in a particular field of knowledge with a specific person (or group of persons) may indicate elements of doctrinal status. A combination of theory, idea, and full name can become axiomatic or be recorded in a textbook. This is a well-known Persona-Doctrine. This is a kind of mythology of research. Many things are taken on faith and cannot be mathematically tested or disproved. The well-known part of the Persona-Doctrine has established information flows using the education and training system, including the full name in the recommended literature in legal education curricula. Before speaking out against this established body of knowledge, one must prepare to defend one's contributions against an indefinite circle of people.

A well-known personified doctrine can be universal in its global significance; it can acquire significance within the legal system, but more often, it has a domestic character. This is because legislation is adopted by public authorities for application on their territory. Accordingly, the object of legal research often has geographical boundaries that coincide with the territory of application of the law. However, the more general the conclusions of the study, the more abstracted the results are from the immediate object of observation, and the more significant the result will be in a territorial sense. This is evident in the possibility of recognizing and applying general theoretical and sectoral research results. Undoubtedly, theoretical-generalizing conclusions are more likely to be taken into account in the general legal sense. This is predetermined by the peculiarities of legal theory as the basis of jurisprudence.

We asked survey participants to assess the term "Persona-Doctrine" in different dimensions: 1) its viability and application, 2) its application in a professional environment, 3) limited use, and 4) not to be used at all.

Most respondents gave a response that was not entirely negative (89.4%), which opens prospects for the term Persona-Doctrine. To a certain extent, realizing this opportunity depends on promoting the term and its introduction into circulation.

We see this possibility, among other things, by approving the special status of "Doctrinal Professor".

Such a designation has been used in the HeinOnline database. According this resource, this status is provided by a university, and is indicated in the HeinOnline database in a notification procedure.

The Doctrinal Professor status is not an academic degree, honorary title, or public office. This arises from recognition of such title by the academic, educational, and other professional communities. For example, a professorial assembly can support such an initiative in Russia. The term Doctrinal Professor may be the equivalent of the status of Persona-Doctrine.

Some respondents expressed a negative reaction regarding the new status. 5.8% rated it as redundant. We can conventionally call this group consistent opponents of the term Persona-Doctrine. An overwhelming majority (94.2%) approved the term to some extent. The novelty of the term is confirmed by 52% of specialists; 29% do not consider it new, and 19% do not consider it excessive.

In fact, the introduction of this term is underway. The initiative was the Expert Survey of outstanding representatives of jurisprudence, whom we selected according to our own criteria and proactively nominated for this status. It is another matter that workers in the field of legal doctrine are often modest people. They do not aspire to dubious titles. This group's adoption of the term Persona-Doctrine is valuable and opens qualified prospects for the extensive use of this term. None of the experts recognized this status as excessive, harmful, or useless.

Experts generally favored using the term Persona-Doctrine but doubted whether they had sufficient achievements to be recognized as Persona-Doctrine. Indeed, it is immodest to nominate oneself and indecent for honest moral people to artificially exaggerate their achievements. However, denying what other people have accomplished is not appropriate. One enthusiastic expert liked the Persona-Doctrine status so much that he introduced it in his professional and service team. As if in jest, organically, but the work of spreading the term has begun.

EVALUATION OF TERM PERSONA-DOCTRINE

Assessing the nominee perception of the new term Persona-Doctrine is essential. Some questions provided indirect information for the study of the adoption of this term. This is a question of other Persona-Doctrines to whom experts could confer such status. In the interviews, we explained to the experts that we were talking about personalities whom they considered to be authoritative. In a 2002 survey of judges, we clarified that we meant such people and works that judges could place next to a normative legal act when writing a court document. Most experts – 93.3% – admit the existence of such people. Only 3.3% of experts categorically denied such a possibility.

Specialists demonstrated the same pattern with some deviations. 94.2% of specialists responded positively to Persona-Doctrine, and 5.8% were categorically opposed.

Diagram 29. (SSLD 54 - ESPD 25). Comparisons of Attitudes to Term Persona-Doctrine

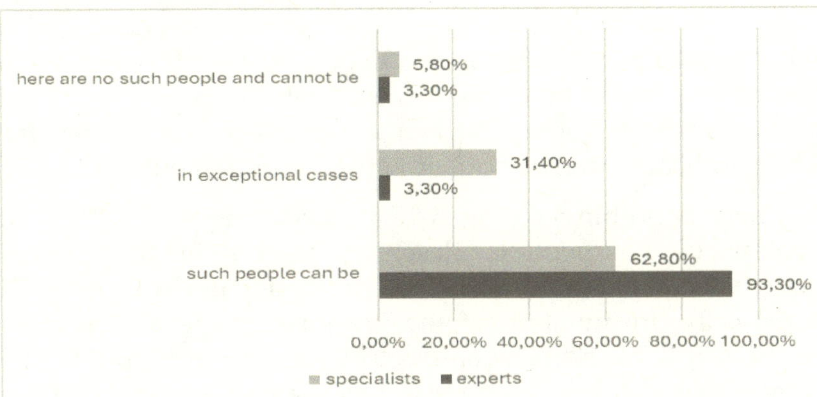

A comparison of opinions on the possibility of recognizing specific people as a Persona-Doctrine showed that experts have a more positive perception of the term Persona-Doctrine – 93.3% agreed that such people can exist. 62.8% of specialists supported this option. 31.4% of specialists admit this possibility only in exceptional cases. The answer "there are no such people" had meager support in both groups of respondents.

Achieving the status of a Persona-Doctrine is a long-term process. It is not easy to establish the beginning, the moment when the formation of a doctrinal persona commences. Perhaps these difficulties are caused by the fact that we evaluate the result and do not track the process. In the questionnaire, we hypothetically created a situation of more or less obvious decision-making for ourselves to move to the heights of a professional career in the form of a doctrinal personality. Based on this hypothesis, the experts were asked, "Are you striving for the status of a Persona-Doctrine?" Possible answers were proposed: 1) consciously created it, 2) sought consciously but not on purpose, 3) instead did not strive on purpose, 4) did not consciously create it, and 5) did not orient himself at all. The purpose of this question is to ascertain whether the attainment of the status of the Persona-Doctrine is the result of deliberate, extraordinary actions. This is an absolutely positive question, as we do not suspect any of the experts we have selected of creating status as an end in itself. Falsified persons on the list of super-cited authors are known, and we avoided interacting with such people. Accordingly, the "pure" Persona-Doctrine who became participants in the Expert Survey did not have a dishonest plan. In addition, it seems natural to plan one's life path, considering some markers of achievements and results. These indicators can be both quantitative and qualitative.

There is nothing wrong with participating in the "Best in Profession" competition. Reaching heights in professional activity is a beautiful result of professional realization. Of course, the formulation of the life goal as the achievement of the status of the Persona-Doctrine could not be put in the foreseeable retrospective simply because such a status had not been suggested before the present study. Our experts avoided the words "deliberately"; nevertheless, 76.7% of the surveyed Persona-Doctrines acted consciously, and 6.7% of them consciously sought. 23.3% of experts categorically deny the orientation towards outstanding achievements. Notably, none of the experts chose the most explicit of the proposed forms of recognition of managed work concerning one's status – they "consciously created it". Perhaps creating such an image as a desired achievement is not done. There are no plans to become the most respected authoritative person to transform their creative ideas into legislation. Such an attitude, according to experts, cannot exist.

The questionnaire asked about the self-assessment of Persona-Doctrine satisfaction with its status. This is a resolutive question. We assess how the expert perceives his nomination for Persona-Doctrine status today. During the interview, we discovered that the expert considers such a nomination unexpected and may be somewhat surprised by the pretentious name of the Persona-Doctrine status. Indeed, this is a new term; we have just invented it and started a public discussion about its viability and applicability.

Accordingly, if an expert follows the attributes of his recognition, he is most likely aware of his status and gets satisfaction from it.

FOCUS ON STATUS OF PERSON. ACHIEVEMENT DATES

Respondents who consciously aspired to their status feel satisfied (50%) or neutral (50%). The highest degree of satisfaction with their status is demonstrated by experts who consciously did not strive for this status (60%). This group of experts shows a very positive assessment. Most subjects are satisfied with their status. 14.3% of experts demonstrate complete disinterest: they have a negative attitude towards their status and have not been guided by it.

There is another vector of observations: the influence of personal qualities on achieving the goal, in this case, the status of the Persona-Doctrine. For example, recognizing that if a person is goal-oriented and hardworking, they are most likely working towards a significant goal. Of course, it cannot be assumed that our experts visualized their goal 25 – 35 years ago as achieving Persona-Doctrine status. First, such a status did not exist. Second, even today, that status is just beginning its journey, and the fate of this term is unknown. However, it is possible to add this new term to the existing markers of success: many good publications, academic authority, recognition in the academic world and at the State level, State awards, notable titles, and so on. Accordingly, the goal setting of the future Persona-Doctrine could fit nicely into markers with an extended application history.

We have data on the role of purposefulness and perseverance, and they can be compared to a significant life result: achieving the status of a Persona-Doctrine. All the experts who have not been focused on achieving the Persona-Doctrine status recognize the strong influence of purposefulness. However, those who have strived consciously recognize the importance of purposefulness, but have different understandings of purposefulness. For one group, the goal was to achieve other significant indicators, and the status of the Persona-Doctrine joined them or materialized in them. Others set a goal for themselves and achieve it.

Comparison with perseverance also seems to be effective. Experts who did not focus on the status under discussion appreciate perseverance. The answers "strong influence" and "influence" correspond to the worldview of experts who consciously aspired to Persona-Doctrine status. Notably, the respondents who value purposefulness and perseverance less did not desire Persona-Doctrine status either intentionally or consciously.

The first group of conscientious workers was reasonably rewarded. The second group of experts, who were not very motivated or goal-oriented, still received a reward they did not seek. They are indifferent or neutral about their status. They can be the most abstracted from human passions, pure researchers who write what they want, when they want, and do not chase after the trappings of recognition. There have been cases of rejection of various awards. The professional formation, development, and achievement of results may correlate with specific periods in the life of the Persona-Doctrine.

Accordingly, it seems logical to connect life stages with achievements. This will allow scholars to identify the most productive periods in the past tense and formulate expectations for future periods. For periodization, we used the moments of obtaining documents on academic achievement – a dissertation (candidate or doctor legal sciences). The period before the candidate thesis is conventionally called the postgraduate period. It includes the period after graduation from the university and before the start of the dissertation research. This is followed by candidate and doctoral dissertations, and the next stage is after the doctoral dissertation. Recognizing the possible value of each stage, we asked experts to rate them from 0% to 100%. Using these periods, they were asked to evaluate their most famous works.

Postgraduates were rarely productive in writing doctrinal material. However, the choice of topic and beginning of research may have commenced during this period. 73.3% of experts considered the period of postgraduate life to be empty from the point of view under consideration. Nevertheless, 26.7% of experts did significant academic groundwork in these years. This suggests that people with outstanding achievements feel ready for a significant career early on. Indeed, in the postgraduate environment, "stars" are sometimes visible from the first year. They are distinguished by preparedness, purposefulness, a severe attitude to the future profession, conscious choice, and other characteristics that are the "natural, pre-established" groundwork for the doctrinal future. The results of expert farrowing identified this group of Persona-Doctrines, who were motivated to super achievements as postgraduates, and constituted more than a quarter (26.7%) of experts.

At the outset of this study, we hypothesized that the most productive period from the point of view of doctrinal groundwork would be the preparation of the doctoral thesis. This was because a doctoral dissertation forms a new academic direction. The study found that 10% of experts achieved full realization (100%) during this period. 26.7% of the experts accomplished 75% of their significant work during the period of writing the doctoral thesis. 46.7% of respondents wrote half (50%) of their doctrinally significant works during this period. This partially supports the preliminary hypothesis, but not completely. The post-doctoral period turned out to be more productive for doctrinal achievements.

A burst of creative activity after the doctoral thesis presumably happened, but only for interested researchers who continued to work actively. The lack of results after the doctoral thesis may indicate the importance of achieving the "Doctor of Legal Sciences" status as the pinnacle of a research career. Indeed, if a person publishes only to defend a dissertation, the defense interrupts this activity. However, if a researcher is looking for the truth and is constantly involved in the research process, regardless of the official record of achievements with the issuance of a final document, he, of course, will continue to work creatively and publish after his doctoral dissertation. Genuine curiosity is not related to the achievement of socially significant calculable markers. They are a by-product. The study identified experts who showed more activity after defending their doctoral dissertations. Moreover, if we take the maximum figure – 100% of doctrinal works – this happened to 43.3% of experts.

To diversify the Persona-Doctrine activity periods, we added the age factor to the data analysis. We lack data on the age at which the experts defended their dissertations. We compared defense, age, and achievement timelines to unify the period. We analyzed the age at which the Persona-Doctrine wrote (or planned to write) their most sought-after works. We had in mind doctrinally significant works and specified the most popular, iconic, quoted, and high-quality ones.

Age is divided into ten-year periods, starting from 20 and up to 90+ years. The highest rates in the age group gradually rise from 20 to 50, peak between the ages of 51 and 60, and then decline to zero after 70.

Table 10. (ESPD 43). Relationship Between Age and Academic Achievements of Persona-Doctrines (Expert Opinion)

formative period	students		PhD	Doctor in Law	after Doctor in Law				
age	up to 20 years	20-30	31-40	41-50	51-60	61-70	71-80	81-90	after 90 years
0	90,00%	36,%	20,0%	10,0%	3,30%	10,0%	26,7%	33,3%	46,70%
25%	6,70%	46,%	30,0%	16,7%	13,3%	6,70%	10,0%	26,7%	16,70%
50%	3,30%	13,%	30,0%	40,0%	23,3%	33,3%	23,3%	13,3%	13,30%
75%	0,00%	0,0%	13,3%	26,7%	46,7%	20,0%	20,0%	13,3%	6,70%
100%	0,00%	3,3%	6,70%	6,70%	13,3%	30,0%	20,0%	13,3%	16,70%

Then, to find the correlation between age and dissertation defenses, we conditionally correlated these periods:

- up to 30 years old – postgraduates
- 30 – 40 years old – Candidate
- 40 – 50 – Doctor of Legal Sciences,
- 50 + – after Doctor of Legal Sciences

This periodization is approximate and does not exclude individual fluctuations.

We have categorized the periods based on well-known data, which generally does not exclude some deviations. For example, a period of 20 – 30 years may be assessed by someone with a candidate of legal sciences, considering the trend toward rejuvenating academic personnel. We also allow defending a doctoral thesis after 60. In addition, the distortion may come from the fact that the respondents look at protection and age differently and do not compare these coordinate systems. We conceived these two questions to determine the period of maximum productivity to form the academic product that would be assessed as doctrinal.

If health and energy were the leading indicators, achievements would be made up to 20, with a maximum of 30. If achievements are based on experience, wisdom, and wealth, then the period of prosperity should come after 50. This conclusion is fully confirmed by the question of the periods of creation of the most significant works – after the doctoral degree – the period from 51 to 70 (46.7%), with a slight drop in the period 61 to 70 (33.3%). Between the ages of 51 and 60, such experts created more than 75% of the most significant works; between the ages of 61 and 70, 50% were created. None of the respondents chose the 100% option. More than half of all significant works were created after the doctorate, meaning 25 – 50% were done earlier. Accordingly, the groundwork for success in adulthood was made in the previous periods, as evidenced by our table: during the candidate dissertation preparation when I was a postgraduate.

Expert questioning has lifted the veil over the sensations (understanding) of one's doctrinal status by the Persona-Doctrine. Experts were asked to report whether they had ever disclosed the fact that they were a Persona-Doctrine to others. The uniqueness of sociological tools is that they allow us to understand the group relationships in a developing, active way. Only a survey and observation make it possible to establish a self-assessment of the subject position in the professional environment. However, the data on the high appreciation of the Persona-Doctrine must come from legislation and incentives (awards, indexes, and so on) and from society. The question opens the channels of information from society. Society transmits a peculiar system of symbols, signs, and markers to the Persona-Doctrine.

This question is more profound than it may seem. It would be necessary to establish the manifestation of the opinion of the people around them, what signs they give, and what actions they perform. In general, these can be forms of recognition of special status: an invitation to events as an expert, provision of speaking at events in the first place, free access to paid events, special seats when seating at events, introduction to other people with all the achievements, positions and awards, the style of conversation from respectful to obsequious. It can also be a request to be photographed, the presentation of books by authors, an invitation to visit a government agency (or an educational or academic organization), particular tasks of a confidential nature from the highest authorities, requests for an autograph, embarrassment during a conversation, expressing special gratitude for communication or some professional cooperation, an invitation in challenging situations for support (for example, to be defended by an official or unofficial opponent, an actor at parliamentary meetings). Hearings, an offer to act as a reviewer of monographs, and others.

Such behavior is noticeable and recorded by the people around the scholar. It can be expressed positively (respect, recognition of authority) and negatively (obsequiousness, flattery, aggressive criticism for opposing views or supporting some State decisions). To an experienced Persona-Doctrine, it seems to us the difference between positive and negative attitudes is noticeable. They are guided by their own ways of mastering signals and decide whether to interact with counterparties or refuse. The Persona-Doctrine must capture the mood of the environment. This likely gives positive emotions signs of apparent merits, but negative emotions are not excluded either.

The results of the expert survey indisputably show that the people around them know that there is a Persona-Doctrine in front of them, and they give external signs of their understanding, which come from the Persona-Doctrine.

Only 3.3% of experts have never faced the fact that they are special people to others. Everyone else experienced varying frequency: very often – 10%, often – 26.7%. Not often, but instead rather – 60% of experts. These responses show that experts read the signs of recognition from the people they encounter, register these facts, and understand them.

Experts have named several forms of recognition as Persona-Doctrine. According to experts, the feeling of their exceptional importance is given to them by high ratings of books and articles by such recognized classics of legal doctrinal scholarship as Harold Joseph Berman (1918-2007), William Elliott Butler, and Vladik Sumbatovich Nersesiants (1938-2005), both oral and written in the form of detailed objective positive reviews.

The traditional form of recognition is the desire for face-to-face interaction at conferences. A signal can be considered a message that people read Persona-Doctrine books and use them in their work. Naturally, they actively participate in sessions of dissertation councils or even supervise them, which is likewise a form of recognition.

After defending a doctoral dissertation before colleagues in various organizations, participation in conferences is recognized. An exceptionally high assessment can be reflected not only in the legal field, but also in the political field. This can be expressed in the elections of deputies and positive assessments by significant actors. Academic high praise is mentions in dissertations, books, and invitations to write textbooks.

Surveys and interviews have revealed a positive attitude towards the new status of the Persona-Doctrine. Despite the novelty of this term, there is a high level of recognition in different groups of respondents. Overall, the term has positive prospects, especially for use in the professional environment. The most optimistic forecast bodes well for the viability of the term and its widespread use.

Achievement of the status of Persona-Doctrine is the result of long-term professional development. The Persona-Doctrine have shown themselves to be single-minded researchers. The overwhelming majority of Persona-Doctrines have consciously acted toward achieving this status. Such a result was not a surprise. To achieve the status of a Persona-Doctrine, they worked hard for a long time (more than 30 years) with a small probability of overachievement. From the point of view of academic and educational periodization, the period after the doctoral dissertation is the most productive for significant works. In terms of age, it is 50 – 70 years, with a peak of 50 – 60 years.

An element of the status of a Persona-Doctrine is an exclusive assessment of the environment, primarily professional. This recognition on the part of an indefinite circle of people does not pass by the Persona-Doctrine. They know about it and get satisfaction from their status.

Chapter 18
Personal Qualities of Persona-Doctrine

The personal qualities of the Persona-Doctrine have been the object of close academic analysis. An expert survey is a self-assessment of Persona-Doctrines. We have had the opportunity in some matters to compare the opinion of Persona-Doctrines, as it were, about their personal qualities, with the opinion of specialists.

The Persona-Doctrine as a person has personal characteristics which, following our hypothesis, impact the achievement of doctrinal status. We asked two groups of respondents – specialists and experts – to assess these characteristics of different origins – to determine the influence of personal qualities on the formation of status.

This question is: do personal qualities matter in forming the Persona-Doctrine? Generally, the relationship between experts and specialists converges only in a generalized assessment – they recognize the importance of personal qualities. 1.8% of experts and 3.3% of specialists do not believe that the role of personal qualities is significant.

Diagram 30. (SSLD 53 - ESPD 20). Comparison of Opinions of Experts and Specialists on Importance of Personal Characteristics in Forming Status of Persona-Doctrine

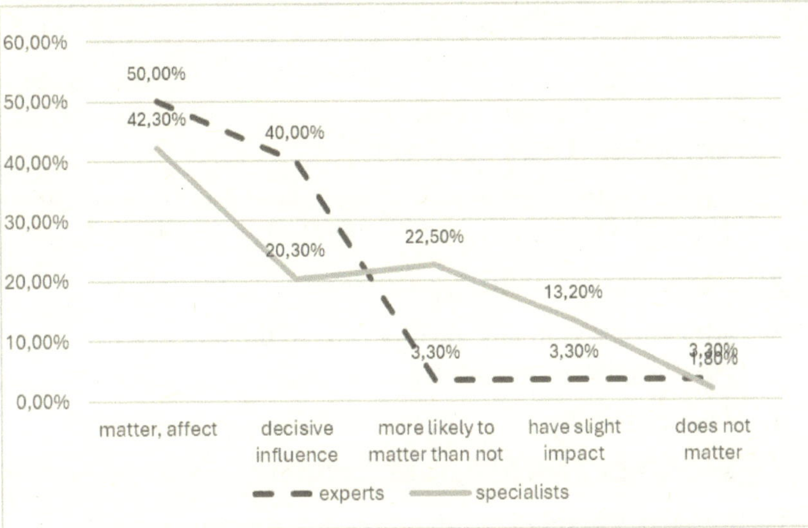

Experts rate the importance of personal qualities more highly than specialists. 90% of experts chose the answer options "decisive" and "matter", and specialists 60.3%. Diametrically opposite assessment: in the opinion of "more likely to matter than" and "have a slight impact". These uncertain options were more often chosen by specialists. The option "has a slight impact" was supported by 13.2% of specialists. 22.5% of specialists do not have a definite opinion. Thus, with an element of originality, both groups of respondents see the key to the success of doctrinal persons in their personal characteristics. However, the degree of confidence in the importance of personal qualities in Personas-Doctrines is very high – 96.7%.

Notably, there are significant differences in recognizing personal characteristics that are of decisive importance. 40% of exports and 20.3% of specialists with such an opinion were identified.

Thus, experts are more focused on personal characteristics in explaining the achievements of the Persona-Doctrine (90%)

than specialists (62.6%). A persona is influenced by internal (personality-related) and external (non-personality-related) factors. Accordingly, a decrease in the effectiveness of personal characteristics as an internal factor is combined with an increase in the effectiveness of external factors.

Several questions are intended to clarify the factors influencing the formation of the Persona-Doctrine. These characteristics can be grouped as follows:

1. education and academic degrees are axiomatic indicators. The expert doctorate for this study is pre-established;
2. publications (quality and style);
3. additional statuses (affiliation with the organization, position, honorary titles);
4. relationships in the team (friendliness, openness);
5. attitude to work (diligence, dedication, perseverance);
6. hierarchical relationships (loyalty, tolerance, flexibility);
7. physical qualities (health).

Specialists have built a hierarchy of factors influencing the Persona-Doctrine as follows.

According to experts, the most influential factor is the quality of publications, which was preferred by 54%. The lowest impact is seen in affiliation with the organization (6.2%) and position (14.6%). This indicates that the status of Persona-Doctrine is perceived as personal, not organizational. This question is cross-cutting with other questions in the questionnaire and survey about the influence of position on work status and personality.

According to experts, the hierarchy of factors is poorly correlated with the ideas of specialists.

Experts once again expressed their distrust of honorary titles. Only 9.7% of experts believe that these titles affect status. This is followed by affiliation with the organization (19.4%) and position (19.4%). Nevertheless, almost 20% of the votes cast for the position role show that one in five experts believes in the power of the position to raise the authority of the author and his works.

The most influential factors are education (64.5%) and the quality of publications (45.2%). The factor of education is fascinating and deserves closer attention. It may be necessary to consider the university where the promising candidate for Persona-Doctrine studied. In our research design we did not ask specifically for the name of the university. However, we can assume that studying at a particular university, which at a certain period becomes a "forge of personnel" of the political and other elite, is a helpful factor. Personal acquaintance, joint study, work under the guidance of a particular successful leader, and learning from the same master create the prerequisites for significant influence of the educational factor on the formation of the Persona-Doctrine.

A comparison of the opinions of specialists and experts is as follows.

Diagram 31. (SSLD 84 - ESPD 10). Comparison of Factors Influencing Persona-Doctrine According to Specialists and Experts

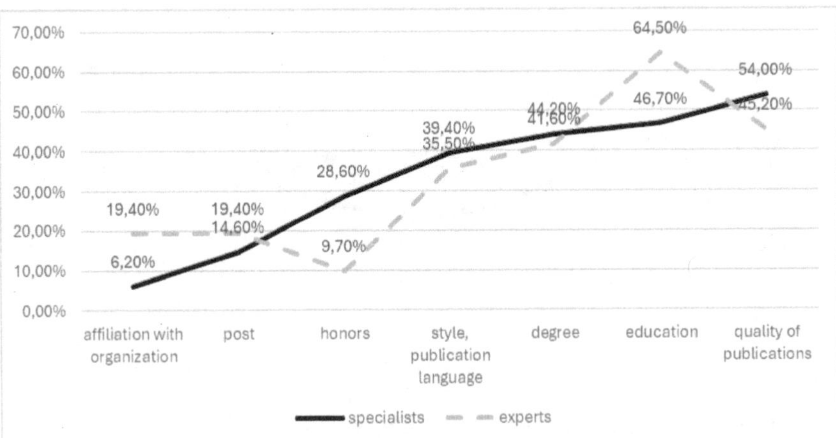

The most significant difference in the opinions of specialists and experts is assessing the factors of education, affiliation with an organization, and honorary titles. Experts rate the importance of education higher (64.5% vs. 46.7% of specialists). According to experts, the role of honorary titles is much lower (9.7%), while specialists see more favorable prospects for honorary titles (28.6%).

The respondent assessed work-related factors, such as dedication, diligence, and others. Other factors are entirely personal, such as health. However, we focus on those personal attributes that influence the attainment of doctrinal status. Affiliation with an organization as an influential factor is rated higher by experts (19.4%) and experts (6.2%).

It is natural to assume that all respondents will select such qualities as diligence, purposefulness, and perseverance to the maximum extent. This is fully confirmed by the surveys.

The following personal virtues influence the achievement of doctrinal status in descending order: 1) purposefulness (71% of experts and 63.7% of specialists), 2) perseverance (67.7% and 58.8%), 3) diligence (64.5% and 54.9%).

Diagram 32. (SSLD 45 - ESPD 11). Comparison of Opinions of Specialists and Experts on Significant Personal Qualities

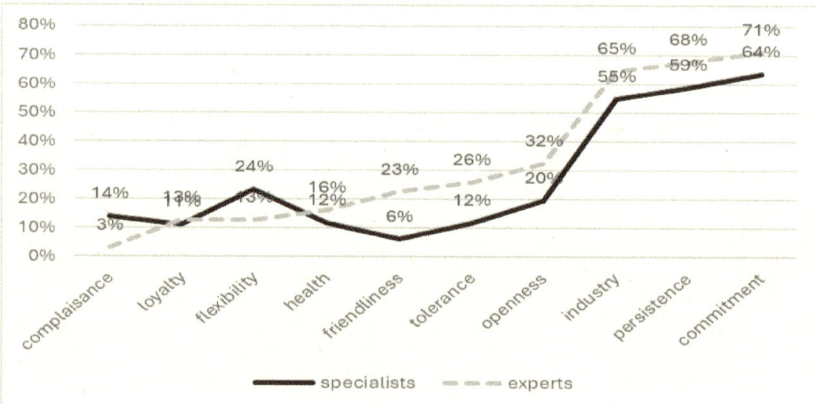

It should be noted that there is an almost complete synchronization of the opinions of specialists and personal doctrines. The only feature that showed significant differences in the assessments of the two categories of respondents was flexibility. Experts noted the greater importance of flexibility.

However, flexibility for these respondents is an even more significant factor in comparison with health (11.9%), friendliness (6.2%), tolerance (11.9%), and openness (32.3%). In the value system of specialists, flexibility follows purposefulness, perseverance, and hard work.

Both groups of respondents showed an insignificant impact of helpfulness. According to experts, friendliness and flexibility are not of great importance. Experts say helpfulness (3.2%) and loyalty (12.9%) have negligible impact. Thus, helpfulness is in the lead in the anti-rating of both groups. As a factor in the movement towards doctrinality, specialists value flexibility more than experts do (23.5% and 12.9%). Perhaps this is because experts already achieved the status of Persona-Doctrine, whereas specialists have not yet done so. Accordingly, specialists can anticipate the status of Persona-Doctrine. They believe their flexibility and non-resistance can collectively lead to doctrinal status.

It should be noted that all these features hinder openness to innovation and confidence in one's position. These are the antipodes of opposition rebellion.

At the design stage of the study, we assumed that respondents would not voluntarily admit that they recognized the effectiveness of flexibility, loyalty, and helpfulness. Much depends on how respondents perceive questions about the role of personal qualities. They may perceive them as questions about them or abstract questions about other people, in general, broadly.

We could assume that respondents would refuse to recognize the values of flexibility. This property is more likely to be regarded as a flaw in everyday consciousness. Contrary to the forecast, experts recognized the tremendous positive value of flexibility.

The respondent understanding of some factors of influence was unexpected. At the stage of developing the questionnaire project, we proposed the influence factor "health" on the assumption that good health creates prerequisites for active and successful research. However, the pilot survey showed that most respondents gave this property the supposed positive content as "good health". Other respondents saw a negative in the question. The meaning is "poor health". Perhaps this is caused by the age and health of the Persona-Doctrines. The 60+ age group may experience natural difficulties with hearing, vision, movement, and other limitations. If, at the same time, the researcher is in good creative shape and has an assistant (which is essential), then he can see the prerequisites for creative activity within his physical limitations. During the interviews, the experts pointed out that health problems, such as restrictions in movement, forced them to focus on intellectual work and acted as a positive factor in this situation.

The environment can influence the formation of the Persona-Doctrine. We formulated the question: "What factors strongly impacted your status as a Persona-Doctrine"? The following answers were offered: "strongly influenced", "insignificantly affected", and "did not affect".

The social environment is represented by the following institutions: family, creative or labor collective, and mentors. The material conditions of the external environment include suitable financing and lack of funds. The factor of "working conditions" is proposed separately.

The financial factor is considered in the "good financing" – funded – variant and "lack of funds". The factors of "good funding" – "underfunding" may or may not be work-related. If we are talking about a young researcher, he would instead not count on the amount of salary because there is no salary or it is small. Scholars can count on financial assistance (more often than family).

76.7% of experts categorically do not recognize the impact of suitable financing, and 23.4% recognize the impact, of which 13.3% consider this impact to be strong. Paradoxically, the exact percentages for groups were obtained for the "lack of funds" factor.

Notably, some experts chose diametrically opposite factors as significant during the interviews. A cross-comparison of the answers revealed that 20% of experts recognize the simultaneous strong influence of two factors (affluence and lack of funds). 70% believe that neither good funding nor lack of funds substantially impacted the development of their doctrinal status. 3.3% of experts attribute the results of their work to sufficient funding. Such a formula is welcome. It explains that sufficiently organized material research work (and perhaps personal well-being) create the prerequisites for intellectual pursuits. A hungry researcher who is always busy trying to obtain simple things is less likely to reach the doctrinal level. It can be assumed that this is the opinion of the materially prosperous Persona-Doctrines. They are not oligarchs; they do not have noticeable wealth in society, but they generally have a higher material comfort than most of the population. 3.3% of such people are a clear minority.

Sociological tools have not identified experts with a socially difficult social start in low material conditions. The struggle for survival and the desire for success in everyday consciousness contribute to forming purposeful and successful individuals. As the saying goes, an artist must be hungry. However, there were not initially "hungry" artists among our experts. This shows that future Persona-Doctrines are recruited in a socially favorable environment, better than the ordinary, well-to-do people in the first generation. Indeed, it is a kind of luxury to surrender to research and expect a delayed ephemeral result. Academic activity requires long-term funding, not funding by the researcher himself, who requires a financially secure environment.

The options "good financing" and "lack of funds" were proposed by the experts at the pilot stage of the project. The seeming contradiction makes it possible to identify what is more important, or more precisely, whether the availability of means can stimulate the formation of the Persona-Doctrine. Good funding as a basis scholarly research is consistent with Marxist logic and generally does not contradict liberal logic. One can realize oneself more effectively in prosperous conditions. When a person does not need to spend time on non-creative pursuits, when there is no concern for satisfying basic human needs, creative talents can flourish. The unconvincing nature of such a thesis globally is evident to us. But despite its illusory nature, it makes sense. The "hungry artist" searches and creates. He is brave, open to innovation, not afraid of shouting, and free since no one pays for his classes, and does not prepay for the desired "result". He is motivated but cannot wager on the result because his achievement is not normative. It is difficult to predict. He may perish before the achievements bring material results. In support of this thesis, we know of famous artists who died in poverty. They never knew that their masterpieces were worth millions.

In psychology, there is a concept of "comfort zone". Psychologists suggest getting out of this zone to activate internal resources. There may not be organic reasons for this change. Escalating this hypothetical situation, we imagined a person who intentionally quits his job, refuses to earn money, breaks social ties, assumes burdensome obligations, sets unattainable goals, and so on. Such an artificial version of the hungry artist was chosen by 3.3% of experts. 10% of experts have the same opinion about good funding and lack of funds. 70% of experts do not recognize the influence of the material factor.

We have investigated the influence of the collective on the achievement of the Persona-Doctrine status. At least two types of collectives could have an external influence on the status of the Persona-Doctrine: "creative collective" and "labor collective". There are nuances of meaning in these two concepts. Labor collective is a Soviet term from the past. A collective of workers, people working at an enterprise in an institution, formed the subject of decision-making. It is not easy to apply this to modern organizations, a term in that historical sense. Today, the "labor collective" is the sum of individualized workers. However, it is necessary to keep in mind the peculiarity of the age composition of the Persona-Doctrines, the formation of which, for the most part, took place in the Soviet State. Accordingly, the definition of "labor collective" can have the same meaning in their vocabulary and consciousness.

We offered this answer taking into account the age representation of Persona-Doctrines 60+. Accordingly, part of their academic activity occurred under conditions of Soviet labor relations, which are dramatically different from modern ones.

Diagram 33. (ESPD 29_3 - ESPD 58). Influence of Age on Understanding of Role of Workforce in Formation of Persona-Doctrine (Expert Opinion)

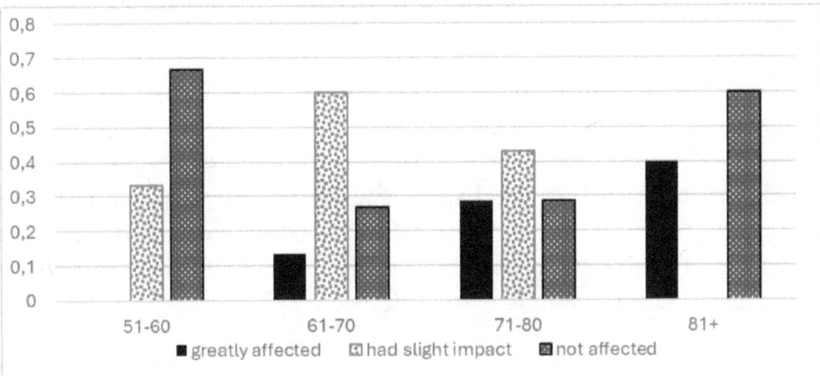

As for the collectives, we assume that the "creative team" option will be more in demand. This assumption is associated with losing the value content of the "labor collective" definition. Today, it is not a team of like-minded people. It is a competitive, aggressive environment. A person is a member of this collective by necessity as an employee. The judicial statistics of court cases of dismissal on disciplinary grounds inspired by hostility, intolerance, envy, and other motives are frightening.

A strong influence on the workforce is recognized by 20% of experts. The impact, although insignificant, is recognized by 43.3% of experts. Influence without diversification is recognized by 63.3% of experts. 36.7% of experts deny the influence of the labor collective.

13.3% of experts consider the creative team to be a decisive influencing factor, and 10% recognize the influence of the creative team. Significantly superior is the group of experts who do not recognize such influences (76.7%).

Respondents aged 61 (28.6%) recognize the strong influence of the workforce, which increases to a maximum of 40% in the 80+ category.

The 51 – 60 age group supports the "slightly affected" and "did not affect" variants. Experts aged 51 – 60 do not feel connected to the workforce, which may be explained by historical conditions, that is, the erosion of this concept from culture and language.

This result is indicated in our hypothesis about the Soviet meaning of the term "labor collective". In 2025, those who were 20 – 30 years old at the date of the dissolution of the USSR will be 51 – 60 years old. Accordingly, their work for hire was carried out in post-Soviet space, without labor collectives in the Soviet sense. There are reasons to foresee the displacement of this term from circulation in the foreseeable future.

Thus, experts focus more on their workforce and overwhelmingly recognize its influence. The low rating of this concept by creative teams is because the term is vague in modern conditions. Persona-Doctrines do not consider themselves members of any creative collectives. Recognizing their doctrinal work as individuals, they are not members of creative collectives.

Working conditions are related to the performance of a job function. 53.3% of experts acknowledge the impact of working conditions, and 46.7% do not. Accordingly, this factor is not essential for respondents. This can be explained by the fact that, as a rule, the performance of creative work occurs not at the employer organization, but at home, in the library, and in other convenient places.

We proceeded from the assumption that the role of the Persona-Doctrine should be high. This assumption is based on the fact that best professional research is carried out in an academic school. It can be a university department or academic circle of researchers. The groundwork is carried out in one's close professional circle. Postgraduate studies are the best way for an aspiring researcher to become a researcher, a center of academic culture. In general, the experts showed the significant role of mentors in their formation as a Persona-Doctrine. The answer option "mentors strongly influenced" was chosen by 76.7% of experts, and "insignificantly influenced" – by 16.7%. 6.7% of experts deny the influence of mentors entirely.

In the questionnaire, much attention was paid to the family. The experts answered a question about family influence on reaching the doctrinal level. 43.3% of experts noted a strong family influence, 23.3% – insignificant, and 33.3% of experts noted that the family did not impact their professional development and outstanding results. Thus, 66.5% recognize the influence of the family to varying degrees.

Experts could understand the word family broadly as all family ties and their own family created by them – the nuclear family. In fact, the general term family needs to be clarified, and we did this by specifying "parental family" in another survey question. This is to emphasize that we are discussing the expert's parents and grandparents in this question. In this version, we are talking about the time of personality formation of the Persona-Doctrine, human qualities in the broadest sense, and not only in research. And in this matter, all forms of influence are allowed. It can be assumed that we are talking about forming such personal qualities of the future Persona-Doctrine as purposefulness, diligence, and others.

In some cases, it is a question of professional involvement in the legal profession in the parental family. The question is: "Were there lawyers in your family who influenced your doctrinal future"?

We cite one example of the influence of the family, the environment, and the country united into a single whole. One expert said he grew up in the South Urals in the 1940s.

At that time, the region and the country, the USSR, were experiencing an remarkable upswing in everything, including industry, research, and production. As he said, everything breathed creativity and pride into the common cause. Under such conditions, all forms of an active, creative personality were involved in collectives from the family, the court, the institution, and the country. Perhaps this is one reason why the Urals of those years generated so many Persona-Doctrines in jurisprudence and other branches of knowledge.

Some experts remembered relatives three or four generations ago. According to their stories, the family memory kept such examples alive and passed them on with pride. One expert outlined four generations, each of which rose to the next step in a legal career and social status.

In the Expert Survey, a clarifying question is formulated: "Did the parental family impact your achievement of the status of a Persona-Doctrine"? A strong influence of the parental family is recognized by 13.3% of experts, a significant influence – by 20%. The parental family did not significantly impact 10% of the experts. Some influence is noted by 26.7% of experts, and 30% deny any influence. Summing up the responses into groups, we recognize a more or less significant influence of 33.3% and little or no 66.7%. The analysis of Persona-Doctrine biographies showed that the experts were strongly influenced by the parental family with outstanding merits, including parents with the status of academician and corresponding members of the Russian Academy of Sciences. Accordingly, the characteristics and achievements of the parental family are essential. Older generations with outstanding achievements provided significant support to the next generation, which is to be expected. In such a family, legal research, groundwork, and topics could accumulate, continuity could be formed, and a kind of family academic school could be formed.

The experts shared the following elements of family influence: 1) the choice of an educational institution, 2) the way of life, 3) the cultivation of respect for knowledge and people, 4) pride in achievements, 5) taught creativity, the need to create, 6) set an example of diligence, 6) created conditions for academic research, 7) the father had experience in public administration, 8) the general life position of the parents, 9) the pedagogical activity of the parents, 10) the situation in the family, constructive character, 11) the forward movement of each successive generation from worker to professor. The outstanding achievements of the parents were recognized with age – after the age of 30. It is noted that the Persona-Doctrine, as in the second generation, continues to develop related items. Wife after husband, children after parents can also inherit the topic (general research direction) and achieve outstanding results.

Specifying the influence of the legal methodology of the older generation as a legal Persona-Doctrine in the second generation, the author notes the family's political influence through experiencing repressions of lawyers of the previous generation. It can be assumed that a heightened sense of justice and a high appreciation of the right to freedom of expression resulted from such a family history.

Some Persona-Doctrines indicated that they were the first example of legal tradition in their family and that the following second and third generations also achieved academic advances. One expert suggested the term for designating such a family group: "the clan of legal scholars of the family". This is the influence of the Persona-Doctrine on their family, the influence moving forward into the future.

One general family theme clarifiers is the question: "Were there any lawyers in your family who influenced your doctrinal future"? It turned out that most Persona-Doctrines are lawyers in the first generation – 76.7%.

Summarizing all the factors that we tested for impact on the status of the Persona-Doctrine by cross-analysis of the answers, the most influential factors identified were: mentors, family, and environment. Financial factors and the creative team turned out to be ineffective. The ineffectiveness of financial factors can be explained by the conditions in the country as a whole. The state of labor resources and the economy allowed a person who has chosen a career of outstanding academic achievements in jurisprudence to have the advantage of relatively favorable material conditions. The threat of poverty and the impossibility of realizing one's plans do not hang over this category of people. They are successful in many ways, including the timely creation of financial conditions.

The influence of the environment can be considered broadly as a country, a State, and local self-government designed to support researchers, especially in the formative period. It should be borne in mind that these are insignificant guarantees. Individuals will be unable to achieve high social and material standards, for an academic career generally does not bring prosperity. But these guarantees are sufficient for modest people focused on academic achievements.

All influential factors belong to the category of the human factor – these are the people around the Persona-Doctrine from whom they seek support, experience dependency, and interact.

Chapter 19
Professional Qualities of Persona-Doctrine

We asked two groups of respondents (experts and specialists) which assessments most strongly influence the formation of doctrinal status. Recognizing the opinion of some subjects as influential, we simultaneously record the sensitivity of creative personalities with respect to these opinions.

Experts recognize the influence of the academic community as the strongest (54.8%). Second place is occupied by public authorities – 38.7%. The degree of influence of the authorities in comparison with the research community is much lower. This is followed by research organizations (32.3%) and professional groups (29%). With regard to recognition among specialists, the research community (60.2%) and the research organization (36.3%) are in first place, followed by professional groups (34.1%) and authorities (26.5%).

Experts put the academic community first (60.2%), and social networks are recognized as the least influential factor (7.1%).

Diagram 34. (SSLD 11 - ESPD 15). Comparison of Opinions of Experts and Specialists on Assessing Influence of External Factors on Formation of Persona-Doctrine

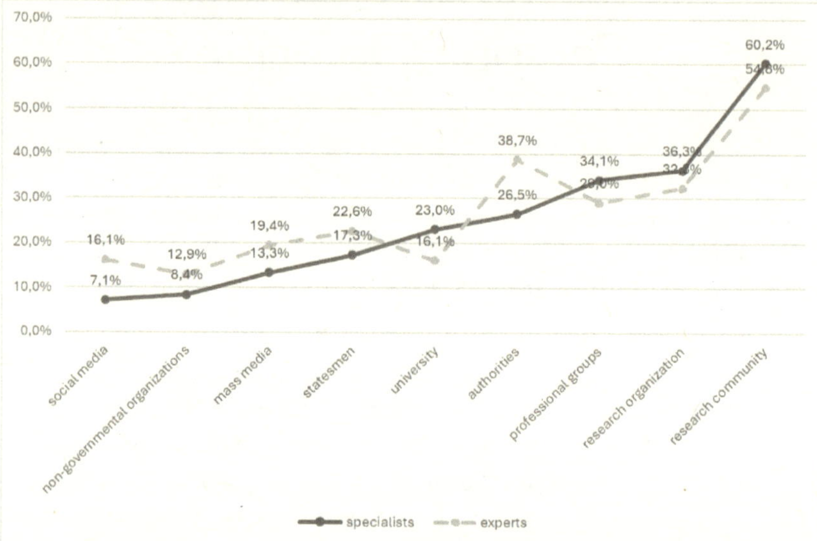

Participants in the survey and expert survey are unanimous about the most significant influence of the assessment of the research community on the formation of the status of Doctrine (60.2% and 54.8%, respectively). The second place in terms of importance for specialists is the assessment of a research organization (36.3%). For experts, it is the authorities (38.7%). This result is a recognition of the role of the administrative resource in forming the status of the Persona-Doctrine. The same is true of the influence of the evaluation of politicians. For specialists, this factor is in the sixth position (17.3%), and for Person Doctrines, it is in the fifth (22.6%). In the comparative diagram, it was evident that the most significant difference is in the assessment of the opinion of public authorities. This reflects the organic connection of many Persona-Doctrines with State authorities and politicians. The same is true of politicians. Experts attribute 22.6% to this factor, and specialists – 17.3%. Experts rate the influence of public authorities more highly than specialists (38.7% vs. 26.5% among specialists). The position of some Personas-Doctrines depends on the decisions of politicians.

The next most considerable difference in the assessments of the two surveys is the role of universities, which specialists estimate to be higher (23%). This may be due to their work in the education system. However, the Persona-Doctrines experience shows this hope's futility (16.1%). Counting on assistance in promotion from State authorities and politicians is more promising.

We have seen the importance of perseverance in attaining doctrinal status. To deepen the understanding of this factor, we formulated a question that clarifies the connection between "persistence" and the sphere and place of its application, namely, persistence in the propaganda of one's proposals.

We formulated the question of what personal qualities influence the achievement of the status of Persona-Doctrine. If the respondent chooses the option "does not depend at all" on perseverance, this can be interpreted as a manifestation of modesty. On the other hand, the option "strongly depends" conforms the importance of active self-presentation. And this question does not involve understanding propaganda in the form of publications. For academic publications, publication is a natural process. But publication in this context is not propaganda. This is normal activity when presenting research results. Propaganda is unusual for academics, but it is managed actively. 47.8% of specialists see the importance of propaganda. Only 16% of specialists do not recognize such an influence. Experts pay much more attention to propaganda. Their figures are 54.9% and 13%, respectively.

Thus, Persona-Doctrines believe that it is necessary to fight for one's reader, a like-minded person. It is necessary to publicly articulate one's proposals. This is the opinion of persons who have achieved doctrinal status.

We have considered the place of active propaganda – media activity. Of those experts who recognize the role of propaganda, 45.2% recognize the importance of media activity. The age of the experts – more than half of whom are in their 60s and 80s – should be considered. Mostly these are not representatives of the Internet generation, which is used to making almost everything publicly available. Accordingly, active propaganda and media promotion will not be typical for modern Persona-Doctrine.

For example, today, researchers send the titles or texts of an article, book, or, at best, a link to the Russian Science Citation Index to disseminate information about their activities. It is uncommon for them to have their own website, blog, or social media channel. Persona-Doctrines have achieved their status without Internet propaganda. However, there is every reason to believe that the information flow of presentations will change. Hard-copy books will give way to other ways of promoting, propagandizing, and disseminating the results of their research. For the discovery of the phenomenon of Persona-Doctrine, the sphere of activity, the place of work, and the type of professional activity are of great importance.

We have studied the activities that form the Persona-Doctrine. Respondents were asked to rate the following types of activities on a scale of "strongly raising" – "raising" – "not raising": 1) teaching activities, 2) research activities, 3) civil service, 4) elective position, 5) leadership of dissertation council, 6) leadership of organization, 7) expert, 8) media activity.

It is possible to roughly group types of activities according to presence or absence of administrative resources. Types of activities in which there may be an administrative resource include: civil service, elective position, leadership of a dissertation council, and leadership of an organization. Types of activities with no administrative resource: pedagogical, academic, expert, and media activity.

All types of activities with administrative resources are classified by experts as unpromising for the formation (or maintenance) of the authority of the Persona-Doctrine: elective position (9.3%), civil service (10.2%), and leadership of the organization (15%). The situation is similar for specialists in that the top three positions of failure are occupied by positions with administrative resources.

We compared the attitudes of two respondents – experts and specialists – to the types of activities that contribute to the formation of doctrinal status.

Diagram 35. Comparison of (ESPD 14 – SSLD 47). Comparison of Opinions of Experts and Specialists on Types of Activities that Form Authority of Candidate of Legal Sciences

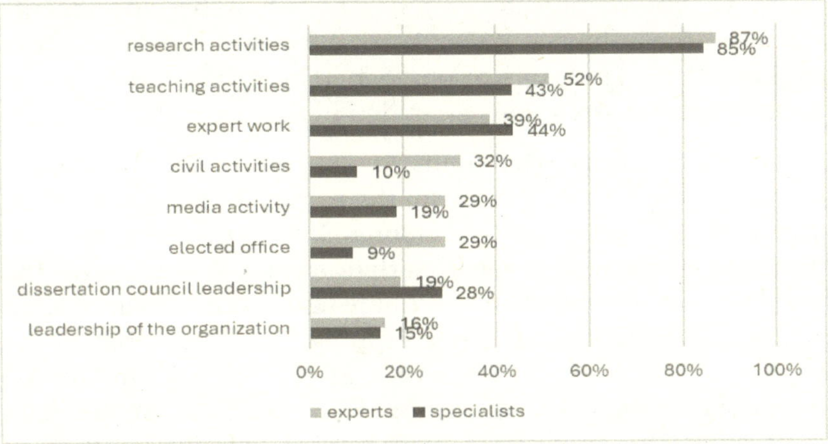

We have identified the types of activities that form (raise) the authority of a Persona-Doctrine. Experts give priority to the following types of activities: research (87.1%), teaching (51.6%) and expert (38.7%). Specialists also put research activity in first place (84.5%). As for the rest, the opinions were distributed as follows: expert work (43.8%) and teaching activities (43.4%). All these activities are without administrative resources.

The comparison shows the unanimity of respondents of both groups in assessing the importance of research work and organization leadership, with similar indicators in assessing the importance of expert work. There is a slight discrepancy in the assessment of the impact of the leadership of a dissertation council in comparison with specialists. We give preference to the opinion of experts, of which 39.4% are members of dissertation councils. The expert, the head of the dissertation council, noted the strong influence of his leadership of the dissertation council on his doctrinal status. Other respondents judge this by indirect data and observations. The admission of the head of the dissertation council about the strong influence of this factor on one's own status confirms the hypothesis that membership and especially the leadership of the dissertation council are converted into elements of doctrinality. Of course, reputation in the academic world and administrative resources are also associated with the leadership of the dissertation council. Let us move on to indicators of doctrinality. The respondents recognize the influence of their association with the dissertation council. At the least, this resource increases the citation rate in abstracts and dissertations defended in this council.

The Expert Survey contains several questions to establish data on labor activity. We mean the presence in the biography during the formation of Persona-Doctrine status of such positions as the head of the dissertation council, the head of the organization, the head of the publishing house, membership of governing bodies, an elective public office, member of the Higher Attestation Commission, judge, head of influential public associations, work in important positions in the State apparatus. The analysis of biographical data shows that all the Persona-Doctrines who took part in our Expert Survey had different types of administrative resources. They were all more or less successful people in their careers. They have held or are holding significant positions. Their active non-recognition of the role of administrative resources in the expert survey is somewhat contradictory to their own position and is refuted by a cross-analysis of the answers to various questions.

We have investigated the influence of public positions on forming the Persona-Doctrine status. Respondents were offered the following answers: "has a positive effect", "no affect", and "has a negative effect". Both experts and specialists noted the positive impact of holding public office (more than 46%) on forming doctrinal status. 50% of experts and 41.2% of specialists deny such influence. Both groups of respondents are in insignificant proportions, which allows for a negative impact of government positions on forming the status of the Persona-Doctrine (3.3% of experts and 12.4% of specialists). Both specialists and experts (46.7 % and 45.6%, respectively) believe that the civil service contributes to achieving doctrinality. The opinion concerning negative impact is insignificant: 3.3% of experts and 12.4% of specialists.

Diagram 36. (ESPD 16 - SSLD 49). Impact of Formation of Persona-Doctrine Status on Holding Public Offices (Comparison of Opinions of Experts and Specialists)

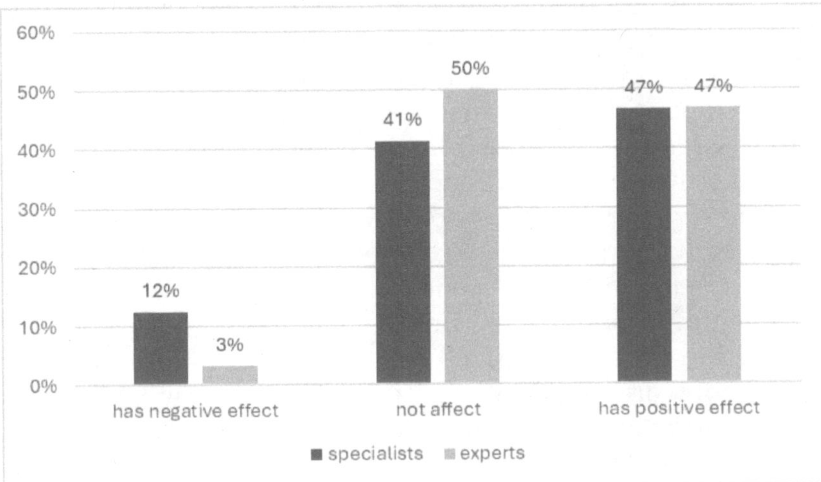

Suppose we remove the assessment of the degree of influence and leave only "affects" and "does not affect". In that case, expert opinions are equally divided by 50%. Specialists have similar indicators. 58.9% acknowledge the influence of government positions, and 41.2% do not recognize any influence of this factor. Respondents were almost divided in half with the opposite opinion, so there was no way to choose the dominant opinion. The intermediate conclusion that the civil service can influence, with a probability of 50%, indicates a significant influence on holding public office in forming the persona-doctrine.

Based on expert answers concerning their civil service experience and biographical data, we divided them into persons with and without civil service experience. 50% of the experts had experience in public service of different durations and in different positions. Experts with public service experience show a higher percentage of assessment of the positive impact of public service – 53.3% compared to persons without such experience (40%). Thus, the civil service has a positive rather than a negative effect on the formation and development of the Persona-Doctrine.

Civil servants, it should be assumed, have no material interest in academic research. With the fully-fledged conscientious performance of official duties, they do not have time for research. The authority of the office strengthens the doctrinal position of the Persona-Doctrine, but is not its source. We consider this influence from the point of view of the content of works, their perception, and promotion. It is difficult to deny that the civil service takes up all working time, as it involves irregular working hours. Accordingly, we must believe that at night, such influential people can create a more enjoyable, meaningful product than professional researchers who are engaged in the same work all day, all the time. From the point of view of work organization, it is not easy to imagine that it is possible to be more efficient in free time than in working hours. All these doubts show that the lack of trust in high quality and independence of civil servant research is justified.

Indeed, civil servants who are not financially motivated have no interest in academic qualifications, are chasing degrees and publications, are busy all day and psychologically overloaded with State tasks, and cannot be authors of high-quality, competitive academic research. However, if such results are obtained, then most likely their source is not related to the personal creativity of the civil servant. The author could have been replaced, the defense conditions could have been softened, and the assessment of the results of such academic work could have been overestimated. Indirect proof of this thesis is the reaction to Dissernet investigations. Most often, unscrupulous dissertation authors are in the civil service or hold elective positions.

We ranked the positive impact of holding public office and public service on forming doctrinal status. In the answer options, only facets of the positive impact of holding public office are presented: "influences in a decisive way", "significantly influence", and "insignificantly affects". We checked the influence of civil service or public office on such elements of the Persona-Doctrine as 1) access to publication, 2) access to information, and the following additional features were seen: 1) more active citation, 2) authority of the position, 3) administrative resource.

Experts practically do not associate access to publication with the civil service since 42.9% and 46.2% give both experience and no experience. The influence of civil service on citations was also not revealed. Access to information is a valuable asset of public service. However, there is no substantial influence. Only 11.1% of experts recognize this.

The authority of the position is an influential factor in the eyes of experts without experience in public service. Thus, 61.5% of experts with no experience and only 35.7% with experience note a significant impact. The same conclusion follows from the indicator "insignificantly influences", This value was chosen by 35.7% of respondents with experience and 7.7% without experience. Thus, experts with no experience in public service exaggerate the positive impact of position on status. Perhaps, without experience, the examiner is less familiar with the constraints associated with the position.

Administrative resources are a positive factor in the formation of the status of a Persona-Doctrine in civil service, as noted by 37% of experts. A significant influence on respondent positions is exerted by their personal experience of public service. 28.6% of experts with civil service experience see administrative resources having a decisive influence. Experts without civil service experience see a more significant influence – 46.2%. Such experts will probably associate the super-significant results of Persona-Doctrines with experience in public service and the availability of administrative resources.

There is a significant difference in the assessment of the administrative resource in the formation of the status of the Persona-Doctrine by experts with and without such a resource. It is considered insignificant by 40.9% of respondents with administrative resources and only 20% without it. It can be argued that experts without administrative resources exaggerate its importance in the formation of the status of the Persona-Doctrine by a factor of two.

In this context, we do not see coercion as a form of action of an administrative resource. We do not mean the deliberate use of administrative resources by the Persona-Doctrines themselves. But latent, this impact still occurs. For outsiders, for authors who cite publications, the indication of the position of the author increases the authority of the statement. Words spoken by a university professor, a retired teacher without a place of work, or mentions of places of work only in the past tense can be perceived differently than the words of the President of the Constitutional Court, senator, or governor.

If, when presenting the results of a study, the position or place of work of the author is indicated, this involves the factor of administrative resources automatically (without actions). In this case, we refer to an influence that does not come from the publication text. It is imperious, influential, and external. Because publications must indicate affiliation with the indication of the author's position, this is an objective factor of influence, even pressure on the reader.

We asked experts about the possible impact of affiliation with an organization on Persona-Doctrine. 32% of experts with administrative resources do not see such dependence. However, 60% of experts without administrative resources are certain that this dependence is strong, and another 40% believe it exists. Thus, respondents without administrative resources believe in its power to promote doctrinalism. Experts with administrative resources do not allow the option "does not depend", which means they fully and unconditionally trust the administrative resource.

It is vital to work out the problem of choosing the object and subject of research that has become the doctrine. We paid considerable attention to studying the motives for determining the main object of research. This question requires the expert to determine the hidden part first: "What is your subject and object of research that has become the Doctrine"? The answer means that the expert knows which of his achievements are valued as a doctrine. Scholars can assume that this is the topic of a doctoral dissertation or monograph. This may be another problem that stands out for its elaboration, depth, and recognition of the author.

Suggested answer options were: "rational – emotional", "objective factors – subjective choice", "random – deliberate", "socially necessary – personally interesting". It is possible to suggest the dominance of the subjective factor because an experienced researcher made this choice as a rule. By that time, the postgraduate experience of the candidate of legal sciences dissertation had been completed. Instead, the object will be characterized as the result of a personal, deliberate decision made under the influence of self-interest.

In the questionnaire, respondents were given a scale to choose an explanation of the object and subject of their research. This is an important question, especially since the choice of topic and doctrinal status are significantly separated by time, often decades. The choice could be: 1) imposed, for example, in the postgraduate school of the police academy, 2) conscious, for example, observing publications and looking for a more promising one, and 3) emotional, that is, according to one's passion and interest, all depending on its dissertation and prospects. At the stage of conceiving a study or formulating a hypothesis, we assumed a more significant role for personal enthusiasm and interest and, accordingly, that the scale would tilt to the side accordingly – emotionally, according to interest. However, the experts showed the exact opposite result. Only 10% of the Persona-Doctrine chose emotionally based on interest in the topic. 60% of the experts acted consciously and rationally. Accordingly, the motive of personal interest was not paramount. Some external objective factors were more at work.

We asked respondents to assess the motives for choosing the topic of the object and research subject at school from "the result of objective factors" to the "personal subjective result". Expert opinions were divided between objective (33.4%) and subjective (23.4%). The influence of objective factors is 10% higher than that of subjective factors when choosing the subject and object of research that brought them recognition. Thus, objective and external factors are more influential than subjective ones.

In choosing the object and research subject, which became Doctrine, two evaluation variants were provided: random and thoughtful. 10% of the experts acted randomly, and 90% acted thoughtfully.

The compilation of the questions made it possible to establish that only 7% of the experts were guided by their own academic interests and made decisions emotionally.

Diagram 37. (ESPD 21 - ESPD 23). Basis for Selecting Object and Subject of Research (Expert Opinion)

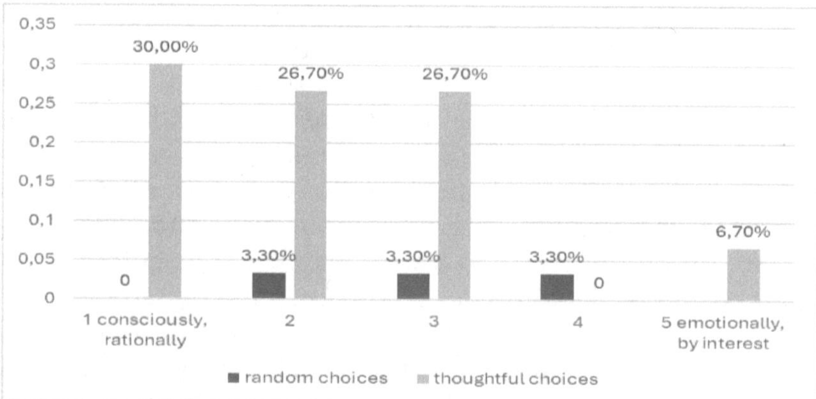

30% of the experts acted consciously, rationally, and deliberately. This result shows the decisive importance of the object and subject of the study. Self-interest does not provide a margin of stability for attaining doctrinal status. It is no coincidence that it is widely believed that choosing the topic of a doctoral dissertation is the most challenging part of the work. This should be a sphere, a topic in which the future Doctor of Legal Sciences will become the founder of his own academic concept and possibly an academic school. Figuratively speaking, this topic, if successful, will be associated with his name. The topic is the result of an analytical search. It will become the foundation of future academic achievements.

An expert survey also investigated the combination of the socially significant and the personal in the motivation of researchers. The experts answered the question about the choice of the object and subject of research, which has become a doctrine. The answer was made by choosing on a scale from 1 to 5, where 1 is "important for society and the State", and 5 is "important, interesting for researchers" with intermediate shades. The results show that self-interest matters significantly. It should be noted that considering the revealed period of the creative flowering of the Persona-Doctrines (51 – 60 years), this is the time of relative freedom of the researcher. By this age, the career groundwork is complete. This is the retirement age, which means that the external impact is reduced. True, the muse does not always come with administrative freedom. However, in conditions of greater freedom and choice during period of creative flourishing, the researcher can act according to his interests.

The option of public motivation for choosing the subject and object of research was chosen by 20% of experts. 23% are inclined to choose a personal interest as a motive. This ratio clearly supports subjective motivation.

For a comprehensive analysis of the motivation of researchers in choosing a subject and an object, we compared different types of interests. "Subjective" and "objective" motives for choice were transformed into "impotent, interesting for researchers" and "important for society and the State".

Thus, the cross-analysis of the answers to the four questions made it possible to identify the priority of the subjective interest of the researcher who made this choice consciously. There are

16.7% of such experts. 13.3% of experts consciously pursued socially significant goals. However, in general, personal interests are in the lead: less than 20% of experts chose interests that interest him personally, emotionally, and rationally.

Plagiarism and unethical borrowing have flourished with the introduction of computers and the Internet. The simple "copy" – "paste" feature from Word heralded the era of mass plagiarism. We are more likely to know the side of the offender. The plagiarist claims he has written a paper, and all the negativity falls on him.

In the questionnaire, we turned to the other side of the plagiarism process – the author of the stolen object – to establish the facts of the unethical use of the achievements of the Persona-Doctrine. It was essential for us to establish the extent of intellectual property theft. In addition, the survey was examined the reaction of Persona-Doctrines to the plagiarism of their works.

Undocumented quotations or the use of theses and words from doctrinal works are typical examples of unethical behavior. However, for doctrinal forms, this unethical behavior has peculiarities. Because of the widespread adoption of the doctrine, the public feels these ideas are common knowledge and do not need to be quoted. Perhaps it is precisely this perception that shows that the idea of the doctrine has acquired a direct normative character.

Along with this generally positive trend, experts note cases of unethical use of their works. The problem of plagiarism exists. Experts on whether others use their achievements for unethical purposes are divided almost half. 50% of experts have encountered unethical use several times, and 6.7% have encountered unethical use frequently. Thus, 56.7% of the participants of the expert pros have a negative experience of plagiarism in their works. 43.3% of experts have never faced intellectual property theft.

It should be borne in mind that, as a rule, Persona-Doctrine does not monitor the ethics of other people's citations. Such cases become known by accident, discovered by the Persona-Doctrine, or informed by others. The question is whether to respond to such cases. My own mentor, G. V. Maltsev, condescendingly reacted to such assumptions: "Rejoice! If something has been stolen from you, you have done something valuable". An identical position was formed as an example by one expert: "They steal texts. But that is a good thing, so they have been useful". But kidnappers do it for profit. In fact, this is theft. Scholars have to make a decision about self-defense. Respondents generally show leniency towards unethical borrowing of their works and refrain from prosecution. Injured experts are not willing to become involved in finding and punishing the offenders.

Experts note that unethical borrowing is most often encountered in the preparation of dissertations. The most common form – plagiarism – is confirmed by the fact that experts have repeatedly found fragments of their work elsewhere without references. Experts complain about implicit plagiarism, which they attribute to stealing ideas and theoretical conclusions.

In the political sphere, political experts considered plagiarism to have occurred when the Administration of the President created a "backup" party of the Russian All-People's Movement. Persona-Doctrine reports the unethical use of materials by their assistants, secretaries, and other support staff. In the journal *Law and Modern States*, we once encountered an investigation of unethical borrowing. It was established that the original source was given to the translator, who passed the translation to the customer and another researcher. This other researcher published a paper with the exact translation in the journal, giving an date earlier.

The authors of the original idea must be vigilant. As experience shows, professors at the doctrinal level are often open-minded, simple-minded people in the good sense of the word. They trust their assistants.

Experts confirm the theft of their works, ideas, and materials, but they do not prosecute offenders systematically. How fashionable it is for big people to be indulgent to the masses of researchers who are scouring for a topic and a faster way to achieve their goals, such as defending a dissertation. In fact, there are negative consequences of general leniency. It breeds impunity and indirectly contributes to the practice of academic dishonesty.

We asked respondents to reflect on whether it is possible to "wrap" the Persona-Doctrine with excessive attention. Recognition of the Persona-Doctrine is an assessment based on an interest in the person, his work, and results, which has grown into an acknowledgment of authority.

In interviews with experts, we discussed this issue many times. And we assumed that the experts, for the most part, concede that they admit the possibility of "winding up" the Persona-Doctrine. The quoted classics of Marxism-Leninism, incorporated into a text of any genre on any subject, can be quoted offhand. For example, the newspaper *Molodost*, 11 April 1970, no 12, published an article entitled "Consulting with Lenin". According to the authors, the article responded to numerous requests for Lenin's works and literature about him. "To help researchers, teachers, graduate students, and students, indexes are offered, including books and articles that consider the development of general research problems and its individual branches in the works of V. I. Lenin". The following selections were proposed: "V. I. Lenin on Chemistry and the Chemical Industry. Moscow, 1969", "V. I. Lenin and Physical and Mathematical Sciences. Moscow, 1969", and an endless series of similar quotation books for every occasion of life. At some point, even a compelling opinion, if used excessively, can become clouded, blurred, and lose its authority.

Another example is S. S. Alekseev, who is often quoted in legal dissertations and other academic research. Simplistic quotations (often without reading) compromise an indisputably deserving person. The extensive unjustified citation of Alekseev led to the question of whether the authors who were citing works had read the publications of this professor and whether they shared his position.

We have seen periods of the rise of works quoted in the wake of a political guiding force and the rapid oblivion of such works. This, combined with the expert answers, will make it possible to recognize the admissibility of this question. Reasonable citation and persuasive authority are likely to endure, and an inflated citation index can easily be shaken in an era of change. "Wound-up" personalities or works include inflated indicators caused by managerial positions. Winding up manifests itself in improperly manipulating the opinions of cheated persons.

It should be noted that the winding up of status, which initially could have been justified, leads to confusion, blurring, insincerity, and lack of authority. Such people are prone to inflated self-esteem, uncritical of their academic achievements, lack immunity to lies, and ingratitude on the part of people. Consider the example of Professor Pavel Astakhov, well-known in Russia. His reputation has nothing to do with academic achievements and academic renown. He does not have any of those, such as 55 publications, Hirsch index 6, the most recent publication for 2021. The profile has not been updated due to a lack of interest. He became famous as a TV presenter. His media fame brought him the position of Commissioner for Children's Rights, in which he failed miserably. In 2022, he returned to TV as a guest on other shows. This is a marker of the importance of this type of activity for him. But he does not act as a lawyer, much less as an expert, a professional authority.

Media demand may be high, but it may be dangerous to use the professional services of such persons. It is the same as seeing a doctor who hosts a medical show on TV (although it happens). In the professional environment, in our case – the legal environment – media involvement is a negative factor. Not a single judge of the Constitutional Court of the Russian Federation or the Supreme Court of the Russian Federation, although retired, not a single significant scholar is hosting a legal show. Thus, our assumption about the possibility of overfatigue from a particular personality, his excessive appearance in public, is confirmed by observation.

Of course, personalities hardened in professional battles are less inclined to get bogged down in the entertainment world. But in general, the scholar should keep such a threat in mind and try to avoid it. 23.3% of experts do not have a definite opinion on this problem. Among those who have spoken, the leaders are Persona-Doctrines who, with varying degrees of certainty, recognize the possibility of becoming obsolete (53.4%). Only 23.2% of experts doubt this possibility, of which 20% admitted that it is impossible to cover up the Persona-Doctrine with excessive attention. The presence of experts is significant because we are talking about them and the challenges they must deal with.

Other specialist answers to the same question differ considerably.

Diagram 38. (SSLD 58 - ESPD 45). Attitude to Possibility of "Winding up" Persona-Doctrine with Excessive Attention (Comparison of Opinions of Expert and Specialist)

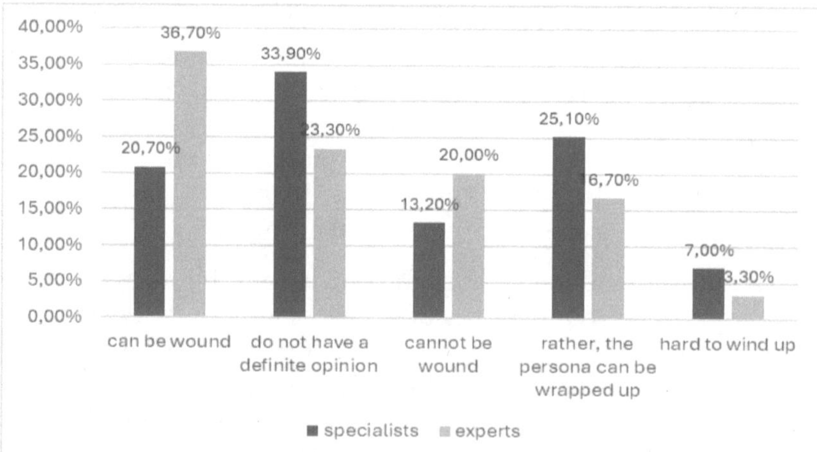

The comparison showed that the number of experts who recognize the possibility of a negative impact of excessive attention is significantly higher for experts: 36.7% versus 20.7% for specialists. Thus, the possibility of "winding up" the Persona-

Doctrine with excessive attention is given by 53.4% of experts and 45.8% of specialists. Accordingly, 23.3% of experts and 20.2% of specialists deny such a possibility, which is almost two times lower than the assumption of the possibility of winding up the Persona-Doctrine. Analysis of the responses suggests the need for priorities for significant people. For doctrinal scholars, justified high citations can be transformed into unfounded, ill-considered citations. This will be the winding-up effect. Recognition of merits can develop into flattery, ingratitude, and artificial elevation of merits to achieve one's goals – the effect of winding up. Presenting a position in one's subject area, brought to an absurd presence in all spheres, is a muddling effect. It is difficult for an exhausted person to position himself in a professional environment, and it is even more difficult to be perceived as a convincing researcher.

Professional burnout depletes a person's resources (emotional, mental, industrial, material, and others). Often the source of professional burnout is work stress. As a result of burnout, what recently seemed interesting, important, and meaningful becomes indifferent and meaningless.

In general, the opinions of experts and specialists are close, confirming the possibility of professional burnout (86.7% of experts and 84.5% of specialists). Many respondents categorically deny this possibility (10% of experts and 8.4% of specialists). Thus, this problem is significant.

Persona-Doctrine is a hard-to-achieve result in which a person experiences heavy burdens. Excessive persistence at work, lack of a clear work schedule (alternating weekends and work days), and other factors lead to stress and, as a result, burnout. Perfectionism is often found in people who take great responsibility for their work. It is not easy to separate personal and working time into creative activities. Many researchers work at home, which territorially mixes personal and work spaces.

The current state of work leads to isolation and emotional loneliness. Collective open academic discussions, banquets after dissertation defenses, joint trips, and other forms of emotional unity of the team are passing into oblivion. Modern team-building technologies are not popular in the academic community, and the old ones are being lost. For example, imagining an academic team playing paintball or bowling is impossible. A significant factor of disunity is the diversification of remuneration: an associate professor receives 20,000 rubles, and a manager receives 2,000,000 rubles. The difference is at least 100 times. They live on different planets and have nothing in common.

Rivalry, unequal relations with colleagues, and conflicts with management can harm the individual. Excessive workload, an increase in the number of tasks, and an increase in intensity, in general, have become a sign of our times. A stress factor in the academic community is the absolutization of publication activity. This is an example of an unfortunate calculation of the effectiveness of a research paper. Calculating the labor standard by the number of units produced is analogous to piece-rate payment for manual labor workers.

This form of calculating the work result has strangely become an effective contract for researchers and teachers. There are reasonable justifications for using this tool. In creative work, a quantitative indicator of performance is not applicable. However, it is officially used to evaluate academic staff and is a factor in professional burnout. These indicators must not matter for career advancement. Moreover, other factors are relevant, of which nepotism is the most significant. The calculation of units of publication activity is comparable to the subsistence minimum, which is adopted for beggars and strangers. And real actors are in no way bound by quantifiable performance indicators: neither minimums nor maximums.

The concept of Persona-Doctrine, to a large extent, is a public status. Accordingly, such people attract unfair competition, envy, and hostility. This is not criticism on the professional plane; these are personal feelings that destroy the comfort of the person-doctrine. In this context, we can see respondent answers to the indicators that can be used to calculate doctrinality.

We have determined whether experts sensitive to professional burnout trust the expert survey to change this status of the Persona-Doctrine. It has been established that those Persona-Doctrines who recognize the possibility of burnout are also distrustful of expert surveys of colleagues.

Thus, Persona-Doctrines that are not sensitive to expert surveys of their colleagues do not allow professional burnout. Accordingly, most experts are at risk of professional burnout as they react to the opinions of their colleagues, which often has nothing to do with research.

As a result of the analysis of survey data, a correlation was established between the recognition of professional burnout and the significance of the academic community assessment of the Persona-Doctrine. If an expert is sensitive to recognition, dissatisfaction with this indicator can be a source of professional burnout.

Diagram 39. (ESPD 46 and ESPD 5_5). Influence of Attitude to Expert Survey on Recognition of Professional Burnout (Experts Opinion)

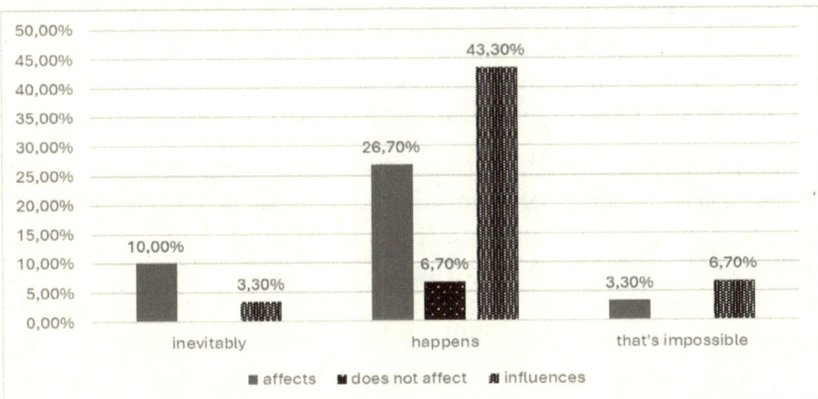

Experts answered the question about the tracking of recognition attributes by Persona-Doctrines. As a result, we identified experts who monitor their own attributes and recognition, and it turned out to be 60% of them. A smaller number of experts (40%) never paid attention to the attributes of their recognition.

Diagram 40. (ESPD 46 – ESPD 33). Impact of Recognition Attributes Tracking Possibility of Professional Burnout (Experts Opinion)

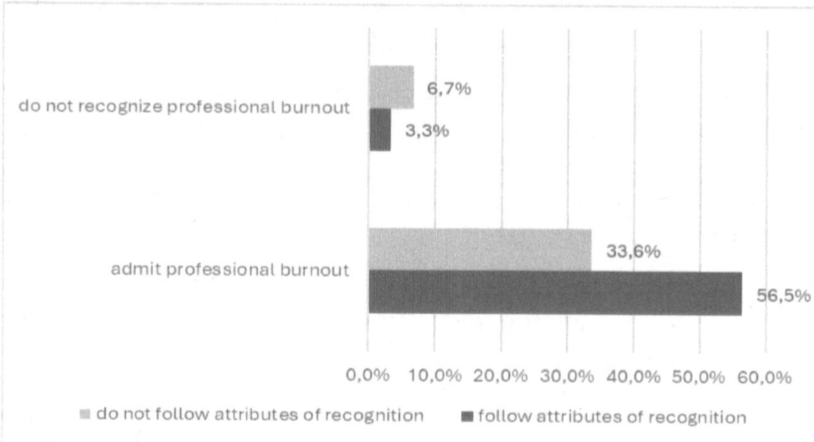

Those experts who monitor recognition attributes show a higher recognition of professional burnout – 56.5%. Thus, if the respondent is sensitive to the human factor, he, as a rule, allows professional burnout. It is non-partnership, hostile, or at least unreasonably critical relationships in the environment surrounding Persona-Doctrines that lay the foundation for their fatigue, withdrawal from active activity, and other negative consequences in psycho-emotional and professional terms.

In connection with the persona doctrine, we see such characteristics as professionalism, which is understood as knowledge of one's business. It is a combination of knowledge, skills, and abilities. A significant motive for long-term and practical work is the researcher's interest. We intentionally amplified the emotional side and offered to appreciate the importance of love for one's work. Moreover, we created an uncomfortable dilemma: "What is more important for forming the Persona-Doctrine: "know" or "love" of what you do"? Of course, knowing and loving the scholar's subject is the best option. But in this case, a situation of choice has been created. Based on their business knowledge (30%), the group prevailed by a small margin. If it is a question of the persuasiveness of doctrine as the result of an action, perhaps the variant "to know" is more accurate. But if we are talking about a choice for a lifetime, or at least for a significant period, "loving" is more motivational. There were 26.7% of such respondents. Almost half (43.3%) of the experts could not decide.

Discarding the uninformative middle version of the harmony "to love + to know", we see a certain majority of experts who believe that it is more important to know and to love than to do one's own business: 26,7% versus 30% who believe that it is more important to know it. Throughout the expert survey, the topic of the duration of work to achieve doctrinal status runs through. The path to a doctoral dissertation is quite long. From the beginning of training, it takes about twenty years the individual is ready for defense. Let us also consider that, according to experts, the most significant doctrinal works are created at ages from 51 to 60 years. The period of effort is at least 30 – 40 years. Accordingly, motivation should be not only strong, but sustainable. The question was formulated to identify what makes the Persona-Doctrine work in this direction. Respondents were offered the following types of motivation: 1) vocation, 2) the duty to the Fatherland, 3) service, 4) interest, 5) personal passion, and 6) expectation of a delayed result.

Conventionally, these motives can be divided into personal ones, including vocation, interest, passion, and expecting a delayed result. The following motives can be socially significant: duty to the Fatherland, service.

Diagram 41. (ESPD 48). All Indicators, Motivation Rating Persona-Doctrine (Expert Opinion)

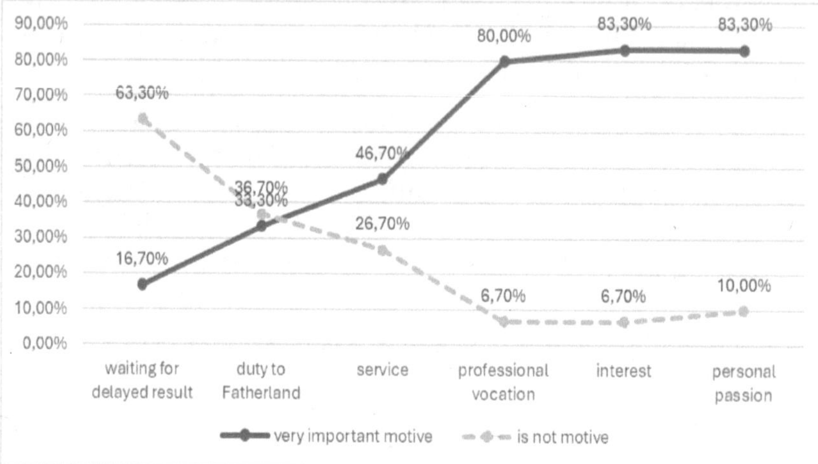

In the above, it is evident that personal motives are foremost. A low level of support for the response "waiting for a delayed result" (16.7% consider it a fundamental motive) may reflect an assessment of this motive and an inaccurate understanding of this construct.

The motive of "waiting for a delayed result" must be explained. It is a reward that can come after an extended period, a goal with a long period to achieve. We have provided for the option of purposeful construction of the status of the Persona-Doctrine. Achieving such a result was planned. The person aspired to this status and worked on it for many years. The duration of the work and the duration of the period are included in the status of the Persona-Doctrine. It cannot happen according to the formula "woke up famous". Accordingly, the programmed Persona-Doctrine expected outcomes, and the expectation of achievement and its evaluation, among other factors, motivated them. Most experts reject the significant role of delayed expectations in their motivation. Only 16.7% recognized such an opportunity for themselves. Perhaps such results are because the term "careerist" in the past, when the personalities of today's Persona-Doctrines were formed, had a negative connotation. His perception has now been transformed into the opposite. Career planning consultants are the companions of advanced workers in today's reality. People do not have to conceal their career aspirations; they do not have to hide them or be embarrassed. However, in general, the expectation of a positive public assessment of the conversation about a career as an end is untenable. A person cannot openly say that he is a careerist and wants to be a member of the government to put the country's budget in his pocket and spit on everyone and everything from a high tribune. Such revelations are impossible.

A careerist must voice socially approved lies that he dreams of serving people, society, country, and the world. It is necessary to cover up personal selfish career interests with concern for the world, the country, people, and humanity. This lie is ubiquitous. It is international, trans-State, and not geographical. It is universal. It is only Alcoholics Anonymous who are obliged to be open and honest and to pour out everything that is in the secret corners of their souls.

It is necessary to publicly indicate the socially significant purposes for using the position to which the Persona-Doctrine strives. For example, someone who plans to become a judge on the Supreme Court or a Doctor of Legal Sciences. Etiquette requires that it be stated that the purpose of these career goals is to serve the interests of fair and lawful justice. It will come as a surprise if a candidate openly declares that he is motivated by a large salary, immunity, and lifetime status, although this is true. It is still impossible to openly declare that a person wants a free apartment of 300 square meters in the center of the capital and other individual perks. Thus, the problem of delayed result motivation remains unsolved, apparently because true motivation is difficult to identify or not revealed at all.

Experts were asked to investigate the possibility of the Persona-Doctrine working in only one direction or the possibility of diversity, which schools can assess from 1 to 5. Uniformity is supported by 10% of experts, and diversity is supported by 66.7%. Whether the Persona-Doctrine can be equally presented as an outstanding authoritative researcher in entirely different fields opens the discussion. We know of cases in an interdisciplinary range. Humanities and social research, such as philosophy, history, political research, and sociology, are more likely to be combined with jurisprudence. At the same time, there are unlikely options for combining jurisprudence with physical, mathematical, technical, medical, and other natural and exact research.

We must acknowledge cases when an epiphany in another (non-legal) research coincides with events of a non-academic but career-like nature in the life of a researcher. Such unexpected talents are often discovered when occupying leadership positions in academic or educational institutions, enterprises, and organizations. Election to the legislature is a factor that stimulates the formation and disclosure of new academic talents. During the XIX convocation of the State Duma, the following mutations occur in candidates of one science, twice candidates of different sciences, or doctors of different sciences. Examples are V. B. Efimov (candidate of technical sciences, doctor of economics), I. N. Igoshkin (candidate of economic sciences, candidate of political sciences), V. M. Kononov (candidate of political sciences, doctor of political sciences), I. I. Melnikov (candidate of fizicheskikh and mathematical sciences, doctor of pedagogical sciences), S. P. Obukhov (candidate of economic sciences, doctor of political sciences), V. N. Plotnikov (candidate of agricultural sciences, doctor of economic sciences).

There are also mutants of academic qualifications, know-it-alls, and all-experts among the graded persons without a deputy mandate. They can produce different multiacademic mutations, but some kinks are problematic for an outside observer to understand. But some people are surprised without words and comments. For example, N. D. Eriashvili is a doctor of economic sciences, has a candidate of legal sciences, and has a candidate of historical sciences. He writes books about environmental law,[1] sanctions,[2] and other unrelated topics. He is also fluent in issues not included in the academic specialties of his various dissertations, such as issues of aesthetics and education.[3] According to the Russian Science Citation Index, his indicators include 1320 works, 18,236 citations, and a Hirsch index of 63. There are also absolute record-holders regarding the number of publications, for example, I. V. Uporov 1,423 and A. P. Ryzhakov 1,340. Third place belongs to Eriashvili.

By right, V. P. Salnikov is a member of the group of multi-specialists. Surprised by his academic outlook, his colleagues at the university point out that his academic portfolio contains "albeit small, but, obviously, necessary manuals on a foreign language, and on physical training, and on the ancient history of the Urals, and on computer technology".[4]

Multidimensionality can be quite diverse; the only question is whether it contributes to strengthening doctrinal status. Here, we can recall Borshchevskii, doctor of legal sciences, professor, and advokat. In the political beau monde, he was noted as the Plenipotentiary Representative of the Government of the Russian Federation (2001 – present). He hosted a program "The Hour of Judgment" (2004) and was a member of the Connoisseurs' Club (2002). He has 35 publications and a Hirsch index of 3 in the Russian Science Citation Index. Its inclusion List of nominees for the status of Persona-Doctrine is even hypothetically impossible due to the absence of prerequisites.

1 Iu. A. Ivanova, N. D. Eriashvili, and I. V. Groshev, Актуальные проблемы современного экологического права [Topical Problems of Contemporary Environmental Law] (2022).

2 E. I. Kuznetsova and N. D. Eriashvili, "Противодействие санкционным угрозам экономической безопасности России [Countering Sanctions Threats to Russia's Economic Security]", Образование. Наука. Научные кадры [Education. Science. Scientific Staff], no. 1 (2023).

3 I. I. Aminov, V. V. Gorokhova, and N. D. Eriashvili, Эстетическая культура и эстетическое воспитание сотрудников правоохранительных органов [Aesthetic Culture and Aesthetic Education of Law Enforcement Officers] (2022).

4 V. Ermykin, "Сальников В.П. великий комбинатор и взяточник [Salnikov V. P. Great Schemer and Bribe Taker]" (available online).

Multidisciplinary specialists are Liudmila Grudtsyna (661 publications) and Iuri Albertovich Dmitriev (412 publications). Of course, we must distinguish between diversity and promiscuity, multi-education, and superficiality. Within the framework of this expert survey, we acknowledge organic diversity is a positive trend. For example, the law theory is perfectly compatible with a branch of law. Alternatively, starting from the native branch of law, the researcher proceeds to generalizations at the constitutional or theoretical level. There are well-known positive examples: Petrazhitsky, Venediktov, and, possibly, other outstanding legal researchers who came to jurisprudence from other disciplines. Yet, in these indisputably outstanding personalities, we see a transition from one knowledge (interest) to another. In the end, a choice was obviously made. The transition, and then the Persona-Doctrine, acted in a new direction, which brought it recognition.

What unites "non-persons – not doctrines" within our framework is that none of the interviewed experts and specialists nominated these multidisciplinary researchers as Persona-Doctrines and did not recognize them as their authority. Of course, two candidates and doctors of different sciences, sometimes related, sometimes not, do not look convincing. Hypothetically, explaining two doctoral theses but two candidate theses is possible. There is simply no logical explanation, but there are examples. Naturally, the question arises – why is the second dissertation not a doctoral dissertation? Why is there an extensive development of the academic field? Each researcher has a personal story that led to this result. But none of them lead to doctrinal status.

We know examples of the emergence of diversity and different directions in specific periods of a researcher's life. This may be due to a change of job, new interests, and a new topical topic. There may be logical deviations from the strategic line that are more or less logical within the framework of the general direction. Some researchers have several degrees, an encyclopedic knowledge, multi-vector thinking, and other advantages. However, there are also negative examples, such as if a respected person attributes himself as a co-author of every work published by his organization or a publisher – every book he publishes. Such a practice creates "diversity", but the result will be negative. As a rule, such owners of falsified authorship are not deterred by image costs. But, as the analysis of profiles shows, over time, their activity decreases under the influence of factors that we have not yet studied. This is probably due to its inorganic origin. For example, the number of people assigned as co-authors is reduced because of available administrative resources.

We have discussed only organic personal diversity with experts. In general, it received a positive assessment from the survey participants.

PROFESSIONAL QUALITIES – RANKING OF COMPONENTS OF LEGAL PROFESSION

We have examined the following components of the legal profession: 1) teaching, 2) judicial, 3) legislative, 4) academic, 5) civil service, and 6) advocacy. One can assume criticism of the choice of these components of the profession because public service (unless in a legal capacity) and the status of a legislator are not, in the strict sense, seen as part of the legal profession. However, it should be considered that these components were assessed when the Doctor of Legal Sciences was considered. We do not exclude the possibility of a candidate of legal sciences becoming a Persona-Doctrine, but this is an exception to the rule.

The question of the legal profession priority was addressed to specialists and Persona-Doctrines simultaneously. This allowed us to compare assumptions (expert opinion) with the actual situation (expert opinion).

In the opinion of 63.7% of specialists, research activity is always conducive to forming Doctrine, teaching – 22.1%, legislative – 10.6%, judicial – 8.0%, advokat – 6.6%, and civil service – 4.4%.

If "always", "as a rule", and "may dispose of" are combined, and "rather, it hinders" and "only gets in the way" are combined into another group, then the doctrinal potential by components of the legal profession are distributed as follows.

Diagram 42. (SSLD 31). Degree of Disposition of Legal Activities to Formation of Doctrine (Specialist Opinion)

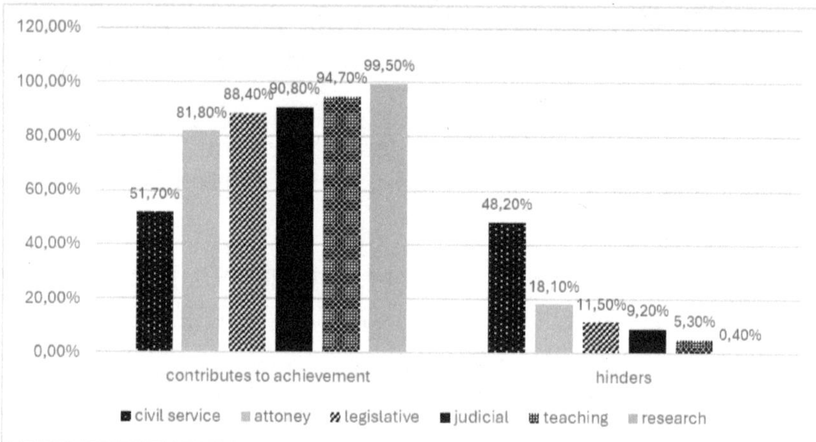

No types of activities that 100% led to Persona-Doctrine status, but research work is close – 99.5%. For the civil service, the positive and negative prerequisites for forming the doctrine coincide: 51.7% contribute to it, and 48.2% somewhat hinder it.

Thus, academic publications are the most promising for persons striving for Persona-Doctrine status (99.4% of specialists). This is followed by teaching (94.7%), judicial (90.8%), legislative (88.4%), advokat (81.8%), and civil service (51.7%).

The anti-rating of legal activity types for achieving the status of a Persona-Doctrine are as follows: civil service, advokat, and legislative activity.

For specialists, speculations about a legal profession conducive to doctrinal achievements are their assumptions. But thanks to the fact that we conducted an expert survey among experts who have already achieved doctrinal status, we can compare the assumption with reality of real Persona-Doctrines.

In the Expert Survey, we asked Persona-Doctrines to identify themselves as a professional representative.

From the meaning of the study, it was assumed that the expert would choose the most significant type of activity, and we presumed the doctrinal status of the experts according to our criteria. Of the experts surveyed, 40% identify as teachers, 37% as researchers, 17% as civil servants, and 6% as other occupations.

In the expert survey, there are several questions about the activities of experts: 1) we asked them to self-identify what type of activity they consider to be their indicator, that is, the most significant for them; 2) the experts determined 100% of what type of activity they were engaged in because all were engaged in different components of the profession consecutively and even simultaneously (for example, 10% judge, who is also 90% a teacher, who is also a researcher – 10%), 3) determine the type of activity in which the primary foundation for achieving their doctrinal status.

One expert survey question identified the types of activities carried out by Personas-Doctrines during the achievement of this high status. In this matter, indirect statistics, because for each type of activity, each expert chooses their employment from 0 to 100%. Accordingly, the experts had the opportunity to be 50% a researcher and 100% a teacher, combining these two types of activities at some point. Half – 50% – of the Persona-Doctrines were teachers, and 20% were free thinkers and researchers. Surprisingly, legislation creates the prerequisites for inadequate statistics, where the employee is employed at more than 100%. For example, any public service is 100% full-time. Combining academic and teaching activities is separated, but in non-working hours, respectively, we get a teacher of night and weekend activities, as a rule, by 25%. Universities which provide night work and weekend employment look comical, but this is the reality. And this 100+ % reality has led us to the corresponding question to the experts. The purpose of the question is to determine the employment of the Persona-Doctrine in the period of movement toward the doctrinal status of creative work. Accordingly, this is a retrospective question for the established Persona-Doctrines.

The results for experts who were 100% employed in one type of activity at the time of the formation of their doctrinal status showed the following types of activity in terms of demand: teacher (33.3%), free thinker (20%), civil servant (13.3%), lawyer and legislator (3.3% each). Full-time employment in politics, judicial, and research activities of the Persona-Doctrine did not give them doctrinal results.

If the experts combined several activities, the picture would be as follows.

Diagram 43. (ESPD 31). Rating of all activities of Persona-Doctrines (Expert Opinion)

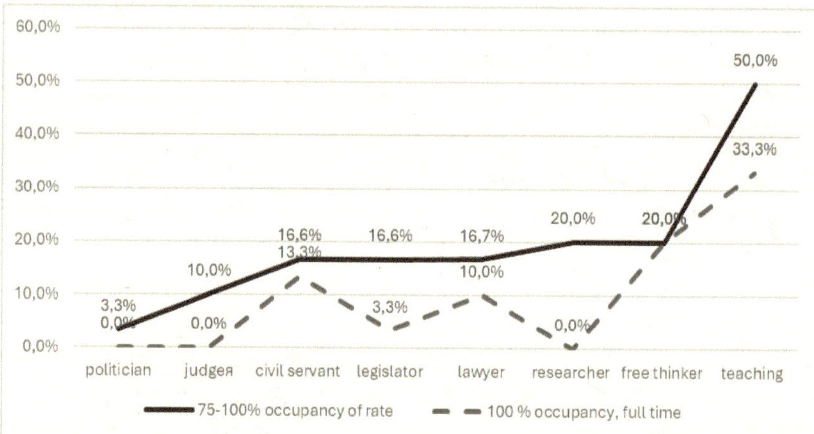

The activities of the teacher, the free thinker, and the civil servant maintain a stable leadership position. Politicians, judges, and researchers are added at the expense of part-time jobs. All mono-employed professionals (except thinkers) are less likely to succeed in doctrinal status. 100% of judges, politicians, and researchers cannot count on doctrinal status. Perhaps judges and politicians are hampered by the lack of a high-quality academic product to promote it authoritatively. The researcher observed the opposite trend. He has the product but does not have the authority or power. The result is the same – the chances of a doctrine are lower.

Let us compare all types of data sources on different issues from Persona-Doctrine. The teachers who combine their employment with other activities can become more successful. The probability of achieving the status of a Persona-Doctrine as a judge, legislator, and in the civil service is possible only on the basis of a part-time job. These activities are authoritative, with administrative resources, and do not make a person a doctrine. However, an explosive effect is formed when a resource is applied to a high-quality academic result.

In general, the opinion of experts seems logical because teaching provides an academic school to students, auditors, and followers. Administrative resources and practical activities in the legal profession enliven teaching and make research results more in demand due to the possibility of their personal lobbying, maintenance, and promotion. However, it is necessary to keep in mind the peculiarity of the legislation – public service is possible only on a full-time basis. Accordingly, it is impossible to be 75% a teacher and 25% a civil servant. When interpreting this analysis, it should be considered that the self-identification of Persona-Doctrine and the actual combination of activities in their lives do not coincide. We know of cases where judges present themselves as researchers or teachers. Perhaps they mean that their research or teaching path is more suitable for the issue under discussion, and they deliberately exaggerate it. Each such distortion must be dealt with individually.

The research conducted allows us to draw several conclusions regarding the admissibility of Persona-Doctrine. The need for this term is confirmed by the results of sociological research: questionnaires, expert surveys, interviews, and embedded observation.

We have identified the need for a term denoting a category of specialists who have reached the doctrinal level. Using comparative legal methods, we have identified a close, comparable term in American legal terminology – doctrinal professor. For the American merit system, our new status as Persona-Doctrine opens new possibilities while retaining the term Doctrinal Professor. A doctrine persona may be a doctrinal professor, but it may also be other nominees. We do not associate the status of a Persona-Doctrine with a specific type of activity in jurisprudence, such as academic, educational, judicial, or public service. Conducting research and publishing results is essential but not exclusively so. During the survey, we identified the types of activities that are more conducive to doctrinal status.

We have created a social portrait of the Persona-Doctrine, typifying doctrinal status subjective and objective prerequisites. This is more often a man over the age of 50, who usually has a candidate of legal sciences scientometric indicators from the Hirsch index: 30+. The place of birth is a small town. The presence or absence of lawyers in the family does not matter. These people consider dedication the highest personality trait, along with perseverance, hard work, and openness. They do not trust new ways of positioning and self-determination. They prefer traditional methods of promoting their ideas through conference publications and speeches.

Scientometric indicators do not attract much attention from jurisprudence authorities. They do not monitor their index intensively and constantly but check it occasionally. They generally do not deal with their Russian Science Citation Index profiles or use artificial inflating methods. This conclusion is based on the profiles of Persona-Doctrines. The expert survey results showed that people of the pre-Soviet and Soviet periods did not have this index, or it is incommensurate with modern indicators. People whose active creative life cycle was at least partially superimposed on the existence of scientometrics and the Hirsch index had and still have the opportunity to actively participate in its formation. Thus, we put aside the unnatural indices of 60+. Even when nominating such a researcher, we will be forced to check the reliability of the scientometric indicator, the lack of administrative resources, and other aggressive deforming factors.

Teachers who combine their work with other (applied) activities are more effective in moving toward Persona-Doctrine status. The age of most outstanding achievement is 51 – 70 years, the period after the doctoral dissertation. These are motivated people who work individually, do not have significant support in the collective, and are not looking for creative cooperation. They do not trust the professional community. Their success is programmed by mentors who laid the foundation for their subsequent successes. The absence of eminent lawyers in previous generations is not an obstacle to outstanding achievements. They are sensitive, vulnerable people who are uncertain about their progress. They may derive satisfaction from public recognition. They have no material problems and highly value human and material self-sufficiency. The revealed lack of fear of insufficient funding indirectly indicates a positive climate for researchers. They recognize the term "Persona-Doctrine", do not refuse to apply it to themselves, and generally demonstrate a positive attitude toward the new status.

Chapter 20

Doctrine-Form as an Object Dimension of Legal Doctrine. A System of Forms of Expression of Doctrine

CONCEPT, APPROBATION, AND ADMISSIBILITY OF TERM DOCTRINE-FORM

We propose introducing a new term into academic discourse: Doctrine-Form. Respondents were asked to rate the novelty of the term and were offered the following options.

Most specialists (56.4%) recognize the term as new. However, they give it a positive assessment by default. The option "such a term is superfluous to us" was chosen by 22.9% of respondents. According to 12.3% of specialists, such a term exists. However, we have not seen this term in academic publications. The Google Book Ngram shows the absence of such a term.

Few specialists (8.4%) know synonyms. We know the term "doctrinal professor" in the American system. We are unaware of the presence of a synonym in Russian legal terminology.

Diagram 44. (SSLD 81 - SSLD 62). Comparison of Novelty of Terms Persona-Doctrine and Doctrine-Form (Specialist Opinion)

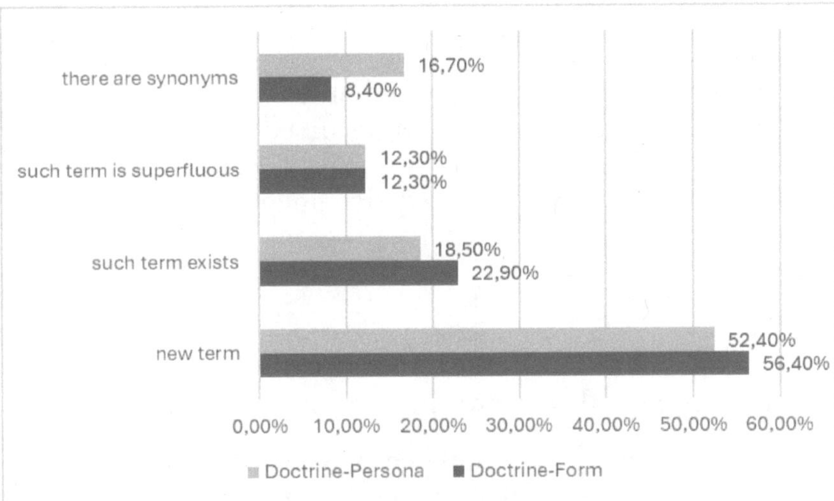

Table 11. Forms of Expression (Shell of Existence) of Doctrine

Type of Doctrine		Forms of Doctrinal Objectification
academic (academic) doctrine		books, articles, monographs, and others; academic research
judicial doctrine		acts issued by courts or organs thereof
ideological doctrine	state (official) doctrine	legal acts of State bodies
	unofficial ideological doctrine	political programs, law of election promises

A doctrine can be objectified and embodied in various forms.

Table 12. Forms of Doctrinal Objectification

Source Sources	A Form of Objectification
ideas	tutorials
views	monographs
teachings	article
principles	performances
legal understanding	court document
behavior	government document
opinion	party document
experience	party program

FORMS OF EXPRESSION OF LEGAL DOCTRINE

The questionnaire formulated a question to establish the optimal form of scholar doctrine. We have listed the works that most often embody the research results in jurisprudence. Recognizing the potential of each form to become a doctrine, we have allowed each type of work to score from 1 to 100%. We asked the same question to experts and specialists to compare their opinions on the most promising materials for a doctrinal start. Afraid to give definite advice, respondents avoided answering 100%. In search of the most promising genre, we compared two variant opinions: "almost unpromising" and "probability is high".

The study established the unanimity of experts and specialists in rating doctrinal forms of academic research. They significantly increase the success of lectures and dissertations. The fact that experts are less likely to succeed in all genres may explain the generally more skeptical attitude toward the success of specific types of content.

The unanimity of experts and specialists increases the value of our conclusions. In addition, this balanced result makes it possible to make informed recommendations to researchers working today about the attractiveness of different genres.

The result shows the common opinion that the textbook is insignificant in the doctrinal process. However, the author refutes the typical opinion about the significant contribution of articles to the promotion of the image of a researcher.

We have calculated the perspectives of each type of genre from dissertation to lecture. We compared the respondent opinions and Persona-Doctrines. A comparison of their opinions allows us to create correct guidelines for writers and motivated authors working from a doctrinal perspective. It will optimize their work for the future.

Diagram 45. (ESPD 3-SSLD 64). Doctrinal Perspectives of Different Works (Comparison of Expert and Specialist Opinions)

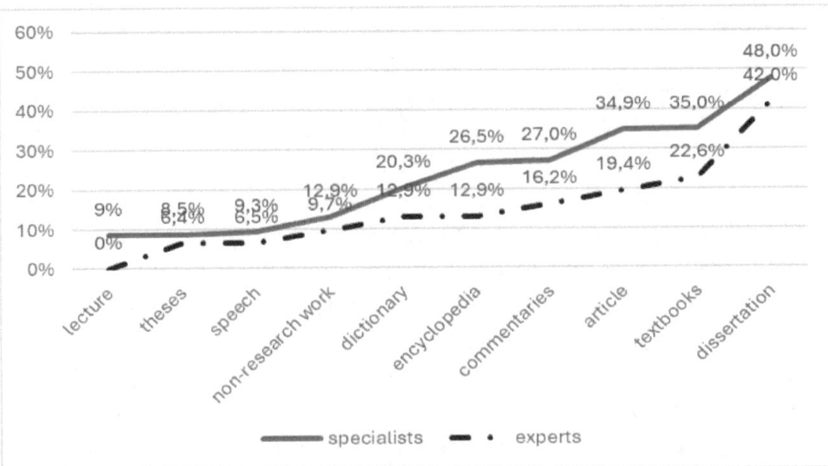

With delayed results (for example, achievement of doctrinal status), dissertations (48% success rate), textbooks (35%), articles (34.9%), and commentaries (27%) should be undertaken. The leading undertaking of the promising doctrinal is the doctoral dissertation, which provides a 48% likelihood of success.

Experts, in contrast to specialists, have more faith in the success of an encyclopedia than in articles. Both specialists and experts consider the chances of dissertations to be the highest among the proposed types of academic publications (42%).

Lectures (8.5% specialists, 0% experts), theses (8.5%/6.4%), and speeches (9.3%/6.5%) are the least likely to become contribute to be coming doctrines.

Textbooks and other genres of publications were also offered for evaluation by respondents. They took a relatively high place in the ranking, second among both experts and specialists. The peculiarity of the textbook (manual) and other works of an educational genre is that they have no requirements for novelty. On the contrary, the author should address the state of the object of exposition based on a well-known doctrine. If appropriate, then it is possible to highlight innovative, authorial, non-traditional trends and views. For example, this can be done in educational publications of increased complexity and advanced level, such as Problems of the Theory of Law and State. However, the reader should be cautioned that the publication presents the author's subjective opinion or alternative theories. A memorable example is: at the beginning of the twentieth century, Professor G. F. Shershenevich (1863-1912) included an annotated list of educational literature in his textbook on civil law, giving an indicative assessment of Diuvernua's readings on civil law. He wrote: "As a textbook, it is unsatisfactory because it does not give a coherent presentation of the subject: it is difficult to convey what has been read. This work is instead a series of successive monographs that seek to elucidate individual issues from the academic point of view".[1] Thus, genres are mixed. In the guise of a textbook, an academic publication containing the author's new ideas or opinions was published. As a rule, a textbook reflects generally accepted opinions with minimal new ideas. Educational literature promotes knowledge rather than creates new knowledge. In ideological totalitarian States, there is no room for creativity in textbooks because only the official position is stated.

[1] G. F. Shershenevich, Учебник русского гражданского права [Textbook of Russian Civil Law] (11th ed.; 1914), I, p. 20.

Nevertheless, according to experts, the textbook has doctrinal potential. The diagram of opinions about the textbook is more detailed.

It is evident from the diagram that 64.5% of experts and 90.3% of specialists left some chance for the textbook to obtain doctrinal status (they gave a non-zero probability). Thus, respondents see considerable potential to acquire reputation and even rise to the level of doctrine for the textbook. This is facilitated by the large circulation of textbooks used in teaching; publishers send them to libraries and use them on library platforms. A textbook can find a larger audience than articles and monographs. There is a debatable custom of citing textbooks in various academic publications, including dissertations. Textbooks are often used to offer a definition. Suppose the dissertation research object is covered by the program of study. In that case, textbooks will be cited without fail.

In almost every Russian dissertation, S. S. Alekseev is mentioned, and his textbook *General Theory of Law* is cited. This is a classic of Soviet jurisprudence, the fame of which rests, *inter alia*, on the laziness of participants in the academic process to turn to modern publications. They do not work with literature. They do not look for new original authors. The demand for textbooks is supported by the descriptive nature of works positioned as research and the low level of academic historiography. Most of Alexeev's cited works were written from the standpoint of communist ideology, under the domination of class theory and the party State. These objective circumstances of Alekseev's work have nothing in common with modern Russian reality. However, the citation trail persists even after the death of Alekseev. This is a negative example of a textbook's high ranking in the system of probable doctrinal forms. Following the well-trodden path of uncritical acceptance, dissertation authors continue to destroy the authority of a respected professor.

Textbooks are used in judicial doctrine. For example, a judge of the Constitutional Court, G. A. Gadzhiev, argues his position with textbooks: E. A. Sukhanov (ed.), Российское гражданское право [Russian Civil Law] (2d ed.; 2011), a textbook in two volumes.[2] Judge S. D. Kniazev quoted the textbook Полицейское право [Police Law. The Law of Internal Administration] by V. V. Ivanovskii published at Kazan in 1911.[3]

An award of the International Commercial Arbitration Court attached to the Chamber of Commerce and Industry of the Russian Federation[4] is based on the opinion of scholars, which, in the opinion of the members of this judicial body, is generally recognized in doctrine and judicial arbitration practice: L. A. Lunts, Курс международного частного права. Общая часть. [Course of International Private Law. General Part] (1973). p. 220; M. M. Boguslavskii, Международное частное право: Учебник [International Private Law: Textbook] (3d ed.; (1998) p. 125. We note the publication dates of textbooks related to doctrine – 1973 and 1998. This literature is not relevant at the date of the award.

References in court documents are made not only to legal literature, but also to medical textbooks. For example, the definition of a defect in the provision of medical care in an appellate ruling is based on a textbook by Stetsenko, *Medical Law* (2004).[5]

In the opinion of many respondents, commentaries can also acquire the status of a doctrinal work and be considered an element of scholar doctrine. The ICAC often relies on this approach to resolve disputes. The award of the ICAC dated 6 September 2004 in case No. 125/2000 is based on the academic

[2] Ruling of Constitutional Court of the Russian Federation, 24 September 2013, No. 1341-O, "On Refusal to Accept for Consideration the Complaint of the Closed Joint-Stock Company "AgroTechResurs" on the Violation of Constitutional Rights and Freedoms by Article 135 of the Civil Code of the Russian Federation".

[3] Ruling of Constitutional Court of the Russian Federation dated 17 July 2012, No. 1286-O, "On Refusal to Accept for Consideration the Complaint of the Limited Responsibility Society "Commercial Bank "Transportnyi" on the Violation of Constitutional Rights and Freedoms by Part 1 of Article 2.6.1 and Part 2 of Article 12.9 of the Code of Administrative Violations of the Russian Federation".

[4] Award of ICAC attached to the Chamber of Commerce and Industry of the Russian Federation, 9 June 2004 in Case No. 125/2000.

[5] Appellate Ruling of the Moscow City Court, 11 October 2016 in case No. 33-33045/2016.

and practical comments of the International Commercial Arbitration Court.[6] This is consistent with doctrine and judicial and arbitration practice and is also reflected in Article 1202 of the Civil Code of the Russian Federation.

The question of whether a commentary could be recognized as a doctrine was raised with survey respondents.

74.5% of experts and 84.5% of specialists gave some chance to obtain doctrinal status. They did not show zero probability.

A commentary is a derivative work that explains primary materials; as a rule, these are legislation, judicial, and other practice. Academic commentaries have become widespread, based on some object or group of objects united by the subject of legal regulation, the period, the issuing authority, and other factors. Commentaries can be article-by-article, consider a group of norms combined into sections, paragraphs, or thematic groups. A commentary can be called academic.

Commentaries on judicial practice are compilations of documents of a judicial body, generalizations of practice, and the like. This type of publication is particularly valued by judges. This source includes reviews of judicial practice and decrees of the Plenum of the Supreme Court of the Russian Federation. The last two are documents that gravitate towards normative legal acts. Bibliographic descriptions are a kind of commentary on academic research and other publications.

An article-by-article commentary on a normative legal act means the presence of the author's opinion on all fragments of the text of the document in each article. This is the most complete, unquestionable commentary. Academic research differs from commentaries because they are based on their own plan; as a rule, they analyze several documents, not only current legal acts but also historical ones. Commentaries are always

[6] Practice of the International Commercial Arbitration Court. Scientific and Practical Commentary (1997), pp. 9–12; Arbitration Practice for 1996-1997 (1998), pp. 162-163, 169-171, 234-239; Practice of International Commercial Arbitration Court attached to the Chamber of Commerce and Industry of the Russian Federation for 1999-2000 (2002), pp. 67-72, 141-147.

bound by the text and structure of the normative legal act, especially if it is an article-by-article commentary. The editors of commentaries published at different times can be analyzed to study the historical path of forming a normative legal act. Academic works refer to the legislation of other countries to summarize foreign law, historical experience, and proposals for possible use in national legislation.

The traditions of many States raise the authority of commentary to an exceptionally high level. In the Anglo-Saxon countries, the search for doctrine is undertaken in the commentaries on codes, individual laws, and "annotated versions" (models) of various normative legal acts. The printing plate has deep historical roots. As Bogdanovskaia rightly noted, commentaries on legislation "were one of the first forms of academic activity that have survived to the present day".[7] She suggested that the development of legal scholarship leads to a further decline in the importance of commentaries. However, Bogdanovskaia's conclusion is not supported by sociological research. On the contrary, the ratings are high and improving.

However, it is not only in the past that that doctrines and commentaries tend to gravitate towards each other. The practice of the Constitutional Court of the Russian Federation and the positions of individual judges confirm this thesis for the Russian Federation. For example, a judge of the Constitutional Court, N. V. Vitruk pointed to two commentaries on the Constitution of the Russian Federation as a source of "doctrinal (academic) interpretation": Iu. V. Kudriavtsev (ed.), Комментарий к Конституции РФ [Commentary on the Constitution of the Russian Federation], p. 477; L. A. Okunkov (ed.), Комментарий к Конституции РФ [Commentary on the Constitution of the Russian Federation] (1996), p. 465.[8]

7 I. Ia. Bogdanovskaia, Прецедентное право [Precedent Law] (2020), p. 86.

8 "Особое мнение судьи Н. В. Витрука к Постановлению Конституционного Суда РФ от 11 декабря 1998 г. № 28-П По делу о толковании положений части 4 статьи 111 Конституции Российской Федерации [Special Opinion of Judge N. V. Vitruk on the Decree of Constitutional Court of the Russian Federation of 11 December 1998 No. 28-P in the Case of Interpretation of the Provisions of Article 111(4) of the Constitution of the Russian Federation]", СЗ РФ (1998), no. 52, item

The Concept of the Classifier of Legal Acts includes scholar doctrine, laws, and decrees, another proof of the recognition of commentaries as equal to academic studies and bearers of doctrinal ideas. The concept developers refer to scholar doctrine as commentaries on legislation and legal practice. In terms of content, doctrine reflects proposals for improving current legislation. This is based on the predictive nature of doctrine, which does not exclude commentaries.

As a rule, a commentary is an interpretation of normative legal acts. Its persuasiveness and depth are determined by the type of interpretation: professional, academic, or doctrinal. In any case, the authors of commentaries give explanations. The informative commentary combines legal norms, academic explanations, analysis of law enforcement practice, and recommendations with regard to application.

The authors of some commentaries try to distinguish them from similar publications by strengthening the title, for example, calling them an academic and practical commentary. In addition, the confusion of academic and commentary tasks leads to other genres being published under the name "commentary": educational, academic. The selective presentation of general theoretical information called "commentary" is distributed in isolation from the full text of the normative act.

For a commentary to be recognized in the Russian context, the author and more often even the editor-in-chief, and the author of the introductory preface is significant, regardless of the authorship of the main text. In the correspondence of the Supreme Arbitrazh Court of the Russian Federation there is an angry letter, whose authors ask: who will be responsible for information in the book that the court did not take into account? The reason for their trust in the selected commentary: the introductory article by V. F. Iakovlev, published under the aegis of the Institute of Intellectual Property and Social Protection attached to the Government of the Russian Federation. And there is no culprit, and cannot be in the sense of legal

6447.

responsibility. It is simply a commentary not tested by judicial practice. It is also possible that the letter authors misunderstood and applied the ideas of the commentary. It should serve as a signal for evaluating the pretentious introductory articles to printed materials.

The appreciation of commentaries is justified. First, the importance of the commentary is traditionally great in Anglo-American countries. Second, the commentary can be academic, referring to relevant judicial practice, positively affecting its quality.

The most cited commentary, according to the RSCI, is V. D. Zorkin (ed.), *Commentary on the Constitution of the Russian Federation* (2011). The authors are judges of the Constitutional Court, authoritative scholars, and leaders. The second most cited commentary is the *Doctrinal Model of Criminal Procedure Evidentiary Law of the Russian Federation and Commentaries to it* (2015), which, according to the annotation, is the fruit of academic research of the Nizhny Novgorod academic school of proceduralists on the problems of the theory of evidence in criminal procedure, criminal procedural principles, organization and activities of the prosecutorial power, judicial control and other problems of legal science.

Particular attention should be paid to the verbal forms of legal doctrine and the oral statements of prominent legal scholars. Indeed, the form of expression of doctrine can be a written text and/or an oral speech such as a lecture. At the intersection of oral and written forms of doctrinal expression, a professor publishes lectures given to some academic, political, or other audience. A well-known example is the speech of Ferdinand Lassalle (1825-1864), *On the Essence of the Constitution*, delivered to the Berlin Burgher District Assembly in 1862. In this lecture, he suggested the doctrine of a de facto constitution. The lecturer wonders what would happen if the printing press that printed the laws burned down, as well as "all the archives, libraries, and bookstores in all the cities; let us suppose the impossible, that in the whole of Prussia, all the repositories of written or printed laws have disappeared, and not a single law in authentic form remains".[9]

Starting from this fantasy, Lassalle depicts the impossibility of adopting laws other than those that have been burned. He calls this phenomenon the correspondence of the text to factual relations. Denying the possibility of borrowing the law from China, he concludes that "such a law would be stillborn, since it would arm public opinion, public conscience, public conscience too much against itself, and is also part of the constitution".[10] The answer is more than interesting. For more than 150 years, this answer has been the most accurate and imaginative description of the economic and political basis of the Constitution.

Despite the verbal account of Lassalle's theses, they are relevant and quoted to this day. However, it should be taken into account that the distribution and citation of the lecture was possible thanks to the publication in the form of a text.

There are many recorded speeches by prominent lawyers in various fields of activity. These are political, judicial, and expert speeches.[11] They are even cited and analyzed in dissertations.[12] There are also examples of the opposite, when people with academic degrees and titles, with teaching experience, cannot connect two words. The tongue does not turn to call such people speakers, much less publish their speeches. Examples are the leaders of legislative bodies. The general quality of their rhetoric decreases. Starting with Sergei Andreevich Muromtsev (1850-1910), the path of the legislators fall from lofty heights

[9] F. Lassalle, О сущности конституции [On the Essence of the Constitution], transl. K. Chekerul-Kusha (1905), p. 7-8.

[10] Ibid., p. 12.

[11] Судебные речи знаменитых русских адвокатов [Court Speeches of Famous Russian Lawyers] (2015).

[12] M. L. Mazurenko, Судебные речи российских адвокатов по уголовным делам и их правовые публикации как феномен общественного правосознания и юридической мысли в пореформенной России: 2-я пол. XIX - нач. XX вв. [Judicial Speeches of Russian Criminal Lawyers and Their Legal Publication as a Phenomenon of Social Legal Consciousness and Legal Thought in Post-Reform Russia: the 2nd half of the 19th - the Beginning of the 20th Centuries] (2012) (abstract of dissertation candidate of legal sciences).

continues today. There is a noticeable decline in the quality of doctrinal speeches by the heads of law-making bodies.

With the help of sociological tools, we have studied attitudes toward lectures. We asked experts and respondents to assess the chances of lectures and speeches becoming the key to the author's doctrinal success.

According to 71.2% of respondents and 77.4% of experts, lectures are doctrinally unpromising. Accordingly, only 8.8% of respondents consider the success of lectures probable; experts do not give lectures any chance – 0%.

Experts consider the speech genre more promising (12.9%) than 9.3% of specialists. However, comparing the chances of speaking in the struggle for doctrinality has shown that they are more hopeless than lectures.

A speech for a researcher has its own peculiarities, as it requires a specific audience. Of great importance is the place, the informational occasion. More often, legal scholars speak at academic conferences and meetings. Listeners are colleagues and researchers. We must admit that conferences are often of a formal nature and have no interest in formulating or resolving any academic problem. Getting a positive effect of citation and authority directly from a speech is difficult. However, an exciting speech can draw attention to the speaker and, therefore, to his works.

First, scholars quote familiar and well-known authors. An additional factor is the publication of the presentation as an abstract or in the conference reviews. This is a different format – a written version of an original oral presentation. Thus, sociological surveys have shown that doctrinal status is not worth wasting energy on speeches due to the low effectiveness of this genre.

It is worth noting the persistence of litigants who, when legislation is uncertain or absent, turn to books as a source of law. These books are of different genres. We have instances of citations and references to textbooks, monographs, commentaries on legislation, and general references to "theory."

The direct effect of scholar doctrine is manifested in its application, on a par with the law, as a legal basis. This can be facilitated by various external (lack of legislation, incompleteness, vagueness, variability) and internal (high quality, authority, recognition as a regulatory factor) circumstances. Specific decisions with such references make it possible to fix the latent application of the scholar doctrine in the judicial system.

Respondents were asked to study these properties of doctrinal forms of law: "What is your attitude to the citation of academic publications in a court session or other State body"?[13] It was not a quotation as an embellishment of speech and argument but as the basis of a legal position in the case. We asked this question in three of our studies, which allows us to compare answers with a difference of 15 years and in different groups of respondents.

In the 2007 – 2008 survey, 44.6% of respondents (civil servants) rated this practice positively and 31.6% negatively. In practice, 15.0% of respondents did not have such experience. And 8.8% of respondents found it difficult to answer.

In the 2022 – 2023 survey, 72.7% of respondents (specialists) assessed this practice positively and 9.7% negatively. In practice, 5.7% of respondents did not have such experience. And 11.9% of respondents found it difficult to answer.

Diagram 46. Comparison of Respondent Attitudes to Citation of Academic Publications in Court Session or Other State Body (2007–2008 and 2022–2023)

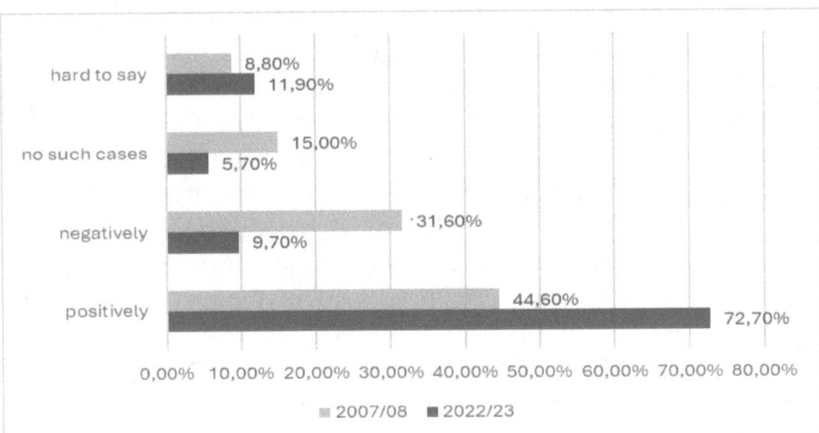

[13] SCS 2007–2008.

A visualized comparison of the 2007 – 2008 and 2022 – 2023 studies shows the following trend. The positive attitude almost doubled, from 44.6% to 72.7%. The number of respondents who have encountered examples of judicial citation of doctrines in their practice has increased, followed by the decrease in those respondents who have never encountered such examples. In 2007 – 2008 – 15% of respondents, and in 2022 – 2023 – 5.7% did not see such examples. Accordingly, the number of respondents who have seen such examples has increased by three times. These statistics indirectly indicate a decrease in the quality of normative legal acts. This conclusion follows from the fact that the scholar doctrine is in demand in the courts when there is a gap, inconsistency, or absence of legislation.

In the 2007 – 2008 survey, young respondents (under 30 years of age) were not so unequivocally in favor of or against citing academic papers (14.7% found it difficult to answer, while the average figure is 8.8%). However, all surveyed representatives of the older generation encountered the practice of citation. Nonetheless, more people had a negative attitude towards such legal argumentation. 46.2% of respondents aged 50 to 59 showed a negative attitude towards the judicial citation of research works.[14]

An exciting dynamic of attitudes toward the citation of academic research in court sessions or other State bodies, depending on the length of public service, was revealed. Respondents with 10 to 15 years of work experience have a more negative attitude towards the practice of citation – 40.9%, and at the same time, a slightly smaller number of people among them. 9.1% have not experienced this phenomenon. Among new entrants (up to 1 year work experience), there is a smaller number of people who have a positive attitude (26.7%) and a more significant number of people who have never encountered this practice (26.7%), thus, they, in fact, know little about what it is, what is called "just in case", and are wary of citations. However, after a short period of work (work experience from 1

[14] SCS code 2007–2008.

to 5 years), civil servants, having familiarized themselves with this practice (9.4% did not meet them), have a more positive attitude towards this practice (50% positively, 21.9% negatively, although among them the most significant number of those who found it difficult to answer – 18.8%).[15]

In 2007 – 2008, 50% of civil servants cited academic research positively. Accordingly, after 15 years, the age group under 30 gained experience and advanced their views from theoretical to practical.

Diagram 47. Respondent Attitude to Citation of Academic Publications in Court Session or Other State Body Depending on Length of Service in Civil Service (2007–2008)

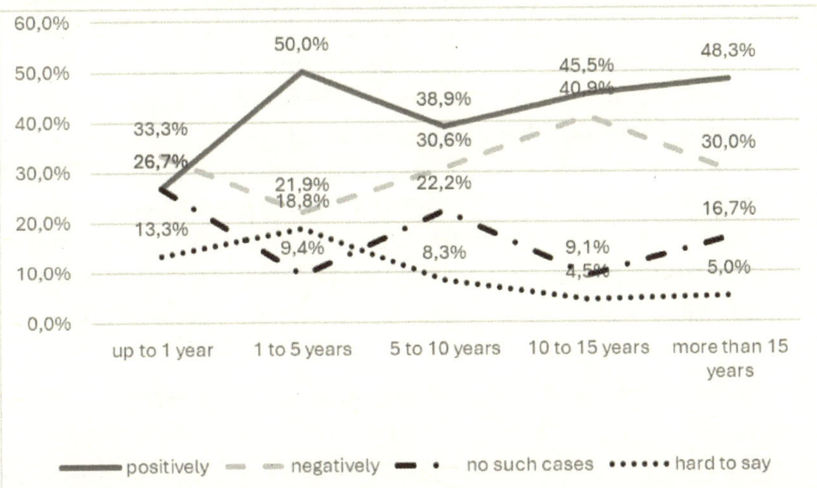

Attitudes towards citation are heterogeneous depending on the type of activity in the civil service. Thus, employees of the legislative (62.5%) and law enforcement (66.7%) departments are more optimistic about this activity. In comparison, only 32.2% of the judiciary have a more positive attitude towards this activity. Among them, a negative attitude to the citation of academic research is characteristic, respectively: 8.3%

[15] SCS code 2007–2008.

(legislative bodies), 22.2% law enforcement agencies, and 40.3% (judicial bodies).

To clarify the attitude of civil servants to the various sources of legal information, a question of which literature is most beneficial to civil servants has been formulated.

The most unpopular genre is monographs (0%). The commentary was recognized as the most valuable (30%). All other genres of academic literature were in demand from 0.5 to 2%. Most respondents do not need academic literature in their professional activities (45% indicated the usefulness of any literature, and 21% found it difficult to answer).

The addition of the age variable yielded the following results. Age groups up to 39 prefer case law materials that are not of interest to older groups. Academic articles that are not interesting to age groups under 39 seem to apply to older age groups (over 40). Monographs as a type of literature were not in demand by the surveyed civil servants. Only 0.5 % of respondents noted the usefulness of textbooks and educational literature. However, in other issues, a reasonably high demand for educational literature was revealed. Perhaps the respondents did not want to advertise their interest in such an insignificant genre, believing that it compromises their educational level.[16]

The literary needs of judges differ considerably.[17] They prefer collections of court practice (35.2%, while the average for all employees is 0.5%). However, judges are less interested in commenting on legislation (5.7%) than others – 30%. Thus, the analysis of judges literary legal interests showed their interest in highly specialized sources.

A question was formulated to determine whether any legal writings are suitable for judges to examine the role of doctrine and research vis-à-vis civil servants.[18]

[16] SCS code 2007–2008.

[17] SCS code 2007–2008.

[18] SCS code 2007–2008.

Half of the civil servants surveyed (50.5%) said that there were works in jurisprudence that were a priori correct. In contrast, only 13.5% of respondents could name specific authors and their works. Less than half (41.5%) of the respondents categorically state that such works should not occur, and 8% have not yet decided on their ideas on this issue (they found it difficult to answer).

Diagram 48. (SSLD 29 – SOGS 2007-2008). Comparison of Respondent Attitudes Towards Legal Doctrine (2007–2008 and 2022–2023)

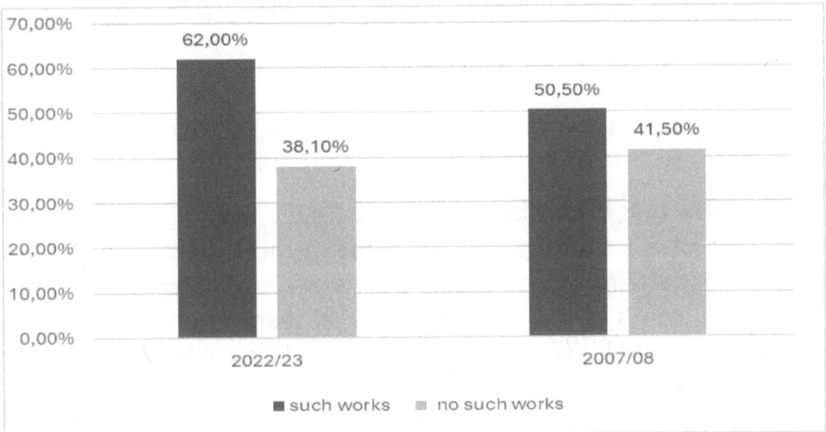

A comparison over the past period shows an increase in the number of respondents who admit the existence of correct works and a decrease in the number of people who distrust doctrinal law.

In the 2022 – 2023 study, the data make it possible to compare attitudes towards legal doctrine with the primary type of activity.

Predictably, respondents engaged in academic and educational activities expressed more acceptance of scholar doctrine through works.

Diagram 49. (SCS 2007 – 2008) Influence of Age on Attitudes to Legal Doctrine

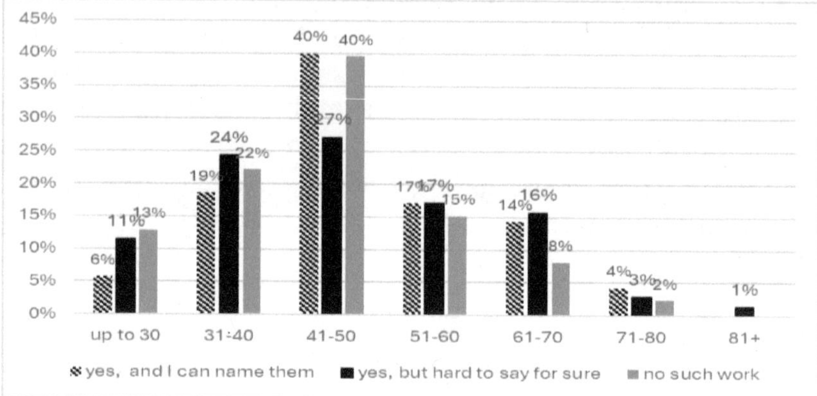

Lawyers express the highest percentage of distrust in legal doctrine – 66.7%, followed by civil servants – 50%.

Of those respondents who said in 2007/08 that legal doctrine was correct for them (13.5% of total number of respondents), 11.1% of respondents named the work of V. V. Vitrianskii, *Contract Law.* The rest of the works were mentioned once, among them: B. Utkin, M. Braginskii, and S. S. Alekseev, *Theory of State and Law;* P. Krasheninnikov; Machiavelli, *The Prince;* Montesquieu; R. David, *Major Legal Systems in the World Today: An Introduction to the Comparative Study of Law;* V. P. Gribanov, *Implementation and Protection of Civil Rights;* Ia. N. Stetsovskii, *Advocacy and the State;* G. F. Shershenevich, *Civil Law;* classical textbooks on Roman law, works by Shatalov, Ia. Skuratov, and others. The list of authoritative works among civil servants is heterogeneous. It includes books, commentaries (P. Krasheninnikov), monuments of legal thought (Machiavelli), classical legal works of the late nineteenth century (G. F. Shershenevich), recognized works of Soviet jurisprudence (S. S. Alekseev). The probability of answering this open-ended question is high only for persons with legal education. It indicates a reasonably high educational level and literary needs of lawyers in the civil service.

Some interesting links were identified between the attitudes of civil servants to legal doctrine and some variables. Thus, the most significant number of respondents who trust doctrinal sources of law and recognize the authority of well-known lawyers (64.5%) was found in the age group under 30 years old (of these, 12.9% of respondents named such works, and 51.6% of respondents found it difficult to name specific names and works) and, accordingly, among civil servants of this age group have a smaller number of respondents who do not have authoritative sources (35.5%).

A more significant number of respondents who have recently entered the civil service (up to 1 year work experience) recognize the regulatory force of doctrinal law – 80.0% (compared to the average value for the sample of 54.9%). However, compared to other internship groups, more respondents found it difficult to name specific authors (66.7% compared to the average value of 45.1%).

It should be noted that law enforcement officers (66.7%) and military personnel (53.3%) were more likely than employees of other agencies to say that they did not have reputable researchers (the average for the sample was 45.1%).[19] Judges are more definite in denying the possibility of using books as a direct form of law (53.8%).

To sum up, the form of a scholar doctrine is the envelope in which it exists, disseminates, and is protected. Legal scholar doctrine exists in printed form, usually in publications. The academic genre is represented by such works as a dissertation and a candidate or doctoral research abstract, articles, textbooks, and comments. We have examined which of these kinds of works are most likely to become doctrine.

Forms of expression of judicial doctrine are acts issued by courts, judges, or judicial agencies. The most traditional form of expression of judicial doctrine in Russia is the Decrees of

[19] SCS code 2007–2008.

the Plenums of the Supreme Arbitrazh Court and the Supreme Court of the Russian Federation.

Decrees of the Plenum are binding on the judiciary. They are likewise considered by State authorities and citizens to be binding. When arguing their positions in judicial activity or oral pleadings, the parties refer to decrees of the plenums along with normative legal acts. In general, the interest of citizens in these acts is quite significant and contradictory.

The most common perception of the decrees of the plenum is that they are binding acts. Reverence for these acts often passes into higher forms when they are proclaimed normative and binding not by virtue of their recognition but by their nature. For example, according to A. B. Vengerov, "the normativity of the guiding explanations lies in the fact that they contain certain legal provisions, principles, considerations that are of a general nature and binding on the judiciary under the specific nature of the judicial activity".[20]

The role of decrees of the plenum increases because it is precisely in these acts that such a complex elaboration of definitions finds expression. This unique role of the supreme judicial bodies is vital because legislation is replete with vague expressions containing quantitative and qualitative characteristics (reasonable, long-lasting, for benefit) or terms that do not have a precise legislative definition (normative legal act, custom). On one hand, formulating definitions and other theoretical and doctrinal provisions is inevitable. On the other hand, they usually become the object of targeted criticism.

For many decades there has been a debate about the status and role in the legal system of decisions in individual cases beyond the specific cases in which they were made. It should be noted that, in summarizing the current trends, the red line of confrontation is the answer to whether a single decision can be considered a judicial doctrine at all. There are several possible

[20] A. B. Vengerov, Роль судебной практики в развитии советского права [The Role of Judicial Practice in the Development of Soviet Law] (1966), p. 126.

answers to this question: 1) may: (a) in any case; b) only on matters of principle; 2) may not under any circumstances.

We adhere to the tradition that categorical options are not acceptable. The average assessment seems more accurate and balanced – some can be considered judicial practice, but not all decisions. Such an assumption makes it possible to classify decisions on cases of principle as forms of expression of judicial practice. In the academic literature, a suggestion has been made to consider cases of public importance as fundamental.[21] In general, in agreement with this position, we must add the following: often the significance of a particular case is understood only by specialists of narrow profile. They distinguish the fundamental case from a series of cases with keen, professional eyes. They can draw attention to a particular case in a variety of ways.

One may conclude that the principle and social significance will generally be typical of court decisions that evaluate normative legal acts. If the court finds the act non-compliant with any requirements, it must be amended in pursuance of the judgment. But even if this happens, in the following case of a party's recourse to the act, which has been evaluated in a certain way by the court, the earlier decision will be used again.

A specific judicial decision in a particular case may acquire doctrinal status in connection with elaborating a legal provision. In the absence of a relevant legal norm, the reasoning of a judicial body may be based on general principles, doctrinal ideas, and other non-normative acts. In this case, the act performs two functions at once. On one hand, a written form is given to another source (a research study, a principle, an idea). On the other hand, this decision becomes a form of expression of judicial practice because the developed legal provisions will be used more than once in subsequent decisions and will become the basis for forming a specific line of law enforcement practice. Consider a few examples.

[21] Ibid., p. 58.

90.3% of experts consider the decrees of the Plenum of the Supreme Court of the Russian Federation to be judicial doctrine, 87.1% to review judicial practice, 83.9% to consider decisions on fundamental cases, and 67.7% to dissenting opinions of judges.

Regarding dissenting opinions, these documents were available until 2020, so experts are familiar with this type of document and, therefore, have a qualified opinion. Notably, the Persona-Doctrina, including the judges of the Constitutional Court of the Russian Federation, named the dissenting opinions of judges among the first five forms of expression of judicial doctrine. This testifies to the importance of publishing dissenting opinions of judges of the Constitutional Court of the Russian Federation. The decision not to publish these documents deprived the legal community and society at large of a valuable source of legal doctrine. In fact, this deprived society of a significant form of expression of judicial practice in the form of dissenting opinions.

A comparison of the answers of specialists and experts visualizes an almost synchronous understanding of the forms of expression of judicial doctrine with minor deviations. For example, there are slight fluctuations in the higher valuation of some sources. Experts highly value any decisions, publications of judges, dissenting opinions, and summarizing acts. The most significant deviation between the opinions of specialists and experts is found in the assessment of generalizing acts.

The most tremendous confidence of specialists in generalizing acts emphasizes the peculiarities of the Romano-Germanic picture of the world. Legislative practice is ambiguous about precedent. On one hand, legislative support is growing. On the other hand, the decisions on specific cases have not been legitimized as a precedent in Russia or applied. Nevertheless, despite the legislator indecisiveness, the sociological survey shows a high level of recognition of decisions in fundamental cases by judicial doctrine – 89.4%.

Moreover, in terms of their level of perception, they have the same level as reviews of judicial practice. 68.1% of experts attribute any decisions to judicial doctrine. These experts recognize the existence of a judicial precedent in the Russian Federation without restrictions.

Predictably, last place was taken by the correspondence of courts (judges). In the article "Judicial Practice: Modes of Expression" (2002), I gave examples of the influence of the correspondence of the Supreme Arbitrazh Court of the Russian Federation, which was taken from the Archive of this court.

There are several possible explanations for the low level of legitimation of this form of activity. First, these sources are little known. They are latent in nature. They can only be consulted in the archives of the judiciary. Second, if these documents are known to respondents, they may not view them as doctrine.

Nevertheless, letters from courts and judges received a relatively high recognition – 25.3%. Such a high positive evaluation shows that respondents are familiar with this type of document and, therefore, have a reasonable opinion. In passing, it should be noted that letters on behalf of other (non-judicial) State authorities and officials also have contradictory assessments by scholars, practicing lawyers, and judges. We have researched the letters many times[22] and concluded that these documents can, under certain conditions, be considered an interpretation. However, many conditions can create obstacles to the use of emails. There is no uniform decision on letters. Each specific example should be evaluated independently.

The results of the survey are as follows. 62.8% of experts unequivocally recognize the decrees of the Plenum of the Supreme Court of the Russian Federation (the answer option "always") and acts summarizing judicial practice (58.4%) as judicial doctrine.

If we add up all the forms of positive assessment of judicial practice ("always" and "sometimes"), the first place in

[22] S. V. Boshno, "Место писем в системе нормативного регулирования [The Place of Letters in the Regulatory System]", Ваш налоговый адвокат. Консультации, рекомендации [Your Tax Attorney. Consultations, Recommendations], no. 7 (2008), pp. 8–16.

legitimation is occupied by acts summarizing judicial practice (97.3%), followed by decrees of the Plenum of the Supreme Court of the Russian Federation (95.6%). 89.4% of specialist respondents recognize reviews of judicial practice as doctrine.

Diagram 50. (SSLD 4 - ESPD 2). Comparison of Opinions of Specialists and Experts on Forms of Judicial Doctrine

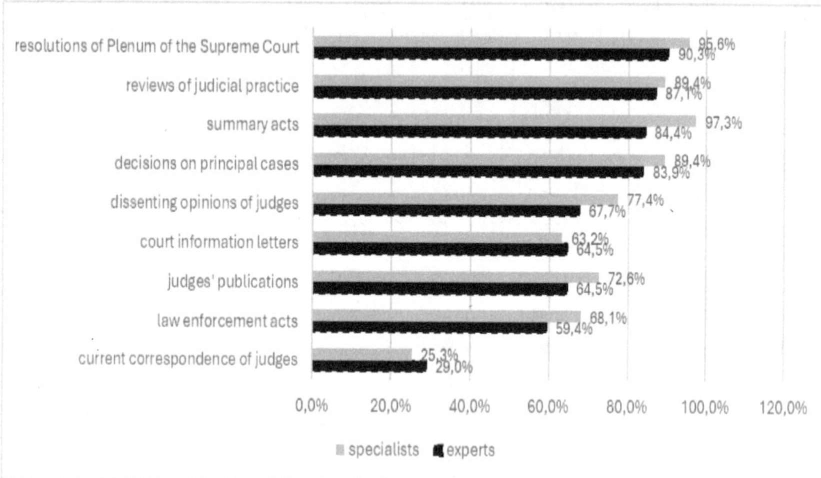

In 2002, in a publication on the forms of expression of jurisprudence,[23] we recorded that the legislator does not see the forms of expression of judicial practice as a channel of high-quality professional information about the needs of the legislative system. In addition, the judiciary of the Russian Federation withdrew from bringing the actual doctrine to the status of law by submitting draft laws to the State Duma. In 2022, the statistics on the participation of judicial bodies confirmed the established strategy – no more than 1% of bills are submitted by the Constitutional Court and the Supreme Court of the Russian Federation. Nevertheless, there is a tendency to increase the functional status of the forms of expression of judicial practice as a form of law. These are amendments to the Code of Arbitrazh Procedure and the Code of Civil Procedure

[23] Boshno, "Формы выражения судебной практики [Forms of Expression of Judicial Practice]." Юриспруденция [Jurisprudence], no. 1 (2002), pp. 14-33.

intended to legitimize various forms of expression of judicial practice.

For example, the 1995 Code of Arbitrazh Procedure of the Russian Federation did not reference judicial practice as a form of law equal in force to the law. Initially, it was established that the court was guided only by laws and other normative legal acts. In 2002, a new Code of Arbitrazh Procedure was adopted. Article 170 of that Code marked the beginning of the finest hour of judicial practice as a form of Russian law. The Article was worded as follows: "The reasoned part of a decision may contain references to decrees of the Plenum of the Supreme Arbitrazh Court of the Russian Federation with regard to questions of judicial practice and decrees of the Presidium of the Supreme Arbitrazh Court of the Russian Federation (Article 170(4), Code of Arbitrazh Procedure of the Russian Federation, dated 24 July 2002, as amended 23 December 2010).[24]

Following the same pattern, in 2010, the wording of Article 170(4) of the Code of Arbitrazh Procedure was changed. References to the decisions of the Presidium of the Supreme Commercial Court of the Russian Federation were allowed in the arbitrazh court decisions. In February 2014 the Supreme Arbitrazh Court of the Russian Federation was liquidated, and the Supreme Court took its place as a source of judicial practice. The unrepealed acts of judicial practice of the Supreme Arbitrazh Court of the Russian Federation remained in force. As a result, the arbitrazh court decisions officially became "Decrees of the Plenum of the Supreme Court of the Russian Federation and Decrees of the Plenum of the Supreme Arbitrazh Court of the Russian Federation on issues of judicial practice that have remained in force, as well as decrees of the Presidium of the Supreme Court of the Russian Federation and decrees of the Presidium of the Supreme Arbitrazh Court of the Russian Federation that have remained in force". Article 170(4), Code of Arbitrazh Procedure of the Russian Federation, as amended 28 June 2014).

24 W. E. Butler, *Russian Civil and Arbitrazh Procedure* (2012), p. 288.

In 2018, this list was supplemented by reviews of judicial practice of the Supreme Court of the Russian Federation, confirmed by the Presidium of the Supreme Court of the Russian Federation (Article 170(4), as amended 28 November 2018).

Following Article 311(1), paragraph 5, of the Code of Arbitrazh Procedure, the grounds for revision of judicial acts pursuant to this Chapter are "the determination or change in a decree of the Plenum of the Supreme Court of the Russian Federation or in a decree of the Presidium of the Supreme Court of the Russian Federation of the practice of applying a legal norm, if the relevant act of the Supreme Court of the Russian Federation contains an indication of the possibility of reviewing judicial acts that have entered into force under these circumstances" (Article 131(1), paragraph 5, Code of Arbitrazh Procedure of the Russian Federation).

Similar amendments have been made to the Code of Civil Procedure. Initially, in 2002, Article 198 of the Code of Civil Procedure indicated that the courts, when deciding, justify their decision only by laws. In this article, the term "law" is used broadly to include all normative legal acts, and in fact this is how the Article was applied. But in 2018, a new element was added to Article 198 – Part 4^1: The reasoning of the court decision may contain references to decrees of the Plenum of the Supreme Court of the Russian Federation on issues of judicial practice, decrees of the Presidium of the Supreme Court of the Russian Federation, as well as to reviews of judicial practice of the Supreme Court of the Russian Federation confirmed by the Presidium of the Supreme Court of the Russian Federation.

On an unspecified date, Article 395 of the Code of Civil Procedure was supplemented by paragraph 5 as follows: grounds for a review of court decisions: 5) a ruling (or amendment) in a decision of the Supreme Court of the Russian Federation, a decision of the Presidium of the Supreme Court of the Russian Federation in a decree. In 2019, this precedent was strengthened by amending Article 395(5): Determination or change in a decree of the Plenum of the Supreme Court of the Russian Federation or a decree of the Presidium of the Supreme

Court of the Russian Federation of the practice of applying a legal norm, if such a decree contains an indication that the legal position formulated in it has a retroactive effect concerning cases with similar factual circumstances (Article 395(5), Code of Civil Procedure, as amended 2 December 2019).

All these changes are made to the functional part of the procedural codes. This is a description of the details of specific rules of conduct. However, the details cannot change the framework general provisions. The principles of law in the General Part of the codes take precedence over the rules of conduct in the Special Part. Nevertheless, the articles-principles in the procedural codes have been preserved in their original form.

In Article 3 of the Civil Code, Article 1 of the Criminal Code, Article 1 of the Code of Civil Procedure, and Article 1 of the Code of Arbitrazh Procedure, there is not a single document of judicial practice in terms of fixing the forms of law of these branches of law.

Acts of judicial practice have crept into criminal proceedings not only without the authorization of a law, but despite it because the criminal procedure code and the criminal code are merely law as a particular type of normative legal act issued by the legislative (representative) body, recognized as a form of SCP and UP. This thesis means that the judicial doctrine has become the starting form of law and is applied directly in considering court cases.

The forms of expression of State ideological doctrine are legal acts of a strategic nature. These are non-normative documents. They are declarative and do not regulate social relations. An ideological doctrine can also be expressed in forms close to a scholar doctrine.

Conclusion

By applying various research methods and knowledge, including jurisprudence, sociology, mathematics, statistics, and computer science, to many objects, original reasoned conclusions have been reached about legal doctrine. New data presented on legal doctrine has the properties of verifiability and objectivity. A model of legal research has been proposed that can be transferred to various objects with minor adaptations. A set of tools combined into a single whole made it possible to collect, analyze, and draw conclusions about the concept of legal doctrine in the space-time continuum.

A questionnaire and an expert survey as part of a continuing sociological research project, commenced in 2002, allowed a unique empirical data collection to be formed and analyzed for the purposes of this study. A variety of questions and answers from various respondents over more than twenty years provides empirical material on the concept and typology of legal doctrine.

The respondent answers to the expert survey represented by the Persona-Doctrine are unique data on the basis of which the portrait of the Persona-Doctrine is formed. This is a human, social, and professional profile. Its value lies in the fact that these elements of the Persona-Doctrine portrait help form a new designation of the Persona-Doctrine according to the formed criteria. The characteristics of the Persona-Doctrine serve as a beacon for the part of the professional legal community oriented towards achieving this status. The study revealed the great importance of the personal, human characteristics of the Persona-Doctrine. These universal positive qualities create prerequisites for achieving great life results, including dedication, diligence, and openness.

Persona-doctrine people are sensitive individuals, which is natural for creative personalities, and does not fit into the idea of people holding high positions with great authority and influence. They are sensitive to their workforce and colleagues. They do not show much confidence in these groups and doubt their objectivity. They foresee rather negative impacts from these groups.

Persona-Doctrines are not alien to the administrative resources that accompanied positions and calling. However, they do not see administrative resources as an elevator to the world of doctrinal achievement. They are related to the policy and leadership of the State and recognize the importance of loyalty, tolerance, and support from officials at the State level.

From time to time, they become acquainted with academic activity statistics such as the Index h, which they recognize due to the lack of other mass quantitative methods. The place of birth and the parental family can be anything, that is, social characteristics are not important. A Persona-Doctrine could be brought up in a village or the capital, in a family of academics or workers. The social picture is diverse and includes all strata. In a parental family, a positive attitude, pride in one's work and country, and shared values are essential. The study revealed the attitude of this group toward material wealth. Persona-Doctrinas are not oligarchs, but neither are they beggars. They have above-average incomes, are not worried about survival, and have resources for creativity and self-realization. In general, a positive perception of one's well-being was revealed. Presumably, in the early years of creativity, the State provided the necessary guarantees for forming an academic reserve.

The path of the Persona-Doctrine is not connected with the super-wealth. It is unsuitable for people striving for quick and/or significant prosperity. Accordingly, reasonable modesty (restraint, self-restraint) is an element of the social portrait of the Persona-Doctrine.

This study establishes the period of creative flourishing of the Persona-Doctrine, measured by the age and periods of dissertation defense. By flourishing, we mean the time when the principal works – the doctrines – were created. The period of creative flowering of the Persona-Doctrine group is 51-70 years. The period from 51 to 60 years is more effective, with a slight decrease but relatively high-efficiency indicators at

61 – 70 years. In dissertation periodization (candidate of legal sciences, SJD), the Persona-Doctrine flowering occurs after the doctoral dissertation defense.

A new term is proposed and tested in this study: Doctrine-Form. This is the outer shell of objectification, the physical existence of legal doctrine, not excluding the oral form of expression; the written form of objectification of modern legal doctrine is still typical. This shell allows the form to be created, spread, acted on, and protected. The form of the external expression of the doctrine – the Doctrine-Form – differs for types of doctrines, although there are universal features of the form for all types:

1. written form,
2. the ability to persist and disseminate,
3. methods of registration, establishing the facts of the emergence of the Doctrine-Form,
4. the personification of the object, individual properties for accounting and identification,
5. channels to make uncertainty accessible to the public,
6. a way of interacting with other forms of law.

Doctrine-Forms are studied on the theoretical basis of the doctrine of sources and forms of law, as well as the typology of doctrines.

Academic doctrine is objectified through academic publications. It has been established that the scholar Doctrine-Form is most likely to be embodied in the following types of materials: dissertations, books, articles, and the like. The probability of becoming a doctrine is most influenced by the following qualities: writing style and unique empirical database. The author's reputation ensures interest in his works and, as a result, increases the likelihood of becoming a doctrine. The doctoral dissertation has the most significant doctrinal prospects.

Promotion and marketing are welcome in various forms. It is established that researchers have traditional (reviews) technological tools (posting on library platforms). The academic community has a negative attitude toward the direct advertising of works. The recommendations of politicians are of great importance in promoting a work or author. Suppose the fact of political engagement of a work to the level of doctrine was unfounded and undeserved. In that case, a sharp surge will be followed by a return to the initial level of demand.

Scholar doctrine may evolve into other types, such as ideological and judicial doctrines. Moreover, scholar doctrine can influence a normative legal act or be included in the text thereof. In the latter case, the scholar doctrine remains in the text of the original source, and its new form is an official document.

A State ideological doctrine as an external expression is a declarative legal document issued, confirmed, or signed by an authorized agency of State power. The legal position of the Constitutional Court of the Russian Federation regarding State doctrine, which has not been revised since 1995, remains unchanged. The Constitutional Court pointed out that the military doctrine was not a normative legal act, and almost half of the respondents remain committed to this position. The legal community is committed to recognizing State doctrines as normative legal acts. In the event of a request to the Constitutional Court of the Russian Federation concerning a more recent State doctrine, the Constitutional Court of the Russian Federation may change its assessment.

Researcher interest in the State official document has increased. Public authorities increasingly are adopting documents that they call doctrines. The form of State doctrine is always in written form. Objects are personified by a number assigned by the issuing authority and the publication date. State doctrines are published like other official documents, such as decrees. They are amended, supplemented, and repealed by legal acts of public authorities. The design, style, and structure must correspond to the law-making technique applied to normative legal acts. In terms of style, they are general and do not contain rules of conduct. State doctrines do not have a direct regulatory impact on social relations. They consist of norms of an introductory nature, such as definitions, goals, objectives, principles, and foundations. State doctrines are declarative and imply the publication of normative legal acts on their basis. The term "doctrine", when applied to a given type of object, is an element of the name. This is not a particular type of normative legal act. The originality of this object in comparison with other Doctrines-Forms allows us to doubt that these legal acts are a legal doctrine. The main argument against is that it is a document of a public authority that gravitates towards normative legal acts. Normative legal acts are another form of law. They are not a doctrine.

Thus, if the State conveys to the legal community in an understandable way that State doctrines are normative legal acts, then the discussion will be completed. These documents will not be typified as legal doctrine. Given the uncertainty and the prerequisites created by the Constitutional Court of the Russian Federation, we conditionally classify legal acts with the word "doctrine" in the title as an ideological State doctrine. This is a Russian phenomenon. There are no American analogues.

Judicial Doctrine-Form is a generalization of acts of judicial power, legal provisions, legal positions, and decisions on fundamental cases. Judicial doctrine in the United States and Russia differs, as it is a continuation of the difference in types of legal system. However, their convergence is apparent. There are points of comparison between legal provisions and precedent (or decisions on fundamental cases).

There is a significant difference in the formation of doctrine, which in American judicial practice has footnotes to academic research and gravitates towards academic citation standards. Such design and the availability of methods for recording judicial doctrine in information databases make it possible to identify and record instances of the citation of research, textbooks, and other materials of academic origin.

The Russian approach to the system of sources and forms of law is based on the conflict between academic sources and judicial practice because academic works have been repeatedly banned from citation in judicial acts. However, we have identified an increased interest in academic publications on the part of the judiciary. Despite the ban, they combine academic doctrine and judicial practice with a subsequent transition to judicial doctrine.

An analysis of the procedural legislation of the Russian Federation for more than twenty years (2000 – 2025) has shown a progressive, growing movement towards legitimizing the judiciary as a law-making body. The Code of Civil Procedure and the Code of Arbitrazh Procedure recognize acts of collective generalization and individual law enforcement acts as a form of law. Because these phenomena are not recognized by normative legal acts, we can regard them as judicial doctrine. This is obviously the Doctrine-Form, which regulates social relations and is recognized by the judiciary as binding. In terms of origin, it is a judicial phenomenon. In terms of the presentation style and the nature of its occurrence, including generalization, interpretation, style of recommendation, and the method of influencing through authority, this is more of a doctrine than a normative legal act until otherwise established by the legislator.

A sociological survey revealed the readiness of the legal community to accept judicial doctrine as a form of law. The prerequisites for legitimizing judicial precedent have been created, and it is possible to finalize this process.

Ideological Doctrine-Form is an idea of the future State and law, which, under certain socio-political conditions, can be transformed into legislation. A feature of this type of legal doctrine is its politicization, which can be associated with the current State or developed outside it. The combination of ideological doctrine and the State is realized in the party State. The ideology of such a State is characterized by uniformity and the prohibition of alternatives and even other ideas. The prerequisites are created by the one-party system. The party documents have greater legal force than normative acts. This connection in the modern State is mainly realized in the relations of State doctrines and normative legal acts. The difference is seen in the fact that ideological documents are issued by party organs. In contrast, State doctrines are issued by State authorities. In the former Soviet Union, Party documents were systematized in the Code of Laws of the USSR and the RSFSR.

Historical forms of expression of ideological doctrine, such as programmatic right, wrong, and anti-law, are still preserved. Sociological studies show the latent effect of the norms of political parties.

Ideological doctrine is experiencing a stage of growth. Its status and relevance are increasing and can move into a phase of active management of normative legal acts of a particular State and international law. It is already evident that in the context of the global geopolitical crisis. Ideological doctrine is activated in the context of the crisis of traditional normative regulation. Expediency, ideas about one's own and others, replace legality.

Wrongness as a concept of future law is known in the history of jurisprudence, in legal acts of transitional periods, and in the practice of State-building. A peculiarity of the ideological doctrine of negation is that wrongness represents a future right, not a criticism or abolition of the existing one. It will become a right in the event of the victory of the corresponding ideological doctrine.

Anti-law negates existing legislation for various reasons which sound progressive and freedom-loving. Anti-law is the abolition of law without providing clear guidelines for future law. Accordingly, we have seen the triumph of anti-law over law.

A Party is not a competitor of anti-law. It is more inclined to be wrong. It advocates and presents effective future models in a generalized form (without specific norms and rules). Its essence is accurately expressed in "the right of pre-election promises". It exists in images of future achievements and political advertising of supposed achievements. For example, the government promises that rivers will flow in the opposite direction, a new person will build a different reality, and artificial intelligence will free people from self-development. These are somewhat extreme, but well-known ideas and images found in past and present programmatic law.

As a result of this study, trends in the correlation of types of legal doctrine are revealed. All types of legal doctrines studied have demonstrated continuing changes. Based on the analysis of sources from 1865, selected by random sampling and processed by textual analysis programs, proposals are made about the direction of movement of certain types of doctrines.

Throughout Russian legal history, judicial practice has not been officially recognized as a form of law. However, its role as a source of law remains. In the twenty-first century, significant changes have occurred, marking Russia's transition to recognizing case law. The Constitutional Court of the Russian Federation played a unique role in this process, substantiating and introducing such forms of legal activity as dissenting opinions of judges, the institution of friends of the court, legal provisions, legal positions, and others. The Court is authorized to give binding instructions to the law-making body to eliminate the unconstitutionality of normative legal acts. In fact, it participates in the formation of legal policy. Its decisions cannot be reversed by anyone but that Court. The rejection of the institution of amicus curae of the Constitutional Court and the ban on the publication of dissenting opinions are unlikely to significantly change the new position of judicial doctrine in the system of forms of law. However, there are other threats.

The threat to judicial doctrine lies in the catastrophic state of the personal composition of the Constitutional Court and the judiciary's apparent tendency to renew or reduce its doctrinality. Faceless judges, without doctoral degrees, proclaim the threat of the leading property of doctrine – authority. Obligation, supported by the coercive power of the State, cannot replace the power of authority as an organic property of doctrine.

Nevertheless, the system of courts of general jurisdiction and arbitrazh courts, merging and dividing, moves towards case law, which is evident in procedural legislation. Decisions in specific cases are expected to be recognized as binding for application in similar cases. However, authority as an attribute of doctrine in the judicial system is only declining. In this way, the State delegates the creation of de facto law to the judiciary, whose representatives are unsuited to this role. If we put the question of judicial doctrine in the abstract, we can see its merits. If we consider the personal composition of the representatives of this group, the judges, this is impossible. For the most part, they are non-authoritative people. Their law-enforcement competence to consider specific cases is based on the qualifications and skills of judges, but not legislators, much less researchers.

The unfortunate relationship between academic and judicial doctrines cannot be easily remedied. The authoritarian and voluntarist nature of judicial doctrine are not balanced by the validity and authority of academic research. Jurisprudence as academic research loses its innovative role; it remains commentary, interpretive. An aggressive ban on presenting academic doctrine in court as a form of law without the necessary legislation and gaps in normative legal acts does not create prerequisites for strengthening the role of scholar doctrine.

However, the academic style of formalization of court decisions in classical countries of case law may take place in the future in the Russian judicial system. This will require a complete change in approaches to legal education, replacing teaching staff with practicing lawyers, and changing the subjects of study in law faculties. Thus, theory and practice must come together to give judicial doctrine an external form that tends to be academic. Future judges will be taught to write analytical essays rather than specific decisions, as this is a necessary skill for doctrinal generalizations. Actual teaching by people without legal experience also discourages academic and judicial doctrinal collaboration.

Academic doctrine itself is undergoing critical changes. Quantitative indicators for assessing the effectiveness of academic activity, combined with continuous multifaceted reforms, have sabotaged the traditions of producing academic materials. Scholar doctrine is under unprecedented pressure from ideology and politics. Loyalty to changing political tasks deprives publications of their academic and innovative character. There is no truth, no good faith, and no freedom.

Creativity requires independence. In jurisprudence, an order for a specific result does not create conditions for fundamental research. Justification, an explanation of the correctness of decisions made, has become the main focus of academic simulations. They may give the impression of doctrines. They can be used in normative legal acts. However, this is not because the academic publications were included in a normative legal act, but because this academic result was ordered by politicians.

There is a tendency to increase the number of people with academic degrees; nonetheless, the number of people with academic degrees is decreasing. New people without academic degrees, who have experience in practical jurisprudence and teaching but no pedagogical education, come to the profession of teaching. These individuals, ready to carry a large teaching load for low wages, have blurred the standard of the faculty, which was previously high and elitist. The innovative, bold, rebellious academic doctrine has no prerequisites. The new cadres are anti-academic and write articles like student essays.

Strengthening the position of case law requires a powerful justification of decisions by scholar doctrine. Perhaps this will lead to the judicial citation of academic doctrine.

But there is a pronounced tendency to strengthen State doctrine. It is a doctrine without an academic basis. It is not the result of the work of the professional community of lawyers. These are legal acts of a general nature. Nevertheless, they are in great demand in political circles because they are presented as abstractly as possible and consist of vague formulations that are easy to arbitrarily interpret when changing everyday tasks.

Ideological doctrine will be strengthened. Perhaps it will take the leading place among all kinds of doctrines. The concept of a legal system in connection with the doctrine of forms (sources) of law has practically exhausted itself. The typology of legal systems is blurred. Halftones, half-systems, and other diffusions have blurred this notion. It has ceased to be a characteristic of the country. States boldly confuse elements of different legal systems without regard to the theory of the issue. Nevertheless, the doctrine of the sources and forms of law continues to be a significant element of the subjective worldview (professional legal consciousness) and State policy.

The fact that the State deliberately withdraws from issuing its precise position on its own forms of law as a normative legal act does not preclude the resolution of this issue without State participation. The situation could be managed if the State explicitly legalized or sanctioned forms of law, such as precedent and doctrine. But in the absence of such a solution, their power only increases.

By filling in the gaps, eliminating contradictions, and explaining other forms of law, doctrine becomes a performance of law. We have called this object Doctrine-Form. Traditional law-making techniques cannot replace, change, or abolish it. In addition to the written form, legal doctrine is preserved and transmitted orally. It exists as an element of legal culture. Lawyers impress the court when they mention a particular author's name or book in their documents. It is a fitting occasion to recall Lassalle's lecture on the essence of the Constitution. The transfer of his idea to the realm of legal doctrine presents the following picture. If, without the full name of the author of a particular book, we do something in a certain way, it has no alternative for us. It is inevitable and absolutely true, so we are impersonally using the legal doctrine without personification. The present legal doctrine manifests itself as a law that exists everywhere.

Legal doctrine is always a source of law. Under certain circumstances, it becomes a form of law. But the attribution of this phenomenon to a source of law or a form of law largely depends on the type of legal system. This was confirmed and clarified during sociological surveys and content analysis. We recognize the organic unity of the terms "source of law" and "form of law", and we divide them according to the degree of influence on social relations, especially law enforcement. If rules are authoritative instructive information, they are a law source. If a rule is binding, its application is axiomatic, inevitable, and coercive. It is a form of law.

The form of law is always a source of law since the data about the law are drawn from it. The source of law may or may not be a form of law. Their relationship can be depicted as ideal and as accurate. Ideal, that is, desirable, is the existence of a source of law, not a form of law, and a source of law, a form of law. Thus, the ideal model does not presuppose the existence of a form of law with no sources. However, in real life, such a phenomenon definitely exists. A form of law without sources is a territory of arbitrariness, voluntarism of State power, which publishes its documents without relying on sources of law. It is precisely such voluntaristic decisions without roots in the sources of law that create the prerequisites for the discussion that this is legislation, not law.

Scholar doctrine is formed and manifested entirely differently in the Romano-Germanic and Anglo-American legal systems. In Russia, scholar doctrine is not a form of law and is not referred to in any other type of doctrine. Nonetheless, jurisprudence belongs to legal scholarship. In the Anglo-American legal system, jurisprudence is a secondary source of law. However, jurisprudence is not legal doctrinal scholarship.

In Anglo-American countries, the doctrine of research academic origin is clearly stated using citations in court documents. The citation system separately counts citations in other studies and in courts. In the footnotes of the court cases, the author and the title of the publications are indicated. The text may contain quotations or an analysis (judicial interpretation) of the idea of the work. In this form, research and judicial doctrines are combined. The second is a form of the first. In the form of a court decision, the publication receives confirmation of its applicability in natural legal relations. At the same time, court decisions may be based on earlier decisions. Initially, references to specific earlier decisions are retained. This means that the correctness of the legal doctrine has been repeatedly emphasized.

Doctrine is formed by abstraction from specific life circumstances. It is generalized and presented as general formulas adopted for an incalculable number of cases. This generalization is the result of abstraction as a method of academic research. Not all doctrines have an academic origin. Despite this, all doctrines formed by abstraction are quite similar. It can be argued that their validity depends on the correctness of the process of abstraction.

A typification is a form of abstraction, the next stage of intellectual activity. The result of abstraction may not be typical. Typing is working with many uniform units. A repetitive nucleus is distinguished in them, which can be called typical. The uniqueness in each unit is discarded since it is not needed for unification and typification. If the commonality is preserved when the unique is discarded, this indicates a typified object.

Typification is an organic method of doctrine formation. However, there is falsification of typing. For example, an insignificant derivative is elevated to the rank of typical. Such typing would be erroneous. Ideological doctrine differs from other types of legal doctrine in that it is most susceptible to misuse in typification. It is created with the participation (by order) of authoritative actors. They are not interested in a reliable typing path but in the presence of a result programmed by the customer. Source data objects for typing are not collected from the actual population. They are selected following the task at hand. The essence of ideology is its impact on the future – to achieve a particular result, as well as to manage today's actions, but also to achieve results in the future. Ideological constructions differ significantly from legal ones because they are not based on law. They create the prerequisites for future law. Wrong and anti-right are probable forms of ideological doctrine.

Scholar doctrine is not accessible in non-democratic States. It does not set tasks for itself, solve, or provide the achieved result. In totalitarian States, the topics for academic research come from the State, and the results must conform to State guidelines. Censorship filters access to the publication of academic results that are disloyal to the authorities. Only academic freedom and active and independent research activity can create the groundwork for forming a doctrine by legal scholars.

Bibliography

Abgomenou, M. M., Концепция права развития в доктрине международного права [The Concept of Development Law in the Doctrine of International Law] (Kiev, 1990) (dissertation candidate of legal sciences).

Alekseev, S. S., *Механизм правового регулирования в социалистическом государстве [The Mechanism of Legal Regulation in a Socialist State]* (M., Legal literature, 1966).

___. *Общая теория права [General Theory of Law]* (M., 1981).

Alekseeva, L. A., and Kasakov, A. B., "К вопросу о роли правовой доктрины в правоприменительной деятельности [On the Issue of the Role of Legal Doctrine in Law Enforcement Activities]", *Международный журнал конституционного и государственного права [International Journal of Constitutional and State Law]*, no. 1 (2019), pp. 48-51.

Alpa, G., "General Principles of Law", *Comparative Law*, no. 1 (1994), pp. 1-39.

Althusser, L., *Lenin and Philosophy, and Other Essays* (New York: Monthly Review Press, 1972).

Aminov, I. I., Gorokhova, V. V., and Eriashvili, N. D., *Эстетическая культура и эстетическое воспитание сотрудников правоохранительных органов [Aesthetic Culture and Aesthetic Education of Law Enforcement Officers]* (M., ЮНИТИ-ДАНА [UNITY-DANA], 2022).

Averianov, L. Ia., *Контент-анализ [Content Analysis]* (2007) (available online).

Barack, A., *Судейское усмотрение [Judge's Discretion]* (M.: Norma, 1999).

Barrick, R., "The Ministerial Exception: Seeking Clarity and Precision Amid Inconsistent Application of the Hosanna-Tabor Framework", *Emory Law Journal*, LXX, no. 2 (2020), pp. 465-519.

Baturina, S. A., "Правовая доктрина как элемент российской правовой системы [Legal Doctrine as an Element of the Russian Legal System]." *Юристъ - Правоведъ [Yurist - Pravoved]*, no. 4 (2008), pp. 31-35.

Baude, W., and Sachs S. E., "The Law of Interpretation." *Harvard Law Review*, CXXX, no. 4 (2017), pp. 1079-1147.

Bell, J., "Sources of Law." *The Cambridge Law Journal*, no. 1 (2018), pp. 40-71.

Belozerov, V. K., "Доктрины и идеологии в системе политических институтов [Doctrines and Ideologies in the System of Political Institutions]." *Вестник Московского государственного лингвистического университета [Bulletin of Moscow State Linguistic University]*, no. 24 (684) (2013), pp. 31-40.

Berliavsky, L.G. "Свобода научного творчества в международном и национальном праве [Freedom of Scientific Creativity in International and National Law]." Взаимодействие международного и российского гуманитарного права в сфере конституционной защиты личности [Interaction of international and Russian humanitarian law in the sphere of constitutional protection of the individual] (Rostov-on-Don: Северо-Кавказская академия государственной службы [North-Caucasian Academy of Public Administration], 2006), pp. 93-97.

Blackstone, W., *Commentaries on the Law of England*: In Four Books. Edited by R. Burn and J. Williams. 11th edition. Dublin: Printed for L. White, William Jones, and John Rice (1794).

Bogdanovskaya, I. Y., *Прецедентное право [Case Law]* (M.: НОРМА ИНФРА-М [NORMA: INFRA-M], 2020).

Bondar, N. S., "Единство теории и практики одинаково важно как для маститых профессионалов, так и для студентов юридических вузов [The Unity of Theory and Practice is Equally Important for Both Venerable Professionals and Students of Law Schools]." *Судья [Judge]*, no. 12 (144) (2022), pp. 4-9.

Borishpolets, K. P., *Методы политических исследований [Methods of Political Research]* (М.: Аспект Пресс [Aspect Press], 2005).

Boshno, S. V. Законодательная инициатива в Государственной Думе Федерального Собрания [Legislative initiative in the State Duma of the Federal Assembly of the Russian Federation] (M., Russian Presidential Academy of Public Administration, 1997) (dissertation candidate of legal sciences).

Boshno, S. V., "Codification." *Право и современные государства [Law and Modern States]*, no. 2 (2014). pp. 44-51.

———. "Доктрина как форма и источник права [Doctrine as a Form and Source of Law]." *Журнал российского права [Journal of Russian Law]*, no. 12 (84) (2003), pp. 70-79.

———. "Доктринальные и другие нетрадиционные формы права [Doctrinal and Other Non-Traditional Forms of Law]." *Журнал российского права [Journal of Russian Law]*, no. 1 (73) (2003), pp. 82-89.

———. "Доктринальные формы и источники права [Doctrinal Forms and Sources of Law]." *Государство и право [State and Law]*, no. 9 (2018), pp. 5-15.

———. "Закон о нормативных правовых актах: прошлое, настоящее и перспективы [Law on Regulatory Legal Acts: Past, Present and Prospects]." *Право и современные государства [Law and Modern States]*, no. 2 (2015), pp. 7-22.

———. "Кодификационные акты и другие источники права: проблемы приоритета [Codification Acts and other Sources of Law: Priority Issues]", in: Международная научно-практическая конференция "Кодификация законодательства: теория, практика, техника" [International Scientific and Practical Conference "Codification of Legislation: Theory, Practice, Technique"] (Nizhnyi Novgorod, 2008), pp. 120-142.

———. "Место писем в системе нормативного регулирования [The Place of Letters in the Regulatory System]." *Ваш налоговый адвокат. Консультации, рекомендации [Your Tax Attorney. Consultations, Recommendations]*, no. 7 (2008), pp. 8-16.

———. "Понятие правовой доктрины [Concept of Legal Doctrine]." *Право и современные государства [Law and Modern States]*, no. 2-3 (2022), pp. 35-45.

———. "Прецедент, закон и доктрина (Опыт социолого-юридического исследования) [Precedent, Law, and Doctrine (Experience of Sociological and Legal Research)]." *Государство и право [State and Law]*, no. 4 (2007), pp. 72-78.

———. "Санкционирование обычаев государством: содержание и классификация [State Sanctioning of Customs: Content and Classification]." *Юрист [Jurist]*, no. 3 (2004), pp. 11-14.

———. "Судебная практика: способы выражения [Judicial Practice: Modes of Expression]." *Государство и право [State and Law]*, no. 3 (2003), pp. 19-29.

———. *Теория государства и права [Theory of State and Law]* (M., 2003).

———. Форма права: теоретико-правовое исследование [Form of Law: Theoretical-legal Research] (M., 2005) (dissertation doctor of legal sciences).

———. "Формы выражения судебной практики [Forms of Expression of Judicial Practice]." *Юриспруденция [Jurisprudence]*, no. 1 (2002), pp. 14-33.

Boshno, S. V., and Vasyuta G. G., "Доктринальные источники служебного права [Doctrinal Sources of Service Law]". *Государственная служба [Civil Service]*, no. 2 (2010), pp. 44-47.

Bracton, H. de., *On the Laws and Customs of England.* Ed. by G. E. Woodbine and S. E. Thorne. (Cambridge, 1968).

Budd, Richard W., and Robert K. Thorp., *An Introduction to Content Analysis: Including Annotated Bibliography*. (Iowa City: University of Iowa School of Journalism, 1963).

Bulmer, M., ed. *Sociological Research Methods*. 2nd ed. (New York: Routledge, 2017).

Butler, W. E, ed. *International Law and the International System*. (Dordrecht; Boston: M. Nijhoff, 1987).

Butler, W. E., ed. *Justice and Comparative Law: Anglo-Soviet Perspectives on Criminal Law, Evidence, Procedure, and Sentencing Policy*. (Dordrecht/Boston/Lancaster: M. Nijhoff, 1987).

———. *Russian Law*. 3rd ed. (Oxford: New York: Oxford University Press, 2009).

———. *Russian Law and Legal Institutions*. Third edition. (Clark, New Jersey: Talbot Publishing, 2021).

Butler, W. E, ed. *Russian Legal Theory. The International Library of Essays in Law and Legal Theory*, 11. (New York: New York University Press, Reference Collection, 1996).

Butusova, N. V., "Государственная идеология России: понятие, содержание, проблемы формирования и правового закрепления [State Ideology of Russia: Concept, Content, Problems of Formation and Legal Consolidation]." *Вестник Воронежского Государственного Университета. Серия: Право [Herald of Voronezh State University. Series: Law]*, no. 1 (2006), pp. 4-19.

Cairns, H., *The Theory of Legal Science*. (Chapel Hill: The University of North Carolina Press, 1941).

Carty, A., *Philosophy of International Law*. 2d ed. (Edinburgh: Edinburgh University Press, 2017).

Chashin, A. N., Правовая доктрина как источник (форма российского права [Legal Doctrine as a Source (Form) of Russian Law]. (M.: INFRA-M, 2022).

———. "Судебная доктрина как источник (форма) Права [Judicial Doctrine as a Source (Form) of Law]." *Европейская двокатура [Eurasian Advocacy]*, no. 5 (24) (2016), pp. 70-75.

Chibizov, V. V., Правоприменительное усмотрение и его роль в преодолении юридических коллизий [Law

Enforcement Discretion and Its Role in Overcoming Legal Conflicts]. (Grozny, 2020) (dissertation candidate of legal sciences).

Chirkin, V. E., *Сравнительное правоведение [Comparative Law].* (M.: NORMA: INFRA-M, 2021).

Coan, A., "Amending the Law of Constitutional Interpretation." *Duke Journal of Constitutional Law & Public Policy* XIII (2018), pp. 83-102.

Coke, E., *The First Part of the Institutes of the Laws of England.* Reprint of the 1823 edition. Vol. 2. (Union, N.J: The Lawbook Exchange, Ltd., 1999).

David, R., and Zhoffre-Spinozi K., *Основные правовые системы современности [The Main Legal Systems of our Time.* (M.: Международные отношения [International relations], 2019).

Devlin, A., *Fundamental Principles of Law and Economics.* (Milton Park, Abingdon, Oxon [UK]; New York, NY: Routledge, 2015).

Dmitriev, A. I., and Butler W. E., *История международного права [History of International Law].* 2d ed. (Odessa: Phoenix, 2013).

Dobrenkov, V. I., and Kravchenko A. I., *Методология и методика социологического исследования [Methodology and Methodology of Sociological Rsearch].* (M.: Академический проект; Альма Матер [Academic Project; Alma Mater], 2009).

Duarte d'Almeida, L., Gardner, J., and Green, L., eds. *Kelsen Revisited: New Essays on the Pure Theory of Law.* (Oxford; Portland, Oregon: Hart Publishing, 2013).

Duncan, W. C., "Colorado Religious School Asks Supreme Court to Take Case on Ministerial Exception." Sutherland Institute (blog), March 16, 2023. (available online).

Durkheim, E., Solovay, S. A., Mueller J. H., and Catlin G. E. G., *The Rules of Sociological Method.* 8th ed. Book, Whole. (New York; Glenco, Ill; Free Press of Glencoe, 1938).

Dvorkin, R. A., *Matter of Principle.* (Harvard University Press. Cambridge, MA, 1985).

Ermykin, V., "Сальников В.П. великий комбинатор и взяточник [Salnikov V.P. Great Schemer and Bribe Taker]." (available online).

Erugina, M. B., Krom, I. L., and Shmerkevich, A. B., "Контент-анализ правовых актов и определение направлений оптимизации паллиативной помощи в современной России [Content Analysis of Legal Acts and Identification of Ways to Optimize Palliative Care in Modern Russia]." *Саратовский научно-медицинский журнал [Saratov Scientific and Medical Journal]*, no. 4 (2015), pp. 506-510.

Fomicheva, O. A., "Экспертиза как форма законотворческой деятельности специалистов в реализации законодательного процесса [Expertise as a Form of Legislative Activity of Specialists in the Implementation of the Legislative Process]" *Российское право: образование, практика, наука [Russian Law: Education, Practice, Science]*, no. 5 (2019), pp. 49-55.

Franzosi, R., ed. *Content Analysis. Sage Benchmarks in Social Research Methods*. (London; Thousand, Oaks, Calif: SAGE Publications, 2008).

Fuller, L. L., *The Morality of Law*. (New Haven: Yale University Press, 1977).

Gadzhiev, G.A. *Онтология права: (критическое исследование юридического концепта действительности) [The Ontology of Law: (a Critical Study of the Legal Concept of Reality)]*. (M.: NORMA: INFRA-M, 2020).

Gambarov, Iu. S., *Курс гражданского права [Course of Civil Law]*. Vol. General Part. 1 vols. (Saint-Petersburg, 1911).

Geller, A., D. Kaplan, and H.D. Lasswell. *The Differential Use of Flexible and Rigid Procedures of Content Analysis.* Library of Congress. Experimental Division for the Study of War Time Communications, Document no. 12. (Washington, 1943).

Gilmullin, A. R., *Правовая доктрина в механизме Российского государства (теория и практика) [Legal Doctrine in the Mechanism of the Russian State (Theory and Practice)]*. Научная мысль [Scientific Thought]. (M.: INFRA-M, 2019).

Glanville, R. de., *The Treatise on the Laws and Customs of the Realm of England Commonly Called Glanvill.* Edited by G. D. G. Hall. (Holmes Beach, Fla., U.S.A: W.W. Gaunt, 1983).

Golovnya, A.I., "Военная доктрина и стратегия национальной безопасности России: контент-анализ с политико-правовых позиций [Military Doctrine and National Security Strategy of Russia: Content Analysis from Political and Legal Positions]." *Право и политика [Law and Politics]*, no. 6 (2011), pp. 944-953.

Google Cloud. "Cloud Natural Language." (available online).

Goriushina, IU. V., and Trofimov V. V., "Регламенты законодательных собраний как документально-фиксированное выражение функциональных направлений современной законотворческой деятельности: начальный исследовательский опыт контент-анализа (на примере Регламента Тамбовской областной Думы) [Regulations of Legislative Assemblies as a Documented Expression of the Functional Directions of Modern Legislative Activity: the Initial Research Experience of Content Analysis (on the Example of the Regulations of the Tambov Regional Duma)]" *Правовая культура [Legal Culture]*, no. 1 (44), (2021), pp. 37-45.

Gotschall, S., and American Association of Law Libraries. *Government Documents SIS. A Survey of Arizona State Legal and Law-Related Documents*. (Chicago, Illinois: Government Documents Special Interest Section, American Association of Law Library, 2021).

Granat, N. L., "Источники права [Sources of Law]." *Юрист [Jurist]*, no. 9 (1998), pp. 6-12.

Green, L., "Positivism and the Inseparability of Law and Morals Symposium: The Hart-Fuller Debate at Fifty." *New York University Law Review*, no. 4 (2008), pp. 1035-1058.

Greenberg, M., What Makes a Method of Legal Interpretation Correct? Legal Standards vs. Fundamental Determinants. (Rochester, NY: Social Science Research Network, January 30, 2017).

Grimm, D. D., *К вопросу о понятии и источнике обязательности юридических норм [On the Question of the Concept and Source of Binding Legal Norms].* (Санкт-Петербург [Saint-Petersburg], 1896).

Gusarova, M. E., and Makarov K. V., "Система компьютерного контент-анализа исторических документов [The System of Computer Content Analysis of Historical Documents]." *Алгоритмы, методы и системы обработки данных [Algorithms, Methods and Data Processing Systems]*, no. 1 (19) (2012), pp. 23-32.

Halstead, T. J., and Library of Congress, eds. *The Separation of Powers Doctrine: Rationale, Applications and Bibliography.* (Hauppauge, NY: Nova Science, 2002).

Hardee, M. D., ed. *Content Analysis as a Research Tool for Higher Education.* (Tallahassee: Dept. of Higher Education, Florida State University, 1972).

Hart, H. L. A., "Positivism and the Separation of Law and Morals." *Harvard Law Review* LXXI, no. 4 (1957), pp. 593-629.

Henszey, B. N., and Benjamin N. Henszey, eds. *Introduction to Basic Legal Principles.* 5th ed. (Dubuque, Iowa: Kendall/Hunt Pub. Co, 1991).

Hosanna-Tabor Evangelical Lutheran Church and School v. EEOC, 565 U.S. 171 (2012) (N.J. Supreme Court 2012).

Ilyukhina, A. V., "Доктринальные принципы права: понятие и специфика [Doctrinal Principles of Law: Concept and Specifics]". *Актуальные проблемы государства и права [Current Problems of State and Law]*, no. 17 (2021), pp. 9-21.

Ivanova, Yu. A., Eriashvili N. D., and Groshev I. V., *Актуальные проблемы современного экологического права [Actual Problems of Modern Environmental Law].* (М.: ЮНИТИ-ДАНА [UNITY-DANA], 2022).

Karapetian, S. A., Источники конституционного права Российской Федерации [Sources of the Constitutional Law of the Russian Federation]. (Rostov-on-Don, 1998) (dissertation candidate of legal sciences).

Katashinsky, V. S., *Методы сбора социальной информации [Methods for Collecting Social Information].* (Ekaterinburg, 2017).

Kerimov, D. A., Источники Советского Социалистического Права [Sources of Soviet Socialist Law]. (Leningrad, 1950) (dissertation candidate of legal sciences).

Khabrieva, T. Ia., "Доктринальное значение российской Конституции [The Doctrinal Significance of the Russian Constitution]." *Журнал российского права [Journal of Russian Law]* CXLVI, no. 2 (146) (2009), pp. 34-38.

Khvostov, V. M., *Общая теория права: элементарный очерк [General Theory of Law: An Elementary Essay].* 6th ed., (Correction and Addition). (M.: тип. Вильде [Vilde Printing House], 1914).

Klishas, A. A. Конституционный контроль и конституционное правосудие в зарубежных странах [Constitutional Control and Constitutional Justice in Foreign Countries]. (M., 2007) (abstract of dissertation candidate of legal sciences).

Koreshkova, T., Семантический анализ для автоматической обработки естественного языка [Semantic Analysis is an Important Subtask of Natural Language Processing], (2021).

Korkunov, N. M., *Лекции по общей теории права [Lectures on the General Theory of Law].* 3d ed. (M.: Н.К. Мартынов [N.K. Martynov], 1894).

Korzun, V., С Богом в космос [With God into Space]. (available online).

Krasheninnikov, P. B., Badulina E., Ovcharova I. A., and Абрамушкина N. A., eds. *Законотворческая история современного Гражданского кодекса [Legislative History of the Modern Civil Code].* (M.: Статут [Statute], 2019).

Kuznetsova, E. I., and Eriashvili N. D. "Противодействие санкционным угрозам экономической безопасности России [Countering Sanctions Threats to Russia's Economic Security]." *Образование. Наука. Научные кадры [Education. Science. Scientific Staff],* no. 1 (2023).

Kvanina, V. V., "Понятие и признаки научной школы [Concept and Characteristics of an Academic School]." *Вестник университета имени О. Е. Кутафина [Bulletin of the University Named after O. E. Kutafin]*, no. 11 (27) (2016), pp. 37-42.

Lafitskiy, V. I., and Boshno S. V., "Беседа Президента Клуба Правовой Доктрины С. В. Бошно с профессором В. И. Лафитским [Conversation by the President of the Legal Doctrine Club S. V. Boshno with Professor V. I. Lafitskiy]." *Право и современные государства [Law and Modern States]*, no. 6 (2022), pp. 9-23.

Laperriere, M.-N., "What Is Civil Law Doctrine: A Feminist Deconstruction of Discourses Surrounding the Legal Capacity of Married Women." *Revue de Droit de l'Universite de Sherbrooke* XLVI (2017), pp. 365-430.

Lassalle, F., *О сущности конституции [On the Essence of the Constitution]*. Translated by K. Chekerul-Kusha. (Kyiv: Типография Петра Барского [Petro Barsky Printing House], 1905)

Lasswell, H. D., and Rogow A. A., eds. *Politics, Personality, and Social Science in the Twentieth Century: Essays in Honor of Harold D. Lasswell*. (Chicago: University of Chicago Press, 1969).

Lasswell, H. D., and Leites N., *Language of Politics: Studies in Quantitative Semantics*. G. W. (Stewart, 1949).

"Law Review: A Discussion of Legal Principles Suggested by Recent Decisions." *Law Review Board of Albany Law School*, no. 4 (1933), w./p.

Lenin, V. I., "Три источника и три составные части марксизма [Three Sources and Three Component Parts of Marxism]." *Просвещение [Enlightenment]*, no. 3 (1913).

Lenta.RU. "Путин закончил "Георгиевскую речь" цитатой русского философа Ильина [Putin Ended the 'St. George's Speech' with a Quote from the Russian Philosopher Ilyin]." (available online).

Littleton, T., *Treatise of Tenures*. (London: S. Sweet, Chancery Lana, Fleet Street, 1841).

Luzan, V. S., "Контент-анализ основных нормативных правовых документов, обеспечивающих реализацию государственной культурной политики (федеральный и региональный аспекты) [Content-Analysis of the Basic Normative Legal Documents, Providing Realization of the State Cultural Policy (Federal and Regional Aspects)]." *Журнал Сибирского Федерального Университета [Journal of Siberian Federal University. Humanities & Social Sciences]*, no. 4 (2011), pp. 342-362.

———. Социально-философский анализ динамики государственной культурной политики Российской Федерации [Socio-philosophical Analysis of the Dynamics of the State Cultural Policy of the Russian Federation]. (Krasnoyarsk, 2011) (dissertation candidate of legal sciences).

Madaev, E. O., Доктрина в правовой системе Российской Федерации [Doctrine in the Legal System of the Russian Federation]. (M., 2012) (dissertation candidate of legal sciences).

———. "Место и роль правовой доктрины в правовой системе Российской Федерации [Place and Role of Legal Doctrine in the Legal System of the Russian Federation]." *Вестник Бурятского Государственного Университета. Педагогика. Филология. Философия. [Vestnik Buryatskogo Gosudarstvennogo Universiteta. Pedagogy. Philology. Philosophy]*, no. 2 (2015), pp. 193-197.

Magaziner, Ia. M., *Лекции по государственному праву: (Общее государственное право) [Lectures on State Law: (General State Law)]*. (Petrograd: Кооперация [Cooperation], 1919).

Malko, A. V., and Gaivoronskaya Ya. V., "Доктринальные акты как основной инструмент правовой политики [Doctrinal Acts as the Main Instrument of Legal Policy]." *Право. Журнал Высшей школы экономики [Law. Journal of the Higher School of Economics]*, no. 1 (2018), pp. 4-25.

Malko, A. V., and Lipinsky D. A., eds. *Юридическая ответственность. Доктринальный словарь [Legal Liability. Doctrinal Dictionary]*. (M.: Проспект [Prospekt], 2019).

Marchenko, M. N., *Курс сравнительного правоведения [Course of Comparative Law]*. (M.: Городец [Gorodets], 2002).

———. *Сравнительное правоведение [Comparative Law]*. Ed. 2. (M.: Проспект [Prospekt], 2013).

Matasar, N. R. A., "Treatise Writing and Federal Jurisdiction Scholarship: Does Doctrine Matter When Law Is Politics?" *Michigan Law Review*, no. 6 (89) (1991), pp. 1499-1519.

Matsko, S. V., Государственная идеология и право современной России: теоретико-правовое исследование [State Ideology and Law of Modern Russia: Theoretical and Legal Research]. (Ufa, 2003) (dissertation candidate of legal sciences).

Mazurenko, M. L., Судебные речи российских адвокатов по уголовным делам и их правовые публикации как феномен общественного правосознания и юридической мысли в пореформенной России: 2-я пол. XIX - нач. XX вв. [Judicial Speeches of Russian Criminal Lawyers and Their Legal Publications as a Phenomenon of Public Legal Consciousness and Legal Thought in Post-Reform Russia: the 2nd half of the 19th - the Beginning of the 20th Centuries]. (Krasnodar, 2012) (abstract of dissertation candidate of legal sciences).

Mostecky, V., and W. E Butler, eds. *Soviet Legal Bibliography*: A Classified and Annotated Listing of Books and Serials Published in the Soviet Union since 1917 as Represented in the Collection of the Harvard Law School Library as of January 1, 1965. (Cambridge, 1965).

Muromtsev, S. A., *Статьи и речи: вып. 1-5 [Articles and Speeches*: V. 1-5]. Vol. Speeches Delivered at the First Congress of Russian Lawyers and the Moscow Law Society (1875 – 1910). 2 vols. (M., 1910).

Nashitz, A., and Fyodor N., "Роль судебной практики в формировании и совершенствовании норм социалистического права [The Role of Judicial Practice in the Formation and Improvement of the Norms of Socialist Law. State and Law]." *Советское государство и право [Soviet State and Law]*, no. 5 (1965).

North, R. C., *Content Analysis: A Handbook with Applications for the Study of International Crisis. Book, Whole.* (Evanston: Northwestern University Press, 1963).

Ohlin, J. D., *International Law: Evolving Doctrine and Practice. University Casebook Series.* (St, Paul, MN: Foundation Press, 2018).

Osipov, M. Ju., "О роли юридической науки в развитии российского права [On the role of Legal Science in the Development of Russian Law]." In Conference materials: in 4 parts (M.: Проспект [Prospekt], 2016), pp. 88-92.

Ovchinnikov, A. I., Dalgatova A. O., and Fathi V. I., "Правовая доктрина как источник права в Российской Федерации [Legal doctrine as a source of law in the Russian Federation]." *Философия права [Philosophy of Law]*, no. 2 (75) (2016), pp. 59-64.

Paddock, LeR., Glicksman R. L., and Bryner N. S., eds. *Decision Making in Environmental Law. Elgar Encyclopedia of Environmental Law*, II. (Cheltenham, UK; Northampton, MA, USA: Edward Elgar Publishing, 2016).

Parsons, F., *Legal Doctrine and Social Progress*. (Littleton, Colo: F.B. Rothman, 1982).

Pashinyan, I. A., "Контент-анализ как метод исследования: достоинства и ограничения [Content-analysis as a Research Method: Advantages and Limitations]." *Научная периодика: проблемы и решения [Scientific Periodicals: Problems and Solutions]*, no. 3 (9) (2012), pp. 13-16.

Peters, C. J., ed. *Precedent in the United States Supreme Court. Vol. XXXIII. Ius Gentium.* (Dordrecht: Springer, 2013).

Petrazhitskiy, L. I., *Теория права и государства в связи с теорией нравственности [The Theory of Law and the State in Connection with the Theory of Morality].* Vol. 1. 2 vols (Saint-Petersburg, 1907).

———. *Теория права и государства в связи с теорией нравственности [The Theory of Law and the State in Connection with the Theory of Morality].* (Vol. 2. 2 vols. Saint-Petersburg, 1907).

Phillipps, C. S. M., *Jurisprudence. Electronic resource.* (London: J. Murray, 1863).

Pinello, D. R., "Linking Party to Judicial Ideology in American Courts: A Meta-Analysis" *The Justice System Journal,* no. 3 (20) (1999), pp. 219-254.

Piszko, R., "Role of Custom in the Formation of the Directives of Law Interpretation." *Juridical Science,* no. 6 (2013), pp. 12-20.

Polyanskiy, D. A., and Puzikov R. V., "Правовая доктрина как особое правовое явление [Legal Doctrine as a Special Legal Phenomenon]." *Вестник Тамбовского университета. Серия: Гуманитарные науки [Herald of Tambov University. Series: Humanities]* CXXVII, no. 11 (127) (2013), pp. 1-10.

Ponkin, I. V., and Lapteva A. I., *Методология научных исследований и прикладной аналитики [Methodology of scientific research and applied analytics].* 2 ed. (M.: Буки Веди [Byki-Vedi], 2021).

Pool, I. de S., ed. *Trends in Content Analysis: Papers.* (Urbana: University of Illinois Press, 1959).

Porter, C., *Automated Content Analysis and the Development and Utilization of Legal Doctrine in the Federal Courts.* (Urbana: University of Alabama Libraries, 2018) (dissertation candidate of Political Science).

Pound, R., "Fundamental Law in the Society of Today." *Tennessee Law Review* XIII, no. 1 (1934), pp. 1-13.

———. "Hierarchy of Sources and Forms in Different Systems of Law." *Tulane Law Review* VII (1933), pp. 475-487.

———. *Jurisprudence.* (St. Paul: West Pub. Co, 1959).

———. "Sources and Forms of Law." *Notre Dame Law Review* CCXLVII (1946), pp. 247-314.

———. "The Economic Interpretation and the Law of Torts." *Harvard Law Review* LIII (1940), pp. 365–85.

Provalis Research. "Text Analysis & Mining Software | Easy to Use Content Analysis | Wordstat." (available online).

Puchta, G. F., *Энциклопедия права Г.Ф. Пухты [Encyclopedia of Law by G. F. Puchta]*. Translated by P. Karasevich. 6 ed. (Yaroslavl: Типография Г.Фальк [Printing house G. Falk], 1872).

Puzikov, R. V., Юридическая доктрина в сфере правового регулирования: проблемы теории и практики [Legal Doctrine in the Sphere of Legal Regulation: Problems of Theory and Practice]. (Nizhny Novgorod, 2003) (abstract of dissertation candidate of legal sciences).

Rastorguev, S. V., "Применение метода контент-анализа к экономическим, социологическим и политологическим исследованиям [Application of the Method of Content Analysis to Economic, Sociological and Political Research]." *Вестник Финансового университета [Bulletin of the Financial University]*, no. 6 (66) (2011), pp. 76-80.

Razumovich, N. N., "Источники и форма права [Sources and Form of Law]." *Советское государство и право [Soviet State and Law]*, no. 3 (1988).

Regelsberger, F., *Общее учение о праве [General Doctrine of Law]*. Edited by Iu. S. Gambarov, A. S. Belkin, and P. G. Vinogradov. Translated by I. A. Bazanova. Library for Self-education, XIV. (M., 1897).

"Research at DeepPavlov." (available online).

Reutov, V. P., Юридическая практика и развитие законодательства [Legal Practice and Development of Legislation]. (Sverdlovsk, 1968) (dissertation candidate of legal sciences).

Roberts, D. LaVon., The Representation of Law Student Information Literacy Definitions in Legal Research Textbooks:

A Comparative Content Analysis. (ProQuest Dissertations Publishing, 2012).

Rostova, M. V., Конституционно-правовое регулирование свободы преподавания и научного творчества [Constitutional and Legal Regulation of the Freedom of Teaching and Scientific Creativity]. (Orel, 2018) (abstract of dissertation candidate of legal sciences).

Sachs, S. E., "The Law and Morals of Interpretation." *Duke Journal of Constitutional Law & Public Policy* XIII, no. 2 (2018), pp. 103-14.

Saidov, A. Kh., *Сравнительное правоведение [Comparative Law].* (Tashkent: Адолат [Adolat], 1999).

———. *Сравнительное правоведение [Comparative Law].* (Moscow: НОРМА ИНФРА-М [NORMA: INFRA-M], 2020).

Salmond, John W., *Jurisprudence*. Electronic resource. 4th ed. (London: Stevens and Haynes, 1913).

Samorodova, N. N., "Контент-анализ посланий В.В.Путина Федеральному Собранию РФ (2000-2014 гг.) [Content-analysis of V.V.Putin's Address to the Federal Assembly of the Russian Federation (20-0–2014)]." *Современные политические процессы [Modern Political Processes]*, no. 2 (15) (2015), pp. 7-13.

Schlag, P., and Griffin A. J., *How to Do Things with Legal Doctrine.* (Chicago; London: The University of Chicago Press, 2020).

Schrage, Eltjo J. H., "Sources of law, the comparative legal history of a concept." *Fundamina: A Journal of Legal History*, no. 1 (2005), pp. 275-84.

Shershenevich, G. F., *Учебник русского гражданского права* [*Textbook of Russian Civil Law*]. 11 ed. Vol. 1. 2 vols. (M., 1914).

Shubert, T. E.,*Доктрина, законотворчество, судебная практика: вопросы взаимовлияния [Doctrine, Law-making, Judicial Practice: Issues of Mutual Influence]*. (M.: NORMA: INFRA-M PUBL., 2019).

Silving, H., *Sources of Law*. (Buffalo, N.Y: W. S. Hein, 1968).

Simic, M., "The Role of Judges in the Interpretation of Law: (Some Issues in the Theory of Interpretation of Law)", *Collection of Papers, Faculty of Law, Nis* no. 15 (1975), pp. 139-44.

Smith, M., Jurisprudence. *Electronic resource*. (New York: Columbia University Press, 1909).

Stephenson, M. C., and Open Society Foundations. *Standing Doctrine and Anticorruption Litigation: A Survey. Book, Whole.* (New York, New York: Open Society Foundations, 2016).

Stumpf, S. E., "Austin's Theory of the Separation of Law and Morals Studies in Legal Philosophy." *Vanderbilt Law Review* XIV, no. 1 (1960), pp. 117-150.

Taribo, E. V., Доктрины Конституционного Суда Российской Федерации в сфере налогообложения: Теоретический и практический аспекты [Doctrines of the Constitutional Court of the Russian Federation in the Field of Taxation: Theoretical and Practical Aspects]. (M., 2005) (dissertation candidate of legal sciences).

———. Проблемы эволюционного развития российской модели судебного конституционного нормоконтроля [Problems of Evolutionary Development of the Russian Model of Judicial Constitutional Norm Control]. (M., 2019) (dissertation doctor of legal sciences).

Text Data Mining | Data Mining Tutorial – Wikitechy. (available online).

Thirlway, H. W. A., *The Sources of International Law. Foundations of Public International Law*. (Oxford, United Kingdom: Oxford University Press, 2014).

Tikhomirov, Y. A., ed. *Правовые модели и реальность [Legal Models and Reality]*. (M.: INFRA-M, 2014).

———. *Теория закона [Theory of Law]*. (M., 1982).

Tiller, E. H., and Cross F. B., "What Is Legal Doctrine?" *Northwestern University Law Review, Northwestern University Law Review*, no. 1 (2006), pp. 517-534.

Udodova, M. A., "Преемственность научных исследований роли воздействия судебной практики на законодательство [Continuity of Scientific Research on the Role of the Impact of Judicial Practice on Legislation]." Материалы конференции в 4-х частях [Conference Materials: in 4 parts], (M.: Проспект [Prospekt], 2016), pp. 52-53.

Van Hoecke, M., and Warrington M., "Legal Cultures, Legal Paradigms and Legal Doctrine: Towards a New Model for Comparative Law." *International and Comparative Law Quarterly* 47, no. 3 (1998). pp. 495-536.

Vasiliev, A. A., Правовая доктрина как источник права: историко-теоретические вопросы [Legal Doctrine as a Source of Law: Historical and Theoretical Issues]. (Barnaul, Алтайский государственный университет [Altai State University], 2007) (abstract of dissertation candidate of legal sciences).

Vengerov, A. B., Роль судебной практики в развитии советского права [The Role of Judicial Practice in the Development of Soviet Law]. (M., 1966) (dissertation candidate of legal sciences).

Vichugova, M., Оцифровываем текст: как превратить слова в числа для Data Mining – 5 NLP-операций Feature Extraction [Digitizing Text: How to Turn Words into Numbers for Data Mining – 5 NLP-operations Feature Extraction. Digitizing the Text]. Big Data, Hadoop, Arenadata, Kafka и Spark (blog), 2019. (available online).

Vlasenko, N. A., Проблемы точности выражения формы права (лингво-логический анализ) [Problems of Accuracy of Expression of the Form of Law (Linguo-Logical Analysis)]. (Ekaterinburg, 1997) (dissertation candidate of legal sciences).

Walker, R., *The English Legal System*. 4th ed. (London, 1976).

West, M. D., ed. *Applications of Computer Content Analysis. Progress in Communication Sciences*, v. 17. (Westport, CT: Ablex Pub, 200)1.

Yadov, V. A., *Социологическое исследование: методология, программа, методы [Sociological Research: Methodology, Program, Methods]*. (Samara, 1995).

———. *Стратегия социологического исследования [Sociological Research Strategy]*. (Moscow: Академкнига Добросвет [Akademkniga Dobrosvet], 2003).

Yembulaeva, N. Yu., and Mikhailik A. A. "Правовая доктрина как источник права и правоприменения [Legal Doctrine as a Source of Law and Law Enforcement]." *Власть закона [Rule of Law]*, no. 2 (30) (2017), pp. 115-123.

Zaitsev, O. V., "Проблемные Вопросы Доктрины Гражданского Права [Problematic Issues of the Civil Law Doctrine]." *Вестник Пермского Университета. Юридические науки [Bulletin of Perm University. Law Sciences]*, no. 1 (23) (2014), pp. 111-116.

Zingis, K. A., "Публикации заключённых: контент-анализ газеты 'новые соловки' (1925-1930 гг.) [Prisoners' publications: Content Analysis of the Newspaper Novye Solovki (1925–1930)]." *Историческая информатика. информационные технологии и математические методы в исторических исследованиях и образовании [Historical Computer Science. Information Technologies and Mathematical Methods in Historical Research and Education]*, no. 3-4 (13-14) (2015), pp. 45-55.

Zozulya, A. A., Доктрина в современном праве [Doctrine in Modern Law]. (Saint-Petersburg, 2006) (abstract of dissertation candidate of legal sciences).

Вести [Vesti]. "Путин возложил цветы к надгробиям Деникина, Ильина и Шмелева [Putin Laid Flowers at the Tombstones of Denikin, Ilyin and Shmelev]." May 24, 2009. (available online).

Методика проведения антикоррупционной экспертизы нормативных правовых актов и проектов нормативных правовых актов [Methodology for Conducting Anti-Corruption Expertise of Regulatory Legal Acts and Draft Regulatory Legal Acts]. (available online).

Методика проведения контент-анализа [Methods of Conducting Content Analysis]. (available online).

Особое мнение судьи Н. В. Витрука к Постановлению Конституционного Суда РФ от 11 декабря 1998 г. № 28-П "По делу о толковании положений части 4 Статьи 111 Конституции Российской Федерации [Special Opinion of Judge N.V. Vitruk on the Decree of the Constitutional Court of the Russian Federation of December 11, 1998 No. 28-P in the Case of Interpretation of the Provisions of Part 4 of Article 111 of the Constitution of the Russian Federation]." Собрание законодательства РФ [Collection of Legislation of the Russian Federation] 52 (1998), St. 6447.

Постановление ГД ФС РФ от 01.22.1998 № 2134-II ГД "О Регламенте Государственной Думы Федерального Собрания Российской Федерации" [Decree of the State Duma of the Federal Assembly of the Russian Federation of 01.22.1998 № 2134-II of the State Duma "On the Reglament of the State Duma of the Federal Assembly of the Russian Federation"]. "Собрание законодательства РФ" [Collection of Legislation of the Russian Federation], 02.16.1998, № 7, St. 801, 1998.

Постановление Конституционного Суда РФ № 10-П от 7 июня 2000 г. "По делу о проверке конституционности отдельных положений Конституции Республики Алтай и Федерального закона "Об общих принципах организации законодательных (представительных) и исполнительных органов государственной власти субъектов Российской Федерации" [Decree in the Case Concerning the Review of the Constitutionality of Certain Provisions of the Constitution of the Altai Republic and the Federal Law "On the General Principles of the Organization of the Legislative (Representative) and Executive Bodies of State Power of the Subjects of the Russian Federation"], no. 10-R (Конституционный Суд Российской Федерации [Constitutional Court of the Russian Federation] June 7, 2000).

Постановление Конституционного Суда РФ № 13-П от 21 декабря 2005 г. «По делу о проверке конституционности отдельных положений Федерального закона "Об общих принципах организации законодательных (представительных) и исполнительных органов государственной власти субъектов Российской Федерации' в связи с жалобами ряда граждан" [Decree "On the Case of Verification of the Constitutionality of Certain Provisions of the Federal Law "On the General Principles of the Organization of Legislative (Representative) and Executive Bodies of State Power of the Subjects of the Russian Federation' in Connection with the Complaints of a Number of Citizens," no. 13-R (Конституционный Суд Российской Федерации [Constitutional Court of the Russian Federation] December 21, 2005).

Постановление Конституционного Суда РФ № № 10-П от 31 июля 1995 г. "По делу о проверке конституционности Указа Президента Российской Федерации от 30 ноября 1994 года № 2137 "О мероприятиях по восстановлению конституционной законности и правопорядка на территории Чеченской Республики)," № 10-R (Конституционный Суд Российской Федерации [Constitutional Court of the Russian Federation] July 31, 1995).

Судебные речи знаменитых русских адвокатов [Court Speeches of Famous Russian Lawyers]. (Moscow: Юрайт [Juright], 2015).

Хабр [Habr]. "Алгоритм извлечения информации в ABBYY Compreno [Algorithm for extracting information in ABBYY Compreno]," (2021). (available online).

Хабр [Habr]. "Назад к микросервисам вместе с Istio. Часть 1 [Back to microservices with Istio. Part 1]." (available online).

Хабр [Hubr]. "ScienceHub #06: Компьютерная лингвистика [Computational Linguistics]." (available online).

Index

www.ingramcontent.com/pod-product-compliance
Lightning Source LLC
LaVergne TN
LVHW100318240926
848810LV00002B/11
9781616196974